The State of the Nations 2008

ALSO OF INTEREST FROM IMPRINT ACADEMIC

Robert Hazell (ed.), *The State and The Nations:*
The First Year of Devolution in the United Kingdom
ISBN 9780907845805

Alan Trench (ed.), *The State of The Nations 2001:*
The Second Year of Devolution in the United Kingdom
ISBN 9780907845195

Robert Hazell (ed.), *The State of The Nations 2003:*
The Third Year of Devolution in the United Kingdom
ISBN 9780907845492

Alan Trench (ed.), *Has Devolution Made a Difference?*
The State of The Nations 2004
ISBN 9780907845874

Alan Trench (ed.), *The Dynamics of Devolution*
The State of The Nations 2005
ISBN 9781845400361

TOCs, reviews and sample chapters:

imprint-academic.com/state

The State of the Nations
2008

Edited by Alan Trench

The Constitution Unit

imprint-academic.com

Published in the UK by Imprint Academic
PO Box 200, Exeter EX5 5YX, UK

Published in the USA by Imprint Academic
Philosophy Documentation Center
PO Box 7147, Charlottesville, VA 22906-7147, USA

ISBN 9781845401269

British Library Cataloguing in Publication Data
A catalogue record for this book is available from the
British Library and the US Library of Congress

Contents

List of Contributors

John Aldridge was formerly a senior civil servant in the Scottish Office and Scottish Executive, holding various posts including principal finance officer. He is a member of the independent expert panel on finance advising the Commission on Scottish Devolution.

Martin Burch is Professor of Government in the University of Manchester, and co-leader of the English Regions Devolution Monitoring team.

Scott Greer is Assistant Professor in the Department of Health Policy and Management in the School of Public Health at the University of Michigan, and an honorary senior research fellow at the Constitution Unit at University College London.

Alan Harding is Professor of Urban and Regional Governance and Director of the Institute of Political and Economic Governance at the University of Manchester. He is co-leader of the English Regions Devolution Monitoring team.

Holly Jarman is Visiting Assistant Professor in the Department of Political Science at the University at Albany, SUNY.

Peter Jones is a freelance journalist, writing principally for *The Scotsman* and *The Economist*. He was leader of the Scotland Devolution Monitoring team between 2005 and 2007.

James Mitchell is Professor of Government at the University of Strathclyde.

Akash Paun is research associate at the Constitution Unit, Department of Political Science, University College London, and writes the Devolution and the Centre Devolution Monitoring Reports.

James Rees is research associate at the Institute for Political and Economic Governance at the University of Manchester, and contributes to the English Regions Devolution Monitoring Reports.

Roger Scully is Professor of Politics at Aberystwyth University, and co-leader of the Wales Devolution Monitoring team.

Alan Trench is research fellow at the Europa Institute in the School of Law at the University of Edinburgh. He is an honorary senior research fellow at the Constitution Unit at University College London, and contributes to both the Scotland and Wales Devolution Monitoring Reports.

Rick Wilford is Professor of Politics at Queen's University Belfast, and co-leader of the Northern Ireland Devolution Monitoring team.

Robin Wilson is co-leader of the Northern Ireland Devolution Monitoring team, and a Ph.D. student in the School of Politics, International Studies and Philosophy at Queen's University Belfast. He was formerly director of the think-tank Democratic Dialogue.

Richard Wyn Jones is Professor of Politics at Aberystwyth University, Director of the Institute of Welsh Politics there, and co-leader of the Wales Devolution Monitoring team.

List of Figures and Tables

CHAPTER 5
THE ENGLISH REGIONS AND LONDON

CHAPTER 6
FINANCING DEVOLUTION: 2008 AND BEYOND

CHAPTER 8
LOST SOULS IN THE LOBBIES?: BACKBENCHERS FROM SCOTLAND
AND WALES IN POST-DEVOLUTION WESTMINSTER

Abbreviations and Acronyms

AM	Assembly Member (member of the National Assembly for Wales)
Asbo	Anti-social behaviour order
BERR	Department for Business, Enterprise and Regulatory Reform
BIC	British-Irish Council
BNP	British National Party
COSLA	Convention of Scottish Local Authorities
CSD	Commission on Scottish Devolution (the Calman commission)
CSR	Comprehensive Spending Review
DCLG	Department of Communities and Local Government
DEFRA	Department for the Environment, Food and Rural Affairs
DETR	Department of Environment, Transport and Regions
DTI	Department of Trade and Industry
DUP	Democratic Unionist Party
EP	English Partnerships
ERA	Elected regional assembly
EVEL	'English Votes for English Laws'
EU	European Union
GCSE	General Certificate of Secondary Education
GDP	Gross Domestic Produce
GVA	Gross Value Added
IICD	Independent International Commission on Decommissioning
IMC	Independent Monitoring Commission
IPPR	Institute for Public Policy Research
IRA	Irish Republican Army
Labgi	Local authority business growth incentive
LCO	Legislative Competence Order
LHB	Local Health Board
MAA	Multi-Area Agreements
MLA	Member of the Legislative Assembly (Northern Ireland)
MP	Member of Parliament (Westminster)
MSP	Member of the Scottish Parliament
NAW	National Assembly for Wales
NHS	National Health Service
NI	Northern Ireland
NIO	Northern Ireland Office

NSMC	North/South Ministerial Council
ODPM	Office of the Deputy Prime Minister
OFMDFM	Office of the First Minister and Deputy First Minister
OTR	'On the run'
PfG	Preparation for Government
PFI	Private Finance Initiative
PQ	Parliamentary Question
PSA	Public Service Agreement
PSNI	Police Service of Northern Ireland
RA	Regional Assembly
RDA	Regional Development Agency
RUC	Royal Ulster Constabulary
SDLP	Social Democratic and Labour Party
SF	Sinn Féin
SI	Statutory Instrument
SNP	Scottish National Party
SSP	Scottish Socialist Party
STV	Single Transferable Vote
UUP	Ulster Unionist Party
UK	United Kingdom
WAG	Welsh Assembly Government

Foreword

Alan Trench

This volume in *The State of the Nations* series focuses on the events of 2007. It surveys what happened during the latter part of the second terms of the Scottish Parliament and National Assembly for Wales, from 2005 to the May 2007 elections, the immediate aftermath, and the first months in office of the new governments, covering events up to the spring of 2008. It also considers a number of issues that will be important during the third term of the devolved governments — including policy-making, intergovernmental relations and finance.

This book is produced as part of the ongoing Devolution Monitoring Programme, which results in three sets of reports each year covering devolution in Scotland, Wales, Northern Ireland, the English Regions, and at the centre. The reports are funded by the Economic and Social Research Council, the Ministry of Justice, the Scotland and Wales Offices and the Scottish Government. We are grateful to each of them for their financial support. We are also grateful to all the members of the monitoring teams, who are too numerous to list here, for their hard work in putting the reports. The reports are available on the Constitution Unit's website, at www.ucl.ac.uk/constitution-unit/research/devolution/devo-monitoring-programme.html. For further information, contact the Unit's Director, Professor Robert Hazell, at r.hazell@ucl.ac.uk .

This book went to press in the summer of 2008, and therefore could not cover some developments that occurred during the final stages of the editing process. These include the resignation of Wendy Alexander as leader of the Labour MSPs and subsequent Labour leadership election campaign in Scotland, the Glasgow East by-election, the resignation of Rhodri Glyn Thomas as Culture and Heritage Minister in Wales and his replacement by Alun Ffred Jones, the appointment of Gerald Holtham to chair the Assembly Government's commission on financial matters, and issues about the devolution of policing and criminal justice in Northern Ireland. For details of these, and for general updates about how devolution works, consult the *Devolution Monitoring Reports*.

For their help in the production of this book, I am grateful to many people. Top of the list are the contributors, for their patience and forbearance as well as their chapters. Close behind them are support staff at the Constitution Unit, including Victoria Spence, the Unit's office manager, and Shokofeh Hejazi and Daniel Broadbent, interns who helped with the copy-editing at various times. I am also grateful to Sandra Good, Keith Sutherland and Anthony Freeman at Imprint Academic, not least for the startling speed with which they have produced this book. My thanks also go to Robert Hazell, and to my new colleagues at the University of Edinburgh, particularly Charlie Jeffery and Drew Scott.

1

Introduction

The Second Phase of Devolution

Alan Trench

2007: THE YEAR WHEN CHICKENS STARTED COMING HOME TO ROOST

This volume of 'The State of the Nations' is concerned first and foremost with the events of 2007, what led up to them and their aftermath and implications. Its main focus is with the 2007 devolved elections which resulted in the restoration of a devolved power-sharing government in Northern Ireland and the entry into government of nationalist parties in Scotland and Wales, and what those governments then did in their first months in office. It also discussed a number of issues that are likely to become important during those governments' terms in office.

This is the first volume in the 'State of the Nations' series to have appeared for three years.[1] The principal reason for this is apparent from the chronology below; between 2005 and 2007, relatively little of interest happened. As Peter Jones outlines in chapter 2, in Scotland, the Labour-Liberal Democrat Executive proceeded to govern, but without attracting much public curiosity, support or enthusiasm. While it may have done worthy things, few of these were particularly noteworthy and it got little credit for what it did do. In Wales, as Richard Wyn Jones and Roger Scully show in chapter 3, a process of complicated if crab-like constitution-making continued, largely away from the gaze of the media, the general public and even many politicians in Cardiff Bay. Labour had to grapple with the problems of governing with only a minority in the Assembly after May 2005 (forcing it into accommodations with the opposition parties and Plaid Cymru in particular over the budget), and with the continuing divisions within the party about devolution. In Northern Ireland, there were long-running attempts to secure disarmament by the IRA and to persuade the long-standing antagonists of Sinn Fein and the Democratic Unionists to share power, so that devolution could be restored, which Rick Wilford and Robin Wilson chart in chapter 4. In 2007, these finally bore fruit.

---

[1] The last was A. Trench (ed.), *The Dynamics of Devolution: The State of the Nations 2005* (Exeter: Imprint Academic, 2005).

From London's point of view, the travails in Northern Ireland were an ongoing source of difficulty. There were also inter-departmental debates and conflicting tendencies in making policy on the English regions (discussed by Martin Burch, Alan Harding and James Rees in chapter 5), which continued to trouble various departments that failed to co-ordinate their policies in any sort of coherent way. But devolution was 'working well' in Scotland and Wales—meaning that in the later years of the Blair premiership it did not trouble the centre of government in any but the most technical of respects. This in turn meant that intergovernmental relations had become even more ad hoc, informal and unsystematic, that the Barnett formula remained unchallenged (if often discussed) as the basis of allocating finance, and that Westminster and Whitehall continued to confuse devolved and non-devolved matters but goodwill between the various institutions (under-pinned by Labour dominance of government) meant that this never provoked open rows or disputes. The centre simply could, and did, disengage from most aspects of government relating to managing devolution. With hind-sight, this seems like astounding complacency on the part of both the UK Government and the Labour Party—complacency which led to what Labour experienced as the cataclysm of the 2007 elections.

**Figure 1.1: Chronology of Major Developments in Devolution,
June 2005–March 2008**

2005	
June	Publication of Wales Office White Paper *Better Governance for Wales*
December	Government of Wales bill introduced into UK Parliament
2006	
March	Scottish Liberal Democrats published Steel Commission report
25 July	Government of Wales Act got royal assent
October	St Andrews Agreement between UK and Irish governments after negotiations with Northern Ireland parties
2007	
7 March	Elections to Northern Ireland Assembly.
3 May	Elections to Scottish Parliament and National Assembly for Wales
8 May	Power (re)transferred to Stormont, with election of executive including Ian Paisley as First Minister and Martin McGuinness as Deputy First Minister

16 May	SNP formed minority administration in Scotland, with Alex Salmond as First Minister
25 May	Rhodri Morgan re-elected as First Minister of Wales
June	Row between Scottish Executive and UK Government about 'memorandum of understanding' with Libya including possible prisoner exchanges
27 June	Gordon Brown replaced Tony Blair as UK Prime Minister
24 July	Formation of Labour-Plaid Cymru 'One Wales' coalition government
July	Publication of UK Government green paper *The Governance of Britain*
August	Publication of Scottish Executive White Paper *Choosing Scotland's Future*
September	Scottish Executive announced its re-naming as 'the Scottish Government'
9 October	UK Government publishes Comprehensive Spending Review for 2008–11
October	Sir Emyr Jones Parry named as chairman of 'All Wales Convention'
30 November	Speech by Wendy Alexander proposed establishment of 'Scottish Constitutional Commission' to review powers and financing arrangements
6 December	Scottish Parliament voted to set up Constitutional Commission
2008	
17 February	Gordon Brown announced support for review of Scottish devolution
25 March	Sir Kenneth Calman named as chairman of Scottish Constitutional Commission
28 April	Membership of Calman commission announced

The 2007 elections are discussed at length elsewhere in the book, and particularly in chapters 2, 3 and 4. As is well known, in Scotland Labour ended up with 46 seats out of 129 in the Scottish Parliament and the SNP with 47; Labour accepted it had 'lost' and allowed the SNP to form a minority government . Yet, as James Mitchell argues in chapter 10, Labour has struggled both to accept that it indeed genuinely 'lost', or to understand the ways in which and extent to which the SNP has changed over the last decade. (If Scottish Labour has failed to grasp that, the problem is all the more pronounced in London.) In Wales, Labour did badly enough to win only 26 seats out of 60 in the National Assembly and Plaid Cymru well enough to win three extra seats and so to hold 15. There followed a protracted period of inter-party negotiations to form a stable government, which resulted in the formation of Labour-Plaid coalition after extensive preparation for a 'Rainbow coalition' of Plaid, the Conservatives and the Lib Dems. As Wyn Jones and Scully show, this process marked a serious process of strategic thought and re-appraisal by the political parties in Wales, a process from which Plaid and the Conservatives emerged with their credibility enhanced and Labour and the Lib Dems did not, mainly because of the way they exposed the depth of their internal divisions and differing forms of disorganisation.[2] Coping with the significant political differences that now exist across the UK will be one of the major issues for the next few years.

The consequence of 2007 was that a number of convenient fudges and efforts to avoid hard issues that had worked effectively since 1999 ceased to work. The smooth progress of devolution (at least from London's perspective) started to look more like luck than good judgement — which means that broader issues become important too. This book considers four such issues: finance and its allocation (by John Aldridge in chapter 6); policy-making and the extent to which emergent 'policy styles' in each part of Britain are likely to prove durable, despite party-political change (by Scott Greer and Holly Jarman in chapter 7); the role of MPs from Scotland and Wales at Westminster, and their failure to carve out a clear role for themselves after devolution (by Akash Paun in chapter 8); and intergovernmental relations, and the differences between the UK's system and that in federal states (by Alan Trench in chapter 9). As a result, it aims both to record what happened between mid-2005 and early 2008, and to identify areas in which developments over the next few years will be particularly important.

DEVOLUTION, THE SECOND PHASE

Although it is still early to judge, we can now start to see what the main feature of the second phase of devolution are likely to be. These differ substantially from phase 1 — and not just in obvious ways, such as the absence now of the broad political consensus and goodwill that hitherto derived from Labour dominance of so many governments.

1. Nationalist Parties Face the Challenges of Government

For both the SNP and Plaid Cymru, entering government office is a huge opportunity, but one that brings with it significant challenges. One is obvious: that of proving that they are competent parties of government, so that

---

[2] See also J Osmond, *Crossing the Rubicon: Coalition politics Welsh style* (Cardiff: Institute of Welsh Affairs, 2007).

supporting them at the ballot box in future elections is more than just a protest vote, whether or not they succeed in making themselves natural parties of government. Both parties need to demonstrate both political and administrative competence in office, and to show that their presence in government makes a tangible difference. Adjusting to such demands is a necessary part of becoming parties of government not just of protest.

That adjustment means, amongst other things, developing a different approach to policy. Policy would appear to have been something of a weak spot for both parties up to now. In each case, the development of policy has hitherto largely been a matter of working out what activists wanted or would attract support from the wider electorate, rather than what was practicable. Entry into government means that policy turns from being a matter of ideology or campaigning into something that involves considerations of consequences and practicalities as well. If a party repeatedly makes policy promises that it cannot deliver, it is unlikely to convince voters that it is a real alternative. The problem both parties face is that they have relatively little to do with established networks of policy development and advice — they may have contacts with some individual outside experts as well as their in-house staff, but their links with think-tanks, the academic community and professional bodies have so far been comparatively weak. How successfully they deal with this may translate into the decisions voters make when they next to the ballot box.

2. The Importance of Party Structures, and the Problems they Create for the Britain-Wide Parties

The three Britain-wide (and unionist) parties—Labour, Conservative and Liberal Democrat—also face serious challenges in this new environment, with which they are trying to grapple. Their dilemma is about how to maintain party unity and a consistent policy platform and image across the whole party, while also allowing their Scottish and Welsh branches (or sections, or whatever they are called) sufficient room for manoeuvre. This is a considerable challenge, much more so than was appreciated before devolution, for two reasons. First, the pressures in the Scottish and Welsh political arenas are quite different to those at UK level—essentially because Labour can be outflanked to its left in Scotland and Wales (by nationalist parties, and also by more left-wing parties and candidates such as 'Labour Forward' in Wales) in a way does not happen in Westminster elections. Second, the 'national' character of those arenas—the fact that Scottish politics is about *Scottish* issues and interests, and similarly in Wales—has a profound effect on the nature of political debate and competition. In a Scottish or Welsh arena, when the issues can be defined primarily in Scottish or Welsh terms, the debate is framed in terms that structurally advantage the nationalist parties. When it comes to arguing about who can best stand up for Scotland or Wales, a party that is only concerned with Scotland or Wales has a huge advantage over ones which are trying to balance those concerns with British or UK ones and which have to ensure that they give out a consistent message across the UK.

So far, the Conservatives have coped with this challenge best. This is partly because the bulk of their electoral strength is in England (as are most of their Westminster seats), and Scotland and Wales are electorally largely peripheral for them in Westminster elections. Consequently, the ways they have established themselves in the Scottish Parliament and National Assembly (described in chapters 2 and 3) have helped the party in Westminster campaigns by giving it a higher profile, a more active role, and perhaps a greater degree of legitimacy. If the price of that has been a degree of internal diversity, it has been well worth while. Nonetheless, there are persistent anti-devolution grumblings, particularly from the present Welsh Tory MPs and also, it appears, from the party's grassroots. The Liberal Democrats, with a federal constitution and aspiration for a federal Britain, have also responded with relative ease to this challenge, though the reluctance of the party in Scotland or Wales to enter office after the 2007 elections (and the divisions and disorganisation that revealed particularly in Wales) will have done it few favours.

The problems are most acute for Labour, which is the only potential party of government to be unionist by electoral interest as well as ideology. Without winning significant numbers of seats from Scotland and Wales, Labour cannot hope to form a government at Westminster (which remains its main goal). Labour appears simply to have counted on the strength of traditional ties and support in both Scotland and Wales, despite many signs that these have been eroding over recent years. (In Scotland, this has been fuelled by the introduction of proportional representation in local authority elections, which has already greatly weakened its position in local government. Loss of control of local authorities will have other consequences, both for maintaining a coherent organisation at local level for Westminster and Holyrood elections, and perhaps for the ability to deliver rewards to Labour supporters through council policies.) The 2007 elections signal a considerable weakening of Labour in both Scotland and Wales—something that has greatly shocked both parties, almost at an existential level. Labour will have to work out what it stands for as a unionist part of the centre-left in Scotland and Wales, and what it has to offer there that is distinctive, if it is to hope to be able to re-establish a powerful position. It will also have to translate that into organisational terms. One likely outcome is the acceptance that Labour cannot function as a monolithic organisation, but needs to become something looser which may have different policies and campaigning strategies in different parts of Britain. This would imply considerable policy and organisational autonomy for the Scottish and Welsh parties, if not a federal arrangement internally. Of senior Labour figures, only Henry McLeish has appeared willing to contemplate such a move so far.

How Labour resolves this remains to be seen—but it will be a major issue for the coming few years, and the solution will have vital ramifications not just for the UK's territorial politics but also for the UK party system more generally, and perhaps even for whether the UK survives as a single state.

3. The Black Hole of England

England remains, of course, largely outside the devolution arrangements. Such attempts as there have been to find answers—whether through elected regional government, reform of institutions at the centre to address 'English' matters more directly, or enhancing the role of local government—have so far had little impact. These problems are starting to become a focus of political and constitutional debate, with a large number of private seminars and think-tank discussions about England that never quite manage to identify what 'the English question' is let alone how to answer it. (The fact that these events are dominated by people from and mainly concerned with life in southern England does not help intellectual clarity either.)

Broadly speaking, the debate seems concerned with two broad sets of issues. One set relates to the Westminster agenda, and particularly the anomaly of the 'West Lothian question'—the ability of MPs for constituencies in Scotland or Wales to vote on matters like health or education for England, but not for Scotland. This has led to some controversial policies including deferred variable fees for universities and foundation hospitals being passed in England by the votes of Scottish and Welsh MPs. In chapter 8 Akash Paun shows how unclear the role of MPs from Scotland and even Wales is after devolution, and how they have failed to carve out clear roles for themselves. He suggests that these MPs who lack an electoral interest in such matters are much more subservient to party discipline than English MPs, who have to balance party and constituency interests which may conflict. This has led to debates about limiting voting on purely English matters to English MPs, favoured in various forms particularly by the Conservatives (who have little electoral interest in Scotland or Wales for Westminster elections, thanks to the first past the post system), including proposals from Lord (Kenneth) Baker and Sir Malcolm Rifkind and further consideration by the party's 'Democracy Task Force' chaired by Kenneth Clarke MP.[3] The administrative obstacles to be overcome to achieve such changes remain formidable

---

[3] Clarke's task force reported on the West Lothian question on 1 July 2008. Its report, *Answering the Question: Devolution, The West Lothian Question and the Future of the Union* is available at www.conservatives.com/tile.do?def=news.story.page&obj_id=145538

(and probably under-rated by the Conservatives; something near a revolution in the preparation and framing of legislation would be needed). It also
remains hard to see the circumstances in which any of this might actually
materialise; the point at which the Conservatives will be able to deliver such
a reform will be when they have a sufficiently strong Commons (and very
largely English) majority that it will not be needed.

The other approach has been to seek to strengthen local or regional
government (or both). 'Localisation' has been favoured by a range of
groups, including the constitutional reform campaign group Unlock Democracy (which incorporates Charter 88 and the New Politics Network), and the
newspaper columnist Sir Simon Jenkins. Rhetorically at least it is also
supported by the Conservatives as well as parts of UK central government.
Regional government has narrower political appeal, having little traction
outside Labour Party circles. However, as Martin Burch, Alan Harding and
James Rees show in chapter 5, the 'regionalisation' agenda continues to
develop for administrative reasons, although in a disjointed and rather inco-
herent way with no clear objectives and action largely determined by the
various responsibilities and differing goals of Whitehall departments.

What may underpin the relative torpor of this debate is the general lack of
public interest in it. Organisations like the Campaign for an English Parliament and parties like the English Democrats may feel strongly about the failure to recognise distinctive English concerns, but there is little evidence as
yet that the wider public shares their concern. Even opinion polling only
tends to show a reaction against the status quo when respondees are
prompted. The issues simply appear to be of low public salience generally,
and excite those engaged in politics more than the wider public.

4. More Contentious Intergovernmental Relations, and a Slow and Grudging Response from the UK Government

It is scarcely news that the lack of political consensus between governments,
and the emergence onto the intergovernmental agenda of a number of difficult fundamental issues, have led to more strained intergovernmental relations. This has, if anything, been more manifest on the level of day-to-day
politics. There are a number of examples, including the early row (in June
2007) between the Scottish Executive (as it still was) and the UK Government over a 'memorandum of understanding' with Libya about which the
Scottish Executive had not consulted.[4] Other examples have included an
argument about gun-control powers between Scotland and UK following the
death of a child by a pellet fired from an air rifle, the obstruction by the

---

[4] This was controversial as it would provide for the transfer of convicted Libyan prisoners to serve
their sentences at home — controversial as the most high-profile such prisoner was Abdelbaset
Al-Meghrahi, convicted in a Scottish court sitting in the Netherlands of the 1989 Lockerbie (Pan Am
flight 103) bombing, and serving a sentence in a Scottish prison.

Scottish Government of the building of new nuclear power stations in Scotland (although this will be pursued elsewhere in Britain), disagreements about both the merits of replacing council tax in Scotland with a local income tax and the consequences for council tax benefit if that happens, or a row between Wales and UK about health policies in March 2008. There have even been a few issues from Northern Ireland, usually involving DUP ministers. None of these are areas where intergovernmental disagreement should come as a surprise; the novelty is that such disagreements now enter the public domain, while before May 2007 they were generally kept behind closed doors.[5]

In fact, what is surprising is how few and how mild such disputes have been, not how many or how acrimonious. Ministers as well as officials from all administrations have been keen to emphasise the consensus between them and their desire to carry on with day-to-day business. Thus the junior UK Government minister responsible for relations with Scotland wrote in January 2008

> The truth is that the business of government is built on daily, weekly, monthly co-operation, consultation and joint working.... The people of Scotland have given ministers north and south of the border the responsibility of working to make Scotland a better place, and they do not want partisan wrangling to get in the way of this task.[6]

Indeed, Scottish Executive/Government officials were instructed early on in the SNP's tenure to continue to be open, frank and helpful to their counterparts at Westminster, not to create difficulties unless there was good reason. At the same time, the SNP sought to make greater use of formal intergovernmental mechanisms (notably the Joint Ministerial Committee) and to abolish the post of Secretary of State for Scotland. This is perfectly comprehensible in the light of the SNP's desire to ensure government continues to work well, as part of its plan to establish itself as an effective party of government, but it clearly came as a surprise to many outsiders, particularly in the media. In chapter 10, James Mitchell emphasises how much the lead for this has come from Scottish not UK ministers. But against this must be put the careful use of intergovernmental issues by the Scottish Government. The row over the Libyan memorandum of understanding sent an early signal that failure to play by the rules would cause considerable difficulty and embarrassment for the UK Government (rather to the annoyance of many officials in Whitehall). Nor has the UK level appreciated that, from a Scottish point of view, day-to-day policy issues are also linked to the constitutional agenda, and

---

5 See A. Trench, (ed.), *Devolution and Power in the United Kingdom* (Manchester: Manchester University Press, 2007), particularly chapter 8, for a discussion of how and why this happened.

6 D. Cairns, 'How Holyrood and Westminster make devolution work', *The Herald* (Glasgow), 11 January 2008.

vice versa. The White Paper *Choosing Scotland's Future* clearly set out an agenda by which failures to take Scottish concerns on a wide range of matters that are presently reserved (set out in chapter 2 of the White Paper) could be used to make a case for devolution of those functions if not full independence.[7] Similarly, the sharp comments made by Alex Salmond (notably not by John Swinney, the Finance Secretary in Edinburgh) after the tight settlement for the Scottish Parliament in the Comprehensive Spending Review were intended to indicate the political importance of the issue. And constitutional restraints on what a devolved government or legislature can do can in fact be used to deflect blame for failure to deliver on policy promises. The UK Government has yet to realise the political astuteness and subtlety of the SNP's intergovernmental agenda, or its potential breadth by linking day-to-day matters to constitutional ones.

The UK has also, it seems, yet to appreciate the sheer skill with which SNP ministers conduct themselves in intergovernmental relations. They play the cards they are dealt extremely well. To understand how well they play the cards it is necessary to understand what the cards are, and that involves a considerable amount of technical detail. One example is the policy on nuclear power stations, where the UK Government accepted in January 2008 that no new nuclear power stations would be built in Scotland even though its policy was to re-establish nuclear power as an element of the UK's overall electricity supply.[8] Devolved powers in this area are limited, and relate to planning functions as nuclear power is a reserved matter. While the UK Government could have overcome Scottish objections, doing so would have involved considerable delay and political pain, would have played into the SNP's hands politically (as opposition to nuclear power is a long-standing SNP policy and is popular in Scotland), and would probably not have produced any more nuclear power stations, because these will need to be built by commercial companies which may well decide that the political risk is excessive. The UK's concession was an understandable practical one, but was not rooted in constitutional factors.

This Scottish skill and deftness in playing what is, in essence, a strong hand politically but often a weak one constitutionally has been matched by tactical maladroitness and gracelessness from the UK Government. The discourtesy of Tony Blair's failure even to acknowledge Alex Salmond's election was remarkable (as James Mitchell discusses). The UK Government has persistently refused to use the term 'Scottish Government' following the

---

[7] Scottish Executive, *Choosing Scotland's Future. A National Conversation. Independence and Responsibility in the Modern World* (Edinburgh: Scottish Executive, 2007). Available at www.scotland.gov.uk/Publications/2007/08/13103747/0

[8] See Department for Business, Enterprise and Regulatory Reform, *Meeting the Energy Challenge: A White Paper on Nuclear Power Cm 7296* (London: The Stationery Office, 2008), particularly para. 3.54; and more generally *Scotland Devolution Monitoring Report May 2008* (London: The Constitution Unit, 2008).

change of name in September 2007 (and hypocritically, since it embraced the term 'Welsh Assembly Government' when that was adopted in 2003 for something that was not even a distinct legal institution). Although Alex Salmond asked the UK Prime Minister (still Tony Blair) to re-convene the plenary Joint Ministerial Committee, on taking office, and put this in writing in August 2007, Blair and Brown failed to do so or even respond to Salmond's request, which was repeated several times in public. While the British-Irish Council met in June 2007, this was largely symbolic and designed to reassure the Northern Ireland unionist parties ahead of a meeting of the North-South Ministerial Conference the following day. When the re-establishment of the JMC was eventually announced in March 2008, no immediate date was set for its first meeting, and it was to be chaired by the new Secretary of State for Justice, Jack Straw, not the UK Prime Minister.[9] Similarly, while administrative arrangements in Whitehall were beefed up somewhat, this took some time to happen and resulted in the appointment of fewer than half a dozen new officials (two of them senior ones), and very limited organisational changes. Although capacity at the centre of government to develop policy and co-ordinate it across government has been boosted (a cabinet committee focussing on devolution and territorial issues, and officials with a remit to improve policy co-ordination), it remains limited. And the partisan engagement of the Scotland Office in constitutional debates has undermined its ability to engage effectively with the Scottish Government as an 'honest broker' on day-to-day issues, however much its minister of state may protest otherwise.

It is inevitable that there will be minor spats and disagreements between governments (like the Wales health issue), and more serious far-reaching disagreements as well. The question is how those are managed. The UK has become relatively poor at managing such differences in recent decades, and has sought to maintain established ways of conducting such relations since devolution even though the context has changed hugely. The result is chastening, not least for those who consider that devolution resembles the operation of federal political systems. In chapter 9 Alan Trench sets out the common features of intergovernmental relations in federal systems, to show how unlike them the UK is. He finds it striking that many systems vary a great deal in both their detailed constitutional arrangements and broader social characteristics have converged on a generally similar approach to handling relations between their various governments. For the future, a key issue will be how the UK as a whole adapts to increasing sources of difference in politics and policy within the state—and in this it may find that emulating some of the mechanisms and techniques used in such systems (as

---

[9] The JMC eventually met on 25 June 2008. The 'joint statement' from the meeting can be found at www.scotlandoffice.gov.uk/our-communications/release.php?id=3676

well as developing the 'more devolutionary political culture' that James Mitchell refers to in chapter 10) offers a way forward, whether or not the UK becomes a federal state in a more formal sense.

5. An Active Role for Parliaments and Legislatures

A surprising aspect of how the UK works is the active role of the various parliaments and legislatures. This is not due so much to the 'Westminster tradition' as to how political tensions between and within parties manifest themselves. In Scotland, the minority government—and the fact that the opposition parties are united in their support of the Union and hostility to independence—has two consequences. One is that what happens in Parliament is inherently uncertain (as it depends on the SNP striking a deal with at least one other party, and often two, to get its business through). Although the position of the SNP as the Scottish Government gives it considerable authority, as does its strong public support, it still cannot assume it has a clear mandate to 'speak for Scotland'. That in turn adds to the drama of political life, and the impact the legislature has. The other is that the Parliament itself becomes an actor in politics, and particularly intergovernmental politics, acting differently to and sometimes in opposition to the government—most notable in relation to the constitutional debate (and the Parliament's decision to set up a 'constitutional commission', now known as the Calman Commission or formally as the Commission on Scottish Devolution).

The existence of a stable majority and effective party discipline make this much less obvious in Wales—but at Westminster, issues of the extent of devolution to Wales will also require extensive parliamentary consideration, and may expose divisions within Labour about devolution.

6. The UK Question

One developing problem—the continuation of a long-standing trend—has been to approach devolution questions as if they were purely bilateral, and did not concern the UK as whole and what sort of state it should be. This trend manifests itself in the fragmented constitutional and financial debates, discussed in detail below, as well as in the UK Government's preference to conduct intergovernmental relations bilaterally rather than multilaterally or avoid change in the state's central institution in Westminster and Whitehall.

Major questions remain about UK-wide issues. Some relate to Parliament. Previous volumes in this series have looked at aspects of the West Lothian question, and the role of Westminster in legislating for the different parts of the UK.[10] In chapter 8 Akash Paun considers what role backbenchers from

---

[10] For example, G. Lodge, M. Russell, and O. Gay, 'The Impact of Devolution on Westminster: If not now, when?', in A. Trench (ed.), *Has Devolution Made a Difference? The State of the Nations 2004* (Exeter: Imprint Academic, 2004), 193–216.

Scottish or Welsh seats actually play at Westminster. He finds that their workloads have clearly declined since 1999, but they have yet to carve out any clear new role for themselves. That reflects a broader lack of clarity about the post-devolution role of the UK Parliament in relation to Scotland, Wales and Northern Ireland. More generally, there is the question of what the United Kingdom is for in the twenty-first century. What, exactly, do the various parts of the UK gain from being part of a single state? Defence, security and military power were one set of reasons, in the eighteenth and into the nineteenth centuries. So were the benefits of the British Empire—trade, resources and administration.[11] After the Second World War the welfare state took on a unifying role.[12] But devolution has meant that a large part of the welfare state is now administered by the devolved institutions, even though key elements (including taxation and redistribution through welfare benefits are not., raising the question of what the UK is now for in terms of social citizenship, let alone more broadly.[13] So far, the UK Government has shown no enthusiasm for taking on the territorial implications of this issue, but instead developed a rhetoric of 'Britishness' (though more recently it seems to be moving away from that).[14]

Several opportunities to join up these debates have been ducked so far, including those presented by the UK Government's role in the Calman commission and the constitutional debate launched shortly after Gordon Brown became UK Prime Minister, by the July 2007 Green Paper on *The Governance of Britain*.[15] The Green Paper scarcely mentioned devolution issues at all, and when it did raise matters that would affect the devolved institutions (like a 'British bill of rights') it did not acknowledge that these would affect devolved concerns.[16] It is hard to avoid the view that the UK Government simply does not want to engage with the UK-wide issues raised by devolution, and hopes that either they will go away or that they can be

---

[11] The role of these various factors is the subject of debate among historians, which is concisely presented in contributions (particularly those by Whatley, Macinnes, Murdoch and Devine) to T.M. Devine (ed.), *Scotland and the Union 1707–2007* (Edinburgh: Edinburgh University Press, 2008).

[12] N. McEwen, 'State Welfare Nationalism: The territorial impact of welfare state development in Scotland', *Regional and Federal Studies* 12(1) (2002): 66–90.

[13] D. Wincott, 'Social Policy and Social Citizenship: Britain's Welfare States', *Publius: The journal of federalism* 36 (1) (2006): 169–88.

[14] 'Britishness' is, of course, particularly problematic in Northern Ireland, where it appeals greatly to the Unionist community but not to the Nationalist one. When 'Britishness' is attached to specific institutions or values that are meant to be neutral between the communities there (as with a 'British bill of rights'), it polarises where it was meant to integrate.

[15] Ministry of Justice, *The Governance of Britain* Cm 7170 (London: The Stationery Office, 2007). Available at www.justice.gov.uk/publications/governanceofbritain.htm

[16] For example, when giving evidence to the Commons Liaison Committee, Brown rejected any need to consult the devolved governments or legislatures about the British bill of rights. See House of Commons, *The Prime Minister: oral evidence, Thursday 13 December 2007 Rt Hon Gordon Brown MP* HC 192–i (London: The Stationery Office, 2008), particularly QQ 44–6. Available at www.publications.parliament.uk/pa/cm200708/cmselect/cmliaisn/192/7121301.htm

dealt with bilaterally. This makes sense from the point of view of a government concerned with maintaining tactical battles against political-party
adversaries. It does not make sense from the point of a view of a state determined to build broad-based consent for its long-term survival, or if the
concern is to ensure an active participatory democracy. The UK state has
long been characterised by taking a passive rather than active approach to
territorial management.[17] Such passivity may now be gravely dangerous to
its survival—even though the questions are hard to answer, intellectually
and politically, and open up a number of difficult issues.[18]

7. The Disjointed Constitutional Debates in Scotland and Wales

The most important implication of the second phase is the way it puts constitutional issues back on the political agenda. (The unwritten constitution of
the UK means that this is easier than in many other systems.) This has been at
its most obvious and dramatic in Scotland—but also at its most dysfunc-
tional. With the White Paper *Choosing Scotland's Future*, the Scottish
Government launched its 'National Conversation'. As both James Mitchell
in chapter 10 and Peter Jones in chapter 2 show, the Conversation was meant
to develop the intellectual and political case for independence, and for
extending devolution considerably on the path to that. However, the lack of
funding and structure means this has been more a theme for ministerial
speeches and a blog more than anything more purposeful. The refusal of the
unionist parties (which together hold a majority in the Scottish Parliament)
to take part has made it all the worse. The unionist parties, following a lead
from the Labour leader Wendy Alexander, have responded by resolving
through the Parliament to establish a 'Scottish Constitutional Commission'
to review devolution ten years on, in a UK context. Thus, independence was
expressly excluded from the remit of the Commission, which was to look at
extending the scope of devolved powers but also potentially reducing them,
in the interest of improving the governance of the UK as a whole—although
when its membership was announced in May 2008 it included no-one from
outside Scotland.[19]

In reality the timescale for the Commission means it is writing for the next
UK Government not the present one, since its final report (even if it is
published on schedule and not delayed) will appear in around June 2009. By
then there will be only a year at most before a UK general election. That is

---

[17] See J. Bulpitt, *Territory and Power in the United Kingdom* (Manchester: Manchester University
Press, 1983; republished Colchester: ECPR Press, 2008) for a stimulating discussion.

[18] See A. Trench, 'Tying the UK Together: Intergovernmental relations and the financial
constitution of the UK' in R. Hazell (ed.), *Constitutional Futures Revisited: Britain's Constitution to
2020* (Basingstoke: Palgrave Macmillan, 2008 forthcoming).

[19] For more detailed discussion of the Scottish constitutional debates, see the Scotland Devolution
Monitoring Reports, particularly for January and May 2007, available at www.ucl.ac.uk/
constitution-unit/research/devolution/devo-monitoring-programme.html

very little time for the UK Government to formulate a response and act on it, and such action is all the harder when the government will be entering 'election mode'.

Figure 1.2: Timetable for the Constitutional Debate, 2007–11

August 2007	Scottish Executive published *Choosing Scotland's Future*
October 2007	Sir Emyr Jones Parry named as chair of All Wales Convention
November 2007	Wendy Alexander proposed establishment of a 'Scottish Constitutional Commission'
December 2007	Scottish Parliament endorsed Scottish Constitutional Commission, with SNP opposing the proposal
February 2008	Gordon Brown announced UK Government support for a commission to review devolution
March 2008	Sir Kenneth Calman named as chairman of Commission on Scottish Devolution (CSD)
March 2008	Alex Salmond 're-launched' National Conversation
April 2008	Membership of CSD announced
October/ November 2008	Interim report of CSD due to be published
May/June 2009	Final report of CSD due to be published
October 2009	Report of All Wales Convention due to be published
2010	Scottish Government proposes holding of referendum on negotiations for independence
May 2010	Final date for holding UK general election
2011	Deadline for holding of referendum on primary legislative powers in Wales (under 'One Wales' agreement)

But the situation is, in truth, worse. What has developed is disjointed, because of the lack of resources available and the extreme partisanship with which the processes is characterised. Neither debate has any funds of its own, as the parliamentary arithmetic at Holyrood means that funds cannot be voted for either cause.[20] In these circumstances the Commission a little better off because it is able to call on support and modest resources from the UK

---

[20] As a minority government the SNP cannot simply allocate funds to this — it would need support from other parties to get the budget through if it did. But if the unionist parties want to appropriate funds for their Commission, they would need to make spending cuts elsewhere, so while they could muster the votes for this they would face huge political criticism for doing so.

Government. The unionist parties are, it must be said, more at fault here than the SNP. While the SNP may seek a single answer from the National Conversation (as Peter Jones suggests, though James Mitchell disputes this), its process has sought to take a range of views into account. The Calman Commission's remit means it must avoid engaging with issues relating to independence. The unionist parties involved seem to believe that somehow arguments for independence can be defeated without repudiating them in open debate. Moreover, while the Calman Commission's remit includes considering issues relating to the governance of the UK as a whole, its membership is exclusively Scottish. Its focus is on the bilateral Scottish-UK relationship, not the UK as a whole. (This will probably aid 'nationalist' positions, because it frames the issue in terms solely of what is best for Scotland—another instance of the constitutional strategy not in fact being appropriate to the purpose it appears to be intended to serve.) The Commission's engagement with the public has been limited—in particular, it is not holding public meetings to engage with the general public and find out what the people at large think, but preferring written submissions and use of its website. While the National Conversation has also been heavily reliant on its website, there have been a number of public speeches and meetings to involve the public directly. But worst is the fact that two distinct processes about the same set of issues are underway, which fail to engage with each other. It is hard to avoid concluding that the pursuit of tactical and partisan advantage has worked against having an open and honest debate about Scotland's constitutional and institutional relationship with the rest of the United Kingdom. Even if these ultimately join up, perhaps through a 'multi-option referendum' which would include an extended form of devolution as well as independence or the status quo, the consequences of the process that leads up to them will persist.[21]

In this, there is an emerging contrast with Wales—where up to now constitution-making has been (as Richard Wyn Jones and Roger Scully show in chapter 3) characterised by a similar focus on an elite up to now. While the Government of Wales Act 2006 may be a carefully-crafted political compromise, it involves an unending constitutional debate: first about the devolution of specific 'matters' to the National Assembly, second about whether and when there should be a referendum to bring in provisions of the Act conferring much broader 'primary legislative powers' on the National Assembly, and third about whether those powers are in fact enough. The first of those remains an ongoing topic, entangled in the day-to-day pattern of relations between London and Cardiff. The All Wales convention is to

---

[21] For the SNP's part, Alex Salmond has opened the door to such a referendum when he launched 'phase 2' of the National Conversation. See A. Salmond, 'National Conversation with Scotland's institutions', Speech at the University of Edinburgh, 26 March 2008; available at www.scotland. gov.uk/News/This-Week/Speeches/First-Minister/nationalconversation

consider the second and perhaps the third of those. That is chaired by Sir Emyr Jones Parry, a former UK Ambassador to the United Nations. During the discussions to establish it, there was a tension about whether the convention would have a narrow composition and agenda, and only consider whether the referendum that the 'One Wales' Agreement pledged would take place before 2011 should go ahead, or should be more open in both composition and the issues it would consider. Certainly, the composition of the executive committee is wide-ranging, and includes representatives of all the major political parties and a wide range of non-party, civil society, groups, and the convention is also going out of its way to find ways of engaging with the public.

But the problem, from a UK point of view, is that none of these debates join up. It is not a particular surprise that debates rooted in Scotland and Wales are predominantly about Scottish or Welsh issues and concerns. But when the UK Government gets involved, it has the opportunity to widen the debate and seek to show what the UK offers people from all parts of it that makes living in one state worthwhile. So far, in keeping with the piecemeal way devolution has developed so far, it has ducked that opportunity whenever it has been presented. The question for the next few years is whether it can continue to do so, and what price will be paid if it does.

8. The Increasing Importance of Finance

It is scarcely a surprise that the territorial distribution of finance, and the nature of fiscal powers, should be areas of difficulty in a decentralised system. In chapter 6 John Aldridge surveys the working of the Barnett formula, how it allocates funding across the UK and how the Scottish Executive/Government has allocated the funding at its disposal. Perhaps what is most intriguing is the extent to which this has *not* been an issue in the UK up to now. Part of the reason for this is the freedom and stability of funding that the Barnett formula system has given, at least up to now, which Aldridge highlights. Another part of the reason is political: Labour politicians in particular, from whichever government, have sought to minimise debate about finance and the Barnett formula. One partial exception was Wendy Alexander, who from the back benches tried to develop policy thinking about Scotland's economic future including possible fiscal powers—but even when Labour ministers have talked about the possibility of new systems (and even in Wales), they have done so very cautiously and emphasised the benefits of the Barnett formula. In general, discussion about whether these arrangements are in fact fit for purpose has largely been limited to the academic and think-tank worlds, with some occasional coverage by the London press (usually linked to opinion polling suggesting developing English concern about higher levels of spending in Scotland).

Martin Burch, Alan Harding and James Rees show in chapter 5 that government spending is distributed very unequally within England as well as between the four constituent parts of the UK.[22] In Wales discussion (largely led by Plaid Cymru) has revolved around the 'unfair' levels of funding Wales receives—in this case, too little rather than too much. Northern Ireland has latched onto the idea of reducing corporation tax to attract inward investment, spurred by the lower rates in the Republic of Ireland.[23] The debate has been at its most sophisticated in Scotland, where considerations of 'getting your share' of expenditure and the more sophisticated but related concept of equity have been balanced by interest in the economic and policy implications of devolving tax powers as well.[24] The cause of fiscal devolution has, unsurprisingly, been embraced by the SNP since it took office, and looms large in the discussion of the 'independence' White Paper as well as the work of the Calman Commission (which is being supported by an 'independent expert panel' on fiscal and financial issues).

In many ways, finance is the most wicked of the issues devolution opens up, especially for the unionist parties. Whatever the problems of the status quo (and there are many), change will mean that there are winners and losers—and the likelihood is that more groups will consider themselves losers than winners. If areas like Wales or the North East of England, which presently have high levels of need that are not matched by public spending there, get some more money but less than they expect, they will consider themselves to be losers as much as somewhere that now appears to be 'over-funded' like Scotland.[25] Politically it is therefore very hard to handle.

It gets more difficult, however. In order to make change happen, there are serious economic and technical problems to be resolved. If taxes are to be devolved, which and how? How will any devolved taxing powers relate to grants from the centre, and how will such grants be calculated? There are no clear answers, and not even many clear questions. But if the United Kingdom is to function as a single decentralised state, such issues need to be addressed and resolved. And that means asking, and answering, a set of even harder questions. What is to be the relationship between the constituent parts of the UK and the state's central institutions in Westminster, Whitehall and

[22] On the territorial distribution of public spending, see also I. McLean, G. Lodge and K. Schmuecker, *Fair Shares? Barnett and the politics of public expenditure* (London: Institute for Public Policy Research, 2008). Available at www.ippr.org/ipprnorth/publicationsandreports/publication. asp?id=619

[23] The Treasury asked Sir David Varney to look at this, and following his report rejected the idea on economic policy grounds. See Sir David Varney, *Review of Tax Policy in Northern Ireland* (London: The Stationery Office, 2007). Available at www.hm-treasury.gov.uk/independent_reviews/varney_ review/varney_review_index.cfm

[24] For a summary of the debate as it had developed to early 2007, see D. Scott and C. Jeffery, *Scotland's Economy: The fiscal debate. A discussion paper* (Edinburgh: Scottish Council for Development and Industry, 2007). Available at www.scdi.org.uk/pi/2007/2584.pdf

[25] See McLean et al 2008.

Downing Street? Within that state, what is to be the relationship between autonomy for the constituent parts, and equity across the state as a whole? What might 'equity' mean—rough parity of life chances, the territorial redistribution of spending according to need or the ability for governments to be able to provide comparable services at comparable levels of taxation? If the first or second of those options are preferred, what sorts of constraints on devolved autonomy might there be, and what would be the political implications, both immediate and longer-term, of those? These are fundamental questions about the nature of the state that the devolved UK has so far ducked, but which cannot be avoided for much longer.[26]

The fact that each of the devolved territories wants to revisit the financial arrangements for devolution, at the same time as pressure for some sort of change mounts within England, means that this will become an increasingly significant issue over the next few years. Its salience may build slowly, but by the time of the 2011 elections it will probably have taken centre stage. And in order to answer it, the wicked issues of what the UK means as a state will have to be opened up as well.

CONCLUSION

What all this means is a complex pattern of territorial politics, different from the previous pattern in significant ways—but still a far cry from the sort of pattern that can be seen in federal systems, even multinational ones like Canada, or profoundly asymmetric ones like Spain or Belgium. The UK Government's approach appears to be rooted in established British ways of operating, including a high degree of political partisanship. And perhaps this helps explain why it does not even seem to understand the questions, let alone have a coherent strategy to answer them. It may believe it can respond by using the same tactics that have worked in the UK in the past, but that was in very different circumstances; the changes that have already taken place mean they are unlikely to be effective now.

The UK has always been a territorially complex state. The early years of devolution have been relatively quiet, and helped conceal that complexity, largely because of the implications of extended Labour dominance. A number of those concerned with devolution have long thought that it would become interesting when (as was inevitable, sooner or later) Labour lost an election somewhere. When that happened in 2007, it happened in a remarkably interesting way. It has been interesting because it has led to nationalist parties (not merely non-Labour parties) entering government for the first time, but because it happened in both Scotland and Wales. Moreover, the

---

[26] For an attempt to address some of these issues from a variety of disciplinary perspectives and come up with some answers, see Greer 2008 forthcoming.

fact that Labour in Wales has chosen to share power means that the Labour Party as a whole has to address questions of how it relates to other parties and political forces, rather than simply wait in opposition for things to go wrong for the parties in office so it could return to power. While the UK Government understands that the new situation raises a set of difficult and serious problems, it has shown no willingness to undertaken the sort of sustained long-term work needed resolve those problems—or indeed of understanding fully their complexity.

Devolution has constituted not just a recognition of the UK's territorial complexity but also of the political failure of other approaches. In particular, it acknowledges that the traditional idea that the Union Parliament could serve as the setting for UK-wide politics, and that administrative and procedural arrangements could deliver adequately tailor that to the different needs of Scotland and Wales, was no longer viable. One could argue that this is because a former skill of compromise disappeared during the political and ideological conflicts of the 1970s and 1980s. However, in a sense devolution is a response to old problems, not new ones. It may prevent a repetition of the sort of Conservative rule of Scotland or Wales without an electoral mandate, which was the concern of the 1980s and 1990s, but that does not constitute a broader agenda for the future.

In particular, what is the United Kingdom *for* in the twenty-first century? Economic integration, particularly in the European Union, mean that the UK-wide economy is less important. Equally, the UK's role in defence and international affairs is not as strong a factor as it might have been thirty or fifty years ago. Devolution means that a large part of the welfare state is now administered by the devolved institutions, even if key elements (including taxation and redistribution through welfare benefits) are not. This raises the question of what the UK is now for in terms of social citizenship, and more broadly. The rhetoric of 'Britishness' can at best be only one part of the answer to this question (and a small part at that). So far, the UK Government has shown no enthusiasm for taking on the territorial implications of this issue. The big long-term issue arising from devolution is not so much about Scotland, Wales or Northern Ireland, but about the UK as whole, and England's relationship to the whole and the other constituent parts. How the UK responds to the increasing territorial challenges it faces will be the big question for the coming years.

Predictions of the future are always risky, with being proved wrong always a major risk. But one can predict, with a degree of confidence, that the second phase of devolution will continue not only to be unlike prove more complicated, more challenging for policy makers and more interesting for students than the first phase did.

BIBLIOGRAPHY

Official Documents and Primary Sources

Cairns, D., 'How Holyrood and Westminster make devolution work', *The Herald* (Glasgow), 11 January 2008.

Department for Business, Enterprise and Regulatory Reform, *Meeting the Energy Challenge: A White Paper on Nuclear Power* Cm 7296 (London: The Stationery Office, 2008).

HM Treasury, *Funding the Scottish Parliament, National Assembly for Wales and Northern Ireland Assembly: A statement of funding policy* 5th edn. (London: HM Treasury, 2007).

House of Commons, *The Prime Minister: oral evidence, Thursday 13 December 2007 Rt Hon Gordon Brown MP* HC 192-i (London: The Stationery Office, 2008).

Memorandum of Understanding and supplementary agreements between the United Kingdom Government, Scottish Ministers, the Cabinet of the National Assembly for Wales and the Northern Ireland Executive Committee Cm 5240 (London: The Stationery Office, 2001).

Ministry of Justice, *The Governance of Britain* Cm 7170 (London: The Stationery Office, 2007).

Salmond, A., 'National Conversation with Scotland's institutions', Speech at the University of Edinburgh, 26 March 2008.

Scottish Executive, *Choosing Scotland's Future. A National Conversation. Independence and Responsibility in the Modern World* (Edinburgh: Scottish Executive, 2007).

Varney, Sir D., *Review of Tax Policy in Northern Ireland* (London: The Stationery Office, 2007).

Secondary References

Bulpitt, J., *Territory and Power in the United Kingdom* (Manchester: Manchester University Press, 1983; republished Colchester: ECPR Press, 2008).

Greer, S. (ed.), *Devolution and Social Citizenship in the UK* (Bristol: Policy Press, 2009 forthcoming)

Lodge, G., M. Russell, and O. Gay, 'The Impact of Devolution on Westminster: If not now, when?', in A. Trench (ed.), *Has Devolution Made a Difference? The State of the Nations 2004* (Exeter: Imprint Academic, 2004), pp. 193–216.

McEwen, N., 'State Welfare Nationalism: The territorial impact of welfare state development in Scotland', *Regional and Federal Studies* 12(1) (2002): 66–90.

McLean, I., G. Lodge and K. Schmuecker, *Fair Shares? Barnett and the politics of public expenditure* (London: Institute for Public Policy Research, 2008).

Osmond, J., *Crossing the Rubicon: Coalition politics Welsh style* (Cardiff: Institute of Welsh Affairs, 2007).

Scott, D. and C. Jeffery, *Scotland's Economy: The fiscal debate. A discussion paper* (Edinburgh: Scottish Council for Development and Industry, 2007).

Trench, A. (ed.), *The Dynamics of Devolution: The State of the Nations 2005* (Exeter: Imprint Academic, 2005).

Trench, A. (ed.), *Devolution and Power in the United Kingdom* (Manchester: Manchester University Press, 2007).

Trench, A., 'Tying the UK Together: Intergovernmental relations and the financial constitution of the UK' in R. Hazell (ed.), *Constitutional Futures Revisited: Britain's Constitution to 2020* (Basingstoke: Palgrave Macmillan, 2008 forthcoming).

Wincott, D., 'Social Policy and Social Citizenship: Britain's Welfare States', *Publius: The journal of federalism* 36 (1) (2006): 169–88.

2

Scotland

The Nationalist Phoenix

Peter Jones

All through Friday 4 May 2007, Labour First Minister Jack McConnell was staring defeat in the face. Labour constituencies such as Central Fife and Cunningham North, thought to be as safe as houses, had fallen to the Scottish National Party (SNP). Labour's last hope lay with the final count of the day — the regional seats in the Highlands and Islands. Labour was allocated three list seats and the SNP two, making the final seat tally Labour 46 and the SNP 47. Labour had lost. The SNP had won. Nationalist activists gleefully recalled a prediction made by George (now Lord) Robertson when he was shadow Secretary of State for Scotland in 1997, that devolution would 'kill nationalism stone dead'. But after the disappointments and reverses of elections in the first eight years of the Scottish Parliament, the SNP was not just arisen from the flames of defeat, it was clutching at the levers of power. The tally of seats won and lost (Figure 2.1) show just how big a change occurred.

Figure 2.1: Seat Gains and Losses by Party 2007

Party	Constituency MSPs		Regional List MSPs		Total seats	Gain/ Loss
	2003	2007	2003	2007	2007	
Labour	46	37	4	9	46	− 4
SNP	9	21	18	26	47	+20
Lib. Dem.	13	11	4	5	16	− 1
Cons	3	4	15	13	17	− 1
Green	0	0	7	2	2	− 5
SSP/ Solidarity	0	0	6	0	0	− 6
Other	2	0	2	1	1	− 3

In terms of seats, the SNP was the only winner. All other parties lost seats. Closer inspection reveals that the tide in favour of the Nationalists was not quite so overwhelming as it seems. Of the 20 seat shift, only six came from the three main rivals, and the remaining 14 came from the small parties and independents.

Nonetheless, this was a dramatic and historic election. Dramatic, because the big lead in the opinion polls that the SNP had built up before the campaign started was steadily eroded throughout as Labour fought back. Historic, because 2007 was the first time Labour had failed to win the biggest haul of seats and votes in Scotland since 1955, opening the door for the first Scottish National Party government in British political history. The counting was also remarkable, for, as is hinted above, it was a complete shambles. The ballot paper, designed to make for speedy tallying by electronic scanning machines, caused dreadful confusion among the voters. A total of 146,097 ballots, or 3.47 per cent of all votes cast, were spoiled.[1] All these features mean that the 2007 Holyrood election will probably be the subject of much debate for years to come.

THE SECOND FOUR YEARS

After a turbulent start to devolved government (the loss of two First Ministers in the first two years), Jack McConnell entered the First Minister's office in 2001 promising to 'do less, better'. By the 2003 election, this mantra was abandoned. He began the second four-year term armed with a manifesto which was strong on criminal justice, particularly dealing with anti-social behaviour, and improvement in health and education. McConnell declared this to be an agenda for 'bold new steps'.[2] Yet by the end of this term, bold-ness of action from the legislative programme turned out to be the exception rather than the rule. Indeed, McConnell's time in office may be remembered more for the non-legislative initiatives taken.[3]

The law-making programme was certainly busy. A total of 66 bills were enacted, or just over 15 per year (see Figure 2.2). Legislation was dominated by the Executive; only three members' bills and one committee bill made it into law. Of the nine private bills, seven provided for rail and Edinburgh tram infrastructure building, all backed by the Executive.

---

[1] S. Herbert and T. Edwards, *Rejected Ballot Papers* Scottish Parliament Information Centre (SPICe) Briefing 07/36, 26 June 2007 (Edinburgh: Scottish Parliament, 2007). Available at www.scottish.parliament.uk/business/research/briefings-07/SB07-36.pdf

[2] 'Labour manifesto targets yob culture', BBC News online, 7 April 2003.

[3] See generally E. Bort, 'Annals of the Parish: The Year at Holyrood, 2005-06', *Scottish Affairs* 57 (2006): 112–34.

The legislative highlight was undoubtedly the bill banning smoking in enclosed public places.[4] Despite vociferous opposition from publicans and sections of the Labour Party, McConnell became convinced that it was a necessary step to improve public health.[5] When it came into force on 26 March 2006, the ban proved popular and was rarely flouted. Dr Mac Armstrong, who retired as Scotland's Chief Medical Officer as the bill became law, described it as 'the most significant measure in a generation to help improve our nation's health.'[6]

Figure 2.2: Bills in the Scottish Parliament 2003–7[7]

	Introduced	Enacted	Withdrawn	Fallen
Executive Bills	53	53	–	–
Private Bills	9	9	–	–
Members Bills	18	3	5	10
Committee Bills	1	1	–	–

The big prize for the Liberal Democrats was the abolition of first-past-the-post elections for local government and the introduction of the single transferable vote. This means that Scottish voters have no fewer than four different election systems to grapple with at various elections, but more importantly, it spelled the end of Labour dominance in local government.

A significant element of the four-year legislative programme dealt with crime and the criminal justice system — nearly a quarter of the Executive's programme was devoted to these topics, highlighting reform of all levels of the courts, and tackling anti-social behaviour.[8] Family law — notably reform of the law relating to cohabiting couples and adoption by same-sex couples — provoked opposition from the Roman Catholic Church.[9] Otherwise, most legislation delivered incremental change, and was relatively uncontroversial. Overall, it was hard to disagree with the verdict of Nicola Sturgeon:

> What is disappointing about the Executive programme is not that any of the proposed bills are particularly objectionable. On the contrary, many of them are eminently supportable … However, taken together, this legislative programme

---

[4] The Smoking, Health, and Social Care (Scotland) Act 2005.
[5] 'Strong move towards smoking ban' BBC News online, 31 August 2004.
[6] 'Positive message on Scots' health', BBC News online, 19 May 2005.
[7] For a full list, see www.scottish.parliament.uk/business/bills/billsnotInProgress-s2/index.htm
[8] Scottish Executive 'Criminal Proceedings Etc. (Scotland) Reform Bill: Policy Memorandum', p. 2, available at www.scottish.parliament.uk/business/bills/55-criminalProceedings/index.htm
[9] The Family Law (Scotland) Act 2006.

does not tackle the big challenges that we face ... It lacks vision and a clear sense of purpose and direction for our nation.[10]

NON-LEGISLATIVE EXECUTIVE ACTION

The McConnell Executive undertook a number of other initiatives which did not need legislation, and relied on executive powers instead. One was a push to tackle sectarianism in Scottish society generally, building on legislation passed in the previous Parliament. Another was aimed a reversing the long gradual decline of the Scottish population. 'Fresh Talent' was an attempt to boost immigration (a reserved area), but by agreement with the Home Office McConnell announced that overseas students could stay for an additional two years after graduating. The initiative also involved a number of other measures aimed at enhancing the attractiveness of Scotland to Scots living outside the country and to immigrants generally.[11]

McConnell sought to establish a programme of development aid and support to Malawi, an African country with historic links to Scotland. This aid included support for teacher training, health service development, and a call for a 'National Fund' to be established to help Malawi.[12] Executive financial support was channelled through non-governmental bodies such as overseas development charities, to get around constitutional and legal problems. Subsequently, after he stood down as First Minister and Labour leader, it was announced that McConnell would in due course become the UK's High Commissioner to Malawi.

But the Executive's declared first priority was improving the economy of Scotland. Measures to try and do this were scattered throughout the Executive's programme. As well as 'Fresh Talent', this included infrastructure improvement (especially the construction of new roads, a passion of the CBI, and railway lines) and a big increase in spending on transport, along with an emphasis on enhancing skills through such things as expansion of the modern apprenticeship scheme. In September 2005 came a promise to cut business rates to the same level as in England and Wales, following a long business campaign.[13] Yet neither the Executive nor McConnell received much political credit for this move.

Moreover, successful politics is not just about legislation, spending money or announcing action plans, but also about implementation. The Executive learned this the hard way from some searching criticism of some of its policies, including the generous teachers' pay settlement in the

---

[10] Scottish Parliament *Official Report*, 7 September 2004, col 9901.

[11] Scottish Executive news release, 'Scotland says welcome to the world' 25 February 2004, available at www.scotland.gov.uk/News/Releases/2004/02/5123. For more detail on the Malawi policy, see *Scotland Devolution Monitoring Reports*, January and September 2006,

[12] www.scotland.gov.uk/News/Releases/2005/11/14081608

[13] 'McConnell vows business rate cut', BBC News online, 6 September 2005.

previous Parliament (criticised for lack of outcome measures to assess improvement by Audit Scotland), and the limited take-up of anti-social behaviour orders (Asbos) by local councils.

Free personal care for the elderly had been one of the Executive's flagship programmes in the previous Parliament. A report in January 2006 published by the Joseph Rowntree Foundation found that in general, the policy had improved the quality of life for older people. This was extracted from a fuller research project by the University of Stirling which also praised the policy for removing many financial uncertainties faced by older people.[14] But the research also pointed out that greater clarity was needed on how to calculate the costs of free personal care and found wide variations between local authorities. Thirteen of 32 councils were found by Age Concern to be wrongly charging people for the costs of food preparation.[15] A report by the Parliament's health committee found there was confusion on who was eligible to receive free personal care, a lack of clear guidance from the Executive, and that half of councils operated a waiting list.[16] A running series of press reports highlighting individual problems and suggesting that care provision was something of a lottery, took the shine off this policy.

A NEW STAGE AND UNSEEMLY NOISES OFF

With a final price tag of £431 million, more than ten times the £40 million cost forecast in the 1997 devolution White Paper, the new home for the Parliament was officially opened by the Queen on 9 October 2004. The ceremony was dignified but not pompous — the Queen was greeted by Aaron Copland's 'Fanfare for the Common Man'. Salmond ruffled some Labour feathers by introducing a hint of politics, reminding the Queen that he led a nationalist party that would seek independence. Her Majesty appeared to be unperturbed.[17]

Three weeks earlier, Lord Fraser of Carmyllie had published his report on why the building cost so much. He found 'no single villain of the piece'. He strongly criticised the type of procurement contract and civil servants for not keeping ministers informed of escalating costs. He contended that 'something in excess of £150 million has been wasted in the cost of prolongation flowing from design delays, over-optimistic programming and uncertain authority'. He concluded, however, 'The Scottish Parliament has a building that meets the vision that I believe Donald Dewar and his colleagues set for

[14] D. Bell and A. Bowes, *Financial Care Models in Scotland and the UK* (York: Joseph Rowntree Foundation, 2006), available at www.jrf.org.uk/knowledge/findings/socialcare/0036.asp

[15] 'Elderly "charged for free food"', BBC News online, 27 February 2006.

[16] Scottish Parliament Health Committee *Care Inquiry* 10th Report, 2006, SP Paper 594. Available at www.scottish.parliament.uk/business/committees/health/reports-06/her06-10-vol01-00.htm

[17] A. Black, 'People and parliament join hands', BBC News online, 30 June 2006.

it. I express the hope that the excellence of the parliamentary activity within the building will reflect the quality of the structure, and that the painful lessons of its procurement are not lost on those privileged to serve there as representatives of the Scottish people.'[18]

The excellence prayed for by Lord Carmyllie did not manifest itself in MSPs' behaviour. Only the SNP and the Greens seemed to be free of scandal (though the SNP did suffer one embarrassment — the expulsion of one MSP, Campbell Martin).[19] In November 2004, after drinking heavily at the Scottish Politician of the Year Awards, Lord Mike Watson, a Labour MSP, bizarrely set fire to curtains in the hotel hosting the event. Ten months later, after admitting wilful fire-raising, he was jailed for 16 months.[20] Liberal Democrat MSP Keith Raffan resigned in December 2004 on ill-health grounds, but this also seemed to have something to do with his expense claims. Expenses also proved to be the downfall of David McLetchie, the Conservative leader. He resigned in October 2005 (see next section) after a long-running media probe led by the *Sunday Herald* into his claims for taxi expenses, not all of which appeared to relate to his parliamentary duties.[21]

But the most spectacular drama was provided by the Trotskyite Scottish Socialist Party (SSP) and its leader Tommy Sheridan. He resigned as leader in November 2004, saying he wanted time to be a 'proper father' to his young child. But rumbling in the background were a series of tabloid newspaper allegations, mainly in the *News of the World*, that Sheridan had a lurid sex life. This developed into a split in the SSP, with one MSP, Rosemary Byrne, backing Sheridan and the remaining four opposing him. In 2006, matters came to a head when Sheridan's action for defamation against the *News of the World* came to court. Sensational claims of group sex were made and denied. Sheridan dismissed his lawyers and conducted the case himself. To the newspaper's evident astonishment, the jury believed Sheridan and awarded him £200,000 damages, though Sheridan's credibility was very seriously wounded. The SSP was terminally divided, and Sheridan's formation of a new party — Solidarity — fatally wounded the far left cause.[22] And subsequently Sheridan and his wife were charged with perjury arising from the evidence they gave during the libel trial.

---

[18] Lord Fraser of Carmyllie. Speech at the publication of the Holyrood Inquiry Report, 15 September 2004. Available at www.holyroodinquiry.org/

[19] 'Nationalists throw out rebel MSP', BBC News online, 10 July 2004.

[20] 'Fire-raising peer sent to prison', BBC News online, 22 September 2005.

[21] 'McLetchie "reviews" taxi expenses', BBC News online, 26 October 2005.

[22] 'Sheridan faced biggest challenge', BBC News online, 4 August 2006.

CHANGES OF LEADER

John Swinney had become the SNP leader in 2001 after the unexpected resignation of Alex Salmond after 10 years as leader. Salmond stood down from his Scottish Parliament seat in 2001 to concentrate on Westminster, vowing emphatically he would not seek to return as leader. Swinney was bright and capable but lacked charisma. Disappointing election results at the 2001 Westminster, 2003 Holyrood, and the 2004 European elections forced him to stand down in June 2004.[23] When it appeared that Salmond's preference, Nicola Sturgeon MSP, might lose the contest to Roseanna Cunningham MSP, Salmond hurriedly entered the fray with Sturgeon as his running mate for deputy leader. The two won convincingly, Salmond gaining 76 per cent and Sturgeon 54 per cent of the votes cast.[24] Salmond's return was a turning point for the SNP which had been losing votes steadily in all elections since a high point in the first 1999 Holyrood election. Though opposition parties tried to taunt the SNP for having an absentee London leader, Salmond proved impervious to such insults. As will be shown later, he set about reinvigorating the party, setting the ambitious (and apparently improbable) target of winning the 2007 elections.

Enforced changes of leader affected the other main opposition parties too. Following the resignation of David McLetchie, the Conservatives debated whether to go for a safe pair of hands in the shape of deputy leader Annabel Goldie MSP or live a little dangerously with Murdo Fraser MSP. In the event, they got both; Goldie and Fraser did a deal and were unopposed as leader and deputy.[25] In May 2005, Jim Wallace decided to quit as Liberal Democrat leader while the going was good. Nicol Stephen, a long-time favourite son of the party, eventually beat Mike Rumbles, winning 77 per cent of the party vote. Stephen, previously Deputy Minister for Transport, stepped up to take over Mr Wallace's roles as Deputy First Minister and Minister for Enterprise and Lifelong Learning.

MORE POWERS?

A constantly-running background debate in the first few years of devolution has been whether the Parliament should have more powers. It is a theme the SNP has plugged away at, but beyond newspaper and academic commentators, it had never stirred much interest.

In summer 2005 Jack McConnell let it be known he had asked his advisors to review whether the Parliament's powers should be enhanced. Issues to be covered included powers over nuclear power stations, casinos, abortion,

---

[23] 'Under-fire SNP leader resigns', BBC News online, 22 June 2004.
[24] 'Salmond named as new SNP leader', BBC News online, 3 September 2004.
[25] 'Goldie "ready to wield handbag"', BBC News online, 8 November 2005.

firearms, broadcasting, election law, and the size of the Parliament. It rapidly emerged that the greatest opposition to further powers might be from within the Labour Party when press reports suggested Labour MPs were opposed to change, and little thereafter emerged about this review.[26] In practice, McConnell allowed important aspects of the existing arrangements, such as meetings of the plenary Joint Ministerial Committee, to fall into disuse. Further indications of McConnell's thinking emerged in October 2006, when he gave the annual lecture set up in memory of John P. Mackintosh. While saying that modification of the settlement might be needed, he ruled out significant change and said, 'It is my considered opinion based on all the evidence before me that a separation of powers, broadly along the lines of the current division of responsibilities between Holyrood and Westminster, is the most advantageous arrangement, not only to improve the lives of ordinary Scots now, but to prepare Scotland for the enormity of the future challenge. ... to abandon devolution here in Scotland after just seven or eight years, to declare the game a bogey, and to take ourselves off in a huff would be to demonstrate quite shocking irresponsibility.'[27] In interviews, there was no mistaking his emphatic dismissal of greater taxation powers, terming calls for them a 'fad'.[28] This scepticism was not shared by all in Labour; after resigning as Minister for Enterprise, Wendy Alexander organised a series of lectures by leading economists (eventually published as a book) on how to improve the Scottish economy.[29] This included a chapter arguing the case for more devolution of taxation, a view which Alexander seemed happy to make known that she shared.

The most significant contribution to the constitutional debate came from the Liberal Democrats. A party commission chaired by Lord Steel of Aikwood (as Sir David Steel, formerly the Parliament's Presiding Officer) reported in March 2006. The Steel Report recommended that the Parliament should be given almost complete control over taxation, firearms, immigration and asylum policy, drugs and some welfare policy. Though it was billed as working toward a 'federal constitution' for Britain, it said little about how the other components of Britain should be constituted, beyond noting that regionalism in England was a difficult question.[30] The media were less

[26] K. Nutt and J. Allardyce, 'Labour MPs to reject more devolved power', *Sunday Times* Scotland 31 July 2005.

[27] J. McConnell, 'In the Interest of Our Nation'. Annual J.P. Mackintosh Lecture, East Haddington, 24 October 2006. Available at www.scotland.gov.uk/News/News-Extras/FM-on-constitution/Q/ViewArchived/On

[28] 'McConnell warning on extra powers', BBC News online, 24 October 2006.

[29] D. Coyle, W. Alexander and B. Ashcroft (eds.), *New Wealth for Old Nations* (Princeton, NJ: Princeton University Press, 2005).

[30] Scottish Liberal Democrats, *The Steel Commission: Moving to Federalism. A new Settlement for Scotland* (Edinburgh: Scottish Liberal Democrats, 2006). Available at www.scotlibdems.org.uk/pages/publications

interested in the policy proposals that in the apparent implication that it made coalition with the SNP much more likely.[31]

LABOUR'S UNIONIST DRUM BEAT

From the outset, Labour's campaign for the 2007 election was dominated by a defence of the Union and an all-out assault on Nationalism. The main themes were signalled at the party's Scottish conference in Oban in November 2006, which featured vehement attacks on the SNP led by Tony Blair, Gordon Brown, and John Reid. They argued that Scotland and the rest of Britain were interdependent, and viscerally linked economically, culturally, and socially. However, Jack McConnell, while making dutiful swipes at the SNP, concentrated on laying out a detailed policy agenda centring on education.[32]

But in contrast to the previous Holyrood elections, when new Labour shone as a bright new force in politics, Labour now looked tired and tarnished. The aftermath of the Iraq invasion and Iraq's descent into civil war exacted a heavy toll on the party's credibility, as did the police investigation into the 'loans for peerages' affair (prompted by a complaint from the SNP Western Isles MP Angus MacNeil), and Blair's decision to renew Britain's nuclear deterrent with a new fleet of Trident submarines and his evident desire to build a new generation of nuclear power stations. The cash-for-peerages probe revealed serious divisions within the Labour hierarchy. One of those quizzed twice by police was John McTernan, Blair's political secretary, who came north in early 2007 to work on the Holyrood campaign — part of a general tendency for 'London Labour' to take over the campaign.

Labour's campaign appeared to be dogged by a tussle to lead it between three groups — Blair/McTernan doom-mongering about the social and cultural ruptures consequent on independence, Brown/Alexander thundering about the economic disasters the Nationalists would cause, and McConnell and his advisors gamely trying to present a constructive agenda for the next four years. The latter two groups were aware that Blair's value on the campaign front was highly questionable and McConnell's discomfiture about this was evident during televised debates. Blair, however, dismissed these concerns, arguing that he was not a factor since voters knew he was soon to leave office. Neither could he believe that people would risk the gamble of voting SNP just to give him a parting kick.[33]

Things were even worse on the organisational front. Campaigners sent from England to assist their Scottish counterparts were aghast to discover that in most of Labour's Scottish seats, there were no records of canvass returns from previous elections. One campaigner was quoted as saying, 'It

[31] H. MacDonell, 'Lib Dems open door to coalition with SNP', *The Scotsman* 7 March 2006. .
[32] 'McConnell makes school leaver vow', BBC News online, 25 November 2006.
[33] Author's personal briefing with Tony Blair.

was a nightmare. No work had been done. Everyone thought these seats were safe and that we didn't need to worry. We basically had to start from scratch finding out who our voters were.'[34] Thus a party with its hierarchy divided, its strategy unclear, and its organisation in tatters, staggered to the election start-ing-line. Though the electorate was clearly disenchanted with Blair, the party determined that he and Brown would lead the assault on the SNP and independence.

Exactly how effective this would be was, however, open to doubt. The SNP had adopted Labour's strategy for defusing Conservative attacks on its plans for devolution in the 1997 election by promising that in government, it would publish a White Paper on independence and then hold a referendum. As with Labour in 1997, it meant that people could vote for the SNP and its manifesto for running a devolved Scotland without worrying whether this meant Scotland becoming independent. Labour strategists took the view that the SNP and independence were so inextricably linked that this was a detail. Labour's 2007 campaign managers were unapologetic. One was quoted in *The Scotsman* as saying, 'In this campaign, after 10 years in government, it is fear, not hope, that will win.'[35]

Jack McConnell's positive agenda came to the fore at Labour's manifesto launch on 10 April. He spoke with passion about education and unveiled radical proposals to increase spending on education by £1.2 billion over the next three years at the expense of other areas. Unfortunately for Labour, the media was more interested in council tax. McConnell proposed various changes at the margins but when the media demanded details he could give none. Because Labour could not produce figures to back its own policy, the figures that it produced on SNP policies were undermined.[36]

Labour Manifesto 2007: Key Points.

Economy: Establish Full Employment Agency to work with UK Government to get 100,000 people into work by 2015; increase proportion of working age population with vocational or academic higher/further education qualification to 51 per cent; invest in science research and conversion of discoveries into products; spend £30 million on cutting small business rates.

---

[34] E. Barnes and M. MacLeod, 'How Jack lost the battle', *Scotland on Sunday* 6 May 2007.

[35] P. MacMahon, 'Labour big guns banking on £13bn fear factor in election', *The Scotsman* 4 April 2007.

[36] M. Linklater, 'Being a maths teacher doesn't mean you have all the answers', *The Times* 11 April 2007.

Education: All 16 and 17 year-olds to be in higher or further education, training work or volunteering; new arithmetic and literacy exams; more emphasis on science and language learning; 250 new refurbished schools; expand number of schools specialising in music and sports; continue reducing class sizes to below OECD average; programme to reduce bullying and violence in schools; real terms increase in finance for further and higher education.

Justice: Establish community police teams in every area of Scotland and double number of community wardens; more use of anti-social behaviour orders by local authorities; reform youth justice system; Sentencing Guidelines Council to bring more consistency to sentencing; put Scottish Crime and Drug Enforcement Agency under one roof with other law enforcement agencies; review a ban on airguns

Health: hospital waiting times to be cut to a maximum of 18 weeks from GP referral; walk-in treatment centres in main commuter hubs; more minor procedures to be carried out by nurses; more services to be provided by GP health centres or at community hospitals; wider consultation by NHS boards on changes to services; direct election of majority of NHS board members to be piloted; reduce amounts payable for prescription charges.

Environment: introduce climate change bill including commitment to reduce carbon emissions by 60 per cent by 2050; 50 per cent of electricity generation from renewable sources by 2020; set target to recycle 70 per cent of waste by 2020.

Rural Affairs: extend community right-to-buy to larger communities; help young farmers enter the industry; increase share of Common Agricultural Policy resources allocated to environmental protection to 15 per cent; legislate to protect definition of Scotch Whisky.

Transport: spend £1 billion a year with 70 per cent devoted to public transport; take forward Glasgow cross-rail project; examine fast link rail services between Glasgow and Edinburgh; consider running Scotrail franchise on a not-for-profit basis; complete major road schemes; abolish tolls on Tay road bridge; build replacement Forth road crossing.

Society: end child poverty by 2020 and fuel poverty by 2016; establish national anti-poverty unit.

Local Government: Cut water and sewerage charges by 50 per cent for all pensioner households within two years

TIME FOR CHANGE IN THE SNP

The SNP's campaign can be traced back to June 2005 when Angus Robert-son, MP for Moray, gathered a group of senior party people and supporters at the Craigellachie Hotel on Speyside. It included bright young people such as the party's former communications director Kevin Pringle, then working for Scottish Gas, and business, public affairs and academic supporters. The aim was to work out where the party had been going wrong and how to put it right. Reports say that the meeting agreed that the party had to stop talking to itself at election time, should concentrate less on protest campaigns and more on positive actions, and should present itself as a party ready for government. The most important factors contributing to previous poor performances were felt to be lack of money and poor communications. Five priorities for action were identified — communications, governance, message, organisation and resource — and teams of staff and politicians were allocated to each. Under governance, the main message was: 'To be ready for government before 3 May 2007, and in government thereafter.'[37]

Many of the tactics adopted by the SNP seem to have been adopted from the New Labour 1997 election guide. Indeed, some of it was written by a former New Labour supporter, Gordon Guthrie, who had switched allegiance to the SNP. A computer expert, he had constructed the software for a programme called 'Activate', which Labour used to identify and track existing and potential supporters. He now built an enhanced version for the SNP. With one exception, the main thrust of SNP election campaigns had been to convert people to the idea of independence by promising that a host of good things — better pensions, lower tax bills, better hospitals — will become possible if only people vote for independence. But, since independence has never appealed to more than, at best, a third of the electorate, the strategy has failed. The exception was the 2003 Holyrood elections, when the SNP downplayed independence and concentrated on policies for devolution, a strategy that did not work either. Guthrie wrote that that the SNP should aim to maintain its traditional electoral base and add to them by constructing a 'coalition of interests'. He advocated, 'The party needs to position itself in the political landscape by understanding and reaching out to segments of the electorate, peeling layers of support from other parties, and binding them into an electoral coalition for independence.'[38]

The SNP used the same tactic as Labour had in 1997, devoting time and effort to talking to Scottish business and promising to use the powers of devolution to make radical cuts in business rates for small businesses. But it did not attempt to hide independence either. Indeed it tried to use independence to enhance its business-friendly credentials by promising that an independent Scotland would cut corporation tax to 20 per cent.

These efforts paid big dividends. In October 2006, the SNP announced that Sir Tom Farmer, founder of the Kwik-Fit chain of car exhaust and tyre fitters, had donated £100,000 in order to ensure a level spending playing field in the campaign. That was followed by £500,000 from Brian Souter, chairman of Stagecoach. Although Souter was a long-time SNP supporter,

---

[37] T. Gordon, 'Wrestling with Independence', *Sunday Times* Scotland 6 May 2007.
[38] Barnes and MacLeod 2007.

Farmer's previous political leanings were towards Thatcherism. Apart from enabling the SNP to claim some heavyweight business backing, the donations meant the party reached its target of £1.5 million to spend on the election.

The reaching-out strategy went much wider than that. The potency of bridge tolls to shift votes had emerged during the Dunfermline West by-election in February 2006. The SNP made abolishing tolls on the Forth and Tay road bridges a campaign pledge. In Ayr and Lanarkshire, health board plans to close hospital accident and emergency units caused much local outrage. The SNP promised to stop any such closures. Discovering that there was a significant body of opposition to plans to spend £1.2 billion on trams and an airport rail link in Edinburgh, the SNP promised to scrap the trams and find a cheaper airport rail link. (This had the handy by-product of meeting with approval in the SNP heartlands north and north-east of Scotland where voters have a strong suspicion that they are losing out on the benefits of devolution while central Scotland is cashing in.)

Some of the SNP's policies did not need changing, but re-modelling. The party has long opposed property-based local council taxes and favoured a local income tax. This has always been open to attacks from opponents claiming that the additional income tax would be penalising. In March 2007, the SNP announced that a fixed rate of 3p extra on the basic rate of income tax would be applied across Scotland, dropping the idea of local power to vary the rate. They also said that council tax bills would be frozen for two years until they were able to introduce the new tax.[39] The new format of an old policy had the merit of simplicity. It had a definite appeal to pensioners and middle-income earners facing rising mortgage payments as a result of interest rate rises. The middle classes were further wooed with promises to abolish the post-graduation student endowment charge of about £2000 per student and eventually to reintroduce a student grant system.

The 'New Labourisation' of the SNP extended to instructing candidates on how to establish a rapport with voters by mirroring their posture, body language, and speech patterns, and by maintaining eye contact.

The SNP's response to Labour's assaults on their financial plans was subtly different to previous campaigns when they did their best to trade numbers, presenting journalists with a mass of competing balance sheets and jostling estimates and counter estimates. In this campaign, the SNP produced their counter-estimate of the state of Scotland's public finances early with two publications in 2006, which reiterated the SNP's claims that an independent Scotland would be among the wealthiest countries in the world and that when oil was included, Scotland's public finances were in

---

[39] P. MacMahon, 'SNP unveil scheme to replace council tax', *The Scotsman* 15 March 2007.

balance.[40] Having done that exercise, the SNP resisted any temptation to do more number-crunching in the election campaign.

SNP Manifesto 2007: Key Points

Government: cut number of Executive departments; reduce cabinet ministers (to be re-labelled cabinet secretaries) from eight to five; review agency structure to reduce bureaucracy; discussions on creation of Scottish civil service on lines of Northern Irish model; early publication of White Paper on independence with aim of a referendum in 2010; produce annual 'health of the nation' report; work constructively with the UK Government, strengthen concordats, restart Joint Ministerial Committee meetings, and seek early negotiation on transfer of responsibility for North Sea oil and gas to Scotland; secure efficiencies of £2.7 billion in 2008–11; introduce not-for-profit Scottish Futures Trust as alternative to private finance for public projects;

Economy: create new Council of Economic Advisors and new National Economic forum; spend £120 million on business rates relief scheme for small businesses; set targets for economic growth to match UK growth rates by 2011 and exceed them by 2017; grow population by 3 per cent over next ten years; proportion of national wealth held by six lowest income deciles to increase; a 10 per cent reduction in wealth disparity of richest and poorest part of Scotland; signal intention to reduce Corporation Tax to 20 per cent when Scottish government has the power;

Transport: 10-year plan to improve road safety; approve second stage Waverley station improvements; cancel Edinburgh trams saving £600 million; cancel Edinburgh Airport Rail Link saving £600 million and substitute cheaper alternative; improve Edinburgh-Glasgow rail journey times, commuter rail routes and Edinburgh-Aberdeen/Inverness rail line; early go-ahead for replacement Forth Crossing; commission study and pilot 'Road Equivalent Tariff' fares for ferries to Western Isles; seek discussions with UK Government on Scotland-London high-speed rail link

Local Government: initially freeze council tax then abolish it and replace with local income tax set at 3p; review community councils; work with lenders to provide loans to first-time buyers and introduce first-time buyers' grant of £2,000; review council housing right-to-buy legislation.

Environment: introduce Climate Change Bill with mandatory 3 per cent annual reduction in carbon output; set target for use of alternative fuels; ban on new nuclear power stations and waste dumps; commitment to renewable energy in every Scottish school; consult on reducing energy footprint in new buildings; seek creation of EU green energy research centre in Aberdeen; support research into carbon capture at power stations and tidal/wave power;

---

[40] Scottish National Party, 'The true wealth of the nation' August 2006, and 'Scotland in Surplus — past, present and future' December 2006 (Scottish National Party, Edinburgh). Both available at www.snp.org

Health and Wellbeing: Patients' Right bill to set 18-week guarantee between GP referral and hospital treatment; more out-of-office hours opening of local health centres; more fast-track diagnostic and treatment NHS treatment centres; presumption against centralisation of core hospital services; introduce direct elections to health boards; seek return of £40 million in attendance allowance payments from UK Government; abolish prescription charges by 2012.

Education: reduce class sizes in P1–3 to 18 or less; pilot free school meals for P1–3 pupils; every pupil to have 2 hours of PE per week; increase nursery provision by 50 per cent; vocational qualifications to have parity of esteem with academic qualifications; abolish graduate endowment fee and replace student loans with means-tested grants; pay off existing Scottish student debt.

Arts and Sport: abolish SportScotland; support Glasgow 2014 Commonwealth Games bid and study feasibility of bidding for 2016 European Football championships; give £2 million to Edinburgh International Festival to promote Scottish art; seek devolution of broadcasting powers and demand creation of Scottish news service.

Justice: raise legal smoking age to 18; stop deep discounting of alcohol in shops and introduce tougher penalties for sales to under-18s; increase funding for drug rehabilitation programmes; recruit 1000 more police; seek devolution of power over firearms and eventually ban air weapons.

Rural Affairs: promote biofuel crops; £10 million fund to support new entrants to farming; introduce ombudsman to police supermarket-supplier relations; merge Scottish Environment Protection Agency and Scottish National Heritage and review farming regulation; work for stronger role in EU affairs including taking the lead at fisheries council meetings; oppose GM crops; work for withdrawal from Common Fisheries Policy.

One tactic from the 1999 campaign survived; direct contact with the electorate, to limit the impact of media hostility. In 2007, direct contact was done much more professionally, using targeted mailings full of individualised messages addressing each voter's concerns, and identified through the 'Activate' programme which was linked to a call centre. This centre was making 25,000 calls a week in the weeks before the campaign and the call rate was upped to 125,000 per week when the campaign began, backed up with leaflet delivery and doorstep contact.[41]

But it was planning that emerged as the key feature of the SNP's campaign. The entire campaign was mapped out minutely long before it began with the aim of controlling the agenda. Planning for the final seven days — regarded as critical by political strategists because it is when wavering voters make up their minds — was begun six months previously. One

---

41 Scottish National Party press release. 'Labour Campaign in disarray as they admit council tax isn't fair.' 10 April 2007, available at www.snp.org/press-releases/2006/labour-campaign-disarray-as-they-admit-council-tax-isn-t-fair/

feature was a series of adverts in newspapers, local and national, with a range of people — pensioners, artists, businesspeople — endorsing the SNP. The idea was to convey to waverers that they were not alone in wanting to vote SNP, indeed that it was the fashionable thing to do.[42] The most striking example of this planning came just before the campaign proper, when in mid-March, Tony Blair visited Edinburgh and Aberdeen to attack the SNP's plans as disastrous for the economy. On the morning of the visit, *The Scotsman* had a scoop — a letter from Sir George Mathewson, a former immensely successful chairman of the Royal Bank of Scotland, endorsing the SNP.[43]

THE CONSERVATIVES COME IN FROM THE COLD

Unlike previous election campaigns, the Conservatives chose not to major on the threat to the Union posed by the SNP. Leader Annabel Goldie did make a big 'state of the union' speech a week before polling day in which she criticised the SNP for seeking to close doors for Scots that had been opened by the Union. But she also critiqued Labour and the Lib Dems as an equal danger to the union because their incompetence in running devolved Scotland had made people question the devolution settlement.[44]

More interesting was Goldie's positioning of the Conservative Party. Since no other party was even remotely likely to do a coalition deal with it, it faced the prospect of being permanently out in the cold and serving little purpose other than being a punch-bag for opponents. But at the Scottish Conservative conference in March 2006, Goldie condemned coalition government as a failure and broached the prospect of minority government. She said her aim was to displace the SNP to become the principal opposition party, and added, 'With proportional representation, no one party will have an overall majority, and there is no reason why a minority administration cannot govern, but then that means the biggest opposition presence is tremendously influential.'[45] The notion was greeted with some horror by many party members, but Goldie quietly reassured them it could have many benefits — keeping the SNP out of power, bringing the Tories in from the cold, and providing an opportunity for the Tories to have a real input into policy-making without soiling their hands with coalition politics. Labour was dismissive, but not overly so. During the summer, Margaret Curran, Minister for Parliamentary Business, had visited New Zealand to learn how its minority government worked and her report seemed to enthuse Jack

---

[42] H. MacDonell, 'Cash and control — the SNP's recipe for campaign success', *The Scotsman* 5 May 2007.

[43] *The Scotsman* 16 March 2007.

[44] 'Blair and Goldie in Union defence', BBC News online, 26 April 2007.

[45] 'Goldie sets out Tory way forward' BBC News online, 4 March 2006.

McConnell, who began privately discussing the prospects for a Labour minority government.[46]

During the campaign, Goldie concentrated on what she termed 'bread-and-butter' issues. The talk of minority government seemed to pay off during the campaign in that the Tories' proposals were listened to more intently than in previous campaigns, and Goldie proved during televised leaders' debates to be more relaxed and mischievously humorous than her matronly image suggested.

LIBERAL DEMS, GREENS AND REDS STRUGGLE

In common with most Lib Dem campaigns, the party chose high-mindedly to stay out of the mire of negative campaigning, concentrating on a positive presentation of their policies. In an 87-page manifesto, there were a lot of them, the boldest of which was an aim for Scotland to convert entirely to 'clean, green energy — the renewables powerhouse of Europe.'[47] The manifesto set out a calendar of action for the first seven months of a Lib Dem government. June was to be about new opportunities for youngsters including an hour a day of physical exercise; July would see new seven-year sentences for knife crime and a tougher regime of community sentences; and so on. It was a not unreasonable assumption that Labour and the SNP could be relied upon to knock lumps out of each other, but would lay off the Lib Dems because they were potential coalition partners. So the Lib Dems could hope to pick up votes equally from disenchanted Labour supporters who could not stomach voting SNP, and would-be SNP voters who could not tolerate voting Labour. The SNP certainly laid off assaulting the Lib Dems, but the party did not reap the rewards it hoped for. This was mainly because the Lib Dems were constantly asked whether they would support a referendum on independence. That confirmed that the SNP were the only real challengers to Labour and also put the Lib Dems on the back foot.

The election was always going to be tough for the Greens, who boldly hoped to win 10 seats.[48] Their big problem was that where their manifesto looked radical and different at previous elections, now the other parties had caught up. Where it was radically different — for example in cancelling major road building schemes or substituting a land value tax for council tax and business rates — it looked out of touch with public opinion.

Things were also going to be tough for the far left, now split into two parties. What was left of the SSP made no predictions about their likely number of MSPs but Tommy Sheridan's Solidarity forecast seven seats.[49]

[46] S. Low, 'Beyond the party conference hall', BBC News online, 15 October 2006.
[47] 'Lib Dems in renewable revolution', BBC News online, 11 April 2007.
[48] 'Greens seek to increase MSP tally', BBC News online, 3 April 2007.
[49] 'Sheridan predicts seven new seats', BBC News online, 3 March 2007.

But the absurdities of the previous year's court case and subsequent vitriolic name-calling between the protagonists meant that neither party had any credibility. The SNP's voter identification efforts targeted people who had previously supported both parties and the Greens. Armed with a manifesto that had elements which appealed to their voters (renewable energy, cutting carbon output, abolishing council tax, free school meals), the SNP had the weaponry to persuade them into the Nationalist camp.

SHAMBLES AT THE COUNT

The remarkable gains being made by the SNP and the closeness of the eventual result were not the only stories to emerge after the polls closed. The two votes under the additional member system had been combined into a single ballot and there was also the local government election with its new single transferable vote system. During the count it rapidly became apparent that there was an abnormally high rejection rate of spoiled papers.

Figure 2.3. Elections 2007, Votes Cast and Rejected[50]

	Votes Cast		Percentage Rejection Rates	
	Total	**Rejected**	**2007 Rate**	**2003 Rate**
SP Regional List Votes	2,102,623	60,455	2.88	0.65
SP Constituency Votes	2,101,638	65,644	4.07	0.66
Local Council Votes	2,099,945	38,352	1.83	0.64

Ron Gould, a Canadian electoral expert, investigated what had happened for the Electoral Commission.[51] His report recommended separating the local and national elections by two years but said that combining the elections was not the main cause of the high spoilage rate. Neither was the electronic count to blame. The main culprit was combining the regional list and constituency votes onto the one paper, particularly in the Glasgow and Lothian regions where the large number of regional candidates caused the voting instructions to be abbreviated.

---

[50] Source: *Electoral Commission Scottish Elections Review 2007*, p. 7.

[51] Electoral Commission *Independent review of the Scottish Parliamentary and local government elections 3 May 2007* (London: Electoral Commission, 2007). Available at: www.electoral commission.org.uk/__data/assets/electoral_commission_pdf_file/0011/13223/Scottish-Election-Rep ort-A-Final-For-Web_27622-20316__E__N__S__W__.pdf

Political and media attention focused on one line in the report: 'What is characteristic of 2007 was a notable level of party self-interest evident in Ministerial decision-making (especially in regard to the timing and method of counts and the design of ballot papers).'[52] The UK Government had retained power over the Scottish Parliament elections (responsibility for local council elections was devolved), so fingers of blame were immediately pointed at Labour ministers, particularly Douglas Alexander, Scottish Secretary at the time, who apologised for 'any actions or omissions on my part' that contributed to the problems.[53] However the report also made it clear that all political parties had been involved in the design of the Parliamentary voting papers and referred to 'months of partisan political discussion.'[54]

The Scottish Parliament debated the Gould report on 10 January 2008, voting by 109 to 15 that the executive and administrative powers for the Parliament and the Executive to run Scottish Parliamentary elections should be devolved.[55] The Liberal Democrats voted against, arguing that the Parliamentary elections should be held under the single transferable vote.

DOWN TO THE WIRE

In the end, the 2007 election result was a damned close run thing. The SNP outpolled Labour in the constituency vote by just 0.8 per cent and in the regional list vote by 1.8 per cent. If Labour had retained Cunningham North, lost by just 48 votes, it would have been the largest party by one seat. Considering that the SNP began the campaign with a five to six point lead in the opinion polls, Labour's campaign can be judged a success. Of course, this turnaround was eclipsed by the triumph of the SNP. This was undoubtedly the best funded, the best organised, the best planned and the most controlled campaign of the SNP's history, and beat the other parties' 2007 campaigns hands down for professionalism. It won 21 constituency seats, the most it has ever done. It won Labour heartland seats, such as Central Fife. It ousted two Lib Dem ministers from their constituencies. But is it a big step forward?

The SNP increased its share of the constituency vote by 9.1 percentage points and its regional vote by 10.2 points. But despite all Labour's disadvantages — a Labour UK Government and Prime Minister perceived to be unpopular, and disillusionment with Labour's performance at Holyrood — Labour's constituency vote fell by only 2.5 points and its regional vote by 0.2 points. The Conservative vote held steady in the constituencies and fell by just 1.6 points in the regional lists. The Lib Dems actually improved marginally. It adds up to a 1.4 percentage point erosion of the major unionist parties'

52 Electoral Commission 2007, p. 17.
53 'Alexander makes election apology', BBC News online, 24 October 2007.
54 Electoral Commission 2007, p. 48.
55 Scottish Parliament *Official Report*, 10 January 2008, col. 4957.

Peter Jones

Figure 2.4. Winning (2003 and 2007) Parties' Seats, Votes and Share of Votes

Party	Constituency Seats and Votes				Regional List Seats and Votes			
	Seats	Votes	%	+/-%	Seats	Votes	%	+/-%
SNP	21	664,227	32.9	+9.1	26	633,611	31.0	+10.2
Labour	37	648,374	32.1	-2.5	9	595,415	29.1	- 0.2
Cons	4	334,743	16.6	0.0	13	284,035	13.9	- 1.6
Lib Dem	11	326,232	16.2	+0.8	5	230,651	11.3	- 0.5
Green	0	2,971	0.1	+0.1	0	82,577	4.0	- 2.9
SSP	0	525	0.0	-6.2	0	13,096	0.6	- 6.0
Solidarity	0	0	0.0	0.0	0	31,096	1.5	+ 1.5
SSCUP	0	1,702	0.1	n.c.	0	39,038	1.9	+ 0.4
MM	0	0	0.0	n.c.	1	19,256	0.9	- 0.5
	73				56			

Note: SSP — Scottish Socialist Party; SSCUP — Scottish Senior Citizens Unity Party; MM — Margo MacDonald; n.c. — no change. Source: BBC News website at http://news.bbc.co.uk/1/shared/vote2007/scottish_parliment/html/scoreboard_99999.stm

constituency vote and a 2.2 point erosion of their regional vote. Where Labour rushed in last-minute constituency organisational support, as in Cumbernauld and Kilsyth or Glasgow Kelvin, it held seats it was expected to lose.

Most of the SNP gains appear to have come from the collapse of minor party support, in particular following the self-destruction of the Scottish Socialist Party. Its constituency vote fell by 6.2 points and its regional vote by 6.1 points, hardly compensated for by the breakaway Solidarity Party which gained just 1.5 per cent of the regional vote. The Greens also lost 2.8 points from their regional vote. But the SNP also had marked success in mobilising people who had previously not bothered to vote. Analysis by the Scottish Centre for Social Research concluded that a quarter of the SNP's vote came from people who had not voted at the 2003 Holyrood election (and about 15 per cent from 2003 Labour voters).[56] These factors suggest that if the three main opposition parties could improve their organisation to match that of the SNP's, the Nationalists might struggle to retain many of their gains.

Opinion polling also suggested that independence became less and less popular as the campaign wore on. For example, a Populus poll for *The Times* published on 20 April showed only 22 per cent backing complete independence. Even amongst SNP voters, 47 per cent wanted a devolved Parliament with more powers, more than the 45 per cent who wanted independence.[57]

So why did the SNP win the election? Commentators agree that while the SNP won the election, it failed to win the constitutional argument. 'The SNP's success in May's election did not signify a growing wish amongst Scots to leave the Union' and ' ... it can safely be suggested that [the SNP's success] was not due to the voters suddenly being converted to the cause of Scottish independence.'[58] There are two caveats to this conclusion. The first is that while the SNP did not convince the electorate of the merits of independence, it was much more successful at persuading the already converted to vote for it than in 2003. Just over three-quarters (76 per cent) of those who favour independence voted SNP in 2007, but in 2003 only half (51 per cent) of pro-independence voters backed the SNP.[59]

The second caveat is that a more subtle analysis reveals that the independence issue can have other effects on voting behaviour. The Scottish Election

[56] See D. McCrone and N. McEwan, 'A Vote for Independence?', presentation at Scottish Centre for Social Research seminar 'The 2007 Election: Earthquake, Misfortune and Revolution?', Edinburgh, 31 October 2007, available at www.scotcen.org.uk

[57] W. Miller, 'How the SNP could win and lose at the same time', *The Times* 20 April 2007.

[58] Scottish Centre for Social Research press release, 30 October 2007, 'SNP election victory not based on increased support for independence', available at www.natcen.ac.uk/natcen/pages/news_and_media_docs/snp.pdf ; D. Denver, ' "A Historic Moment"? The results of the Scottish Parliament's elections', *Scottish Affairs* 60 (2007), p 78.

[59] Scottish Centre for Social Research 2007.

Study 2007 used a 'valence politics' model to explain the result.[60] Unlike position political analysis (where voters are identified as for/against/neutral on a particular issue such as the Iraq War) valence political analysis assumes that voters share the same overall objective (such as reducing crime) but have different views of the parties' ability to deliver that objective. The authors argue:

> ... 'standing up for Scotland's interests' is more or less the SNP's raison d'être, and so even those opposed to independence are nonetheless inclined to believe that the party could deliver benefits to Scottish voters. Thus, the SNP's stance on independence might win it valence support from voters, regardless of their own personal constitutional preferences.[61]

To summarise, the SNP won the election because of five factors: much better organisation and funding, winning the votes of both 'full-strength Nationalists' and 'Nationalist-lites', a perception it would stand up more for Scotland than Labour, having the most popular leader, and a perception it would do a better job on devolved issues.

INTO AN UNCERTAIN FUTURE

Following the pattern of previous Holyrood elections, the immediate focus was on whether the SNP could form a coalition government. Labour hopes of forming an anti-SNP coalition were never really possible.[62] The SNP had 47 votes in the 129-seat Parliament and was 18 votes short of a majority. With the political gulf between Labour and the SNP being deep and visceral, any arrangement with Labour was out of the question, particularly after Salmond declared that Labour had lost the 'moral authority' to govern.[63] The Conservatives stuck to their pre-election position, opposing coalitions and favouring a minority government. That left the Greens (two seats), the Liberal Democrats (16 seats) and perhaps the independent nationalist Margo MacDonald as the only hope for a coalition with a wafer-thin majority.

The Greens refused to entertain coalition, offering instead to support the SNP in votes of confidence and on crucial budget votes — 'confidence and supply', as their position became known. (This approach had, of course, already been explored by Labour before the elections.) By 11 May, a deal was struck; the SNP agreed that the Greens should have some advance consultation on legislative and budgetary issues, to oppose new nuclear power stations, to introduce early legislation to reduce climate change, and

[60] D. Denver, R. Johns, J. Mitchell and C. Pattie, 'The Holyrood Elections 2003: Explaining the results'. Paper presented at EPOP conference, University of Bristol, September 2007. Available at www.scottishelectionstudy.org.uk/ paperspubs.htm

[61] Denver et al 2007, p. 6.

[62] 'SNP begins coalition discussions', BBC News online, 5 May 2007.

[63] 'SNP beats Labour in Scottish poll' BBC News online, 4 May 2007.

to nominate a Green MSP for a Parliamentary committee using SNP nominating rights. (Patrick Harvie duly became convener of the Transport, Infrastructure and Climate Change committee.) While there was media expectation that the Lib Dems would also agree a deal, the Lib Dems continued to insist on their opposition both to independence and an independence referendum, and would only talk to the SNP if the referendum plan was dropped.[64] This precondition was completely unacceptable.[65]

On 16 May, the Parliament voted in Alex Salmond as First Minister by 49 votes (47 SNP and two Green votes) to 46. Both the Conservatives and Lib Dems abstained. Salmond became Scotland's fourth First Minister, the first SNP member in the party's history to be elected to government.[66]

List of Scottish Government Departments and Ministers, May 2007

Office of the First Minister
First Minister: Alex Salmond
Minister for Europe, External Affairs, and Culture: Linda Fabiani
Minister for Parliamentary Business: Bruce Crawford

Finance and Sustainable Growth
Cabinet Secretary: John Swinney
Minister for Enterprise, Energy and Tourism: Jim Mather
Minister for Transport, Infrastructure and Climate Change: Stewart Stevenson

Education and Lifelong Learning
Cabinet Secretary: Fiona Hyslop
Minister for Children and Early Years: Adam Ingram
Minister for Schools and Skills: Maureen Watt

Health and Wellbeing
Cabinet Secretary and Deputy First Minister: Nicola Sturgeon
Minister for Public Health: Shona Robison
Minister for Communities and Sport: Stewart Maxwell

Justice
Cabinet Secretary: Kenny MacAskill
Minister for Community Safety: Fergus Ewing

Rural Affairs and the Environment
Cabinet Secretary: Richard Lochhead
Minister for Environment: Michael Russell

---

[64] 'Lib Dems rule out SNP coalition', BBC News online, 7 May 2007.
[65] I. MacWhirter, 'Referendum? Salmond's too busy making history', *The Herald* (Glasgow) 7 May 2007.
[66] 'Salmond elected as first minister', BBC News online, 16 May 2007.

Law Officers[67]
Lord Advocate: Elish Angiolini
Solicitor General: Frank Mulholland

SNP IN OFFICE, BUT IN POWER?

The biggest risk for the SNP as its leaders moved into government for the first time was that the Parliamentary arithmetic meant it was seen as weak and powerless. The seat numbers meant that, if Labour opposed a measure, the SNP had to gain Green and either Conservative or Liberal Democrat support. That meant that, unlike the previous two administrations, Salmond was not able to announce a legislative programme shortly after taking office, and even by January 2008 only five bills had been presented to the Parliament.[68] One, a bill to abolish tolls on the Forth and Tay road bridges, met no significant opposition and was speedily passed. However, for the government to be weak, the opposition has to be seen as strong. The SNP's ace card is that the three main opposition parties have to unite to defeat the government, whereas the SNP, with Green support, only needs the support of one other party.

An early Parliamentary dogfight exposed these positions. The SNP manifesto pledged that it would cancel two major transport projects — a tram system for Edinburgh costing about £600 million and a complex tunnelled main line rail link to Edinburgh airport costing another £600 million. Both were projects of the previous administration, so Labour and the Lib Dems were determined to preserve them. The Conservatives were also supporters, but with provisos that the projects should provide value for money and avoid expensive cost over-runs. After several unsuccessful earlier attempts, on 27 June 2007 a third opposition attack succeeded in forcing the government to accept the trams scheme, but could only delay a decision on the airport rail link until September time which the Government used to develop plans for a cheaper alternative, said to cost about £210 million.[69] With Conservative support, this enabled the SNP to cancel the original project, in a Parliamentary vote on 27 September.[70] The result could be described as a score draw; the SNP ended up saving only about £400 million (rather than £1.2 billion), but the opposition could save only one of the two schemes.

---

[67] Elish Angiolini had been appointed as Lord Advocate by the Labour/Lib Dem coalition in 2001, and re-appointed by the new government. Frank Mulholland is a professional lawyer with no known party-political affiliations. Neither is an MSP.

[68] These were the Budget (Scotland) Bill (Budget); Glasgow Commonwealth Games Bill; Graduate Endowment Abolition (Scotland) Bill; Public Health etc. (Scotland) Bill; and Abolition of Bridge Tolls (Scotland) Bill.

[69] Scottish Parliament *Official Report,* 27 June, 2007, col 1192.

[70] Scottish Parliament *Official Report*, 27 September 2007, col 2308.

The SNP's ability to take executive action which does not require Parliamentary approval has turned out to be its strongest card. It established momentum by cutting the number of Executive departments, and cabinet ministers, from nine to six (see list of departments and ministers). Its immediate headline-grabbing announcements included:

* reversing of the previous Executive's plans to close accident and emergency units at Ayr and Monklands hospitals,
* abolishing the Forth and Tay road bridge tolls
* abolishing the £2000 graduate endowment fee, and
* acting to raise the legal age for buying cigarettes from 16 to 18 years.

Salmond also re-branded government north of the border by changing the public name from 'Scottish Executive' to 'The Scottish Government' (although the legal name, enshrined in the Scotland Act 1998, remains unchanged).[71]

As the SNP settled into office, Jack McConnell decided to withdraw from the political stage. On 15 August, he resigned as leader of the Scottish Labour MSPs and by 14 September, Wendy Alexander, the sole nominee for the post, was confirmed as his successor.[72] Alexander was widely regarded as the brightest of the Scottish group and was close to Gordon Brown, the new UK Prime Minister. Yet scarcely had Alexander taken up the leadership than she was engulfed in a scandal about improper cash donations (albeit of small amounts) raised for her leadership campaign. While she was eventually cleared of wrongdoing by the Electoral Commission, the controversy continued to undermine her leadership.

FINANCIAL SETTLEMENTS

Budgets and the hard realities of finding the money to pay for manifesto promises brought everything back to earth. The UK Government had long made it known that the Comprehensive Spending Review (CSR) covering 2008–11 would produce much smaller spending increases than the previous spending reviews. But the SNP government was outraged when the CSR was announced on 9 October 2007 (see also chapter 6). Salmond fumed that Scotland had been 'squeezed and short-changed by the Treasury.' The real increase over the three years, he argued, was not the 1.8 per cent claimed by the Treasury but, because of a redrawing of the baseline for English health spending, only 1.4 per cent. Worse still, he raged, the annual increases were 0.5 per cent in 2008–9, 1.6 per cent the next year, and 2.3 per cent in the final

---

71 Scottish Government press release, 3 September 2007, 'The Scottish Government — It's official.' Available at www.scotland.gov.uk/News/Releases/2007/09/31160110

72 'Alexander leads Scottish Labour', BBC News online, 14 September 2007.

year, making things exceptionally difficult in the looming year.[73] Independent analysis, however, suggested that the 1.8 per cent increase was the correct figure and that Scotland had got a worse deal than Wales, but a better deal than Northern Ireland (see Figure 2.5). Nevertheless, the outcome gave Salmond much less room for manoeuvre than his predecessors.

Figure 2.5. Departmental Expenditure Limits (£ million), Devolved Administrations, 2006–11[74]

	2006–7 Estimated Outturn	2007–8 Plans	2008–9 Plans	2009–10 Plans	2010–11 Plans
Current prices					
Scotland	24,806	26,059	27,244	28,399	29,784
Wales	12,949	13,588	14,272	14,964	15,772
Northern Ireland	9,264	9,596	10,025	10,359	10,796
Total UK DEL	321,539	344,600	361,100	377,500	396,900
2007–8 prices					
Scotland	24,207	26,059	26,528	26,925	27,496
Wales	13,299	13,588	13,897	14,188	14,560
Northern Ireland	9,515	9,596	9,761	9,821	9,967
Total UK DEL	330,273	344,100	351,607	357,912	366,412
Percentage real growth per annum					
Scotland	6.5	7.7	1.8	1.5	2.1
Wales	5.3	2.2	2.3	2.1	2.6
Northern Ireland	4.1	0.9	1.7	0.6	1.5
Total UK DEL	3.5	4.2	2.2	1.8	2.4

[73] Scottish Government press release, 9 October 2007. 'FM comments on UK spending review', available at www.scotland.gov.uk/News/Releases/2007/10/10084746. See also *Scotland Devolution Monitoring Report*, January 2008, section 8.

[74] Source: Adapted from Centre for Public Policy for Regions, Updated analysis of the 2007 Comprehensive Spending Review (CSR) with particular emphasis on Scotland, October 2007, available at: www.cppr.ac.uk/centres/cppr/newsandevents/

Notes: For 2007–8 actual prices figures, the original baseline before CSR 2007 for Scotland was £26,271 million, for Wales was £13,790 million, for Northern Ireland was £9,700 million, and for total UK DEL was £344,100 million. Inflation is assumed at 2.7 per cent per annum 2008–11.

Though the settlement was not as stringent as the SNP claimed it was, the Government had to make some hard choices. The manifesto pledge to increase police numbers by 1000 officers was trimmed back to 500 new officers.[75] The promised £2000 grant to first-time home buyers was dropped, the pledge to write off all existing student debt disappeared and the commitment to reduce class sizes in primaries 1–3 was watered down. Nevertheless, by the time John Swinney, Cabinet Secretary for Finance and Sustainable Growth, announced the budget for 2008–11 on 14 November, it contained plenty of additional spending allocations. But the big headline items which eclipsed the dropped spending promises were a freeze on council tax bills and reductions for business rates, the latter phased over three years rather than introduced in one go as promised.[76]

The keystone of the budget was an agreement, billed as a 'concordat', between the Government and the Convention of Scottish Local Authorities (COSLA) aimed at giving councils enough money to freeze council taxes. The big carrot on offer was to reduce the amount of ring-fenced funding (central government grant which can only be spent on specifically ear-marked functions) from £2.7 billion (about 25 per cent of grant-aided expenditure) in 2007–8 to £300 million in 2010–11.[77] This was warmly welcomed by many council leaders who have long resented not having control over large parts of their budget and it also divided Labour council leaders from Labour MSPs who argued ring-fencing was necessary.[78]

Not everyone was happy however. The universities complained bitterly that having asked for £168 million over the three years, which they said was essential to maintain research and teaching levels, they had only been given £30 million.[79] The Government managed to find small sums of unallocated money within the budget to give universities an extra £10 million for

---

[75] 'Funds to recruit 500 new officers', BBC News online, 12 November 2007.

[76] For full budget statement and debate, see Scottish Parliament *Official Report*, 14 November 2007, cols. 3324-3383. For the budget document, see Scottish Government, *Scottish Budget: Spending Review 2007* (Edinburgh: Scottish Government, 2007), available at www.scotland.gov.uk/Publications/2007/11/13092240/0 . See also *Scotland Devolution Monitoring Report*, January 2008, section 9.

[77] Scottish Government/COSLA 'Concordat', November 2007, available at: www.cosla.gov.uk/attachments/aboutcosla/concordatnov07.pdf

[78] 'Labour hits out at funding change', BBC News online, 13 January 2008.

[79] F. MacLeod and H. MacDonell, 'Crisis for Scottish Universities after SNP budget blow', *The Scotsman* 16 November 2007.

2008–9.[80] A pattern gradually emerged that the SNP was interested only in making concessions only to the Conservatives and Greens. The Conservatives limited their ambition to achievable goals which were consistent with their manifesto, and succeeded: 1000 additional new police officers, a shift in drugs policy to abstinence and recovery treatments, and faster cuts in business rates for small businesses. The Greens sought more money for climate change policies and cuts in road building plans. They got the former, didn't get the latter, and abstained in the final vote.[81]

**Figure 2.6. Scottish Government Departmental
Expenditure Limits 2007–11. £ Million, 2007–8 Prices[82]**

	2007–8	2008–9	2009–10	2010–10	% p.a real increase
Health and Wellbeing	10,776	10,925	11,125	11,264	1.5
Local Government	8,784	8,925	9,076	9,205	1.6
Finance and Sustainable Growth	2,682	2,279	2,812	2,801	1.5
Education and Lifelong Learning	2,358	2,344	2,355	2,377	0.5
Justice	979	1,014	1,029	1,025	1.5
Rural Affairs and Environment	530	600	604	600	4.3
Office of First Minister	266	273	278	282	1.9
Administration	241	239	237	236	–0.7
Crown Office etc	101	107	112	111	3.3
Scot. Parl't. and Audit Scotland	107	107	107	108	0.2
Total DEL	26,824	27,265	27,738	28,009	1.5

Note: These figures include allowances for depreciation and thus the Total DEL figure is different to that in Figure 2.5.

[80] See Scottish Government news release, 'Funding boost for higher education' 28 January 2008, available at www.scotland.gov.uk/News/Releases/2008/01/28103341
[81] See *Scotland Devolution Monitoring Reports*, May 2008, section 8, for a fuller account.
[82] Source: J. Armstrong and R. Harris *The Scottish Government's Budget 2007: How it Has Been Funded*, CPPR Briefing No. 3 (2007), available at www.cppr.ac.uk/media/media_54616_en.pdf

In the end, the price of meeting these demands seemed remarkably small. John Swinney announced an increase of £8 million for the Justice portfolio (mainly for extra police officers) and £4.3 million for the environment portfolio (to finance more community renewable energy projects), paid for by reductions elsewhere.[83] Providing a 'capital city allowance' for Edinburgh secured Margo MacDonald's vote, and with Conservative votes and a tactical error by Labour, the SNP won by 64 votes to one (a sole Labour MSP voting in error) with 60 abstentions.[84]

THE CONSTITUTIONAL DEBATE:
A CONVERSATION AND A COMMISSION

Could Alex Salmond, up against a unionist majority, make any serious moves towards independence? He certainly intended to try. The 'National Conversation' was opened on 14 August 2007 when Salmond published a White Paper which did not simply set out the case for independence, but also set out how the existing devolutionary settlement could be taken further.[85] This was, he said, because 'there are a range of options which carry support — from greater devolution to fiscal autonomy to full independence' and 'as a democrat … I believe in the sovereignty of the Scottish people and their right to choose the status of the country in which they live.'[86] In other words, if the Scottish people said that they wanted more devolution and not independence, he seemed prepared to settle for that.

Much of the White Paper appeared to be little more than a long shopping list of extra powers that Scotland might wish to see transferred from Westminster. A first list set out the powers needed to take Scotland up to the limits of devolutionary power. The second list added the powers needed to move from 'maxi-devolution' to independence: control over foreign affairs, defence, and macro-economic matters.[87] This section seemed a little vaguer than the previous section. The White Paper stated that there would be negotiations between the Scottish and UK Governments over 'apportionment of the national debt, allocation of reserved assets such as the UK official reserves, the BBC, and overseas missions of the Foreign Office; future liabilities on public sector pensions, and social security benefits; the split of the

[83] J. Swinney, 'Letter to Andrew Welsh MSP, Convener, Scottish Parliament finance committee', January 2008. Available at www.scottish.parliament.uk/s3/bills/05-Budget/index.htm

[84] Scottish Parliament *Official Report*, 6 February 2008, col. 5906.

[85] Scottish Executive, *Choosing Scotland's Future: A National Conversation. Independence and responsibility in the modern world* (Edinburgh: Scottish Executive, 2007). Available at www.scotland.gov.uk/Topics/a-national-conversation

[86] A. Salmond, 'The Launch of a Public Debate on Scotland's Constitutional Future', Speech at Napier University, Edinburgh, 14 August 2007. Available at www.scotland.gov.uk/News/This-Week/Speeches/a-national-conversation/

[87] Scottish Executive 2007, chapter 3.

defence estate and the equipment of the armed forces.'[88] However, there was no discussion of a Scottish central bank or currency beyond stating that these were matters presently reserved to the UK Government. The discussion on foreign affairs maintained the SNP's certainty that an independent Scotland would 'continue in the European Union and bear the burdens and fulfil the responsibilities of membership.' But it also said that there would be 'negotiations on the detailed terms of membership', implying that EU membership was not entirely certain.[89]

Salmond reiterated that 'independence or arguably a substantial shift in power will require a referendum.'[90] The White Paper was imprecise on when a referendum would be held or what question would be asked, canvassing the possibility that it might be a multi-option referendum on a choice between independence, the status quo, or substantial more devolution. An annex set out a draft referendum bill proposing that the only question to be asked was about negotiations for independence.[91]

If Salmond's aim had been to draw the other parties into a devolution-enhancing discussion, the first signs were disappointing. A statement on 13 August from the three unionist party leaders — Jack McConnell, Annabel Goldie and Nicol Stephen — rejected the White Paper as a 'nationalist crusade' that could only damage Scotland, but also signalled the formation of a loose unionist coalition seeking a new devolution settlement: 'We are willing to enter into debate jointly about the way in which devolution within the UK can best develop in the years to come and we believe that colleagues in Westminster have a role to play in that debate.'[92] In a lecture at Edinburgh University on 30 November, Wendy Alexander took this a step forward when she announced a proposal for a 'Scottish Constitutional Commission' to produce plans for enhancing the devolutionary settlement. The Commission would be very different from the National Conversation: .an 'expert-led', largely independent, group of people, but with independence excluded as an option for consideration. It would also have a 'Westminster dimension' and be about the rest of the UK, not just Scotland. That includes the possibility that some powers might flow back from Scotland to Westminster.[93] This proposal was supported by the other unionist parties at Holyrood (there had been several meetings between the party leaders to shape the strategy in the weeks between the joint opposition statement and the speech), and unsurprisingly, the Scottish Parliament endorsed it in a vote

---

[88] Scottish Executive 2007, p. 21.

[89] Scottish Executive 2007, p.23.

[90] Salmond 2007.

[91] Scottish Executive 2007, pp. 44-48.

[92] The statement in full can be viewed at http://news.bbc.co.uk/1/hi/scotland/6944185.stm

[93] W. Alexander, 'A New Agenda for Scotland.' Speech at University of Edinburgh, 30 November 2007. Available at: http://wendy.intraspin.com/2007/11/30/a-new-agenda-for-scotland/?cat=20

on 6 November, by 76 votes to 46 with three abstentions.[94] For the SNP, Nicola Sturgeon, claimed as a victory that the Labour Party, which had stoutly defended the status quo at the election, was now in favour of more powers. The SNP was leading the constitutional debate, she said and all other parties were trailing in its wake.[95] However, the Alexander plan clearly sparked considerable disquiet within the Labour Party (and particularly Scottish Labour MPs at Westminster), and led to wider questioning of her leadership — questioning fuelled by the allegations of improper acceptance of campaign donations and poor performances at First Ministers' Question. For the rest of 2007, and the first months of 2008, there was considerable debate within the Labour Party about whether and how the constitutional debate should be taken forward. That debate largely ended when Gordon Brown gave an interview to BBC Scotland on 17 February 2008, in which he announced his support for what was now dubbed a 'review', and implied that leadership of it would be taken over by the UK Government.[96]

CONCLUSION

So far, the SNP has proved an effective government: canny in its manage-ment of a difficult parliamentary situation, but with a shrewd eye for popular measures and so far successful in establishing for itself a reputation for competence. It has failed to cause the sort of intergovernmental chaos some had predicted, it has sought maximum publicity from disputes on issues where the UK Government is weak. The response from London has been often graceless and carping — with Tony Blair failing to contact Alex Salmond to congratulate him on his election, Gordon Brown failing to respond for many months to Salmond's attempts to revive the Joint Ministe-rial Committee, and UK Ministers insisting on referring to the 'Scottish Executive' rather than 'the Scottish Government' since its renaming.

The constitutional battlelines for the third session of the Scottish Parlia-ment are set. On one side the SNP minority government has its National Conversation aimed at independence or a major gain in devolved power, versus the other parties and their Constitutional Commission aimed at a re-ordering of the devolution settlement which may or may not produce more devolved powers. Both positions have their weaknesses. The National Conversation is ill-shaped, there is no obvious point at which it might be declared to have come to a conclusion, it is lacking in activity (it largely consists of a blog) and postings on its website hardly speak of a coherent,

---

94 Scottish Parliament *Official Report*, 6 December 2007, col. 4289.
95 Scottish Parliament *Official Record*, 6 November 2007, col 4138.
96 See 'PM backs Scottish powers review', BBC News online, 17 February 2008, and also J. McIvor 'What Westminster gives... it could take' BBC News website available at http://news.bbc.co.uk/1/hi/programmes/politics_show/7242422.stm

informed discussion. However, having built up expectations on a wide front — from promising free higher education to faster economic growth — Alex Salmond and the SNP Government now have to deliver. As the first Labour/Lib Dem Executive found out, expectations can be very hard to fulfil.

On the unionist side there are perhaps more problems. The Constitutional Commission must win early respect and authority. Securing that depends on the three supporting parties being seen as determined to push through such changes as the Commission may recommend. At the outset, the biggest question marks hung over the Labour Party. Will it allow the Commission free rein to extend devolution, and is the party leadership of one mind about this?

BIBLIOGRAPHY

Official Documents and Primary Sources

Alexander, W., 'A new agenda for Scotland', Speech at University of Edinburgh, 30 November 2007.

Electoral Commission, *Independent Review of the Scottish Parliamentary and Local Government Elections* (London: Electoral Commission, 2007).

Herbert, S. and T. Edwards, *Rejected Ballot Papers*, Scottish Parliamentary Information Centre (SPICe) briefing 07/36, 26 June 2007.

McConnell, J., 'In the Interest of Our Nation', J.P. Mackintosh annual lecture, 24 October 2006.

Salmond, A., 'The launch of a public debate on Scotland's constitutional future', Speech at Napier University, Edinburgh, 14 August 2007.

Scottish Executive, *Choosing Scotland's Future: A National Conversation, Independence and responsibility in the modern world* (Edinburgh: Scottish Executive, 2007).

Scottish Government, *Scottish Budget: Spending Review 2007* (Edinburgh: Scottish Government 2007).

Scottish Government and Convention of Scottish Local Authorities (COSLA), *Concordat* (Edinburgh: Scottish Government and COSLA, 2007).

Scottish Labour Party *Scottish Labour Party Manifesto: Building Scotland* (Glasgow: Scottish Labour Party, 2007).

Scottish Liberal Democrat Party, *The Steel Commission: Moving to federalism a new settlement for Scotland* (Edinburgh: Scottish Liberal Democrat Party, 2006).

Scottish National Party, *Scotland in Surplus — past, present and future* (Edinburgh: Scottish National Party, 2006).

Scottish National Party, *The True Wealth of the Nation* (Edinburgh: Scottish National Party, 2006).

Scottish National Party *Manifesto 2007: SNP, It's Time* (Edinburgh: Scottish National Party, 2007).

Secondary Sources

Bell, D. and A. Bowes, *Financial Care Models in Scotland and the UK* (York: Joseph Rowntree Foundation, 2006).

Bort, E., 'Annals of the Parish: The Year at Holyrood, 2005–06', *Scottish Affairs* 57 (2006): 112–34.

Coyle, D., W. Alexander and B. Ashcroft (eds.), *New Wealth for Old Nations* (Princeton, NJ: Princeton University Press, 2005).

Denver, D., '"A Historic Moment?" The Results of the Scottish Parliament Elections', *Scottish Affairs* 60 (2007).

Denver, D., R. Johns and C. Pattie, 'The Holyrood Elections 2003: Explaining the results'. Paper presented at EPOP conference, University of Bristol, September 2007.

Gordon, T., 'Wrestling with independence', *Sunday Times* Scotland, 6 May 2007.

Linklater, M., 'Being a maths teacher doesn't mean you have all the answers, *The Times*, 11 April 2007.

MacDonell, H., 'Cash and control — the SNP's recipe for campaign success', *The Scotsman*, 5 May 2007.

MacWhirter, I., 'Referendum? Salmond's too busy making history', *The Herald*, 7 May 2007.

McCrone, D. and N. McEwan, 'A Vote for Independence?', presentation at Scottish Centre for Social Research seminar, 'The 2007 Election: Earthquake, Misfortune and Revolution?', Edinburgh, 31 October 2007.

Miller, W., 'How the SNP could win and lose at the same time', *The Times*, 20 April 2007.

3

Welsh Devolution

The End of the Beginning,
and the Beginning of...?

Richard Wyn Jones and Roger Scully

The result of the Welsh devolution referendum on 18 September 1997 — a desperately narrow victory for the Yes campaign — has widely, and rightly, been understood as marking the beginning of a new era in Welsh politics. It now seems equally clear that 31 March 2004 heralded what we might term 'the end of the beginning'. On the latter date, the Commission on the Powers and Electoral Arrangements of the National Assembly for Wales, chaired by Labour peer Lord (Ivor) Richard, published its report.[1]

The report of the Richard Commission has, in many important ways, defined the parameters of Welsh politics ever since. This does not mean that all of the Commission's (unanimous) recommendations have been accepted and acted upon. To the contrary, and as we detail below, several key elements were subsequently rejected by the Labour UK Government. It was the fact that the Commission (whose membership included representatives of all Wales' major political parties, plus several distinguished independent figures) recommended radical changes to the devolution 'settlement' established by the Government of Wales Act 1998 that proved to be most important. This emboldened devolutionists within the Labour Party to propose — and ultimately secure in the Government of Wales Act 2006 — changes to the legal and institutional structure of Welsh devolution that are, in some respects, even more far-reaching than those proposed by Richard.

Indeed, the terms of the 2006 Act, and in particular Part 4, which allows for the transfer of primary legislative powers to the National Assembly following an affirmative vote in a referendum, provided the common ground upon which Labour would ultimately agree a coalition deal with Plaid Cymru after the May 2007 National Assembly election. Chapter Two of the Coalition agreement, *A Strong and Confident Nation*, binds both parties '... to proceed to a successful outcome of a referendum for full law-making powers under Part IV as soon as practicable, at or before the end of the

---

[1] Commission on the Powers and Electoral Arrangements of the National Assembly for Wales (Richard Commission), *Report of the Richard Commission* (Cardiff: National Assembly for Wales, 2004). The Richard Commission was established in 2002, in accordance with the coalition agreement that brought the Welsh Liberal Democrats into government alongside Labour in the autumn of 2000.

Assembly term.'[2] But whatever the fate of that pledge (and whatever the result of any referendum), Part 3 of the 2006 Act meant that, come what may, extensive Measure-making powers *will* be transferred to the National Assembly through orders in council (and also through primary legislation at Westminster) over the coming years. With Assembly Measures amounting to primary legislation in all but name, the die has been cast. When one also bears in mind that Parts 1 and 2 of the 2006 legislation definitively erased the various elements of local government structures and practices that were incorporated into the 1998 Act (elements that have characterised Labour's various devolutionary schemes for Wales since the 1960s), the conclusion is clear. The political and constitutional foundations of Welsh devolution may have been shaky, with the 1997 referendum result and the 1998 legislation. But in the aftermath of the Richard Commission report, a more solid, parliamentary edifice is emerging, and emerging much more rapidly than could have been imagined a decade ago. Moreover, as we will detail later, this edifice is emerging with the broad support of the Welsh population as a whole, as well as most—though not all—of the nation's political class.

In this chapter we will explore the key period in Welsh political and constitutional life, between 2005 and the summer of 2007, when Wales began to move beyond the 'end of the beginning'. We will do so in five sections. The first two are concerned with the constitutional architecture of devolution. First, we will briefly explore the Labour Party's response to the Richard Commission report in the period leading up to the 2005 UK general election. Secondly, we will discuss the evolution of the Government of Wales Act 2006, from White Paper to Royal Assent. We then move on to consider other aspects of political life in Wales. The third section focuses on the 2007 election, while the fourth examines the remarkable post-election machinations that led, eventually, to the formation of the Labour-Plaid coalition. Finally, the fifth section examines the development of public attitudes towards devolution over recent years, and what the evidence on public opinion tells us about prospects for the proposed referendum on primary powers.

THE RICHARD COMMISSION AND THE LABOUR PARTY

The Richard Commission's report presented a powerful, evidence-based and well-argued case for its recommendations. For current purposes, they can be simplistically summarised as falling under three headings:

---

[2] The 'One Wales Agreement' is available online at: http://onewales.blogspot.com/ and at http://wales.gov.uk/about/strategy/strategypublications/strategypubs/onewales/?lang=en It is also reproduced as an appendix to John Osmond's useful account of the extraordinary interregnum that followed the 2007 National Assembly election *Crossing the Rubicon: Coalition politics Welsh style* (Cardiff: Institute of Welsh Affairs, 2007).

- Internal organisation;
- Powers; and
- Electoral arrangements.[3]

Regarding the first, the Commission recommended that full separation of the legislature and the executive should be brought about. The 'single body corporate' established in the 1998 Act should be formally abolished, and both the National Assembly as a parliamentary body and the Welsh Assembly Government as the executive established on an appropriate legal basis. To those observers schooled in the British constitutional tradition (or indeed most other constitutional traditions), this recommendation will appear utterly unremarkable — the reassertion of 'normality' after a period of idiosyncratic experimentation. But in the context of the historical development of Welsh devolution, the recommendation is far from anodyne. From the mid-1960s through to the 1997 referendum, every devolutionary scheme proposed by the Welsh Labour Party had stressed the 'local government' character of the proposed Assembly. In large part this worked to succour sceptics or opponents of devolution that any National Assembly would be secondary in form as well as status to the 'proper' parliament, Westminster.

That the Richard Commission could advocate eliminating the local government features of the Assembly's organisation, less than five years into its life, is striking. That this recommendation met with no serious opposition is equally so. But that this was indeed the case is testimony to two factors. The first is the basic instability of the structures established by the 1998 Act, which at a rather late stage in proceedings had grafted a parliamentary-style cabinet onto the body corporate envisaged in the 1997 pre-referendum White Paper, *A Voice for Wales*.[4] This led to some predictable frustration and confusion among those charged with understanding and operating the structures. The second factor was the shared determination of the Assembly's Presiding Officer, Lord Elis-Thomas, and First Minister Rhodri Morgan, that devolved governance in Wales develop in a more parliamentary direction, notwithstanding the letter and spirit of the 1998 Act. The impact of their determination was that by the time that Richard reported, a division of powers was already a de facto reality. Rendering that division de jure proved entirely uncontroversial.

[3] For more considered analyses see, *inter alia*, R. Rawlings, 'Richard's Radical Recipe,' *Agenda: Journal of the Institute of Welsh Affairs*, Summer 2004, pp. 27-31 and the various contributions to J. Osmond (ed.), *Welsh Politics Come of Age: Responses to the Richard Commission* (Cardiff: Institute of Welsh Affairs, 2005).

[4] Welsh Office, *A Voice for Wales: The Government's proposals for a Welsh Assembly* Cm 3718 (London: The Stationery Office, 1997). The definitive analysis of the 1998 Act and the early years of the National Assembly is R. Rawlings, *Delineating Wales: Constitutional, legal and administrative aspects of national devolution* (Cardiff: University of Wales Press, 2003).

In marked contrast, the issue of powers was, and remains, highly contro-versial. The Richard Commission went much further than most expectations, in recommending the transfer of primary legislative powers to the National Assembly in those areas in which it was already exercising secondary powers. Both inside and outside the Commission, this recommendation was interpreted in terms of 'adopting the Scottish model' of devolution — a formulation that serves to occlude some subtle but important differences between Scotland and Wales that would persist if and when the primary legislative powers step is eventually taken.[5] The Commission further recom-mended that primary powers be transferred by 2011, although it made no recommendation as to whether or not such a development would require popular approval through a referendum. In the intervening period before 2011, an interim dispensation was suggested that would allow the National Assembly to develop the necessary competence and experience in drafting and scrutinising legislation. This interim dispensation — later to become known as '13.2' after a Summary Box in the Report text — would involve the development of a 'new model of framework-legislative devolution'.[6] Specifically, this would mean 'including in future primary legislation new framework provisions designed to allow the Assembly to, for example, make through secondary legislation any changes it wished within the field covered by the Act. The aim would be to construct broad delegated powers that reflect the democratic mandate and scrutiny powers of the Assembly.'[7]

Finally, on electoral arrangements, the Commission argued that the trans-fer of primary powers to the Assembly, and concomitant growth in its responsibilities for the proper scrutiny of legislation, would require an increase in the size of the chamber. A total of 80 members (compared with the current 60) were advocated, with the Commission arguing that they should be elected by a version of the single transferable vote system in multi-member constituencies.

Comprehensive accounts of Labour's response to the Richard Commis-sion have been given elsewhere.[8] What they make clear is that the broad

---

[5] This important point is briefly flagged in A. Trench, *Better Governance for Wales: An Analysis of the White Paper on Devolution for Wales* Devolution Policy Paper no. 13 (Edinburgh: ESRC Devolution and Constitutional Change programme, 2005). The key difference is that 'Even if such a change [to primary law-making powers] were to take place, what Wales would end up with would resemble the Scotland Act 1978 more than the Scotland Act 1998...The Assembly would only have the powers to act where it was expressly authorised to do so, unlike the situation for Scotland where the Scottish Parliament may legislate on all matters except those expressly reserved to Westminster' (para. 2.26). The impact of this would be to ensure that even when fully empowered, the National Assembly will enjoy significantly less freedom of manoeuvre than the Scottish Parliament.

[6] Richard Commission 2004, p. 244.

[7] *Ibid.*, p. 243.

[8] See, in particular, the *Wales Devolution Monitoring Reports* for March 2004, June 2004, September 2004, December 2004, April 2005 and January 2006 (London: The Constitution Unit), all available at www.ucl.ac.uk/constitution-unit/publications/devolution-monitoring-reports/index.html ,

thrust of Labour's *initial* response to Richard was far from positive. As already suggested, the proposed changes to the internal organisation of the National Assembly were welcomed and regarded as unobjectionable. But in other respects the reaction was very different. The recommended reforms to the electoral arrangements of the devolved chamber (80 members, and STV) were simply dismissed; indeed, the Labour Party barely engaged with the substantive arguments advanced by the Richard report.

The issue of powers generated more serious engagement. Initially, Rhodri Morgan conceded that a referendum would be necessary for primary powers to be introduced, while making abundantly clear his lack of enthusiasm for any such referendum. At an academic conference in Cardiff in June 2004, Morgan went on to propose the development of a more expansive version of Richard's 13.2 proposal — '13.2-plus' — to allow for the transfer of further powers to the Assembly short of full primary powers. Details on this mechanism were notably vague, but the clear implication of the First Minister's suggestion was that some such arrangement might well be the maximum achievable for the foreseeable future.

Expectations were lowered further when Labour published a party document entitled *Better Governance for Wales* in August 2004. The contrast between the clarity and intellectual rigour of the Richard report, and that of the governing party's formal response to it, could not have been more marked. Several features of that response appeared at the time to be particularly important. The first was a palpable reluctance to consider the expansion of the National Assembly's powers with the issue posed as a choice between primary powers, on the one hand, and Henry VIII powers to amend or repeal existing legislation in areas of Assembly responsibility, on the other.[9] The second was the insistence on the requirement for a *post*-legislative referendum before primary powers could be transferred to Cardiff.[10] The latter requirement had apparently been insisted upon by Welsh Labour MPs, and their success in ensuring that this appeared in the party's formal response was regarded by many — not least the MPs themselves — as a particularly significant victory. To understand why, one must recall the difference between the two devolution referendums in 1979 and 1997. In 1979, a post-legislative referendum followed the comprehensive rubbishing of the UK Government's proposals during an elongated period of parliamentary

and A. Trench, 'Rhodri's Retreat,' *Agenda: Journal of the Institute of Welsh Affairs*, Summer 2004, pp. 40–1.

[9] With regard to the latter, the Labour Party's policy document makes the point in the following terms: 'One option would be to grant the Assembly enhanced Order making powers to make new legal provision for Wales in defined fields within the responsibilities currently devolved to it, including a power to amend or repeal relevant earlier legislation in these fields. This would in effect apply the principle of framework legislation retrospectively.' Welsh Labour Party, *Better Governance for Wales* (August 2004), para. 26 (p. 8).

[10] Welsh Labour Party 2004, para. 29 (p. 8).

scrutiny-cum-bloodletting.[11] Eighteen years later, a pre-legislative referendum soon after a sweeping general election victory meant that opponents were given scant opportunity to raise objections to the devolution proposals, whether in their generalities or particulars. In the summer of 2004, it appeared that the MPs had secured a re-run of 1979 rather than 1997, seemingly undermining any realistic prospect of attaining the Richard Report's goal of primary powers for many years to come.

Another element of Labour's response that gained particular notoriety was its attack on 'dual candidacy', the practice whereby individuals could offer themselves as Assembly candidates both in a particular constituency and on the regional list. During the first Assembly, dual candidacy had not been regarded as problematic. Prominent Labour figures, including Rhodri Morgan, had been dual candidates themselves in the first Assembly election, while all four main parties had both constituency and regional list members elected to the Assembly. After the 2003 election, however, the status of regional members became the subject of much hostile comment from Labour AMs; it should perhaps be borne in mind that no Labour members were returned through the regional lists in 2003. In particular, the Clwyd West result was seized upon as highlighting a particularly iniquitous anomaly whereby 'failed constituency candidates' could enter the Assembly through the 'back door' of the regional list (in Clwyd West, three candidates defeated by Labour's Alun Pugh were returned through the North Wales regional list). *Better Governance for Wales* proposed a ban on dual candidacy arguing that the present system was 'both confusing and frustrating for the electorate.'[12]

A special conference of the Welsh Labour Party in September 2004 approved a promise for further legislation to be included in Labour's 2005 UK election manifesto. The contrast between the vagueness of the manifesto's commitment on powers — the Assembly's legislative powers were to be 'enhanced' — contrasted sharply with the specificity of the document's uncompromising stance on dual candidacy. Labour would

> prevent candidates from standing on both the list and in a constituency in order to make all candidates genuinely accountable to the electorate, and to end Assembly Members being elected via the backdoor even when they have already been rejected by the voters.[13]

This all served to ensure that few, if any, expectations persisted of any dramatic changes to the 1998 Act. The prevailing mood is captured nicely in the contributions by two shrewd observers of the Welsh political scene in a

---

[11] On the Wales Act 1978 and subsequent referendum see D. Foulkes, J.B. Jones and R.A. Wilford (eds.), *The Welsh Veto: The Wales Act 1978 and the referendum* (Cardiff: University of Wales Press, 1983).

[12] Welsh Labour Party, *Better Governance for Wales* (August 2004), para. 9, p. 5.

[13] The Labour Party, *Britain Forward Not Back* Wales Labour Party Manifesto, (London: The Labour Party, 2005), p. 108.

previous *State of the Nations* volume. Writing soon after the 2005 UK general election, Alan Trench expressed surprise at the way Rhodri Morgan — 'hitherto regarded as strongly supporting devolution' — had reacted to the Commission's report.[14] Morgan's reaction, he suggested, had served to ensure

> that decisions about Wales's constitutional future are not to be made in Wales, but principally in Whitehall and Westminster, by the Secretary of State. This is not a friendly setting, as interest in Wales there is limited, and there is considerable hostility toward the Assembly from a number of Welsh Labour MPs to whom Peter Hain looks for support. Securing time for new legislation and the passage of that legislation will not be straightforward, and the position taken by the First Minister…risks further dilution of in the course of the drafting of the White Paper and translating that into legislation…[15]

Meanwhile, John Osmond hypothesised that 'altering the political governance of Wales so as to remove the Labour Party from its dominant position may prove to be a necessary precursor for full implementation of the Richard Commission recommendations.'[16] The Richard Commissioners, it appeared, had laboured mightily but to little avail.

THE GOVERNMENT OF WALES ACT 2006: FROM WHITE PAPER TO ROYAL ASSENT

Given how the Labour Party had responded to the Richard Commission report, the contents of the June 2005 UK Government White Paper, *Better Governance for Wales*, came as a major surprise.[17] Nothing in the internal Labour Party debate over the proceeding year would have led observers to expect proposals as radical and far-reaching as those contained within the White Paper. The White Paper may have shared the title of Labour's initial August 2004 response to the Richard Commission, but in fact the two documents could hardly have been more different in tone or ambition.

Such was the wholly unexpected scope of the proposals in the White Paper that the most single striking element of them — that the UK Parliament should legislate immediately for the transfer of primary legislative powers to the National Assembly, those powers to be 'unlocked' after an affirmative vote in a referendum, to be held at some unspecified point in the future—was missed almost entirely in initial media reactions.[18] Moreover, by legislating

---

[14] A. Trench, 'Introduction: The dynamics of devolution', in A. Trench (ed.) *The Dynamics of Devolution: State of the Nations 2005* (Exeter: Imprint Academic, 2005), p. 15.

[15] Trench, 2005, p. 17.

[16] J. Osmond, 'Wales: Towards 2007,' in Trench *Dynamics of Devolution*, p. 43.

[17] Wales Office *Better Governance for Wales* Cm 6582, (London: The Stationery Office, 2005).

[18] It is surely no coincidence that the proposal to legislate immediately for primary powers was dealt with in only one sentence (on page 4) of the 7-page Wales Office press release that accompanied

for primary powers immediately, while simultaneously guaranteeing that a referendum would be required before such powers come into force (and by stating that Wales would not be ready for such a referendum for several years), Welsh Secretary Peter Hain effectively outflanked those Welsh Labour MPs who had regarded the pledge of a *post*-legislative referendum as a major victory for their devolution-sceptic position. The third devolution referendum would be no 1979 redux, and the Richard Commission's proposed end point had survived, after all!

Debate on the desirability or otherwise of primary powers was largely side-stepped during the parliamentary passage of the Government of Wales Bill, on the basis that it was for the Welsh people to decide at some future point. The only point that attracted Parliamentary attention was the fact that wording of the referendum question was to be set out in the order in council for the referendum, and was not set out in the bill. Furthermore, it was clear that the referendum would only be likely to occur at a time when supporters of primary powers believed that it would probably be won. Given that most devolutionists had long-since conceded that a referendum would be necessary before any move to primary powers, Hain's solution was elegant, ingenious and potentially highly favourable to their cause. Though there were some — largely ritualistic — denunciations of the various 'locks' insisted upon before a referendum could be held (the requirement of a two-thirds majority in the Assembly in favour, as well as the agreement of a Secretary of State and the UK Parliament as a whole) there can be no doubting the fact that, on powers, the White Paper was a major victory for devolutionists.[19]

Indeed, in one important respect, the White Paper went further than the Richard proposals. A form of Rhodri Morgan's 13.2-plus mechanism (to transfer powers short of full primary powers to the Assembly) also found its way into the UK Government's legislative proposals. But while Morgan had implied that this mechanism might be a *substitute* for the Richard goal of primary powers, in the White Paper they became the interim dispensation. Moreover, the operation of this dispensation would almost certainly mean that, even if primary powers were rejected at a future referendum, substantial new powers would continue to accrue to Cardiff. These powers would constitute primary law-making powers in all but name — or rather by a

the publication of the White Paper. It is not mentioned at all in press release's bullet point summary of the White Paper proposals (on page 2). See 'White Paper takes forward Welsh devolution,' Wales Office Press Release, 15 June 2005.

[19] The ability of Westminster to refuse an Assembly request for a referendum has raised the ire of devolutionists. And the requirement for an Assembly super-majority represents a de facto Labour veto. But as Peter Hain has pointed out, in reality it would very difficult to win a referendum without overwhelming support in the Assembly, as demonstrated by a two-thirds majority. And given popular attitudes in Wales (see final section of this chapter), any decision by Westminster to refuse a referendum request backed by two-thirds of the Assembly would surely increase support for Cardiff at the expense of London. Westminster would have little to gain and much to lose in provoking such a confrontation.

different name, as legislation by the Assembly on this basis would be known as 'Measures' rather than 'Acts'.

The 13.2–plus mechanism finally decided upon was one whereby the Assembly could request Measure-making powers in certain policy areas; if this request was approved by Westminster, powers could be transferred to the Assembly through an Order in Council. As ever, the devil is in the detail. The White Paper's pledge to allow MPs to undertake 'pre-legislative scrutiny' of such requests, remained (and remains) vague, and an obvious potential point of friction. But the potential of such orders (which have subsequently become known as Legislative Competence Orders, or LCOs) to empower the National Assembly is considerable. The LCO mechanism also has clear benefits for those managing parliamentary business at Westminster, as orders demand relatively little parliamentary time, and could potentially reduce the time UK Government departments must spend co-ordinating with the Assembly Government. Indeed, should the use of LCOs prove to be extensive, and if those orders are widely drawn, then any future referendum on primary powers may well be, in practice, largely about confirming what already exists, rather than heralding a major step-change. This would not only represent another significant difference from the two previous devolution referendums, but is also potentially favourable to the devolutionist cause.

Other aspects of the White Paper were much less surprising. The abolition of the body corporate established in the 1998 Act was proposed, with the separation of executive and legislative functions of devolved government in Wales made explicit. The UK Government also proposed to ban dual candidacy in Assembly elections, claiming that dual candidacy 'both devalues the integrity of the electoral system in the eyes of the public and acts as a disincentive to vote'.[20] And, as expected, the White Paper made no serious engagement with the possibility of increasing the numbers of Assembly Members, nor with adopting the single transferable vote electoral system.[21]

The recommendations of the Richard Commission regarding the electoral arrangements for, and size of, the National Assembly are, however, the exception to the rule. These aside, it is evident that the White Paper accepted and attempted to enact the Commission's main proposals. The radical and

[20] Wales Office 2005, p. 29.

[21] With regards the former, and if only for the sake of historical record, it should be noted that in July 2005, Peter Hain publicly suggested that active consideration was being given to incorporating a mechanism in the Bill that would allow an increase in the size of the Assembly at some future point—presumably after the unlocking of primary powers. The occasion was a conference organised by Aberystwyth University's Institute of Welsh Politics. No such mechanism found its way into the published Bill. We may speculatively suggest that the consequential issues of electoral arrangements, as well as the very considerable political difficulties (for Labour) caused by the obvious corollary of the ending of Welsh over-representation at Westminster, served to dissuade Ministers from pursuing this possibility.

ambitious nature of the White Paper, and the stark contrast it offers to the tone of the Labour Party's initial response to the Richard Commission, raises an obvious question. How did such a dramatic change of heart on the part of Labour occur? This story remains, as yet, untold. In a recent interview, however, Peter Hain has spoken of having to overcome opposition at cabinet level:

> some arm twisting was required but that's in the nature of government. There's nothing particularly conspiratorial about this, but there were one or two very senior members of the government — one particular senior member of the government — with whom I had to have some serious engagements; and a bit of a kind of stand-off at one point; and a bit of a kind of power struggle. But that person was persuaded in the end and all to the good.[22]

It is also clear that Hain's Wales Office co-operated closely with the Welsh Assembly Government, both in formulating the White Paper proposals and in lobbying for their adoption. A number of well-informed sources have hinted that Rhodri Morgan's influence was particularly important in the latter regard. While these suggestions cannot be confirmed, they are certainly plausible. On the operational level, the bill team was largely seconded from the Assembly Government.

Public and political debate on the White Paper focussed to a substantial extent not on the issue of powers, but the proposed ban on dual candidacy. Unsurprisingly, the other parties attacked the ban as deeply partisan. Adding further spice to the debate was the collapse of successive attempts by the UK Government to construct any form of intellectual case for their position. Having initially claimed that the ban reflected deep public disquiet at the 'Clwyd West' issue, Hain was subsequently forced to admit that there was in fact no public opinion data in Wales that supported this claim.[23] Evidence collected by the Scottish Arbuthnott Commission was cited in support, even though that Commission's report explicitly rejected a ban on dual candidacy.[24] Comments by Lord David Steel and even the Electoral Reform Society were invoked to justify the ban — much to their surprise and even indignation.[25] Attempts to justify the ban descended into the farcical by

[22] Interview with Peter Hain conducted by Richard Wyn Jones on 13 July 2007 for the S4C television series *Datganoli*.

[23] See 'Route Map to Power,' Interview with Peter Hain by Richard Wyn Jones in *Agenda: The Journal of the Institute of Welsh Affairs*, Winter 2005/2006, pp. 24-28.

[24] *Ibid.* See also Commission on Boundary Differences and Voting Systems, *Putting Citizens First: Boundaries, Voting and Representation in Scotland* (Edinburgh, The Stationery Office, 2006), paras 4.55–4.61, pp. 42–5.

[25] Contrast Peter Hain's Oral Evidence to the House of Commons Welsh Affairs Committee on 10 November 2005, especially Q. 245 (available at www.publications.parliament.uk/pa/cm200506/cmselect/cmwelaf/uc551-iv/uc55102.htm) with Lord Steel's intervention in a Lords debate on the Bill (at HL Deb, 22 March 2006, col. 263). Contrast also Peter Hain's comments to the Welsh Grand Committee meeting on 23 June 2005, (HC Deb, 23 June 2005, col. 5) with the submission from the Electoral Reform

January 2006, when research produced by the Bevan Foundation on behalf of a Labour MP was hailed as evidence in support of the UK Government's case.[26] This claim was rapidly discredited. The UK Government also came under almost unprecedented criticism from the Electoral Commission who, along with the current authors, pointed out the rare and highly inauspicious international precedents for the UK Government's proposal (notably the banning of dual candidacy in pre-Orange revolution Ukraine). This all added to the UK Government's discomfort.[27] Unsurprisingly perhaps, given both the second chamber's political composition and Labour's failure to establish any plausible case for the ban on dual candidacy, beyond crude partisan advantage, the House of Lords voted to overturn the ban in April 2006. Ultimately, however, the fact that the ban was specifically trailed in the 2005 manifesto — as well as a notably helpful intervention from Assembly Presiding Officer Lord Elis-Thomas — saw the Lords drop their objection.[28]

The granting of Royal Assent in July 2006 meant that the second major piece of Welsh constitutional legislation in only eight years had been successfully marshalled through Parliament.[29] With the benefit of hindsight, it is evident that the dual candidacy controversy served as a major distraction from the real substance of the Bill. Whether this was by accident or design remains a moot point. But the furore undoubtedly served Peter Hain's wider purposes. It is striking, given the unexpectedly radical nature of the Bill, that it reached the statue book with few if any hostile or unsolicited amendments. Most particularly, Part 4 of the Bill, conferring primary powers on the Assembly subject to an affirmative vote in a referendum, scarcely raised a murmur.[30] The majority of Welsh Labour MPs, who remain largely unreconciled to devolution at all, never mind enhanced powers for the National Assembly, were comprehensively out-manoeuvred.

Welsh Secretary Peter Hain's publicly stated ambition is that, unlike its predecessor, the 2006 Act will last a generation. Only time will tell whether

Society: Electoral Reform Society, *Much Better Governance for Wales*, September 2005 (available at http://walesoffice.gov.uk/bgfw.html)

[26] See *Public Attitudes to dual candidacy in the elections to the National Assembly for Wales, Occasional Paper No. 5*, Bevan Foundation, January 2006.

[27] See, respectively, *The Electoral Commission's response*, September 2005 (available at http://walesoffice.gov.uk/bgfw.html) and Oral Evidence to the House of Commons Welsh Affairs Committee on 18 October 2005 by Richard Wyn Jones and Roger Scully, especially Q. 61 (available at www.publications.parliament.uk/pa/cm200506/cmselect/cmwelaf/uc551-i/uc55102.htm)

[28] See 'Call to end election 'ping-pong,' BBC News online, 23 June 2006 .

[29] For an analysis of the Act and its implications see A. Trench, 'The Government of Wales Act 2006: the next steps in devolution for Wales', [2006] *Public Law* (winter), pp. 687-96.

[30] A fact that appears even more striking in retrospect now that several Labour MPs have begun to rail against the possibility of proceeding to a referendum on primary law-making powers. See, for example, the remarks by Foreign Office Minister Kim Howells as reported in 'Howells in attack on Plaid pact,' *Western Mail* 4 July 2007

this ambition proves well-founded.[31] But it seems highly unlikely that the issue of the number of Assembly Members (and, therefore, also the method of their election) can be avoided for that long, even though this issue currently elicits palpable and understandable caution among pro-devolutionists. Nevertheless, the sheer inventiveness of the 2006 Act, and the great flexibility inherent within it, may well ensure that it continues to set the broad parameters of government and politics in Wales for many years to come. The fact that such a far-reaching, and constitutionally novel, measure could reach the statute book with such relative ease offers testament to Peter Hain's very considerable political skills.

But the passage of the 2006 Act also testified to another central reality of politics in Wales. It offered confirmation that, although 'one-partyism' has been weakened by devolution, it retained a considerable grip on Welsh politics. The Richard Commission, in the processes it followed and the final report it produced, appeared to embody a new, more pluralistic Welsh politics. But subsequent events — from the publication of that report to the final passage of the Government of Wales Act — demonstrated the resilience of a different and far less inclusive politics. The 2006 Act is, as stated, a major piece of constitutional legislation, one intended to provide the basic building blocks for Welsh political life for a generation. However — notwithstanding all the sound and fury surrounding dual candidacy — the only debates that *really* mattered with regard to the final content of the Act were those held inside the Labour Party. To the extent that they were relevant at all, prominent devolutionists in Wales's other political parties mattered for how they orientated themselves around the divisions within Labour (Lord Elis-Thomas's previously-mentioned intervention being only one of several cases in point). Such behaviour is characteristic of what political scientists term one-party dominant political systems (or sub-systems) — ones where the most important cleavages occur within the dominant party rather than between parties, and where other political actors are required to provide implicit recognition of this state of affairs, orienting their behaviour around shaping the battles occurring within the dominant political force.[32] There remains some distance still to be travelled before a mature and pluralistic democracy may be said to exist in Wales.

The iron grip maintained by Labour on the progress of the Government of Wales Act contrasted sharply with the faltering and undistinguished progress of Labour in government during the National Assembly's second term.

---

[31] See for example, the Secretary of State's remarks in the Commons second reading debate; HC Deb, 9 January 2006, col. 45.

[32] On one-partyism in Wales see Iain McAllister's still unsurpassed paper 'The Labour Party in Wales: The dynamics of one-partyism,' *Llafur* 3(1) (1980), 79–89. More generally see T.J. Pempel (ed.), *Uncommon Democracies: The one-party dominant regimes* (Ithaca, NY: Cornell University Press, 1990).

Labour was deprived of its Assembly majority by the expulsion of Peter Law, following his decision to stand against the official Labour candidate in Blaenau Gwent in the 2005 UK general election. Labour's candidates were humiliated in the Assembly and Westminster by-elections that followed Law's untimely death in April 2006. Acting as a minority government for its final two years, Labour became highly risk-averse, and did little more than limp over the finishing line at the end of the second term.

The most obvious public sign of the now-minority government's difficulties was the way in which the annual budget process became the subject of protracted — and factious — inter-party haggling in the autumns of 2005 and 2006. In both cases the opposition parties demanded, and won, considerable concessions before a budget was eventually passed. In general, there was little obvious direction to the Welsh Assembly Government's activities. Much Assembly time was taken up with numerous policy reviews, some of which (most notably a review of science policy) led to little substantive action by the government.[33] Even potentially significant constitutional developments such as the empowering of the Assembly in the field of transport — following the 2006 Transport (Wales) Act—had little immediate impact. The Assembly Government's announcement in February 2006 that it intended to renege on its manifesto commitment to eliminate all charges on home care services for disabled on the grounds of 'equity' and cost, served to further undermine its credibility.

Even a much-vaunted 'bonfire of the quangos' proved something of a damp squib. Although the Welsh Development Agency, Welsh Tourist Board and ELWa were brought 'in house' from April 2006, doubts about this policy had increased to the point that the Assembly Government was forced to accept that the Welsh Language Board — initially another target for executive annexation — should be spared this fate. Nor did the announcement in late 2005 that part of Wales would be eligible for significant EU Convergence Fund funding between 2007–13 bring much respite for the government, given that 'failure to achieve sufficient income growth is the reason that the West Wales and Valleys region has qualified again for support.'[34]

The sense of drift was captured in an outburst by the Assembly's Presiding Officer Lord Dafydd Elis-Thomas on 22 May 2006: 'it's very difficult', he proclaimed, 'to point out anything that has happened recently...we are not really loved out there by the Welsh public, they are not getting value for money and therefore we need to do something about it.'[35] Such outbursts by Elis-Thomas have been a regular feature of Welsh public life for more than

[33] See *Wales Devolution Monitoring Reports* (London: The Constitution Unit) for 2005, 2006 and April 2007, and in particular the analyses of 'Public Policy' and 'Economic Development'.

[34] *Wales Devolution Monitoring Report*, January 2006, (London: The Constitution Unit), p. 51.

[35] Cited in *Wales Devolution Monitoring Report*, September 2006 (London: The Constitution Unit), p. 9.

three decades, but it was clear that he was voicing widespread sentiment. Not all the Assembly Government's travails were of its own making. The furore in the first half of 2006, surrounding the Home Office's abortive attempt to force the amalgamation of the Welsh police forces with neither proper consultation nor adequate consideration of the financial and accountability implications of such a move, amounted to what Rhodri Morgan might call (in other circumstances) a 'hospital pass' from the UK Government. But it was a palpably tired Welsh Labour Party that prepared to fight the third National Assembly election in May 2007.

THE 2007 ASSEMBLY ELECTION

As the third election to the National Assembly approached, there were a number of reasons to expect that Labour would struggle to sustain the position it had held four years previously. The first was simply the 'time for a change' factor. By May 2007, Labour had been in power in London for ten years, and in Cardiff for eight. As many political scientists have shown, there is generally an electoral cost from being in power; it was plausible to expect that Labour would have to pay some of this price. Labour had also lost a particular advantage it had enjoyed in 2003, when it had possessed — in Tony Blair and Rhodri Morgan — the two most popular political leaders in Wales. Four years on, both men enjoyed far lower levels of popular support. Finally, there had been growing evidence that the Labour Party machine in Wales was in significant decline. Declining party membership and activism levels were problems for Labour across the UK. So also was a sharp decline in the financial resources available to the party. But the party's electoral results since 2003 also indicated that public support for Labour was slipping. In the 2005 UK general election, Labour in Wales saw its vote share fall by 5.9 per cent to 42.7 per cent, a decline that translated into a loss of five Parliamentary seats in Wales. While Labour remained the dominant party in terms of parliamentary representation, its vote share in Wales was its second lowest at a general election (only just beating its result in 1983) since the mid-1920s. Moreover, the Blaenau Gwent by-elections — where, in a historic party bastion, two lavishly-resourced Labour candidates were decisively beaten by two inexperienced and poorly-resourced independents — pointed to particular troubles in the traditional Labour heartlands.

The only feature of the electoral landscape that seemed unambiguously encouraging for the Labour Party was the opposition that they would have to face. Plaid Cymru had been deeply disappointed by their 2003 election performance, with the party's overall share of the vote falling dramatically in comparison to 1999, and its number of seats in the Assembly reduced from 17 to 12 in 2003. The reasons for this decline in electoral fortunes have been discussed elsewhere.[36] As a consequence of this poor performance, however, the party was embroiled in internal strife over leadership, strategy and policy for most of the Assembly's second term. By 2007, some key lessons had been learned. Plaid's election campaigning had been substantially up-dated, encompassing a more effective targeting of key seats and use of voter identification software, a new party logo and much improved leaflets and advertising materials, and an election manifesto with more appealing policies. Other lessons, however, had not been taken on board. In particular, Plaid retained as their leader Ieuan Wyn Jones—a man who, whatever his other qualities, had shown in previous elections that he lacked widespread voter appeal.

The Conservative Party entered the 2007 campaign with realistic expectations of making some ground. Their Assembly Members had generally performed effectively during the 2003–07 term, while the party was experiencing growing popularity across the UK. However, the Welsh Conservatives were also fighting against a history of weak electoral performances (relative to their counterparts in England) that stretches back at least to the 1880s, and against a deep-rooted perception in much of Wales that they are an essentially English party. The Liberal Democrats had some hopes of gaining an additional Assembly seat in the election. However, they were campaigning against the background both of a generally lacklustre performance during the Assembly's second term and the modest poll ratings of the Britain-wide party under the uninspiring leadership of Sir Menzies Campbell.

The election campaign itself offered further signs of devolution in Wales maturing. The election campaign was more intellectually serious than in 1999 and 2003; all four main parties produced manifestos that displayed at least some aspects of a distinctly Welsh policy agenda. In other respects, the quality of the party campaigns varied substantially. The Labour Party fought a poor campaign. Welsh Labour were hardly helped by the fortunes of the UK-wide party (fighting an election in the dog days of the Blair government, and with issues like Iraq and the 'Cash for Honours' affair continuing to rumble in the background). Nonetheless, expectations were absurdly over-inflated, with Labour continuing to insist until polling day that they might win an Assembly majority when this was never a serious proposition. The central coordination of the campaign was also weak, and the essentially nostalgic central message of the campaign seems to have fallen on largely fallow ground. The 'Welsh Labour' brand appealed to 'classic Labour' values. This *may* have helped shore up the party's traditional base in the Valleys constituencies, but its broader resonance appears both geographically and socially limited. Furthermore, though the Valleys loom large

---

[36] R. Wyn Jones and R. Scully, 'Minor Tremor but Several Casualties: the 2003 Welsh Election', *British Elections and Parties Review* (2004) 14; 191–210. See also J. Osmond 'Nation Building and the Assembly: The emergence of a Welsh civic consciousness' in A. Trench (ed.) *Has Devolution Made a Difference? The State of the Nations 2004* (Exeter: Imprint Academic, 2004).

symbolically — for both Labour partisans and their Plaid Cymru opponents — their real importance is limited and declining.

Plaid Cymru had most reason to congratulate itself on its election campaign. Most observers considered that Plaid (notably election co-ordinator Adam Price MP, and outgoing chief executive Dafydd Trystan) ran the best campaign at both national and local levels. With strong financial support from a buoyant UK party, the Welsh Tories also ran strong local campaigns in key constituencies, although their national campaign never quite matched the slickness of Plaid Cymru. The Liberal Democrats' national campaign was generally unexciting, but the party did place great effort into its key target constituency seat of Ceredigion, having captured the Westminster seat from Plaid Cymru in 2005.

Welsh-specific opinions polls are rare. However, two polls published a week before the election were broadly in line with the picture painted by private polling conducted by some of the parties for several months prior to the election.[37] The final polls showed Labour averaging 34 per cent on the constituency vote, and 34.5 per cent for the second (regional list) vote. Plaid Cymru were on 26 per cent for the constituency vote and 25 per cent for the list vote. The Conservatives scored 19 per cent for both votes, while the Liberal Democrats averaged 14 per cent and 13.5 per cent respectively. Applied uniformly across Wales this suggested that Labour might win 26 seats, Plaid 15, the Conservatives 10 and the Liberal Democrats 7.[38] However, previous elections had indicated a tendency for polls to under-estimate the Conservative vote in Wales, and the Tories remained optimistic of challenging Plaid for second place in both votes and seats.

Table 3.1: Vote Shares and Seats (Change from 2003), 2007 Election

Party	1st Vote (%)	2nd Vote (%)	Seats
Labour	32.2 (-7.8)	29.6 (-7.0)	26 (-4)
Plaid Cymru	22.4 (+1.2)	21.0 (+1.3)	15 (+3)
Conservatives	22.4 (+2.5)	21.5 (+2.3)	12 (+1)
Lib. Dems	14.8 (+0.7)	11.7 (-1.0)	6 (-)
Others	8.3 (+3.6)	16.3 (+4.5)	1 (-)
Turnout = 43.5% (+5.3%)			

[37] The two polls were both telephone polls—conducted, respectively, by NOP for ITV-Wales and Beaufort Research for the Western Mail. The authors have also seen, on a confidential basis, results from private polling from several of the parties, conducted over several months leading up to the election.

[38] The final two seats were expected to be retained by the independents, Trish Law in Blaenau Gwent and John Marek in Wrexham. In the event, while Law won comfortably, Marek was defeated in what was the Labour Party's sole constituency gain of the election.

The aggregate results of the election are presented in Table 3.1. They show that the Labour Party comfortably retained its position as the largest party in the National Assembly. However, the party fell well short of the majority which Rhodri Morgan had insisted throughout the campaign was Labour's realistic goal. Plaid Cymru and the Conservatives both made some advance in vote share and in seats, while the Liberal Democrats' position as only the fourth party in Wales was reinforced as they failed to make any gains whatever.

One feature of the election result, from which most participants and observers drew some comfort, was the rise in turnout. The increase was only modest, and still left voter participation rates in devolved elections well below those for UK general elections. Turnout is particularly disappointing given both the fact that Welsh voters have traditionally participated at slightly higher rates than the rest of Britain in other elections, and also that democratic renewal was a stated objective of Welsh devolution.[39] But even a modest rise was better than further decline, and survey evidence also indicated that the perceived importance of the devolved institution had increased significantly during that period.[40]

That Labour made a net loss of only 4 seats on 2003, and remained much the largest party, might cause many to fail to recognise the scale of the electoral setback experienced by the party. The Labour Party in Wales is used to dominance, even hegemony, to a greater extent than just about anywhere else in the UK. But Labour's vote share in 2007 fell back sufficiently for the result to constitute the party's worst performance at any Westminster or devolved election in Wales since the general election of 1918.[41] Although Labour held onto many constituencies, its decline in support left many of its Assembly Members looking vulnerable; of the 12 most marginal constituency seats in the new Assembly, 10 were held by Labour AMs. This was a new and highly uncomfortable position for many in the party.

Another notable feature of the election result was the high degree of uniformity in Labour's performance. Prior to the elections, most observers had anticipated a 'patchwork quilt' of results, with no very clear patterns emerging. Yet for the Labour Party at least, this was not true. Labour's vote share fell back in all five regions of Wales on the second vote, and in 39 of

---

[39] See discussion in R. Scully, R. Wyn Jones and D. Trystan, 'Turnout, Participation and Legitimacy in Post-Devolution Wales', *British Journal of Political Science* 34 (2004): 519–37.

[40] A telephone poll conducted by ICM for the BBC prior to the election, which replicated a question used in previous academic surveys, found the highest-ever level of respondents (35 per cent) choosing the 'National Assembly for Wales' when asked which level of government 'has most influence over the way Wales is run'. (The other alternatives offered were the European Union, the UK Government in London, and local councils).

[41] Indeed, given that — partly due to the peculiar circumstances of the 1918 UK election — Labour did not stand candidates in one quarter of all the Welsh seats, 2007 was in reality Labour's worst ever result in a devolved or parliamentary election in Wales. 2007 was also the first year that Labour's vote share in Wales had not been higher than its vote share in Scotland at a devolved or UK election since 1924.

the 40 constituencies on the first vote.[42] Wales has long been a country renowned for its internal divisions and differences. But on one thing at least, in 2007, it was united. Across the north and the south, the east and the west, in both urban and rural parts of Wales, Labour was in decline.

Why did Labour's decline not produce an even worse final result for the party? Put simply, Labour was saved from far worse by the lack of a credible and appealing alternative. Both the Conservatives and Plaid Cymru made moderate gains. The Conservatives continued on the trajectory of modest progress that they have set since their nadir in the UK general election of 1997, while Plaid Cymru managed to recuperate some of the losses of 2003. Both parties also effectively targeted certain constituency seats. But both Plaid and the Conservatives fell well short of a serious breakthrough across Wales. Neither was strong enough to turn evident dissatisfaction with Labour into significant gains for themselves.

Although 2007 brought some undoubted electoral successes for Plaid Cymru, it would be realistic to describe these as important tactical victories amidst an accompanying strategic failure. Plaid succeeded in almost all its key target seats, and fought particularly effective defensive campaigns where its representatives faced possible difficulties. Among the latter cases, Labour was pulverised in the (redrawn) Arfon constituency, while in Ceredigion, Plaid's overwhelming defeat of a strong Liberal Democrat candidate undoubtedly contributed to the latter's post-election trauma. But the successes of the party's campaign should not mask its broader strategic failure — of failing to find a political message that could translate widespread dissatisfaction with the Labour Party into support for Plaid candidates. Despite the heavy fall in Labour support, across Wales Plaid only saw a modest rise in its vote. The contrast with Plaid's Scottish sister party is stark, as the Scottish National Party largely defined the agenda in Scotland's devolved election. Plaid benefited from Labour's difficulties, but could not dominate the Welsh election in the same way. While devolution has changed many things, the party's decades-old conundrum remains unresolved; how to advance a programme that appeals throughout Wales?

The Conservatives were very close to having a very good result. Conservative challengers lost to Labour AMs by 83 votes in Vale of Glamorgan, 92 in Vale of Clwyd, 511 in Delyn, 1,119 in Clwyd South, and 1,192 in Gower. Although disappointment will persist at the failure to increase the party's representation in the National Assembly by more than one seat, or to displace Plaid as the second largest party, wiser heads will surely point to the party's overall progress in a country that has historically been difficult territory for Conservatism. The Tories' image as the English party in Wales has very deep roots, and it will not easily or quickly displaced.

---

[42] The only seat where Labour's vote share increased was Cardiff Central, where it rose by 2.0 per cent.

Despite a strong local candidate and campaign, the Liberal Democrats were comprehensively defeated in their key target seat of Ceredigion, and by a margin sufficient to indicate that the party may struggle to retain the Westminster seat at the next UK general election. For all the party's confident noises in the months prior to the election, the Lib Dem performance in Wrexham and Swansea was ultimately disappointing. But even more alarming was exposure of the party's chronic weakness across much of Wales. In Ynys Môn, for example, the British National Party won more list votes than the Liberal Democrats. Indeed, across Wales increasing numbers of voters turned towards independent candidates and to the political fringes. An independent candidate finished in the first four (thus beating at least one main party candidate) in five constituencies in 2003, but in eleven in 2007. And the share of the list vote going to 'Others' rose substantially, with the far-right BNP — which, like many extremist parties often serves as an outlet for protest votes — gaining 5.1 per cent of the list vote.

A further noteworthy consequence of the pattern of results was a significant rise in the disproportionality of the final outcome. The National Assembly is elected under a system that might be described as semi-proportional representation, as although the allocation of list seats via the d'Hondt formula does take account of the number of constituency seats won by each party in that region, the fact that only one-third of AMs are elected via the list means that the system cannot be guaranteed to provide a high degree of proportionality. This not only provides a high effective threshold for the representation of minor parties, which would have to win seven per cent or more across a region to stand a realistic chance of winning a seat. It also creates a situation in which, with only four list AMs per region, the allocation of such seats cannot wholly compensate for significant disproportionalities in the constituency results in particular regions. In the three south Wales regions (South Wales West, South Wales Central, and South Wales East), Labour won 19 of the 23 constituency seats in 2007, from just over 38 per cent of the vote. The 12 list seats across these regions were all won by the three main opposition parties, but even this was not remotely sufficient to provide them with proportionate compensation for the very high — one might reasonably say grotesque—disproportionality of the constituency results. It is thus unsurprising that the overall outcome of the NAW election produced a Gallagher Index of Disproportionality figure of 9.9 — up from 8.7 in 2003, and very high by international standards for countries operating 'proportional representation'.[43]

---

[43] The Gallagher Index is the standard political science index for the calculation of the disproportionality of parliamentary elections results: that is, the disparity between the proportion of votes cast for parties and the proportion of seats they gain.

THE CONSEQUENCES OF THE 2007 ELECTION

The period following the election revealed that, while devolution in Wales is now well-established and broadly accepted, the political parties and much of the broader political class still have much to learn about the politics that follows from devolution. The failure of the election to produce a majority party led to several weeks of confusion about which parties would take power. A minority Labour administration took office in late May, but this was almost universally expected to be in office for only a short period of time. The main alternatives to emerge were a 'Red-Green' coalition between Labour and Plaid Cymru, or a 'Rainbow' coalition encompassing Plaid, the Conservatives and the Liberal Democrats. But while the outcome of coalition negotiations remained uncertain, several things were strikingly clear to most observers in the weeks after the election. Leading politicians in a number of parties — and in particular, paradoxically, in those parties with most invested in the current settlement — appeared notably unprepared for managing the difficulties imposed by the politics of coalition negotiations. It was also evident that many in the small community of political journalists in Wales were largely ignorant about a type of politics which may be relatively unfamiliar in recent UK experience but which would be regarded as wholly unexceptional 'normal politics' in a great proportion of the democratic world.

Labour's election campaign was poor, but its performance during the post-election interregnum often bordered on the inept. It seems extraordinary that a party long privately conceding defeat in key constituencies (such as Cardiff North and Clwyd West) had not done more to prepare the ground for a post-election situation in which it had fallen far short of an overall majority. But this is precisely what occurred. It is also extraordinary that leading Labour figures saw fit to insult potential coalition partners in the immediate aftermath of the election (describing Plaid and the Lib Dems as 'inedible', and 'unpalatable'), and then to ignore them, through Rhodri Morgan going on a post-election break. And it is inexplicable that Labour did not do more immediately after the election to try to secure a coalition with the Liberal Democrats, before the prospect of a Rainbow coalition involving the other three main parties began to solidify.[44]

In defence of Rhodri Morgan, however, it may be suggested that much of Welsh Labour's problem is cultural, even psychological. Labour has long been the hegemonic party in Welsh politics, its dominance in terms of votes being underpinned and reinforced by innately disproportional electoral

---

[44] Osmond 2007 provides a detailed account of the processes by which a Labour-Lib Dem coalition crept onto the agenda, was superseded by the Rainbow coalition, and then the Red-Green coalition came to be agreed.

systems.[45] Large and influential sections of the Welsh Labour Party remain resolutely 'in denial' about the implications of devolution and its semi-proportional electoral system. Working with this sort of party behind him, Morgan would have found it difficult to have moved faster even had he attempted to. Only when faced with the realistic prospect of losing power did his party accept, reluctantly, the necessity of compromising with erstwhile enemies.

By this time, Plaid Cymru was the only available partner. The agreement reached with Plaid was strongly endorsed at a specially-convened party conference, a result which represented an unambiguous victory for Labour's devolutionist wing. But while the constitutional balance of power between UK and Welsh devolved government remains as it is, and different electoral systems remain in place at both levels, the internal party tensions of the past few weeks and months are likely to be recurring feature of Welsh Labour Party politics. The many Welsh Labour parliamentarians who remain utterly unreconciled either to coalition with Plaid or to devolution retain a significant capacity for mischief-making. Rhodri Morgan's health problems in the summer of 2007 added another potentially destabilising element to this already-combustible mixture.

The contrast between Plaid and Labour's post-election behaviour could not have been more marked. Plaid's leadership was determined to keep as many options as possible on the table. The only possibility that had been explicitly disavowed prior to the election was Plaid serving in government under a Conservative First Minister, but this formulation still permitted Tory-Plaid cooperation in various forms. The stance of the leadership — along with the behaviour of the other parties — made Plaid central to all coalition negotiations, and ultimately enabled Plaid to make the choice between alternative coalition agreements. Both agreements allowed for the implementation of large parts of the party's election manifesto, and, more generally, bore the stamp of the party's strong negotiating team. (According to one close observer, Plaid greatly benefited from the experience of leader Ieuan Wyn Jones in the negotiations at Westminster surrounding Parliamentary ratification of the Maastricht Treaty in the early 1990s.)

Whether the party made the right choice in opting for the role of junior partner in a Labour-led government, rather than leading a Rainbow government, will be debated by Plaid activists for many years to come. The party leadership's ultimate decision to go for the 'Red-Green' deal was endorsed overwhelmingly by activists in a special conference. But this does not mean that no reservations persist within the party. For instance, the former leader, Dafydd Wigley, used a high-profile speech at the National Eisteddfod in

---

[45] Labour has won at least a plurality of the vote in Wales at every election since the general election of 1922.

August 2007 to voice concerns about the extent to which the commitments of the coalition agreement were deliverable. More generally, party members and supporters at all levels will have to adjust their ways of thinking and operating substantially now that Plaid is, for the first time in its more than 80-year existence, a party of government.

Table 3.2: Members of the Labour-Plaid Cymru Cabinet, formed July 2007

Minister	Portfolio	Party
Rhodri Morgan AM	First Minister	Labour
Ieuan Wyn Jones AM	Deputy First Minister and Minister for the Economy and Transport	Plaid Cymru
Jane Davidson AM	Minister for Environment, Sustainability and Housing	Labour
Andrew Davies AM	Minister for Finance and Public Service Delivery	Labour
Dr. Brian Gibbons AM	Minister for Social Justice and Local Government	Labour
Edwina Hart MBE AM	Minister for Health and Social Services	Labour
Jane Hutt AM	Minister for Children, Education, Lifelong Learning and Skills	Labour
Carwyn Jones AM	Counsel General and Leader of the House	Labour
Elin Jones AM	Minister for Rural Affairs	Plaid Cymru
Rhodri Glyn Thomas AM	Minister for Heritage	Plaid Cymru
Deputy Ministers		
Leighton Andrews AM	Deputy Minister for Regeneration	Labour
Jocelyn Davies AM	Deputy Minister for Housing	Plaid Cymru
John Griffiths AM	Deputy Minister for Skills	Labour
Gwenda Thomas AM	Deputy Minister for Social Services	Labour

In the post-election horse-trading, the Conservatives were both canny and lucky. They were canny in playing their hand well. Past efforts to maintain cordial relations with their potential coalition partners in Plaid Cymru and the Liberal Democrats were continued, with the Tories contributing positively towards the negotiation of the 'Rainbow' deal between the three parties. But they were also lucky that the deal collapsed for reasons that could not be blamed on them. Holding power in Wales alongside Plaid Cymru—indeed, under the leadership of a Plaid Cymru First Minister—would surely have created substantial and public divisions in the Conservative Party, significant sections of which remain unreconciled to devolution. As matters transpired, the Conservatives emerged from the coalition negotiations in a stronger formal position (as the official opposition in the National Assembly), and being able credibly to claim that they had worked in good faith for an alternative, non-Labour government.

However, the Conservatives' luck may run out. The party leadership has managed to paper over persisting internal divisions on devolution in recent years. But a referendum on enacting Part 4 of the Government of Wales Act 2006 would be likely to bring Tory divisions fully into the open. Given the party leadership's strident and fundamental criticism of the status quo, any decision by the party to oppose further constitutional change would inevitably open the party to ridicule. But could the party really stomach campaigning for primary legislative powers for Wales, given the persistent opposition to devolution among a significant group of party activists as well as the party's three Welsh MPs? While media speculation has inevitably focused on the divisions a referendum could open up within Labour, its repercussions for the Welsh Conservatives might be equally momentous. Not the least of those is that any outbreak of public hostilities on the devolution issue would inevitably undermine the entire political strategy of the Welsh Conservatives under Bourne's leadership, namely to present the party in a more 'Welsh' light. The party clearly faces some very difficult choices in the months and years ahead.

Of the four main parties, the Lib Dems have been the most damaged, even discredited, by the coalition negotiations. For the party apparently to reject the Rainbow deal that had been negotiated by its leadership made the Lib Dems look merely silly; for them then to try to reverse their position, and resurrect the Rainbow deal once it was too late, smacked of a particularly highly-developed brand of incompetence. Perhaps most worrying for the party's future prospects was that, in the absence of commanding leadership in the Welsh (or indeed UK-wide) party, the Welsh Liberal Democrats appeared to be behaving as an increasingly loose collection of local parties rather than a coherent national force. Attitudes towards the prospective coalition deal seem to have been almost wholly determined by local electoral circumstances, rather than issues of principle or policy. Forcing Plaid into bed with Labour was the earnest hope of Ceredigion Liberals looking to the next Westminster election, while most Brecon and Radnor Liberals seem to have concluded that a deal with the Conservatives would have made it more difficult for them to squeeze the constituency's residual Labour vote in subsequent elections, and so on. No party is immune from such considerations, of course, and differences of opinion within parties are axiomatic. But with the same old faces returned to the Assembly, the party's MPs wholly unable to offer leadership, and little to distinguish the party programmatically in the crowded centre-left of Welsh politics, it is very difficult to see where the party goes next. It is not an exaggeration to suggest that the Welsh Liberal Democrats face an existential crisis.

PUBLIC ATTITUDES IN WALES

A central foundation for the conclusions and recommendations of the Richard Commission was the evidence presented to them of a substantial shift in public attitudes in the years following the 1997 referendum. This evidence showed that opposition to devolution in Wales fell substantially between the referendum and the end of the National Assembly's first term, and also offered a significant indication of a public appetite for taking devolution further.[46] In the years since publication of the Richard Report these trends have been reinforced and even extended further.

A main measure of public attitudes on devolution is a question on 'Constitutional Preferences' that has been used consistently in every major survey in Wales since 1997.[47] This questions asks respondents to choose between four broad options: 'Independence', 'a Parliament with substantial law-making and some tax powers', 'an Assembly with only limited law-making powers', and 'No Devolution'. As can be seen from Table 3.2, over the decade since the referendum, there has been no significant trend in support for 'Independence' for Wales, or in support for the 'Assembly' option. However, the proportion of respondents choosing the 'No Devolution' option has fallen by more than half — down to well under 20 per cent from nearly 40 per cent within the span of a decade. Alongside this change, support for the 'Parliament' option has more than doubled, comfortably topping 40 per cent in 2007.

---

[46] Much of this evidence is presented and discussed in Chapter 3 of the Richard Commission report.

[47] The Institute of Welsh Politics at Aberystwyth, working with the National Centre for Social Research, conducted a detailed academic survey of public attitudes immediately after the 1997 referendum, and after the 1999, 2001, 2003 and 2007 elections. These surveys were all supported by grants from the Economic and Social Research Council of the United Kingdom. The Electoral Commission also convened a detailed survey of public attitudes (fieldwork conducted by GfK NOP) during 2006. All figures on public attitudes cited in this section of the chapter come from these surveys.

Table 3.3: Constitutional Preferences in Wales, 1997–2007[48]

Constitutional Preference (per cent)	1997	1999	2001	2003	2006	2007
Independence	14.1	9.6	12.3	13.9	11.5	12.2
Parliament	19.6	29.9	38.8	37.8	42.1	43.8
Assembly	26.8	35.3	25.5	27.1	25.0	27.5
No elected body	39.5	25.3	24.0	21.2	21.3	16.5
Weighted N of respondents	641	1173	1044	935	955	837

Opposition to devolution has actually fallen more substantially in Wales over the last decade than it has in Scotland, and opposition in Wales is now lower than it was in 1997 in Scotland.[49] This decline has been most noticeable among groups who were most likely to oppose devolution in the referendum. This includes those who see themselves as primarily British (rather than Welsh) in terms of national identification, and also women. The latter were significantly more likely to oppose devolution in 1997. But by 2006, research for the Electoral Commission was showing women about 5 per cent *less* likely to do so.[50]

Our conclusions about public attitudes do not rely merely on answers to one question on Constitutional Preferences. Answers to a number of other questions, over several surveys, all point in the same direction. Particularly interesting responses have come from a pair of questions asked in several recent surveys. These questions ask about which level of government (local councils, the National Assembly, Westminster, or the EU) firstly 'Have the Most Influence over Governing Wales', and secondly which 'Should Have the Most Influence over Governing Wales'. As is shown in Table 3.3, perceptions of the actual importance of the Assembly have been steadily rising. Nonetheless, there remains a stark disparity between how people think things are and how they would like them to be.

[48] Source: Institute of Welsh Politics/National Centre for Social Research surveys; see note 47 for details.

[49] In Scotland, the proportion of respondents choosing the No Devolution option in the standard constitutional preference question was 18.1 per cent in their 1997 post-referendum survey; by 2006 (the most recent year for which figures were available, this had declined to 9.0 per cent).

[50] The reasons why attitudes to devolution may have moved more rapidly among women than men have yet to be explored seriously. Obvious potential candidates for an explanation include the symbolic impact of the large number of female AMs and ministers in the National Assembly (something that stands in stark contrast to the heavily male-dominated history of politics in Wales), and the impact of specific policies of the devolved administration in areas like health and education.

It is relatively easy to show that there has been a substantial shift in public attitudes to devolution over the last ten years. It is more difficult to explain precisely *why* there has been such a change. However, we can rule out some possible factors, and identify others that are of some relevance.

First, it seems fairly clear that support has *not* risen because devolution has helped to revitalise democracy in Wales. That may have been the stated ambition of the 1997 White Paper.[51] However, there are few, if any, signs of democratic renewal—whether one looks at electoral turnout, or other indices of political interest and participation among the public. Secondly, support for devolution has not risen because of widespread perceptions of great policy successes in the major areas of public policy. Public perceptions in areas like health, education and the standard of living are, at best, only modestly positive.[52]

Table 3.4: 'Most Influence over How Wales is Run'[53]

A: Has Most Influence			
Response (per cent)	**2001**	**2003**	**2007**
National Assembly for Wales	17.0	22.4	35.6
UK Government	64.4	57.9	53.2
Local councils	15.5	15.0	5.4
European Union	3.2	4.7	5.9
Weighted N of respondents	1033	917	827

B. 'Ought to Have Most Influence'			
Response (per cent)	**2001**	**2003**	**2007**
National Assembly for Wales	56.2	56.0	74.3
UK Government	26.3	29.1	17.7
Local councils	16.5	13.8	7.7
European Union	1.0	1.2	0.2
Weighted N of respondents	1033	917	857

[51] Welsh Office 1997.

[52] For further details, see R. Wyn Jones and R. Scully, 'Y Farn Gyhoeddus/Public Opinion', paper presented to conference on *A Decade of Devolution*, Cardiff, 2007.

[53] Sources: Institute of Welsh Politics/National Centre for Social Research surveys; see note 47 for details.

So what has happened? Devolution has not lived up to the worst fears that were raised in 1997. In the Parliamentary debates prior to the Scottish and Welsh referendums, the Conservative spokesman, Michael Ancram warned of 'the dark, cold night' that would follow 'Yes' votes. But few people in Wales (or Scotland for that matter) believe that devolution has actually delivered the dark, cold night. And while government in Cardiff is not generally viewed as a fantastic success, neither for that matter is government in London. Where the two levels of government are viewed as distinct, however, is in their relative degree of concern with the interests of Wales. As is shown in Table 3.4, in this regard the level of trust in the devolved body is much higher. It may also be because of this disparity in trust that there is also a disparity in attributions for policy outcomes; voters are disproportionately likely to attribute policy successes to the National Assembly and the Assembly Government, and failures to London.[54]

Table 3.5: 'Trust to Govern in Wales' Best Interests', 2007[55]

Response (per cent)	UK Govt	Welsh Assembly Govt
Just about always	4.2	19.5
Most of the time	31.9	53.0
Only some of the time	51.5	24.2
Almost never	12.5	3.2
Weighted N of respondents	872	872

To summarise, there has been a substantial change in public attitudes to devolution in Wales over the last decade. There is no longer any serious question over whether the majority of the Welsh people support some degree of self-government. They do. If devolution was the 'settled will' of the Scottish people in 1997, it certainly is so for the Welsh ten years on. What remains at issue is how much more self-government the public would be willing to support.

Does this evidence have direct implications for a referendum on primary legislative powers for the National Assembly? A substantial body of research on referendums around the world shows that opinions on the matter

[54] For instance, in our 2007 survey, slightly more than 60 per cent or those perceiving improvements in the NHS attributed this to the National Assembly/Assembly Government, compared to only one-quarter attributing this to the UK government. However, of those who thought things had become worse, almost half blamed the UK Government and only about 15 per cent attributed blame to Cardiff! Very similar figures also apply for the policy areas of education and the economy.

[55] Source: Institute of Welsh Politics/National Centre for Social Research surveys; see note 47 for details.

ostensibly at stake are far from the only thing that influences referendum results. The circumstances of the campaign can also have a huge impact. The evidence on changes in public attitudes does indicate that a referendum on primary powers would be *winnable*. But in the absence of prior knowledge as to the context of such a referendum, we cannot say for certain that it would be won.

CONCLUSION

Devolution in Wales has, over the past decade, been developing in a very different way than in Scotland. In Scotland, the formal establishment of devolution was preceded by the existence of a substantial Scottish civil society and distinct Scottish institutions. The referendum itself followed years of work in developing a broad-ranging consensus on the matter among social and political elites, and within the Scottish public. In Wales, the process has worked almost in reverse. Rather than *following* years of preparatory work, and delivering formal recognition of a distinct political sub-system that largely already existed, in Wales formal devolution has largely been the spur for such things. The last decade has seen—from a rather low base—rapid development of political and governmental institutions, as well as of a more distinctive Welsh civil society. *Avant la lettre*, devolution has also become the settled will of the Welsh public. And the Richard Commission offered the closest thing that Wales has seen, thus far, to Scotland's Constitutional Convention.

The last few years have seen the 'end of the beginning' of devolution in Wales, and the beginning of something rather different. This something includes the establishment of a more solid institutional basis for substantial self-government for Wales. It also shows every sign of including the gradual erosion of one-party dominance, so long a feature of Welsh political life, and the development of a more internationally normal type of partisan politics. Above all, Wales is now moving into an era in which the *fact* of devolution is no longer of great interest. What is of interest, increasingly, is its character and form, and what is done with self-government for the people of Wales.

BIBLIOGRAPHY

Official Documents and Primary Sources

Commission on Boundary Differences and Voting Systems, *Putting Citizens First: Boundaries, Voting and Representation in Scotland* (Edinburgh, Stationery Office, January 2006).

Commission on the Powers and Electoral Arrangements of the National Assembly for Wales, *Report of the Richard Commission* (Cardiff: National Assembly for Wales, 2004)

Welsh Office, *A Voice for Wales: The Government's proposals for a Welsh Assembly* Cm 3718 (London: The Stationery Office, 1997).
Welsh Labour Party, *Better Governance for Wales* (August 2004)
Wales Office *Better Governance for Wales* Cm 6582, (London: The Stationery Office, 2005)

Secondary Sources

Foulkes, D., J.B. Jones and R.A. Wilford (eds.), *The Welsh Veto: The Wales Act 1978 and The Referendum* (Cardiff: University of Wales Press, 1983)
McAllister, I., 'The Labour Party in Wales: The dynamics of one-partyism,' *Llafur* 3(1) (1980), 79–89.
Osmond, J., 'Nation Building and the Assembly: The emergence of a Welsh civic consciousness' in A. Trench (ed.) *Has Devolution Made a Difference? The State of the Nations 2004* (Exeter: Imprint Academic, 2004).
Osmond, J., *Welsh Politics Come of Age: Responses to the Richard Commission* (Cardiff: Institute of Welsh Affairs, 2005).
Osmond, J., 'Wales: Towards 2007' in A. Trench (ed.) *The Dynamics of Devolution: The State of the Nations 2005* (Exeter: Imprint Academic, 2005).
Osmond, J., *Crossing the Rubicon: Coalition politics Welsh style* (Cardiff: Institute of Welsh Affairs, 2007).
Pempel, T.J., *Uncommon Democracies: The one-party dominant regimes* (Ithaca, NY: Cornell University Press, 1990).
Rawlings, R., *Delineating Wales: Constitutional, legal and administrative aspects of national devolution* (Cardiff: University of Wales Press, 2003).
Rawlings, R., 'Richard's Radical Recipe,' *Agenda: Journal of the Institute of Welsh Affairs*, Summer 2004.
Scully, R., R. Wyn Jones and D. Trystan, 'Turnout, Participation and Legitimacy in Post-Devolution Wales', *British Journal of Political Science* 34 (2004): 519–37.
Trench, A. *Better Governance for Wales: An Analysis of the White Paper on Devolution for Wales* Devolution Policy Paper no. 13 (Edinburgh: ESRC Devolution and Constitutional Change programme, 2005).
Trench, A. 'Rhodri's Retreat,' *Agenda: Journal of the Institute of Welsh Affairs*, Summer 2004.
Trench, A, 'Introduction: The dynamics of devolution', in A. Trench (ed.) *The Dynamics of Devolution: The State of the Nations 2005* (Exeter: Imprint Academic, 2005).
Trench, A. 'The Government of Wales Act 2006: the next steps in devolution for Wales', [2006] *Public Law* (winter), 687–96.
Wyn Jones, R., and R. Scully, 'Minor Tremor but Several Casualties: the 2003 Welsh Election', *British Elections and Parties Review* 14 (2004), 191–210.
R. Wyn Jones and R. Scully, 'Y Farn Gyhoeddus/Public Opinion'. Paper presented to conference on *A Decade of Devolution*, Cardiff, 2007.

4

Northern Ireland

Devolution Once Again

Rick Wilford and Robin Wilson[1]

INTRODUCTION

Following the 2007 electoral round, it was one of the more arresting ironies of the devolved UK that Northern Ireland — unlike Wales and Scotland — appeared to have secured a stable, power-sharing administration. Its third Assembly election on 7 March 2007 confirmed that Northern Ireland had become a dominant two-party system, with the Democratic Unionist Party (DUP) and Sinn Féin (SF) significantly ahead of their respective ethnic-bloc rivals, the Ulster Unionist Party (UUP) and the Social Democratic and Labour Party (SDLP). Thus, what the former UUP First Minister, David Trimble, had once envisaged as the 'nightmare scenario' had come to pass — the prospect of an Executive led jointly by the DUP leader, Rev Ian Paisley, and the leading republican Martin McGuinness.

Yet, it was uncertain at the time of the election whether devolution would be restored by 26 March 2007, the target date set by the Northern Ireland Secretary, Peter Hain. In the event, and as so often before and since the Belfast Agreement of 1998, that deadline slipped to 8 May 2007, when powers were formally transferred to the Assembly.

Figure 4.1: Chronology of events

2005	
28 July	IRA announces end to its paramilitary campaign
26 September	IICD announces decommissioning of IRA weapons
13 October	Northern Ireland Secretary, Peter Hain, says UK Government will proceed with security 'normalisation'
23 November	Stormy second reading at Westminster of Northern Ireland (Offences) Bill, which gives de facto amnesty for post-agreement 'terrorist' offences

[1] As ever, we are dependent on the valued contributions of all other members of the Northern Ireland devolution monitoring team: Lizanne Dowds, Greg McLaughlin, Elizabeth Meehan and Duncan Morrow. And, as ever, the responsibility for the contents is our own.

2006	
11 January	UK Government withdraws Northern Ireland (Offences) Bill, following withdrawal of SF support over provision for soldiers and police
16 February	Peter Hain introduces Westminster Bill to permit devolution of policing and justice
6 April	London and Dublin set goal of restoration of devolution by 24 November 2006, allied to warning of 'joint stewardship' if not accomplished
20 April	Northern Ireland Bill introduced to establish transitional 'Hain Assembly' and to enshrine 24 November 2006 as deadline for resumption of devolved government
15 May	Assembly elected in November 2003 recalled for first of three, six-week sessions to prepare for devolution before November deadline
22 May	SF president, Gerry Adams, fails to secure DUP compliance with nomination of Rev Ian Paisley (DUP) and Martin McGuinness (SF) as First Minister and Deputy First Minister respectively
13 October	London and Dublin unveil 'St Andrews Agreement' after still further talks with the parties in Scotland — though none of the latter signs up to the proposals — setting new 'devolution or dissolution' deadline of 26 March 2007
21 November	St Andrews Bill rushed through Commons
24 November	As 'Transitional Assembly' comes into being, Ian Paisley declines to nominate himself as First Minister, indicating his conditions not yet met, but two governments persist with post-St Andrews timetable
2007	
28 January	Special SF conference endorses policing and criminal justice system
7 March	Third Assembly election consolidates polarisation of party system around DUP and SF
26 March	What had been presented as absolute deadline for renewal of devolution allowed to slip on foot of inter-party agreement to 8 May, with devolution order signed the previous day countermanded by emergency legislation passed the next
8 May	Power transferred to Stormont, with appointment of Ian Paisley and Martin McGuinness as First Minister and Deputy First Minister, smiling before world's media

The restoration of devolution was enabled by three factors:

- the (revised) consociational framework set out in the St Andrews Agreement of October 2006;[2]
- the stated readiness of 'mainstream' republicanism, through SF, to endorse the police and criminal justice system in Northern Ireland; and
- the preparedness of the DUP to participate fully in an inclusive power-sharing Executive and agree a date for the devolution of policing and justice powers (itself contingent on SF's endorsement of the criminal justice system of Northern Ireland).

These effective preconditions presented difficulties for each of the two major parties and both suffered some (minor) defections in the run-up to and the wake of the election, though not to an extent that frustrated the realisation of their prospective political cohabitation. Their internal critics brushed aside, the First and Deputy First Ministers designate, Messrs Paisley and McGuinness respectively, along with ten other ministers and two juniors, took the revised Pledge of Office on the floor of the Assembly on 8 May 2007, thereby setting the new administration on its intended four-year course.

While the plain people of Northern Ireland had, like the White Queen in 'Through the Looking Glass', grown accustomed to believing six impossible things before breakfast, this turn of events meant they had to believe six more at the breakfast table and another half-dozen thereafter. It *is* remarkable that the two major parties are now in office together and, in the DUP's case, prepared to participate fully in each of the three post-agreement institutional strands, something it did not do during the first devolved mandate.

The obvious question is: 'Why now?' Indeed, as some observers have mused, if the 1998 Belfast Agreement was a case of 'Sunningdale for slow learners', the 'Agreement at St Andrews' was for those who were even slower on the uptake. The former characterisation is, though, highly misleading since the Belfast Agreement was much more intricate in several key respects than its 1973 predecessor.

The more recent version tabled by London and Dublin at St Andrews, however, differs in procedural degree — rather than in kind — from its 1998 progenitor. What *had* altered was the context: not only was it transformed by the IRA's decision in July 2005 to decommission its arsenal, to the satisfaction of the Independent International Commission on Decommissioning (IICD) and the two governments, but also by its endorsement in January 2007 of the police and the courts, in both Northern Ireland and the Republic.

---

[2] Because Northern Ireland is a divided society, devolution to the region has never been solely about how power would be transferred from London to Belfast but how it would then be shared at Stormont. The 'consociational' model of power-sharing, as classically set out by A. Lijphart, *Democracy in Plural Societies* (New Haven, CT: Yale University Press, 1977), claims that politics in divided societies should be based on ethnic divisions rather than seeking to bridge them.

That altered reality did make the difference, not just between the St Andrews and Belfast Agreements, but also between the former and the ill-fated 'Comprehensive Agreement' of December 2004, which itself carried forward a number of proposals contained in the Anglo-Irish 'Joint Declaration' of May 2003. There is, then, a lengthy paper trail leading to St Andrews which, though it has followed a serpentine course, has had a clear trajectory towards the realisation of an inclusive administration founded upon consociational principles.

The restoration of devolution was not, however, arrived at freely, especially in the DUP's case. While it remains committed to its preferred outcome, a freely negotiated voluntary coalition, it was constrained — some might claim coerced — into the four-party Executive by two things. First, there was the apprehension that the alternative to devolution styled, but not defined, by the UK and Irish governments as their 'joint stewardship' of Northern Ireland would evolve into some form of joint authority, thereby weakening the union.[3] Secondly, like the other parties, the DUP reflected the electorate's mounting disquiet about policy changes instituted by the hyperactive Northern Ireland Office (NIO) since the reinstitution of direct rule in October 2002. The shift to a domestic rating regime based on capital values and, in particular, the impending introduction of water charges in April 2007 were high on the electorate's agenda and proved equally unpopular among the Northern Ireland parties.

Together with the reform of the region's system of public administration — including the planned cull of district councils from 26 to seven — and the ending of academic selection for post-primary schools, these were sticks brandished with some relish by Peter Hain and his ministerial colleagues to induce the parties into government.[4] At the same time, the Secretary of State made plain that the restoration of devolution would enable regional politicians to revisit these issues and resolve them to their mutual satisfaction and that of their respective electorates.

That invitation, plus the prospect of some sort of devolution dowry from the exchequers in London and Dublin, comprised the incentives, to be set against a raft of disincentives if the offer were refused: unpopular policy changes, loss of salaries and allowances and, more worryingly for unionists, the uncertainties of 'joint stewardship'. There was, in short, little subtlety evident in this British-Irish exercise of statecraft.

---

[3] During an interview on BBC Northern Ireland (4 April 2007), Ian Paisley ascribed the threat of 'joint government with the south of Ireland...the Union destroyed' to the Northern Ireland Secretary, Peter Hain. 'It would', he claimed, 'be curtains for our country'. In 2006, a senior Northern Ireland official had suggested to the authors that 'Plan B' would likely be 'a greener form of direct rule'.

[4] More properly, the unionist parties, since both SF and the SDLP would support the ending of academic selection, while SF, alone amongst the parties, endorsed the proposed reduction to seven district councils.

THE PATH TO ST ANDREWS (SUMMER 2005 — OCTOBER 2006)

The path to St Andrews was strewn with obstacles and, since June 2005, the UK and Irish Governments had laboured to remove as many as they could. An already difficult task, it was compounded by the outcome of the 2005 UK general election, which in Northern Ireland was a triumph for the DUP and represented a measured advance for SF. It was evident, therefore, that any prospect of the return of devolution would require an accommodation between the constitutional extremes.

The first breakthrough came with the announcement in July 2005 that the IRA had ordered an end to its armed campaign, instructed its units to 'dump arms' and directed its 'volunteers' to 'assist the development of purely political and democratic programmes through exclusively peaceful means'.[5] Two months later, General John de Chastelain, the head of the IICD, reported that 'the arms decommissioned represent the totality of the IRA's arsenal', a conclusion reinforced by two independent witnesses, Rev Harold Good and Fr Alex Reid.[6]

With decommissioning accomplished, the British and Irish Governments mounted a renewed push, contingent upon reports by the Independent Monitoring Commission (IMC) verifying that the IRA was embarked on the cessation of all paramilitary and criminal activity.[7] In October 2005, the Secretary of State announced, consistent with undertakings provided in the 2003 Joint Declaration, that he would:

* proceed with the updated 'security normalisation' programme, designed to reduce the Army's establishment progressively to around 5,000 personnel;
* renew discussions with the parties on the devolution of policing and justice;
* appoint a Victims' Commissioner; and
* most controversially, publish legislation to deal with those individuals connected with paramilitary crimes committed before the 1998 Agreement who had evaded arrest and trial (known as 'on the runs' or OTRs).

Seemingly committed to tackling this latter issue, the UK Government acknowledged that it would 'be painful for many people'. But it justified its

---

[5] BBC News Online, 28 July 2005.

[6] IICD, *Report of the Independent Commission on Decommissioning*, 26 September 2005 (Dublin and Belfast: IICD, 2005), available at www.nio.gov.uk/iicd_report_26_sept_2005.pdf [accessed 13 June 2007]. The statement by the two witnesses is available at BBC News Online on the same date, as is the terse statement from 'P O'Neill' representing the IRA Army Council, which confirmed that 'the process of putting arms beyond use has been completed'.

[7] IMC reports are available at www.independentmonitoringcommission.org/index.cfm. They have confirmed that the IRA has forsworn violence and that its leadership is committed to the use of exclusively peaceful and democratic means in pursuit of Irish unification.

proposal on the grounds 'that it is a necessary part of the process of closing the door on violence forever'.[8]

On 23 November 2005, the proposed legislation, the Northern Ireland (Offences) Bill, received its second reading, which proved an ill-tempered affair. Construed as an effective amnesty for the OTRs, it was opposed by the Conservatives, the unionist parties and the SDLP. Crucially, though, when the Secretary of State disclosed at second reading that the Bill would also apply to soldiers and police charged with terrorism-related offences, thereby putting them on a par with republican and loyalist paramilitaries, SF withdrew its support for the legislation and Peter Hain was forced to withdraw it in January 2006.

He remarked, however that 'the Government remains of the view that this anomaly will need at some stage to be faced as part of the process of moving forward' and that it would 'take stock in the Autumn'.[9] If that stock-taking did occur, it had produced no tangible outcomes by the time the DUP and SF were to state their intent to participate in a re-devolved administration, in November 2006.

On 26 January 2006, the UK Prime Minister, Tony Blair, and the Irish Taoiseach, Bertie Ahern, announced that talks would begin in early February, with the aim of restoring the devolved institutions later in the year: 2006 was, according to the two premiers, 'the decisive year for this process'.[10] On 16 February, Peter Hain introduced a bill paving the way for the devolution of policing and justice, together with other provisions, each intended 'to prepare the ground for devolution by ensuring there are no legislative barriers to progress'.[11]

Between February and early April, the two governments held discussions with all the Northern Ireland political parties, culminating in the publication of a joint statement setting out a timetable for the restoration of devolution by 24 November 2006.[12] To that end, the Assembly, elected in November 2003, was to be recalled on 15 May and would be permitted to meet for a maximum of 18 weeks, one six-week bloc before the summer recess and two further six-week blocs thereafter.

[8] HC Deb, 13 October 2005, col. 451.

[9] HC Deb, 11 January 2006, col. 289.

[10] NIO news release, 26 January 2006.

[11] HC Deb, col. 119WS, 16 February 2006. The Northern Ireland (Miscellaneous Provisions) Bill included provisions for a wholesale electricity market on the island of Ireland and the funding of sustainable energy in Northern Ireland. Alongside the Bill, the NIO published a document on the devolution of policing and justice designed to facilitate inter-party discussions on the model for the new department (or departments) — Northern Ireland Office, *Devolving Police and Justice in Northern Ireland: A Discussion Paper* (Belfast: NIO, 2006), available at www.nio.gov.uk/devolving_police_and_justice_in_northern_ireland_a_discussion_paper.pdf [accessed 13 June 2007].

[12] 'Joint statement by the Prime Minister and the Taoiseach — Armagh, 6 April 2006', available at: www.nio.gov.uk/joint-statement-by-the-prime-minister-and-the-taoiseach-armagh-6-april-2006/media-detail.htm?newsID=12944 [accessed 13 June 2007].

The 'Hain' Assembly

According to the joint statement, the primary purposes of the recalled Assembly would be to:

- elect a First Minister and Deputy First Minister 'as soon as possible';
- allocate ministerial posts through the d'Hondt proportionality rule and make other preparations for government, including in relation to the North-South and 'East-West' strands of the 1998 Agreement; and
- consider issues on the agenda for a devolved administration, including water charges, the reform of public administration and education.

The statement made plain, however, that the process was finite:

> If by 24 November the Assembly has failed [to form a power-sharing Executive] we do not believe that any purpose would be served by a further election at that point or a few months later in May 2007. We do not think that the people...should be asked to participate in elections to a deadlocked Assembly. There would be no choice but to cancel salaries and allowances for MLAs and to defer restoration of the Assembly and Executive until there is a clear political willingness to exercise devolved power ... If restoration ... has to be deferred, the Governments agree that this will have immediate implications for their joint stewardship of the process. We are beginning detailed work on British-Irish partnership arrangements ... [which] will be shaped by the commitment of both Governments to a step-change in advancing North-South co-operation and action for the benefit of all.[13]

The die was cast: it was to be devolution, by 24 November 2006, or dissolution and the imposition of an undefined joint stewardship arrangement — or so it seemed. On 10 April, the eighth anniversary of the Belfast Agreement, Peter Hain announced the appointment of Eileen Bell, the Alliance Party deputy leader, as Presiding Officer of the Assembly (when it was recalled in May) and a week later said that an emergency Bill would be introduced on 20 April, arranging for MLAs to be recalled to deal with the matters set out by Tony Blair and Bertie Ahern on 6 April. If they failed to do so then, as Peter Hain put it, 'the Government will be forced to close the book on devolution for the foreseeable future'.[14]

The emergency Bill, according to the Secretary of State, set 'an immovable deadline of 24 November 2006' as he warned that 'otherwise...we will have to move on'.[15] The Northern Ireland (St Andrews Agreement Bill thus rapidly completed its parliamentary passage, enabling the Assembly to be recalled on 15 May. On that day, Peter Hain reiterated his warning that

---

13 *Ibid.*
14 HC Deb, 18 April 2006, col. 19.
15 NIO news release, 20 April 2006. In the event, 24 November did of course prove to be movable.

failure to establish the devolved Executive by the deadline would mean that all salaries and allowances for MLAs would stop.[16]

At the Assembly's third plenary session, consistent with the key purpose of the legislation, the SF president, Gerry Adams, moved that the DUP leader, Rev Ian Paisley, be appointed as First Minister and Martin McGuinness as Deputy First Minister on the restoration of the devolved administration — an offer which, at this stage, Rev Paisley refused. Asked by the Speaker if he accepted the nomination, the DUP leader was unequivocal: 'Certainly not, Madam Speaker. It goes without saying that my reasons are well known across this Province, and they have been endorsed by the majority of unionist voters.'[17]

It was labelled the 'Hain Assembly' since the Secretary of State determined the majority of its business, and after discussions with the parties he established a 'Preparation for Government' (PfG) Committee. This was 'to scope the work which, in the view of the parties, needs to be done in preparation for Government' and, if it so chose, 'to develop this remit by consensus over time or to establish sub-groups to address particular issues', which could be referred for debate in the Assembly.[18]

The PfG Committee held its initial meeting on 5 June 2006 but, in the face of the refusal of the Speaker to chair its proceedings, was unable to agree on an alternative arrangement. After three meetings at which it failed to resolve the issue, the Secretary of State directed on 12 June that it be chaired, in turn, by the Deputy Speakers, Francie Molloy (SF) and Jim Wells (DUP), whom he had also appointed.

It was an inauspicious start, yet the Committee met throughout the summer, established a sub-committee to address the economic challenges facing Northern Ireland and produced six reports. Three of these were on the economy, and there was one each on law and order issues; on rights, safeguards, equality and victims; and on institutional matters (i.e. reform of the three strands created by the 1998 Agreement).[19] While there were sharp differences among the parties over preferred recommendations, the reports did identify common ground. In relation to the economy, for instance, members agreed that responsibility for development should be centralised within a single department or agency and that the economy should be tilted towards the private sector.[20] On law and order, although they were much

---

[16] NIO news release, 15 May 2006.

[17] Northern Ireland Assembly *Official Report*, 22 May 2006.

[18] NIO news release, 25 May 2006. The committee comprised three members each from the DUP, SF, the SDLP and the UUP, and two from Alliance.

[19] Each of the reports is available on the committee page of the Assembly, www.niassembly. gov.uk/theassembly/CPFG/cpfg_commpage.htm [accessed 15 June 2007].

[20] Executive responsibility for the economy straddles the Department of Enterprise, Trade and Investment and the Department of Employment and Learning; the Department for Regional Development is involved in terms of public infrastructure, and rural development comes under the

divided, the parties did agree that there should be one devolved department to administer policing and criminal justice rather than two. They could not, however, reach a consensus on whether there should be two co-equal ministers — as in the Office of the First Minister and Deputy First Minister (OFMDFM) — or rotating ministers, or a minister and a junior minister in the nascent department. The Committee's report on institutional issues also disclosed important areas of agreement, including that the Committee of the Centre (which scrutinises the OFMDFM) should be changed from a standing to a statutory committee, that there should be fewer MLAs and that multiple mandates — MLAs and MPs overlap in ways that would be unconscionable in devolved Scotland and Wales — should be phased out.

There were thus measured successes in securing agreement at committee level, which is where the bulk of the Assembly's work was undertaken.[21] In retrospect, its activities combined to create a relatively upbeat prelude to the talks that were to occur at St Andrews, though few anticipated that a resolution to the outstanding difficulties was within sight. The Assembly reconvened in September for a further six plenary sessions, the last held on 3 October. With the deadline of 24 November fast approaching, the determination of the governments to dissolve the Assembly was undiminished — if, that is, no Executive was to be formed by that date.

THE AGREEMENT AT ST ANDREWS (OCTOBER 2006)

In the run-up to the talks at St Andrews, which were co-hosted by the UK and Irish Governments, the Independent Monitoring Commission (IMC) — a key arbiter of the 'peace process' — published its 12th report.[22] A little over a year after its final act of decommissioning, the IMC reported, the IRA had no wish to return to violence, no longer held the capacity to mount a sustained campaign, was 'clamping down' on criminal activity by its members and had dismantled key parts of its structure. The Chief Constable of the Police Service of Northern Ireland, Sir Hugh Orde, 'broadly welcomed' the report, and while he was cautious about the extent to which

Department of Agriculture and Rural Development. A number of arm's-length economic-development agencies were, however, merged into Invest NI in April 2002, during the previous period of devolution.

[21] There were six plenary sessions of the Assembly before the summer recess and six further sessions in the autumn during the run up to St Andrews. Most of the issues for debate arose from the PfG Committee's reports, though that on rural planning (23 May 2006) gave members the opportunity to criticise the NIO's draft 'Planning Policy Statement 14', which proposed to halt the erection of (almost) all single dwellings in rural areas, an initiative strongly supported by environmental NGOs. In populist vein, MLAs were almost universally opposed to the proposal and called on the Assembly's Business Committee to establish a working party, 'to develop a balanced policy for the sustainable development of the countryside and the protection of the environment'.

[22] IMC, *Twelfth Report of the Independent Monitoring Commission* (London: The Stationery Office, 2006), available at www.independentmonitoringcommission.org/documents/uploads/IMC%2012th%20Report%20pdf.pdf [accessed 13 June 2007]. The other key arbiter has been the IICD.

IRA members were still engaged in criminal activities, also said the organisation was 'winding down'.[23]

Together with the IMC report, Sir Hugh's judgment helped frame the immediate context as the party delegations arrived at St Andrews on 11 October 2006. Two days later, however, when the 'agreement' was unveiled, it emerged that it was not an agreed package negotiated among the parties but rather the best estimate by the UK and Irish governments of the way forward.[24] It was a working agenda, for the DUP and SF primarily, as the apparent deadline neared.

St Andrews in Context

The Agreement comprised a three-page preamble and five annexes, four of which — on institutional reform; human rights, equality, victims and other issues; a financial package for the restored Executive; and a timetable for implementation of the proposals — were prepared by the UK and Irish Governments. The fifth, on future 'national security' arrangements, which related to a mixture of 'reserved' and 'excepted' matters, was drafted by the UK Government alone.

It was apparent from the documents that the confidence of key policy-makers in the 1998 template remained undiminished. Indeed, the succession of London-Dublin initiatives after the re-introduction of direct rule in October 2002, though containing some important differences of procedural detail and, necessarily, of timing, were consistent in nailing the Belfast Agreement's 'consociational-plus' colours to the mast.[25]

In that respect, and with some justification, St Andrews can be described as 'the long Good Friday Agreement'.[26] Like its 1998 parent, it sought to manage rather than resolve mutually exclusive constitutional projects within a consociational framework. As such, it must be understood as a contingent arrangement rather than a definitive settlement. It is, in effect, an agreement to disagree over the future of Northern Ireland, the constitutional status of which remains subject to the 'consent principle'.

The strategic issues at St Andrews were entangled. First, was the DUP prepared to participate in a power-sharing administration alongside SF? Secondly, was the latter, having steered the path to decommissioning by the IRA and an end to its involvement in paramilitary and criminal activities, willing to endorse Northern Ireland's police and its criminal justice system

---

[23] BBC News Online, 5 October 2006.

[24] Northern Ireland Office, *Agreement at St Andrews* (Belfast: NIO, 2006), available at www.nio. gov.uk/st_andrews_agreement.pdf [accessed 13 June 2007].

[25] The key policy statements during this period are the Joint Declaration (2003) and the Comprehensive Agreement (2004). Both are available at www.nio.gov.uk.

[26] Or, as one of the UUP's negotiating team put it to one of the authors, 'St Andrews is the Good Friday Agreement in a kilt' (private information).

— this itself being conditional on the DUP's agreement to set a date for the devolution of powers in this domain? Meeting those preconditions meant that the agreement at St Andrews had to be drafted in a way that dovetailed reforms sought by the DUP with others demanded by SF. That is to say, there needed to be a certain symmetry in devising a mutually acceptable set of proposals which, on the one hand, would enable the DUP to claim that St Andrews was a *new* agreement and, on the other, allow SF to contend that it represented the *implementation in full* of the 1998 model.

Policing and the Suspensory Power

St Andrews was not a *tabula rasa*, but rather represented the most recent incremental step from the Belfast Agreement *via* the Joint Declaration of 2003 and the Comprehensive Agreement of 2004. Each prior attempt to revive devolution had, for instance, included the commitment by the UK Government to devolve policing and criminal justice and, in the case of the 2004 proposals and those at St Andrews, set out a timetable for implementation — in the latter case by May 2008, provided a 'stable inclusive partnership government' was in place.[27] All parties supported the transfer of such powers, but it was SF that pressed at St Andrews for a definite date.

Equally, the 2006 proposals reiterated the UK Government's readiness to repeal the Northern Ireland Act 2000, an undertaking already given in 2003 and 2004, thereby removing its power to suspend the devolved institutions. This matter had been at the top of SF's, and the SDLP's, agenda since the suspensory power was introduced and, in February 2000, the Act was implemented for the first time.[28]

The Ministerial Code and Pledge of Office

Like the Comprehensive Agreement, St Andrews also proposed to amend the Northern Ireland Act 1998, which implemented the Belfast Agreement, to provide for a *statutory* ministerial code. This was of particular concern to the DUP, which had consistently contended that there was an absence of ministerial accountability and collectivism within the Executive during the first mandate.

---

[27] *Agreement at St Andrews*, para. 3. The Comprehensive Agreement proposed a two-year timetable for the devolution of policing and criminal justice.

[28] There was some intellectual dishonesty in this: in the absence of a written UK constitution and in the context of the sacred cow of 'parliamentary sovereignty', emergency legislation reintroducing direct rule could of course be implemented if the restored devolved administration were to collapse once more. Indeed, if such a capacity did not exist, Northern Ireland would stare into a constitutional black hole should one or other of its ethno-nationalist camps defect from the arrangements, as unionists progressively did between 1999 and 2002. Ironically, otherwise nationalists would be locked in to supporting indefinitely an Assembly where there is still no bill of rights and the DUP was effectively granted a veto at St Andrews over initiatives from nationalist ministers it opposed (see below) — albeit that provision also applies to SF in reverse.

Of course, the absence of collective responsibility within the 'cabinet' was in no small measure aggravated by the DUP's decision during 1999–2002 to boycott all meetings of the Executive Committee and the North/South Ministerial Council (NSMC) — enabling its rotated ministers and the wider party to act as both government and opposition, as it saw fit. But its status as the region's leading party and, therefore, the very real prospect that Ian Paisley would become First Minister and that the DUP would have the largest number of ministers — making it, in effect, a gamekeeper rather than a poacher — reinforced its insistence on a statutory code.[29] It was not alone, however, in pressing for revisions to the complementary ministerial pledge of office.

In 2004, the UK and Irish Governments had proposed that the pledge in the 1998 Agreement be amended to include a requirement that ministers would participate fully in the Executive, the NSMC and the British-Irish Council (BIC), and that they would observe the joint nature of the OFMDFM. Those requirements were aimed particularly at the DUP, given its dilettantish approach to the Executive and the NSMC during the first mandate. Moreover, the likelihood that the DUP and SF would hold the posts of First Minister and Deputy First Minister respectively, given their electoral ascendancy at the 2003 Assembly election and the Westminster and local-government elections in 2005, led to the reinforcement of the obligation on the co-equal incumbents to work in unison.

Those two requirements were also included in the St Andrews Agreement, thereby assuaging both governments and SF. But the issue of SF support for the police service and the criminal justice system was at the heart of the DUP's agenda (and those of the other proto-Executive parties) at St Andrews — indeed, it was a 'deal-breaker' as far as the DUP was concerned. Consequently, at the DUP's insistence as well as that of the UUP and the SDLP, the Agreement included a paragraph — subsequently included in the revised pledge — to meet that demand:

> We believe that the essential elements of support for law and order include endorsing fully the Police Service of Northern Ireland and the criminal justice system, actively encouraging everyone in the community to co-operate fully with the PSNI in tackling crime in all areas and actively supporting all the policing and criminal justice institutions, including the Policing Board.[30]

Its inclusion placed enormous pressure on the SF leadership. It would need to convince the bulk of 'mainstream' republicans, not only that its

---

[29] The SDLP was opposed to a statutory ministerial code, largely on the ground that it would lead to serial challenges in the courts, not just by political parties but the citizenry. For an elaboration of its opposition, see Mark Durkan's contribution to the debate on the Northern Ireland (St Andrews Agreement) Bill, HC Deb, 21 November 2006, cols. 446–7.

[30] *Agreement at St Andrews*, para. 6.

leaders should take the pledge but that they be involved actively — not just tacitly — in the governance of law and order in Northern Ireland. It implied they would play their part in ensuring that the PSNI and the courts would be regarded as a part of society, particularly its Catholic component, rather than apart from it.

Executive Formation

Elsewhere, St Andrews revisited the procedure for appointing the Executive. The 1998 Agreement required that the largest party in the largest 'designation' (*i.e.* 'unionist', 'nationalist' or 'other') in the Assembly nominated the First Minister and the largest party in the second largest designation the Deputy First Minister, and that the nominees would be endorsed, on a joint ticket, by a parallel-consent vote.[31] Subsequently, all the other 10 ministers would be nominated by the d'Hondt proportionality formula but would not be subject to a legitimising vote by MLAs.[32] In 2004, the Comprehensive Agreement proposed an amendment to this procedure. As before, the largest parties in the largest and second largest designations would respectively nominate the First Minister and the Deputy First Minister, but thereafter the remaining (10) ministers were to be nominated in d'Hondt-governed order and, together with the two nominees for the top posts, endorsed by a cross-community vote in the Assembly.

While this would have supplied a very public endorsement of the whole Executive, the revised procedure — had it been implemented — would have spared the DUP's embarrassment at having to subject its nominee for First Minister to a vote in tandem with SF's nominee for Deputy First Minister. This would have been especially acute in the absence of the verifiable completion of IRA decommissioning.

The St Andrews proposals departed from the tried and the untried procedures in that they did not require a legitimising vote for any Executive member. Instead, the largest party would nominate the First Minister, the second largest party the Deputy First Minister and the remaining 10 ministers would be nominated, as before, via d'Hondt. There the process would stop, except of course that each minister was required to affirm the revised pledge of office. It was a serial anointment of the whole Executive, which

[31] That is, the nominees had to be endorsed by a majority of both those designating themselves as 'unionists' and as 'nationalists' and by an overall majority in the Assembly — as distinct from the alternative test of 'cross-community' support in the Belfast Agreement, the 'weighted majority' arrangement, in which a 60 per cent super-majority had to comprise at least 40 per cent of each bloc to carry.

[32] This was the procedure applied when the first Executive Committee was formed in November 1999. The parallel-consent test was re-applied to the election of David Trimble and Mark Durkan in November 2001 as First Minister and Deputy First Minister respectively, following the resignation of Séamus Mallon who had held the latter post.

did not oblige the blessed to be acclaimed by the decidedly mixed congregation.

Executive Decision-making

Other Executive-related changes related to decision-making procedures. A recurring and justifiable criticism of the 1998 Act was that the vesting of executive authority in the devolved departments, rather than the 'cabinet' as a whole, enabled ministers to embark on policy solo runs and deprived the Executive of collective responsibility. While St Andrews did not amend the provision, it did address the issue of collectivism.

It proposed, first, that 'where a decision of the Executive could not be achieved by consensus and a vote was required, any three members of the Executive could require it to be taken on a cross-community basis'.[33] Secondly, in relation to the NSMC and BIC, any minister would have the right to seek discussion on any decision paper submitted by a ministerial colleague relating to North-South and/or 'East-West' matters and, inferentially at least, to seek support within the Executive for a cross-community vote if that paper provoked dissensus. Thirdly, it proposed an amendment to the 1998 Act enabling 30 MLAs to initiate a referral from the Assembly to the Executive in respect of 'important ministerial decisions', subject only to certification by the Speaker that the referral 'concerned an issue of public importance'.[34]

The last of these proposals was included in the Comprehensive Agreement, whereas the first two were novel. Taken together, they may be understood as a means of engineering the politics of accommodation between and among ministers and so of manufacturing the practice of collective responsibility within the Executive, if only in the sense of bridling ministerial autonomy. On the other hand, they do carry an attendant risk of slowing down decision-making and potentially creating gridlock within the Executive, even if an Assembly referral can only be made once in respect of any particular issue.

Other Institutional Matters

As in 2004, St Andrews proposed that the Committee of the Centre which scrutinises the OFMDFM should be changed from a standing to a statutory committee — which had already been agreed on an all-party basis in the Preparation for Government Committee. It also reiterated:

• that the First Minister and Deputy First Minister should review the number of functions exercised by their own departments and seek

---

[33] *Agreement at St Andrews*, Annex A, para. 2.
[34] *Agreement at St Andrews*, Annex A, para. 6.

agreement for their transfer to other departments, subject to Executive and Assembly approval (this was a proposal also endorsed by the PfG Committee);

- that an institutional review should be established to examine the operational aspects of the 'strand one' (internal) institutions; and
- that a review, under the auspices of the NSMC, be carried out to examine the efficiency and value of the North-South implementation bodies and the case for additional bodies and areas of co-operation 'where mutual benefit would be derived'.[35]

The latter review, originally included in the Comprehensive Agreement, managed to square the circle between, on the one hand, the DUP's desire to curtail the growth of what it has referred to, witheringly, as 'North-Southery' and, on the other, the aspiration shared by SF and the SDLP to strengthen the North-South aspects of the 1998 Agreement.

Other continuities between the 2004 and 2006 proposals included:

- provision for the chairs and chief executives of the North-South bodies to appear before the relevant Assembly (and Oireachtas) committees when called upon and at least annually;
- encouragement of the Assembly parties by the Northern Ireland Executive to establish a North-South parliamentary forum and a parallel consultative forum;
- creation of a standing secretariat to service the BIC;[36] and
- an 'East-West' inter-parliamentary framework, to embrace Westminster and the Dáil, the three devolved legislatures and those of the Isle of Man and Channel Islands.

In summary, the St Andrews Agreement stands in direct line of descent from the Belfast Agreement, via the Joint Declaration and, more particularly, the 2004 Comprehensive Agreement. The crucial difference, of course, was the changed context: IRA decommissioning, though by no means transparent, had created a more enabling environment. That left the unfinished business of SF and IRA support for policing and criminal justice, which would govern the implementation of the revised proposals.

There was, however, one novel 'carrot' at St Andrews — the ostensible readiness of both governments to consider proposals for increased expenditure from the parties, designed to 'make the most of new opportunities arising from greater peace and stability'.[37] Thus, in the context of the 2007 Comprehensive Spending Review, there was a commitment that the

---

[35] *Agreement at St Andrews*, Annex A, para. 12 and para. 19.

[36] This was otherwise left to the governments in London and Dublin, which could explain its infrequent convocation hitherto.

[37] *Agreement at St Andrews.*, Annex C.

Chancellor of the Exchequer would meet the parties to consider their proposals and that both governments would further consider proposals for joint investment initiatives. Additionally, the UK Government undertook to introduce a cap on domestic rates under the new capital-values regime — inevitably making the scheme less progressive — and to examine the possibilities for further rate reliefs for pensioners on lower incomes. Decades of direct rule have engendered a populist-oppositionalist political culture in Northern Ireland, to which these responses were genuflections.

Timetable

As in 2004, the St Andrews proposals set out a timetable for implementation and, on this occasion, made plain — so it seemed — that the schedule was unalterable. If the DUP and SF failed to nominate their candidates for the posts of First Minister and Deputy First Minister by 24 November 2006, then the UK and Irish Governments would 'proceed on the basis of the new British-Irish partnership arrangements to implement the Belfast Agreement'.[38]

The first step was for the DUP and SF to confirm their acceptance of the proposals by 10 November 2006 and to agree 'definitively to restore the power sharing institutions'. One week later a new 'Programme for Government' committee was to meet, its membership to include the leaderships of the proto-executive parties. It was tasked to agree priorities for a restored Executive and to make preparations for restoration, including agreement on the necessary arrangements relating to ministerial responsibilities, 'ensuring that d'Hondt can be run and the Executive can operate immediately'.[39]

On 20/21 November 2006, under the timetable, the UK Government would give legislative effect to the Agreement. On 24 November 2006, the Assembly would meet to nominate the First Minister and Deputy First Minister. In March 2007, after the publication of a report by the IMC in January, there would be endorsement of the agreement by the electorate.[40] On 14 March 2007 the ministers would be nominated by the party leaders, and on 26 March 2007 power would be devolved and d'Hondt run. To push the point home, the two governments reminded the parties that failure to agree to establish the Executive would lead to 'immediate dissolution of the Assembly, as will failure to agree at any stage'.[41]

The proposals were unveiled by the two premiers at St Andrews, with the party leaders, most notably Ian Paisley and Gerry Adams, giving measured

---

[38] *Agreement at St Andrews*, Annex C, para. 12.

[39] *Agreement at St Andrews*, Annex C, para. 10.

[40] At this stage it was not entirely clear whether the electorate's endorsement would be *via* a referendum or an election to the Assembly. During the passage of the St Andrews Agreement Bill, Peter Hain said the DUP had strongly favoured an election while SF had preferred that there was 'no consultation prior to restoration … but if there had to be consultation…they preferred an election to a referendum' — HC Deb, 21 November 2006, col. 427.

[41] *Agreement at St Andrews*, Annex D.

responses. The DUP leader, borrowing a phrase from a former Prime Minister of Northern Ireland, spoke of the region being at the 'crossroads' and insisted that the onus fell on republicans. He claimed they had to 'deliver on the pivotal issue of policing and the rule of law' — a process 'that starts now…it is deeds not deadlines that count'. To steady the nerves of those within his own camp and the wider Protestant electorate, he said that 'unionists can have confidence that their interests are being advanced and democracy is finally winning the day. The days of the gunmen in government are hopefully over for ever'.[42] To reassure his supporters further, he disclosed that he had sought and been given an assurance by Tony Blair that the future of academic selection would be a matter for the new Assembly to determine (see below).

For his part, Gerry Adams urged republicans and nationalists to study the proposals, make their views known and 'be part of the effort to resolve these matters' — chief among them support for the PSNI and the wider criminal justice system. In direct reference to the DUP's position, he remarked that 'sometimes there's a lot of talk about delivery. Republicans have delivered big time in recent times. We have a moral responsibility to keep delivering, but it's a collective responsibility.' He concluded: 'Sometimes I think in order to be part of a progressive way of finding a solution we have to acknowledge we've been part of the problem.'[43]

THE TRANSITIONAL ASSEMBLY

In the wake of the negotiations — which had threatened throughout to end with no indication of progress — it was clear that both major parties had a significant amount of work to do in convincing their respective electorates to support the proposals, whereas endorsement by the lesser parties, the SDLP and the UUP was, in effect, a given.

Gerry Adams was especially careful not to rush to judgment, at least in public. Speaking at a republican commemoration on 15 October, he told the gathering that 'so far, no-one has agreed to these proposals except the British Prime Minister and the Taoiseach'. Referring to support for law and order, he chose his words carefully: 'Issues of this importance, with such major implications, require careful study. They need comradely debate and thorough discussion.'

For his part, acutely aware of disquiet within his ranks at the prospect of governing in tandem with SF, Ian Paisley drove home the 'delivery' theme to his party's advantage: 'Let no-one be deceived by statements from the Secretary of State that there will be any move by myself or the DUP to enter into

---

[42] BBC News Online, 13 October 2006.
[43] UTV News Online, 13 October 2006.

any government until Sinn Féin has delivered up front on policing. What is more, the final say...will be with the people of Northern Ireland.'[44]

Faltering Steps

With such caution in the air, it came as little surprise that in the run-up to 10 November 2006, the first date in the timetable, instead of an explicit statement of support for St Andrews, both SF and the DUP chose equivocal formulae. On 6 November 2006, SF indicated that the proposals 'have the potential to deliver the full implementation of the Good Friday Agreement'.[45] Three days later, the DUP merely affirmed that 'aspects of the proposals require further work'.[46] An additional sign of unease, especially within the DUP camp, was that the first meeting of the new Programme for Government Committee, scheduled for 17 October, was postponed by the Secretary of State after a meeting with Rev Paisley earlier in the day.

The immediate cause of the postponement was the DUP's concern that SF had not, at that point, indicated that its nominee for Deputy First Minister, Martin McGuinness, would take the pledge of office which, inter alia, committed all ministers to support the police and the courts. Peter Hain responded by asking the Preparation for Government Committee to reconvene to try to resolve the issue. Thus, the planned head-to-head between the party leaders, which would have been the first time they had met, was shelved.

The NIO's response demonstrated that the UK and Irish Governments were prepared to be flexible to try to overcome the outstanding difficulties. Undeterred, the UK Government published the St Andrews Agreement Bill, which was rushed through the Commons on 21 November. During its passage, Peter Hain demonstrated even more suppleness or, as some had it, slipperiness. Whereas the proposals had stipulated that the First Minister and Deputy First Minister would be nominated in the 'Transitional' Assembly on 24 November, he remarked that the UK and Irish Governments would be satisfied that the process would be carried forward if the two major parties expressed an *intention* to nominate: 'The DUP and Sinn Féin...will indicate who the First Minister will be come the restoration on 26 March. That indication will trigger the transitional Assembly which can get down to the real work of preparing the Programme for Government.'[47]

---

[44] BBC News Online, 15 October 2006.

[45] SF news release, 6 November 2006.

[46] DUP news release, 9 November 2006.

[47] HC Deb, 21 November 2006, col. 420. The Northern Ireland (St Andrews Agreement) Act passed in May 2006 had set the deadline of 24 November 2006 in statute and had associated it with the nomination of *all* ministers, not just the First Minister and Deputy First Minister, on pain of dissolution and indefinite postponement of the third Assembly election then scheduled for May 2007.

All that was clear at this stage was that implementing St Andrews was shrouded in uncertainty — not least the preparedness of SF (and the IRA) to endorse the proposals, including, most importantly, the revised pledge of office. The Bill having completed its parliamentary passage, the scene shifted to the Transitional Assembly, which came into being on 24 November. Before its first session the DUP's 120-member Executive had passed (by a majority of 9:1) a resolution, which included the following:

> The DUP holds to its long standing position that there can only be an agreement involving Sinn Féin when there has been delivery by the republican movement, tested and proved over a credible period, in terms of support for the PSNI, the Courts and the rule of law, a complete end to paramilitary and criminal activity and the removal of terrorist structures...Clearly, as Sinn Féin is not yet ready to take the decisive step forward on policing, the DUP is not required to commit to any aspect of power sharing in advance of such certainty.[48]

In the light of the resolution, Ian Paisley said in the Assembly that 'the circumstances have not been reached in which there can be a nomination or a designation *this day*' (authors' emphasis). But 'if and when commitments are delivered', he went on, 'the DUP would enter government'. The statement, though hedged with caveats, was construed, correctly, by the Speaker as a statement of intent to take up the post of First Minister, all other things being equal — much to the discontent of several DUP MLAs. For his part, Martin McGuinness readily accepted his nomination by Gerry Adams as prospective Deputy First Minister.

As events unfolded — including a pathetic attempt by the maverick loyalist Michael Stone to disrupt proceedings — the disquiet in the DUP's ranks became more evident and Mr Paisley was constrained to issue a statement to settle nerves, not least in London and Dublin. He confirmed that 'if policing and all of the other outstanding issues are settled [and] delivered, I would accept the First Minister's nomination provided the election results are favourable'.[49]

Programme for Government Committee

The die was cast: the outstanding issue for the third Assembly election to proceed as planned was SF's support for policing and the criminal justice system. Pending that outcome, on 27 November — more than a month after the planned date — the Programme for Government Committee held its first meeting, picking up the threads of the *Preparation* for Government Committee's work. But it differed in a number of respects from its predecessor.

First, its membership was restricted to the four prospective Executive parties, a provision at odds with the inclusiveness of the Belfast and St

---

[48] BBC News Online, 24 November 2006.
[49] Northern Ireland Assembly *Official Report*, 24 November 2006.

Andrews Agreements. Secondly, it was, in the words of Gerry Adams, to be 'leadership-led' — he, together with the SDLP leader, Mark Durkan, and the UUP leader, Sir Reg Empey, attended the inaugural meeting, along with key figures from each of their parties, though Rev Paisley's place was taken by his deputy, Peter Robinson, flanked by senior colleagues. Thirdly, the committee's remit was more focused since it was charged by the Secretary of State to 'agree priorities for a restored Executive', although — like its predecessor — it was also to 'make preparations for restoration'. Finally, and a signal that it was to be the forum within which difficult negotiations would occur, its proceedings — unlike those of the Preparation for Government Committee — were to remain confidential; only its decisions would be published.

The Committee met ten times before the Transitional Assembly was dissolved at the end of January 2007, as provided by the St Andrews Act. To expedite its work, its members agreed six sub-groups tasked to address key items that would face a new administration, including one on the economy.[50] Its agenda was structured by the outcome of the meeting on 1 November 2006 between the parties and the Chancellor of the Exchequer, Gordon Brown, as signalled in the St Andrews Agreement.

On reflection, the Committee took the agreed view that the economic package on offer at that meeting 'was insufficient to create the new fiscal and investment environment required to address decades of under-investment' and proposed an alternative one.[51] It centred on three strands: fiscal reform, including 'a competitive rate of Corporation Tax' (i.e. reduced to the 12.5 per cent level of the Republic),[52] an investment package 'to strengthen and rebalance the NI economy' and a reform of the funding arrangements for public expenditure in the region.[53]

While this prompts comparison with Oliver Twist asking Mr Bumble for an extra helping, it is of interest that the nascent Executive parties could agree their wish list, indicating a disposition towards accommodation — even if merely confirming that 'rent-seeking' is alive and well in Northern Ireland. Indeed, the parties had earlier agreed that the impending introduction of water charges should be deferred and 'that the public services funding

[50] The sub-groups were: economic issues; the Comprehensive Spending Review, the Programme for Government, rates and water charges; the civil-service estate programme Workplace 2010 and public-sector job location; school admissions policy; policing and justice; and the review of public administration and rural planning.

[51] Transitional Assembly, Committee on the Programme for Government, press notice 31/07, 4 January 2007.

[52] It is one of the peculiarities of the 'peace process' that the DUP and the UUP took as their measure of fiscal reform the rate of corporation tax in the Republic. Invest NI reports that workforce competences, rather than the corporation tax rate, represent the biggest concern for prospective investors in Northern Ireland — C. Casey, 'NI investment agency secures 3,500 jobs from overseas firms', *Irish Times*, 26 April 2007.

[53] Committee on the Programme for Government, press notice 31/07, 4 January 2007.

gap caused by this deferment and the capital backlog be paid for by Government as additional funding'.[54]

After the meeting with the Chancellor, an at first sight incredible '£50 billion' package was trailed in the next day's headlines. But it quickly became evident that this was a decade-long plan which merely represented the total which the UK Government expected to allocate over that period. Neither on the capital nor the current side did it signal an increase in resources over and above projections and it was dismissed, among others, by the Northern Ireland region of the Confederation of British Industry. The employers' organisation said it was little more than 'nuisance money'.[55]

Yet as the former chief adviser to David Trimble, the Cambridge economist Graham Gudgin, subsequently pointed out, the restoration of devolution was coinciding with Gordon Brown 'turning off the taps' in public expenditure: 'What local politicians are discovering in their dealings with the Chancellor is that the Treasury is in the business of holding down spending, not showering what they regard already as a pampered and ungrateful region with yet more cash.'[56]

While the parties did cohere around an economic package, the sub-committee dealing with policing and justice made less headway. Its members failed to achieve consensus on the ministerial arrangements under devolution, the appointment procedure for the relevant minister or the timing of the transfer of policing and justice powers — though they did 'agree by consensus that all parties should support the rule of law'.[57] Though there were extensive areas of agreement, including the principle of devolving these powers, the report appeared before the endorsement of the PSNI and the criminal justice system by SF — the remaining obstacle in the path of devolution, pending the outcome of the planned election.[58]

SF and Policing

While the DUP embarked on carrying its supporters into an election that, barring accidents, would mean its participation in an administration alongside SF, the SF leadership began to bring its members, including the IRA Army Council, into the pro-PSNI fold. On 29 December 2006, SF's *ard*

---

[54] Press notice 01/06, 20 November 2006.

[55] BBC News Online, 2 November 2006.

[56] G. Gudgin, 'Unravelling the final package', *Fortnight* 452, May 2007, pp. 4–5.

[57] *Report on the Devolution of Policing and Justice 03/06r*, Transitional Assembly, 22 January 2007, p. 4.

[58] *Ibid.*, pp. 4–5.

chomhairle (executive) met in Dublin to agree privately a resolution to be put before a special *ard fheis* (conference) in January. The life of the Transitional Assembly was limited to the end of that month, when it was to be dissolved in preparation for the election.

The special *ard fheis* was held, again in Dublin, on 28 January 2007 and delegates overwhelmingly endorsed the *ard chomhairle* motion, subsequently published. This expressed critical support for 'civic policing through a police service which is representative of the community it serves, free from partisan control and democratically accountable', encouraged all in the community 'to co-operate fully with the police service (north and south) in tackling crime and actively supporting all criminal justice institutions' and authorised SF's elected representatives to participate in the Policing Board and the district policing partnerships.[59] Two days later, the 12th IMC report gave, in effect, the 'green light' for the election.

THE ASSEMBLY ELECTION

Disquiet in SF and DUP ranks rumbled on during February and early March 2007 but, with few high-profile defectors in either camp, the election duly took place on 7 March. The campaign discourse itself centred on what became labelled as 'bread and butter' issues rather than matters of constitutional principle, with health care, the rates and water charges leading the way. But no one was suggesting for a moment that this would translate into electoral outcomes, since all the parties were offering similar populist-conservative platforms — agreeing in particular on the iniquity of asking private citizens to pay collectively for the public good of a modernised water and sewerage system.

---

[59] There were prior indications that SF's leadership was committed to securing support for the motion. On 13 December 2006, a SF delegation led by the party president, Gerry Adams, met the Chief Constable, Sir Hugh Orde, a meeting recorded on camera for the first time. At the end of November, SF had announced that seventeen of its southern councillors and two of its TDs would take their seats on the new generation of policing committees established as liaison groups advising on law enforcement — a signal event in itself. The full text of the long motion is available at www.sinnfeinonline.com/news/ 3189. It endorsed both the PSNI and the Garda Síochána and was, in that respect, a double first.

Figure 4.2: Assembly Votes, Vote Shares (%) and Seats — 1998–2007

Election	UUP		DUP		SDLP		SF	
	Votes (%)	Seats	Votes (%)	Seats	Votes (%)	Seats	Votes (%)	Seats
1998 Assembly	172,225 (21.3)	28	145,917 (18.0)	20	177,963 (21.9)	24	142,858 (17.6)	18
2003 Assembly	156,931 (22.7)	27*	177,944 (25.7)	30	117,547 (16.9)	18	162,758 (23.5)	24
2007 Assembly	103,145 (14.9)	18	207,721 (30.1)	36	105,16 (15.2)	16	180,573 (26.2)	28

Note: Following the election (in November 2003), three of the UUP's MLAs defected to the DUP in January 2004, thereby increasing the seat differential between them to nine

Only one opinion poll appeared during the campaign. It forecast a 25 per cent share of first-preference votes for the DUP, 22 per cent for SF, 20 per cent for the SDLP and 16 per cent for the UUP. In terms of rank order this was accurate, though not as to vote shares.[60] The DUP topped the poll, with a strong performance by SF consolidating the trend towards polarisation evident in Assembly, and indeed other, elections in recent years (see Figure 4.2). The minor non-sectarian parties held their own however: Alliance picked up an extra seat in South Belfast (representing the first Chinese candidate elected to any parliament in Europe), to hold seven, while the Greens secured their first Assembly toehold, in North Down.

To put the UUP's plight in perspective, its aggregate vote has fallen from 258,349 at the 1997 UK general election to its present nadir — a truly dramatic decline, matched only by that of the SDLP, whose vote over the same decade has fallen from 190,814 to its current low. In 1999, when powers were transferred to the first Executive, the UUP and the SDLP each had four ministers, while there were two for both SF and the DUP, yielding a 6:6 balance between unionists and nationalists. The outcome of the 2007 Assembly election meant that the Executive (including the First Minister and Deputy First Minister) would, through d'Hondt, yield a 'cabinet' of five DUP, four SF, two UUP and one SDLP — a 7:5 unionist majority.[61]

At this early stage, however, with the exception of Ian Paisley and Martin McGuinness, there was no indication which of the MLAs from the prospective parties would become ministers, nor which departments each of them favoured. Moreover, uncertainties remained about whether the target date of 26 March for the formation of the Executive would be met.

Post-election Negotiations

There was, however, evidence of continuing momentum, including a second all-party meeting with the Chancellor to press for an enhanced 'peace dividend'. It took place the day after the budget statement, with the outcome an offer of £1 billion — or, rather, £600 million from the UK Treasury supplemented by £400 million from the Republic's exchequer, designed to assist in bridging the infrastructure deficit bequeathed by direct-rule. On closer inspection, it emerged that £200 million of the Treasury's contribution was to be derived from end-of-year flexibilities and a further £200 million from the sale of public assets, leaving a residual figure of just £200 million — a

---

[60] The results of the Ipsos/Mori poll were published serially in the *Belfast Telegraph*, beginning on 1 March.

[61] Had an Executive been formed in the immediate wake of the 2003 Assembly election it too would have had a 7:5 unionist: nationalist weighting, with 4 DUP, 3 UUP, 3 SF and 2 SDLP ministers. The subsequent defection of 3 UUP MLAs to the DUP would have altered the party balance within the Executive to the benefit of the DUP, which would have gained an extra ministerial role at the expense of the UUP.

long way from the '£50 billion' which Peter Hain had spun as 'extraordinary' after the previous meeting between the parties and Gordon Brown.

Presented with the renewed case for the reduction of corporation tax levied in Northern Ireland, the Chancellor responded by establishing a review of the impact of fiscal policies in the region, to be chaired by the former head of Revenue and Customs, Sir David Varney. His background suggested he was unlikely to be overly receptive to suggestions that the UK's unitary taxation regime should be dismantled.[62]

In the event, and after intensive, separate discussions involving both premiers and the leaderships of the DUP and SF, on 24 March the DUP Executive met to endorse the party's participation in the power-sharing administration. The Executive resolution acknowledged that 'a significant opportunity exists to have devolution returned in a context which can make real and meaningful improvement in the lives of the people in NI'. It therefore recommended that the DUP 'would support and participate fully in a NI Executive if powers were devolved to it on an agreed date in May'. It continued: 'We are willing to bridge the short gap between now and then with preparatory work, including departmental pre-briefings and finalising a Programme for Government. This firm commitment is offered within an environment where no-one, including the Government, goes back on any of the advances and commitments made.'[63]

Having spent the year, including the period beyond St Andrews, insisting that 26 March 2007 was the absolute, immovable deadline, Peter Hain now acceded to the DUP's insistence that 'D-day' be deferred to 8 May. But with the devolution order signed on 25 March, the deferral required the passage of emergency legislation in Parliament, duly accomplished on 27 March.[64]

Over the weekend, delegations from the DUP and SF met at Stormont Castle to iron out the modalities of transferring power and the timetable for effecting a transition to devolution by 8 May. On 26 March, for the first time, Ian Paisley and Gerry Adams met face-to-face in the unlikely but neutral setting of the members' dining room in Parliament Buildings to confirm the

---

[62] Peter Hain rehearsed the objections to a change in corporation tax when he appeared before the Northern Ireland Affairs Select Committee on 18 April 2007, though he was careful not to pre-empt the outcome of the Varney review. See the uncorrected evidence at www.parliament.the-stationery-office. co.uk/pa/cm/cmniaf.htm. A subsequent report in the *Financial Times* ('Corporation tax blow for N Ireland', 30 May 2007) suggested that Sir David Varney had 'poured cold water' on the proposed reduction in corporation tax, because it 'would encourage transfer pricing' — as indeed it has, egregiously, in the Republic where US corporations have ensured that huge profits have been made by their Irish subsidiaries, even where these have had relatively few employees, thereby avoiding the 35 per cent corporation tax rate on profits posted at home. There is increasing European annoyance, particularly in France and Germany, at the beggar-my-neighbour Irish tax shelter, which may well prove to have had substantial intangible costs in lost international goodwill.

[63] DUP news release, 25 March 2007.

[64] Northern Ireland (St Andrews Agreement) (No2) Act 2007.

deal. Shortly afterwards, they appeared in angular proximity before the TV cameras to commit their parties to the restoration of devolution.

The six-week delay (affording the DUP the claim that it had secured an additional period to test the IRA's commitment to exclusively peaceful and democratic means) did not, however, signal a hiatus in the unfolding process. During his remarks on 26 March, Ian Paisley indicated that his party would 'participate fully with the other [Executive] parties in making full preparations for the restoration of devolution', including regular meetings with the incoming Deputy First Minister, Martin McGuinness — though he was quick to reassure his electors that the relationship with 'my Deputy', would be 'a work-in not a love-in'.[65]

Within a week, the parties had informally run d'Hondt to arrive at departmental allocations, and by mid-April they had all announced their ministerial representatives.[66] Thus, unlike in 1999 — which was the first successful running of d'Hondt — when the nomination of ministers took place without an agreed allocation of departments, the announcements betokened the outcome of inclusive, all Executive-party negotiations prior to devolution. Given the nominations of Ian Paisley and Martin McGuinness as First Minister and Deputy First Minister respectively, this enabled them and their ministerial colleagues in waiting to be briefed in advance by their relevant officials and allowed d'Hondt to be run without incident on 8 May.

Thus, the new Executive comprised the following ministers and departmental appropriations (d'Hondt order in brackets):

- DUP: Peter Robinson — Finance and Personnel (1); Nigel Dodds — Enterprise, Trade and Investment (3); Arlene Foster — Environment (7); Edwin Poots — Culture, Arts and Leisure (9);
- SF: Caitriona Ruane — Education, (2); Conor Murphy — Regional Development (6); Michelle Gildernew — Agriculture and Rural Development (8);
- UUP: Michael McGimpsey — Health, Social Services and Public Safety (4); Sir Reg Empey — Employment and Learning (10); and
- SDLP: Margaret Ritchie, Social Development (5).

---

[65] BBC News Online, 26 March 2007. The patronising tone of Rev Paisley's address of Mr McGuinness as 'Deputy', unsurprisingly, raised sensitive Catholic hackles.

[66] While the leaders of both unionist parties (Messrs Paisley and Empey) were to be in the Executive, neither Gerry Adams nor Mark Durkan, the leaders of SF and the SDLP respectively, were to take ministerial posts, though Mr Durkan (a former Minister of Finance and Personnel) chaired the Finance and Personnel Committee. Mr Adams (as in the first mandate) did not participate in any committee; nor did his party colleague, Pat Doherty, the former chair of the Enterprise, Trade and Investment Committee. Were there to be any sense in the Catholic community of disaffection from devolution, arising from a perceived association with deadlocking DUP behaviour, this would not help bind SF and the SDLP to the arrangements.

An equally positive sign was inter-party agreement over the d'Hondt governed allocation of the chairs and deputy chairs of the Assembly's statutory and standing committees, again prior to the transfer of power, and the nomination by Messrs Paisley and Adams of Ian Paisley Jr and Gerry Kelly as junior ministers from their respective parties in the OFMDFM. To some extent, this outbreak of sweet reasonableness rather belied Gerry Adams's anticipation that devolution would be 'a battle a day', although he had in mind a number of substantive policy gaps between and among the parties over issues including academic selection and the reform of public administration.

MLAs and the Assembly

Amidst extensive media coverage, and attended by sundry luminaries — including Bertie Ahern and Tony Blair — the new Assembly began its proceedings on 8 May with the election of the new Speaker, Willie Hay of the DUP, and three Deputy Speakers (David McClarty (UUP), Francie Molloy (SF) and John Dallat (SDLP)), after which Ian Paisley and Martin McGuinness took the revised pledge of office.[67] Thereafter, d'Hondt was run and each ministerial nominee affirmed the pledge, as did the two junior ministers. The following day, the chairs and deputy chairs of the 11 statutory and six standing committees were nominated and the membership of each of the committees was disclosed.[68]

The process of Executive formation lacked the drama and theatricality of 1999, testament to the extensive preparatory work following the events of 26 March. Of the 12 ministers, five (Messrs Dodds, Empey, McGimpsey, McGuinness and Robinson) had cut their ministerial teeth in 1999–2002. Unlike the Assembly as a whole, which returned just 18 female MLAs — at 16.6 per cent, by far the lowest proportion of the devolved assemblies, mainly because of the appalling unionist showing — the Executive included four women, Ms Foster, Ms Gildernew, Ms Ritchie and Ms Ruane, who constituted exactly one-third of the total.

The new MLAs began their mandate on something of a positive note.[69] But of the new intake of 108 MLAs, only 48 had served in the first Assembly; the

---

[67] This was another subtle, but not insignificant, sign that the co-equal ethos of the Belfast Agreement had been shaded by St Andrews under the DUP's enhanced power. In the previous period of devolution, the Speaker, Lord Alderdice, was drawn from the constitutionally impartial Alliance Party.

[68] See Northern Ireland Assembly *Official Report*, 9 May 2007. The additional statutory committee is the Committee of the Centre, previously a standing committee. There is a new standing committee, established following the St Andrews Agreement, *viz.*, the Assembly and Executive Review Committee.

[69] The proceedings were, however, overshadowed by the death of George Dawson (DUP, East Antrim) on the eve of the transfer of power. He was replaced by Alastair Ross with effect from 14 May.

remaining 60 faced a steep learning curve.[70] When the total of 184 committee allocations were announced, it was clear that some could anticipate a
heavy workload. Only 19 members will serve on one committee, with 51 on
two, 19 on three and one, Willie Clarke (SF), nominated to five committees.

An End to Activism

A remarkable feature of the prior period of direct rule, from 2002 to 2006,
was the associated ministerial activism.[71] This translated itself, inter alia,
into the emergence of cross-departmental strategies to address the key policy
challenges facing Northern Ireland — sectarianism and social exclusion —
as well as the key challenge facing the world: sustainability.[72]

Each of these strategies fell vulnerable to the absence of party collegiality
within the devolved Executive. They each depended on the OFMDFM being
able to coordinate departmental efforts but, unlike in Scotland, the head of
the civil service in Northern Ireland has no power to direct the departmental
permanent secretaries if they have political cover from their ministers.

Moreover, the abiding problem remains that, however much 'bread and
butter' issues were at the top of the electorate's agenda, the ethno-nationalist
focus of the party system means the parties are policy-light and lack the
political compass that the left-right divide provides in 'normal' democratic
societies. Hence their tendency to default to 'rent-seeking' — demanding
additional expenditure, while at the same time resisting any tax imposts. In
effect, this becomes a politics of 'spend but don't tax'.

Within days of the new Executive being formed, the finance minister,
Peter Robinson, was thus warning his colleagues, in public, to stop supporting unfunded proposals — the Assembly having just voted in principle to
follow Scotland on free personal long-term care for the elderly.[73] On the other
side of the balance, ministers had no concrete proposals for alternatives to the

[70] Seventy-six of the new MLAs had been elected to the 2003 virtual Assembly, but when it was convened in May 2006 its body of work focused on efforts to restore devolution, rather than performing the extensive repertoire of roles enacted between 1999 and 2002.

[71] R. Wilford and R. Wilson, 'Northern Ireland: while you take the high road ...' in A. Trench (ed.), *The Dynamics of Devolution: The State of the Nations 2005* (Exeter: Imprint Academic Press, 2005), p. 82.

[72] Office of the First Minister and Deputy First Minister, *A Shared Future: Policy and Strategic Framework for Good Relations in Northern Ireland* (Belfast: OFMDFM, 2005), available at www. asharedfutureni.gov.uk/pdf_documents/gprs.pdf); *First Steps Towards Sustainability: A Sustainable Development Strategy for Northern Ireland* (Belfast: OFMDFM, 2006), available at: www.ofmdfmni. gov.uk/sustain-develop.pdf; and *Lifetime Opportunities: Government's Anti-Poverty and Social Inclusion Strategy for Northern Ireland* (Belfast: OFMDFM, 2006), available at: www.ofmdfmni.gov. uk/antipovertynov06.pdf.

[73] 'Robinson warns budget-breaking ministers', *News Letter*, 19 May 2007.

reformed rates and new water charges, and so inevitably set in train further reviews instead.[74]

Also kicked into the long grass was the reform of public administration, with the parties unable to agree on whether to reduce the number of councils from 26 to seven, as proposed by the outgoing regime, but now only supported by SF among the regional parties. It was suggested that the elections to the new authorities, due in 2009, might not now take place until 2011.[75] Meanwhile, an Assembly motion from Alliance to endorse the 'community relations' policy, *A Shared Future*, was amended merely to take note of it.[76]

The difficulty was crystallised by the publication of the draft Programme for Government in October 2007. The document covered only 16 pages (double-spaced to boot) — a marked contrast with the first PfG under the earlier devolution mandate, which ran to more than 70. There were lots of aspirational targets and some actions but no new policies. Implying that Northern Ireland's sectarian problems were solved by the renewal of power-sharing, the draft asserted: 'Our primary focus over the lifetime of this Programme for Government will be on growing the economy.'[77] It was therefore to be all the more bitter a blow when, as expected, the Varney review rejected wholesale the clamour for corporation-tax cuts.[78]

The Executive creaked as the UUP and SDLP supported an unsuccessful Alliance amendment in the assembly debate on the programme and associated budget, attacking its 'limited vision'. The two party leaders, Sir Reg Empey and Mark Durkan, respectively, staged a joint press conference to protest about the budget allocations to their ministers. While the DUP finance minister, Peter Robinson, threatened that 'without an agreed programme for government, there cannot be government', the Alliance leader, David Ford, bemoaned the 'inactivity' of the executive, telling his party conference: 'The question is how long will this inadequacy be tolerated by the two Governments?'[79]

---

[74] Department of Finance and Personnel and Department for Regional Development news releases, 11 June 2007.

[75] N. McAdam, 'Reduction in number of councils may be heading towards two-year reprieve', *Belfast Telegraph*, 12 June 2007.

[76] Northern Ireland Assembly *Official Report*, 4 June 2007, available at www.niassembly.gov.uk/record/reports2007/070604.htm.

[77] Northern Ireland Executive, *Building a Better Future: Draft Programme for Government 2008–2011* (Belfast: OFMDFM, 2007), available at www.pfgbudgetni.gov.uk/pfg241007new.pdf, p. 5.

[78] D. Keenan, 'Disappointment at Varney's findings', *Irish Times*, 18 December 2007 For the report, see Sir David Varney, *Review of Tax Policy in Northern Ireland* December 2007 (London: The Stationery Office, 2007), available at www.hm-treasury.gov.uk./media/1/3/varney171207.pdf.

[79] G. Moriarty, 'McGuinness tags SDLP, UUP as problem parties', *Irish Times*, 28 November 2007.

THE BLAIR EFFECT

The realisation of devolution on 8 May 2007 appeared to be a triumph for the tenacity of Tony Blair and Bertie Ahern and their fixity of purpose in respect of the consociational-plus formula elaborated in 1998 and only marginally adjusted by the terms of the St Andrews Agreement. To chafe at the achievement seems curmudgeonly and out of touch with the *Zeitgeist* that prevailed on 8 May, embodied in Tony Blair's invocation of an opportunity to 'escape the heavy chains of history'.[80]

Yet probing beneath the surface of the glowing international media coverage reveals a less edifying picture. The most obvious point is the counter-factual: 8 May happened not because the parties in Northern Ireland had finally committed themselves to a process of reconciliation but was driven, ultimately, by the UK Prime Minister's increasingly palpable search for an historic legacy — one associated with peace in Ireland, not violence in Iraq. What had repeatedly been described as utterly implacable deadlines, which if broken would mean the Assembly would be dissolved indefinitely and the political class dispersed, were broken. And not just once, but twice — with regard to 24 November 2006 and 26 March 2007. Moreover, a DUP walkout from St Andrews in October, which would have collapsed the talks, was reportedly only prevented by a raft of concessions by Tony Blair, granted out of fear of the next day's headlines.[81]

Further evidence as to how much events in Northern Ireland were being driven by not just domestic UK but personal, prime-ministerial considerations came when it was revealed in April that Mr Blair would not announce his retirement until after the Scottish and Welsh elections — despite the obvious damage this would do to the Labour Party in those polls, and which was undoubtedly to contribute to the post-electoral instability there with which we began this chapter.[82] He would, rather, delay for all of a week … until after the Assembly convened. He duly made the announcement that he was to step down on 10 May.[83]

Yet, ironically, it was all in vain. A poll for the *Independent* on Tony Blair's 10th anniversary as premier found 69 per cent of respondents thought his enduring legacy would be Iraq. Just 6 per cent volunteered Northern Ireland.[84]

And was Northern Ireland, finally, really a done deal? Of the agreement between the DUP and SF on 26 March, Tony Blair said:

In a sense, everything that we've done over the last 10 years has been a preparation for this moment. This won't stop republicans or nationalists being any

80 BBC News Online, 8 May 2007.
81 H. McDonald, 'Blair's last-ditch deal saved Irish talks', *The Observer*, 15 October 2006.
82 W. Woodward, 'Blair to wait until week after May elections to quit', *The Guardian*, 7 April 2007.
83 S. Lister, 'PM quits after his triumph in Ulster', *Belfast Telegraph*, 10 May 2007.
84 A. Grice, 'Blair's bloody legacy: Iraq', *The Independent*, 1 May 2007.

less republican or nationalist, or make unionists any less fiercely unionist. But what it does mean is that people can come together, respecting each other's point of view, and share power, make sure politics is only expressed by peaceful and democratic means.[85]

This was, however, subject to an obvious rejoinder. How could the protagonists genuinely share power, more stably than before, if they were still as 'fiercely' determined as ever to pursue their antagonistic constitutional *desiderata* — not the inherent uncertainty of shared government but assimilation of the 'other side' to a taken-for-granted 'Britishness' or 'Irishness', through the copper-fastening of partition or a transition to a united Ireland?

CONCLUSION: DIVIDED THEY STAND

There was evidence within weeks of the new dispensation that not everything was rosy on the ground. It emerged that another 'peace wall' was to be constructed in north Belfast — on, of all places, the playground of an integrated school. This suggested that, at neighbourhood level, young people might not be finding it such a glib matter to 'escape the heavy chains of history'. According to Jarman, since the paramilitary ceasefires of 1994, nine new barriers have been built in Belfast and 11 strengthened or extended.[86]

Shortly before the transfer of power, the NIO admitted there were now 46 of these barriers all told — and another 11 gates — physically dividing neighbourhoods along sectarian lines.[87] Indeed, research based on interviews with fully 9,000 individuals in 'interface' areas of Belfast has painted a picture of sustained polarisation and low-level violence — untouched by the comings-and-goings at Stormont since 1998 — in just those working-class heartlands where the victims, and the protagonists, of the 'troubles' have been most concentrated. Two thirds of the respondents believed 'community relations' had *deteriorated* since the paramilitary ceasefires of 1994 and substantial majorities believed that violence in their area, coming from the 'other' side, had increased over that time.[88] The researchers concluded: 'Despite the cessation of most paramilitary violence we are left with a situation within which the creation of territorial division and rigidified ethno-sectarian communities means that fear and mistrust are still framed by a desire to create communal separation.'[89]

---

[85] O. Bowcott, 'Northern Ireland's arch-enemies declare peace', *The Guardian*, 27 March 2007.

[86] N. Jarman, *Working at the Interface: Good practice in reducing tension and violence* (Belfast: Institute for Conflict Research, 2006), p. 5.

[87] S. Lister, 'Divided by 57 peace lines', *Belfast Telegraph*, 26 April 2007.

[88] P. Shirlow and M. Murtagh, *Belfast: Segregation, violence and the city* (London: Pluto Press, 2006), pp. 92–3.

[89] Shirlow and Murtagh 2006, p. 181.

Why should this be? Shirlow and Murtagh argue that the 'fundamental flaw' in Northern Ireland's constitutional architecture is that 'it placed traditions and group equality before the higher and more dignified principle of individual rights'.[90] It is, ultimately, because in the consociational schema the unit of society is the 'community', not the citizen — the unit, as Bobbio points out, of every democratic constitution in the world — that consociationalism is just that: a schema with few empirical referents, outside of Northern Ireland and (as witnessed by the aftermath of the 2007 elections) the slowly but steadily fracturing Belgium.[91] Consociational constitutions can only always be provisional barometers of an ethnic power balance, which the protagonists have every incentive to seek to shift in their favour in a zero-sum game.

A particularly worrisome instance in Northern Ireland is the long-running political sore of the '11 plus' transfer test: 'academic' selection for post-primary education still, uniquely, applies in Northern Ireland.[92] The existing test will be run for the last time in 2008–9, following legislation under direct rule. But the fact that the decision to abolish the '11 plus' was first announced by Martin McGuinness, then as education minister — cocking a snook at his unionist Executive colleagues on the eve of the collapse of devolution in October 2002 — ensured subsequent debate would take a highly sectarian form. This despite the way the existing system clearly disadvantages most members of the Protestant working class who fall within the unionist parties' clientele.

The problem, as the clock for anxious citizen-parents of primary-school children ticks down, is that in the absence of agreement in the new Executive an already Balkanised education system could become increasingly messy — with 'maintained' (de facto Catholic) schools foregoing formal selection but some 'controlled' (i.e. Protestant) and 'voluntary' grammars introducing individual tests for 'academic' competence.[93] The DUP secured the three-ministers veto arrangement at St Andrews precisely to prevent a rerun of the McGuinness episode, even though his party colleague, Caitriona Ruane, assumed the education portfolio.

By the same token, the DUP has refused to act to introduce legislation to promote the Irish language, having selected (as did the UUP in the previous devolved period) the small but symbolically-critical Department of Culture, Arts and Language during the d'Hondt picking of ministerial straws.[94] This

[90] *Ibid.*, p. 41.

[91] N. Bobbio, *The Age of Rights* (Cambridge: Polity Press, 1996).

[92] This is a literally meaningless procedure ever since the introduction of the core curriculum in secondary schools, applied to Northern Ireland via the 1989 Education Reform Order: all post-primary pupils now undergo the same curriculum, regardless of any supposed facility for 'academic' rather than 'vocational' study. The '11 plus' now functions purely as social sifting.

[93] K. Torney, 'Ulster school pupils facing uncertain future', *Belfast Telegraph*, 7 June 2007.

[94] M. McHugh, 'We will veto Irish Language Act — DUP', *News Letter*, 21 May 2007.

was despite a commitment to legislation in the St Andrews Agreement and widespread support expressed in a consultation initiated by the direct-rule administration — which, however, maladroitly passed the political hot potato to its devolved successor by the stratagem of announcing a second consultation when the first one had hardly ended.

For decades after partition, in Catholic minds devolution connoted Protestant-majority rule. With that parliament being abolished and the civil-rights reform programme implemented, however, it became increasingly possible for Catholics to dissociate devolution from any idea of ethnic 'lock-in'. This was reflected in the overwhelming support for the Belfast Agreement in 1998, on which the Protestant community was evenly split and from which it increasingly defected, until the collapse in 2002, as London and Dublin were seen to indulge the demands of SF, backed by the threat of the IRA.

Yet the resurgence of the DUP, and the willingness of London and Dublin to indulge its demands in turn, now that the IRA threat has gone, has not only been reflected in increasing electoral polarisation. It has also been associated with a marked swing in ethnic opinion between the Northern Ireland Life and Times Surveys of (late) 2005 and 2006.[95] These saw a shift from 66 per cent to 81 per cent in support among Protestants for devolution as their constitutional preference for Northern Ireland. By contrast, however, Catholic support for devolution fell from 35 per cent to 29 per cent, while support for a united Ireland rose from 39 per cent to 48 per cent.

Figure 4.3: Changing Constitutional Preferences — 2001–6

	2001	2003	2005	2006
	%	%	%	%
ALL				
Northern Ireland should become...				
Independent	10	9	11	6
Remain part of the UK with own Parliament	31	30	31	42
Remain part of the UK with own Assembly	12	22	21	16
Overall pro-devolution	43	52	52	57
Remain part of the UK with no Assembly	13	12	10	5
Unify with the Republic of Ireland	21	17	17	23
Don't know	13	11	10	9

95 Data available at www.ark.ac.uk/nilt. We are indebted to Lizanne Dowds for this analysis.

PROTESTANTS				
Northern Ireland should become…				
Independent	8	6	10	5
Remain part of the UK with own Parliament	47	37	39	59
Remain part of the UK with own Assembly	18	31	27	22
Overall pro-devolution	65	68	66	81
Remain part of the UK with no Assembly	17	17	15	6
Unify with the Republic of Ireland	1	2	1	2
Don't know	9	7	8	5
CATHOLICS				
Northern Ireland should become…				
Independent	13	12	12	7
Remain part of the UK with own Parliament	14	18	23	22
Remain part of the UK with own Assembly	4	9	12	8
Overall pro-devolution	18	27	35	29
Remain part of the UK with no Assembly	7	7	3	3
Unify with the Republic of Ireland	49	38	39	48
Don't know	13	15	10	13

Given the unevenness of results in recent years among Catholic respondents, it is too early to detect a trend. But there is a warning signal: if the DUP is seen to be manipulating the deadlocking vetoes built into the consociational system — indeed boosted by St Andrews — to communal advantage on issues such as the '11 plus' or the Irish language, among the minority community the feeling could grow that, once again, the ethnic cards are stacked against it.

The elections in the Republic in May 2007 will only add to that sense of frustration. Few 'northern nationalists' have much grasp of southern politics and certainly no one in the northern-based SF leadership saw coming the rebuff it would face. Its Dáil representation fell from five to four — making a mockery of Gerry Adams' pre-election pretensions when he had announced, somewhat prematurely, that the party was appointing a negotiating team with a view to being part of a government in the south, as well as in the north. Now that the forward momentum of the 'peace process' has halted, the prospect of unification before the centenary of 1916, through participation in coalitions north and south — the core of the Adams 'peace strategy' — has proved to be a chimera.

Where all this will lead is impossible to say. But it can be guaranteed that the DUP will behave in sectarian ways that anger even moderate Catholics. A talismanic moment came when the Executive split on the issue, inherited from direct rule and Peter Hain, of whether to fund a 'conflict transformation initiative' in north Belfast linked to the paramilitary Ulster Defence Association.

The SDLP minister for social development, Margaret Ritchie, insisted in August 2007 that the project would not be funded unless the UDA decommissioned its weapons within 60 days, and when the deadline passed denied the funding, with widespread public support. But Mr Robinson, DUP deputy leader as well as finance minister, claimed Ms Ritchie had acted in breach of the ministerial code and pledge of office, while she implied he was 'the person who likes to think he controls the Executive'.[96] In advance of an Executive meeting which addressed the issue (and which could not even agree on the relevant minute of its previous meeting, with the UUP and SDLP dissenting), Ms Ritchie insisted: 'I will not be bullied by Peter Robinson.' She left the five-hour meeting early to take to the TV studios, accepting she was accusing ministerial colleagues of 'fabricating minutes', while Nigel Dodds of the DUP emerged at the end of the meeting to describe her behaviour as 'scurrilous'.[97]

The next day, the respected Northern Ireland journalist Dan Keenan encapsulated the situation in the *Irish Times*:

> Indeed there was a collective sigh of relief when Sinn Féin and the DUP agreed to share power, with many observers (especially those resident outside Northern Ireland) choosing to believe that the Northern problem was now effectively resolved. What has become clear, as this week's events show, is that hitherto implacable enemies agreeing to share office does not guarantee stable government. Perhaps Alliance leader David Ford is right when he alleges that the current executive arrangement is not about powersharing (working together) at all, but rather power-splitting (a carve up).
>
> The Assembly does not have a formal role for an opposition. Therefore what opposition there is to any given measure has to come from within. In normal parliamentary set-ups this is called a split and it appears there is no push to patch up this damaging split around the Stormont executive table at this point.[98]

---

[96] M. Purdy, 'Tensions laid bare in UDA debate', BBC News Online, 16 October 2007; D. Keenan, 'Uproar as Ritchie ends funding for loyalist plan', *Irish Times*, 17 October 2007.

[97] D. Keenan, 'DUP may censure Ritchie's decision', *Irish Times*, 18 October 2007.

[98] D. Keenan, 'UDA stand-off tests the power-sharers', *Irish Times*, 19 October 2007.

BIBLIOGRAPHY

Official Documents and Primary Sources

Independent International Commission on Decommissioning, *Report of the Independent Commission on Decommissioning*, 26 September 2005 (Dublin and Belfast: IICD, 2005), available at www.nio.gov.uk/iicd_report_26_sept_2005.pdf.

Independent Monitoring Commission, *Twelfth Report of the Independent Monitoring Commission* (London: The Stationery Office, 2006), available at www.independentmonitoringcommission.org/documents/uploads/IMC%2012th%20Report%20pdf.pdf.

Northern Ireland Executive, *Building a Better Future: Draft Programme for Government 2008–2011* (Belfast: OFMDFM, 2007), available at www.pfgbudgetni.gov.uk/pfg241007new.pdf.

Northern Ireland Office, *Devolving Police and Justice in Northern Ireland: A Discussion Paper* (Belfast: NIO, 2006), available at www.nio.gov.uk/devolving_police_and_justice_in_northern_ireland_a_discussion_paper.pdf.

Office of the First Minister and Deputy First Minister, *A Shared Future: Policy and Strategic Framework for Good Relations in Northern Ireland* (Belfast: OFMDFM, 2005), available at www.asharedfutureni.gov.uk/pdf_documents/gprs.pdf.

Office of the First Minister and Deputy First Minister, *First Steps Towards Sustainability: A Sustainable Development Strategy for Northern Ireland* (Belfast: OFMDFM, 2006), available at www.ofmdfmni.gov.uk/sustain-develop.pdf.

Office of the First Minister and Deputy First Minister, *Lifetime Opportunities: Government's Anti-Poverty and Social Inclusion Strategy for Northern Ireland* (Belfast: OFMDFM, 2006), available at www.ofmdfmni.gov.uk/antipovertynov06.pdf.

Sir David Varney *Review of Tax Policy in Northern Ireland* December 2007 (London: The Stationery Office, 2007), available at www.hm-treasury.gov.uk./media/1/3/varney171207.pdf

Secondary Sources

Bobbio, N., *The Age of Rights* (Cambridge: Polity Press, 1996).

Jarman, N., *Working at the Interface: Good practice in reducing tension and violence* (Belfast: Institute for Conflict Research, 2006).

Lijphart, A., *Democracy in Plural Societies* (New Haven, CT: Yale University Press, 1977)

Shirlow, P. and M. Murtagh, *Belfast: Segregation, violence and the city* (London: Pluto Press, 2006).

Wilford, R. and R. Wilson, 'Northern Ireland: while you take the high road …' in A. Trench, (ed.), *The Dynamics of Devolution: The State of the Nations 2005* (Exeter: Imprint Academic Press, 2005), 63–89.

5

The English Regions and London

Martin Burch, Alan Harding and James Rees

THE EXAGGERATED DEATH OF ENGLISH REGIONALISM

When governance between the centre and the locality in England was last examined in this book series, the people of the North East had recently rejected the option of establishing England's first Elected Regional Assembly (ERA). The 'no' vote in the North East referendum was so resounding that the UK Government promptly abandoned its plans for 'democratic regionalism' outside the UK's non-English nations and London. As Sandford and Hetherington noted at the time, however, the process of English regionalisation and the broader reform of sub-national governance within which it fitted did not begin, nor did it end, with the idea of creating ERAs.[1] This is not to argue that the stillbirth of elected regional government was inconsequential. What it meant, rather, was that the questions to which ERAs were seen, by some, to be at least a partial answer had to be addressed in different ways. In the process, the fragile and unspoken 'deal' that the former Deputy Prime Minister, John Prescott, and his allies had brokered in getting the ERA initiative to its first — and, as it turned out, last — major hurdle has become progressively unstitched.

What the ERA package managed to achieve, on paper, was an uneasy alignment of three rather different 'drivers' of reform in sub-national governance and spatial development policy. These were:

1. *Devolution*, based on the contention that citizens of the English regions outside London, like every other part of the UK before them, should be entitled to exercise rights to greater levels of self-government and/or that Westminster and Whitehall were too distant or overloaded to be able to make informed decisions about strategic priorities at the regional scale.

2. *Efficiency and effectiveness*, based on the idea that the region provided potential economies of scale and/or the most appropriate territorial level at which certain strategic services might be

---

[1] M. Sandford and P. Hetherington, 'The Regions at the Crossroads: The Future for Sub-National Government in England' in A. Trench (ed.), *The Dynamics of Devolution: The State of the Nations 2005* (Exeter: Imprint Academic, 2005) pp. 91–113.

delivered, irrespective of whether delivery was by directly elected bodies.

3. *Redistribution* of economic activity and growth, based on the recognition that tangible mechanisms were needed to realise the UK Government's commitment, set out in the PSA target on Regional Economic Performance, to at least arrest, if not also reverse, the growing gap in economic performance between English regions.

In finessing matters so that ERAs would have taken over a limited range of economic development and related functions from various Non-Departmental Public Bodies and been 'offered', in the first instance, to the three lagging regions in the north of England, the UK Government could claim to tick each of these boxes, however faintly. What has happened since, however, is that because the three original strands of the 'regional agenda' can no longer be delivered through a single 'fix', each of these prerogatives has become associated with a modified set of initiatives that point in different directions.

The first section of this chapter examines the evolution of regionalism and regionalisation in the period since further regional devolution within England dropped off the Government's agenda. In so doing, it draws a distinction between explicit and implicit change; that is to say, between what the UK Government has done and said in terms of formal, sub-national institutional and spatial policy reform and the way its actions and proposals in other areas have interacted with — and indeed in some senses, counteracted — them. It distinguishes between two strands of English regional development, institutional and economic policy, and reviews developments in both these areas. The next section assesses actual and proposed institutional reforms in the post-referendum period and the extent to which they have created, or might create, a new settlement based on the search for a more efficient and decentralised — as opposed to devolved — approach to sub-national governance. The third section examines recent changes in the way the UK Government has understood and explicitly sought to shape spatial economic development trends and sets them alongside other, more implicit ways in which it responds to and influences sub-national development. The fourth section then presents a balance sheet which assesses progress against the UK Government's stated regional policy aims and anticipates the way performance in this regard is likely to unfold in the future. The concluding section then reflects upon the nature and direction of both explicit and implicit forms of regionalisation in assessing implications for the future of the English regional agenda. It then goes on to ask whether current and proposed arrangements are likely to prove robust and what their spatial impacts are likely to be.

REGIONAL DEVELOPMENT — THE INSTITUTIONAL STRAND

On the surface, the North East referendum seemed to sound the death knell for the idea of devolving further powers and/or responsibilities from the 'centre' to the regions. In practice, though, this proved to be the case only in the sense that the UK Government was forced to reinterpret what 'devolution' means, in ways that sometimes stretch dictionary definitions of the concept past breaking point, and to accept that administrative regions are not the only spatial scale at which it can be applied. Thus, on one hand, the language used in particular by HM Treasury suggests that 'devolving decision making' need not entail the transfer of responsibilities to a popularly elected body, but can equally seek to empower unelected public agencies or even non-statutory organisations. Here, 'decentralisation' seems a more appropriate term than 'devolution'. On the other hand, alternative scales of government or governance — whether on the local authority level, or the less institutionalised city- or sub-regional one — have variously been lauded by the major national political parties and other interests as deserving of greater trust and responsibility.

Figure 5.1: Chronology of Events — 2005–7

2005	
23 September	Mayor of London publishes proposals for extra powers
9 November	DfES announces a greater departmental presence in Government Offices for the Regions
18 November	David Miliband, Minister for Communities, writes to Regional Assemblies requesting proposals for streamlining
30 November	ODPM publishes consultation document on review of GLA
2006	
13 February	Commission on London Governance produces final report
22 March	Government Office Review published
31 March	Submission of South-East Plan
3 April	Olympic Delivery Authority goes live
5 May	David Miliband replaced by Ruth Kelly and ODPM renamed DCLG
26 October	Publication of local government White Paper *Strong and Prosperous Communities*

22 November	Culture Secretary reveals £900 million increase in projected costs of the 2012 London Olympics
28 November	Publication of Greater London Authority Bill
1 December	Publication of Eddington Review of Transport
5 December	Publication of Barker Review of Land-Use Planning
8 December	Department of Health names the locations of new Health Research Centres of Excellence
12 December	The Northern Way announces change in focus and approach
13 December	Publication of Local Government and Public Involvement in Health Bill
2007	
30 January	Manchester chosen as the venue for Britain's first supercasino by the Casino Advisory Panel
14 March	The Communities and Local Government Select Committee releases its report into the Future of Regional Government
15 March	Culture Secretary Tessa Jowell tells Parliament that the budget for the London Olympics has risen to £9.35 billion
21 March	Publication of the Lyons Inquiry final report into local government finance
28 March	Lords defeat for the government over the Gambling Order, throwing the decision to site the supercasino in Manchester into uncertainty
28 June	New Gordon Brown administration announces plans for Regional Ministers and Regional Select Committees
17 July	Review of sub-national economic development and regeneration published
5 October	UK Government announces £5 billion commitment to Crossrail
9 October	UK Government's Comprehensive Spending Review (CSR) published
7 November	DCLG announces designation of first 13 cross-local authority Multi Area Agreements (MAAs)

Development Agencies, Government Offices and Assemblies

Any idea that the survival of two of the principal regional organisations — Regional Development Agencies (RDAs) and Government Offices for the Regions — would be under threat once directly elected regional assemblies were off the Government's agenda was quickly dispelled. Instead, both have been refashioned in an attempt to ensure that they fit more securely within a regional decentralisation agenda. RDAs have been the principal beneficiaries. They have continued to acquire programme responsibilities, for example in the fields of European funding, rural policy, training and support for small businesses, thereby cementing their place as the principal regional quango. Indeed, the degree of Governmental faith placed in RDAs as purposeful, 'business-led' bodies continued to increase to the point whereby the promise to 'strengthen the regional level' contained within the July 2007 Sub-National Review of Economic Development and Regeneration concentrated almost entirely upon RDAs, for example in promising to make them responsible for the production of a single regional strategy.[2] Government Offices for the Regions, whilst they have continued to expand in terms of the number of central departments represented within them, had a tougher ride. They were set ambitious staff reduction targets by the UK Government following the Gershon review, as part of which they were expected to become more 'strategic' and less engaged in programme delivery.[3]

The principal regional casualties, somewhat ironically given the rhetorical emphasis placed upon 'devolution', have been the partially indirectly elected Regional Assemblies (RAs) — the only regional agencies with direct links to non-national politicians. The abolition of RAs, announced in the Sub-National Review, will see their planning functions transferred to RDAs and their role in scrutinising RDAs passed to networks of local authorities within the relevant region.

Although debates about regional decentralisation have tended to focus upon the sorts of activities that ERAs would have been engaged in, narrower concerns with achieving economies of scale are evident in a number of largely unrelated developments in specific policy areas. Thus, the recent period has witnessed attempts to regionalise aspects of service planning and/or delivery. This was nominally successful in the case of fire and emergency services, with the creation of Regional Management Boards, health services, with the creation of Strategic Health Authorities, and housing, with the creation of Regional Housing Boards. It was resisted, from below in the case of policing, where services continue to be controlled at the sub-regional

2 HM Treasury, *Sub-National Review of Economic Development and Regeneration* (London: The Stationery Office, 2007).

3 Sir P. Gershon, *Releasing resources to the frontline: Independent Review of Public Sector Efficiency* (London: The Stationery Office, 2004).

level rather than the regional one favoured by the UK Government. In none of these cases, however, do new regional arrangements bear much relation to one another.

City-Regions

Perhaps the biggest potential departure since the North East referendum, and one where debate has been more influenced by the notion of redistribution, is the rediscovery of 'city-regionalism'. The concept of the city-region is driven by the observation that the realities of economic and social geography, and the regular 'boundary hopping' that is a day-to-day reality for an ever-larger proportion of the population, are not captured effectively by existing, administrative units of governance, be they local or regional. It is not a new concept, the most significant antecedent being Derek Senior's memorandum of dissent to the Redcliffe-Maud Report in 1969.[4] However it has recently been 'pushed', in different ways, by a variety of forces internal and external to government, largely as a means to address the UK Government's nominal commitment to reduce inter-regional disparities in economic growth rates. Underpinning the somewhat diffuse case for city-regions is a large volume of work that has demonstrated (a) the growing importance of the larger cities and their hinterlands to patterns of spatial economic change in the emerging 'knowledge economy', and (b) the fact that neither local authority areas nor administrative regions are units that even begin to approximate functional economic areas. Put simply, the argument supported by many proponents of city-regions is that if the Government is serious about eroding inter-regional economic disparities, its focus should be upon the larger, more economically diversified and better connected provincial city-regions which have greatest growth potential in the medium term and that, if such areas are to 'punch their weight' and be led more effectively, further thought needs to be give to forms of city-regional governance.

The key protagonists within the 'city-region debate' include a number of inter-local authority alliances, especially but not exclusively in the north of England, which see advantages in developing city-regional coalitions and strategies, partly in recognition of the inter-connected fortunes of their areas and residents and partly in presenting a stronger united front to government and regional agencies. Other key contributions have come from various left-of-centre think tanks and academics. Arguments for enhanced 'city-regionalism' differ in important respects. Some proponents advocate city-regions as an alternative (and selective) scale for devolution through the

---

[4] Royal Commission on Local Government in England, *Report, Volume 2, Memorandum of Dissent*, Cmnd 4040–I (London: HMSO, 1969).

creation of new, formal city-regional authorities.[5] Others favour more voluntaristic forms of horizontal city-regional governance created through non-statutory, cross-district collaborative arrangements (such as the Association of Greater Manchester Authorities) or the creation of vertically integrated policy frameworks and the use of inter-governmental incentives to encourage city-regional co-ordination and co-operation.[6] The messages occasionally conveyed by a small number of national politicians and civil servants and via official position statements on the importance of city-regions to national economic prosperity have been critical to creating a climate of expectation around the institutionalisation of city-regions.[7] However, the only muted statements of Government intent thus far came in a White Paper on Local Government and in the Sub-National Review of Economic Development and Regeneration, both of which referred to the city-region as a particular form of sub-region rather than a special category in its own right.[8] These announced a number of initiatives — a strengthening of the governance of city-regional transport, a facilitating of the ability of local authorities to work together through Multi-Area Agreements (MAAs)[9], the potential establishment of City Development Companies at a cross-district scale — but fell short of either favouring a particular city-/ sub-regional governance model or overtly suggesting particular territories in which new arrangements might be most beneficial.

London Governance

Given that the case for enhanced 'city-regionalism' has been seen largely as a means to rebalance the UK — or, at least, English — spatial economy, it is something of a paradox that the greatest institutional and policy change has taken place in the area in which economic power is concentrated. The metropolitan area of London remains the only complex, cross-district urban area in the country with its own, directly elected strategic authority. Though the achievements of the new London governance arrangements have tended to be overstated, perhaps because of the high political profile of the Mayor, there is no doubt that in comparison to provincial cities the capital is forging ahead, with significant central government support, in terms of the clout and

[5] Institute for Public Policy Research, *City Leadership: Giving city-regions the power to grow* (London: IPPR, 2006).

[6] Association of Greater Manchester Authorities (AGMA), *City Regions Governance in Greater Manchester: the Way Forward* (Wigan: AGMA, 2007); SURF-CUPS, *A Framework for City-Regions* (London: ODPM, 2006).

[7] HM Treasury, Department for Trade and Industry and Office of the Deputy Prime Minister, *Devolving Decision Making: 3 – Meeting the economic challenge: The importance of cities to regional growth* (London: The Stationery Office, 2006).

[8] Department for Communities and Local Government, *Strong and Prosperous Communities: The Local Government White Paper* (London: The Stationery Office, 2006); HM Treasury 2007, *Sub-National Review* , note 2 op cit.

[9] In November 2007 the first 13 MAAs were designated by the DCLG.

coherence of its governing arrangements. This was emphasised in 2006 when the UK Government, following a review of the powers of London's Mayor and strategic authority, announced a strengthening of its functions in respect of housing, skills, planning and culture. This was later legislated in the Greater London Authority Act 2007. As the section after the next makes clear, what is less remarked upon, but no less observable, is the fact that UK Government support for the future development of the most economically powerful area of the country does not stop at the boundary of Greater London but comprises a broader, if implicit, strategy for the super-region that has the capital at its heart.

Regional Ministers and Oversight

One other institutional gap left by the rejection of the Elected Regional Assembly (ERA) option in the North East referendum concerns accountability. ERAs were intended to provide democratic accountability through oversight of a range of appointed bodies in the regions. Little was done to try to address this problem until the arrival of the Brown Government in June 2007, upon which a number of (mostly junior) ministers were appointed who, in addition to their departmental duties, have also been designated as the ministers for specific regions. These regional ministers were tasked with 'providing a clear sense of strategic direction' for their region as well as giving each region a voice in the UK Government, especially on policies relating to economic growth. They are able to take questions in Parliament on the work of regional bodies and on regional strategies. It is also proposed that a new system of regional Select Committees, one for each region, be established to give oversight and scrutiny of regional bodies and activities and the work of regional ministers.[10] How this will work in practice remains to be seen. A moot point is whether the House of Commons select committee system has enough resources to undertake these new tasks. Moreover, how representative of his/her region a minister will manage to be, given their other responsibilities, remains untested at the time of writing. It would certainly help for regions to have a champion able to put their case at the very heart of UK Government (as London has long been able to do), but the effect may be to further draw the threads of regional policy-making upward into Westminster and Whitehall.

Overall, do the institutional developments noted above create, or have the potential to create, a new decentralised settlement for sub-national governance in England? Since the collapse of the ERA project, change has been piecemeal and sporadic. In one sense what is emerging is much more organic than what went before, and the move towards city-regions from the bottom

[10] Ministry of Justice, *The Governance of Britain* Cm 7170 (London: The Stationery Office, 2007), pp. 37–8.

up should therefore be applauded. The problem with such conditional arrangements, however, is that the lower tier may lack the resources and incentives to take the initiative. The outcome could be a sub-national system of governance which remains diffused and in transition between one model of regionalism and another. In sum, institutionally speaking, English region-alism outside of London is messy, lacks clear direction and is somewhat contradictory in terms of aims and purpose. In this latter feature it has much in common with regional development policy, to which we now turn.

REGIONAL DEVELOPMENT — THE ECONOMIC POLICY STRAND

The second strand of English regionalisation, alongside the institutional one, has been economic. Spatial economic policy has had two main foci: the Treasury's initiative to address national productivity variations and the Public Service Agreement (PSA) target which commits the UK Government to maximising sustainable economic development in all regions on the one hand, whilst also reducing the gap in economic performance between regions on the other. Given the hold-up on the institutional front following the North East referendum, the Treasury dominated economic agenda has, during the period since November 2004, loomed larger in the development of regional policy.

Treasury Policy and the PSA target

The development of Treasury policy can be traced back to the 2000 Spend-ing Review which produced a PSA target for the period 2001–4, jointly designated to the then Department of Trade and Industry (DTI) and the then Department of Environment, Transport and Regions, aimed at improving 'the economic performance of all regions, measured by the trend in growth of each region's GDP per capita.'[11] The Treasury's own position was more clearly revealed in November 2001 with the publication of a paper on regional productivity.[12] This made it clear that the Treasury does not see regional policy as being about the redistribution of existing economic activ-ity but rather about ensuring that the weaker regions, as well as the more successful ones, do better by redressing market failures in areas such as skills, competition, innovation, enterprise and investment. In pursuit of this objective the paper commits the UK Government to 'tackling the persistent differentials in economic performance across and within the countries and regions of the United Kingdom'[13] and reveals the Government's 'long term

---

[11] HM Treasury, 'Department of the Environment Transport and the Regions' in *Spending Review 2000: Public Service Agreements 2001–2004* (London: The Stationery Office, 2000), para. 17.

[12] HM Treasury, *Productivity in the UK: 3 – the Regional Dimension* (London: HM Treasury, 2001).

[13] HM Treasury 2001, p. 55.

ambition of reducing the persistent gap between regions by increasing the growth rate of the worst performing regions.'[14] A further paper was published in July 2003 which sets out the role that local authorities might be expected to play in encouraging economic growth in their areas.[15] This kind of thinking was enshrined in the PSA target jointly agreed by the Treasury, the DTI and the then Office of the Deputy Prime Minister for the 2002 Spending Review, which was then made more precise in the 2004 Spending Review by specifying a date (2008) for sustainable improvement in economic performance across all the regions.[16] Thus the current Regional Economic Performance PSA committed the UK Government to:

> Make sustainable improvements in the economic performance of all English regions by 2008 and over the long term reduce the persistent gap in growth rates between the regions, demonstrating progress by 2006.[17]

The key point to note about the Treasury's productivity policy and the PSA target is that they constitute an inherently contradictory set of policy aims. At heart this reflects tension between the desire to reduce inter-regional disparities and being seen, politically, to treat all regions even-handedly. In practice it is difficult to identify the mechanisms through which it is intended that inter-regional disparities will be reduced and the main focus has been upon the first part of the Regional Economic Performance PSA.[18]

The Northern Way

The one partial exception has been the Northern Way initiative. This was an attempt — on however small a scale — to redress the 'treat all equally' bias of policy by developing a more discriminatory approach favouring three of the less prosperous regions. Originally conceived within Whitehall at a time when there was growing nervousness about the level of government attention that was being devoted to issues of growth management in the greater south east, the Northern Way, driven largely by the three northern RDAs, is, at least in principle, an ambitious attempt to close the economic 'gap'

---

[14] HM Treasury 2001. In this paper the Treasury highlights the role of Regional Development Agencies as the key agents in driving forward 'the new regional industrial policy.'

[15] HM Treasury, *Productivity in the UK: 4 – the Local Dimension* (London: HM Treasury, 2003).

[16] HM Treasury, 'Office of the Deputy Prime Minister' in *Spending Review 2002: Public Service Agreements* (London: The Stationery Office, 2002), objective 1:2. See also J. Adams, P. Robinson and A. Vigor, *A New Regional Policy for the UK* (London: IPPR, 2003), pp. 3–5, and J. Adams and P. Robinson, 'Regional Economic Policies in a Devolved United Kingdom' in A. Trench (ed.), *The Dynamics of Devolution: The State of the Nations 2005* (Exeter: Imprint Academic, 2005), pp. 242–4.

[17] HM Treasury, *2004 Spending Review PSAs* (London: The Stationery Office, 2004), p. 17. The 2004 PSA Target is in operation over 2005–8. See also BERR, *PSA Target 7 – Regional Economic Performance*, available at www.berr.gov.uk/files/file14298.pdf.

[18] See for example HM Treasury, *2004 Spending Review: Meeting Regional Priorities – Response to the Regional Emphasis Documents* (London: The Stationery Office, 2004) p. 5 and para. 4.25.

between the north of England and the best-performing southern regions. Whilst initial discussions about what an overarching development strategy for the whole of the north of England should look like concentrated upon generic, rather than spatial, issues (skills, infrastructure, innovation, entrepreneurialism, employment rates, etc.), a significant 'city-region' component was quickly added in an ostensible recognition that not all areas of the North could be expected to play an equal role in driving economic innovation and growth. Its practical effect has, however, been muted due to the fact that:

- It has been chronically under-resourced: the budget for the Northern Way for the spending period 2006–8 was just £100 million, only £50 million of which was new government money, and no additional funding will be devoted to it in the next spending period.[19]
- There exists no obvious mechanism whereby the Northern Way can have an impact upon 'productive' government spending, that is to say expenditure which might be expected to support economic development rather than being purely distributive.
- It is difficult to establish any sharp spatial priorities due to the political fudge which saw the identification of eight city-regions across northern England, which together cover ninety per cent of its population.

The Comprehensive Spending Review and the Sub-National Review

While the Northern Way initiative constituted a slight shift in the underlying commitment to managing growth evenly across England, it has been the latter approach, especially as expressed in the PSA target, that has dominated policy. As indicated above these targets were in part refined in response to each expenditure review. Consequently, a key driver in the development of regional policy at the national level has been preparation for each expenditure review. The 2007 Comprehensive Spending Review (CSR) led to the commissioning by the Treasury of a number of enquiries into specific areas of policy some of which bear on regional policy. At the same time, in the build up to the CSR, submissions were made to the Treasury by, or on behalf of, various English regional organisations including the Greater London Authority, The Northern Way, the 'Core Cities' group of local authorities, the RDAs and the RAs.

As part of the CSR process, in early 2006, the Treasury, the DTI and the Department of Communities and Local Government (DCLG) launched a comprehensive review of sub-national economic development and regeneration. This was tasked with examining ways in which the UK Government's Regional Economic Performance PSA target could best be achieved and

---

[19] The Northern Way initiative is likely to be reduced to a research and analysis function at the end of its current funding period.

evaluating the effectiveness of existing sub-national structures in England in helping to achieve this target.[20] Feeding into this and the CSR were the reviews of aspects of policy affecting sub-national development. The most significant of these were reviews of transport policy by Sir Rod Eddington, of land-use planning by Kate Barker, and of local government functions and finances by Sir Michael Lyons. The Eddington study essentially argued that transport investments that aim to alleviate congestion represent the most reliable route by which transport policy can support national economic competitiveness. In support of this approach, it called for changes in the planning process for major transport projects through the introduction of a new Independent Planning Commission to take decisions on projects of strategic importance.[21] The Barker review of land-use planning also examined how planning policy and procedures could better deliver economic growth and prosperity. The report called for a more simplified and streamlined planning process to assist economic growth and, like the Eddington study, proposed an Independent Planning Commission to determine major infrastructural applications.[22] The Lyons review of local government recommended that local authorities be encouraged to pursue 'place-shaping' policies, including economic development initiatives.[23] In particular it recommended the introduction of better incentives for local authorities to promote economic prosperity and growth.

The Sub-National Review of Economic Development and Regeneration, published in July 2007, built upon the findings of these studies. Its main proposals were to:

- Empower all local authorities (alongside local partners) to promote economic development and neighbourhood renewal, and to create better incentives to help achieve these ends.
- Support local authorities in all areas to work together more effectively where they so wish and to encourage the development of robust decision-making at this level.
- Streamline the regional tier outside London by creating more effective and accountable RDAs which would be responsible, in liaison with local authorities, for preparing a single strategy for the region. RDAs will also support local authorities and sub-regions in delivering sustainable economic development. Regional assemblies or chambers are to be phased out.

[20] HM Treasury, *Terms of Reference for the Sub-National Economic Development and Regeneration Review,* available at www.hm-treasury.gov.uk./media/5/E/csr07_subnatecon_tor.pdf.

[21] Sir R. Eddington, *The Eddington Transport Study* (London: The Stationery Office, 2006).

[22] K. Barker, *Barker Review of Land Use Planning: Final Report – Recommendations* (London: The Stationery Office, 2006).

[23] Sir M. Lyons, *Lyons Inquiry into Local Government: Place-shaping: a shared ambition for the future of local government. Final report*, (London: The Stationery Office, 2007).

- Sharpen the focus of central government departments through clearer objectives and responsibilities, and provide more effective support and better coordination for economic development and neighbourhood renewal at all spatial levels.[24]

In most respects, however, it added little in the way of further detail as to how these imperatives would be achieved in practice.

Notably, none of these reports move outside of the implicit, dominant policy assumption of even-handed growth incentives. Nevertheless, the thrust of Kate Barker's recommendations have been carried into the Housing and Regeneration Bill published in autumn 2007, and have substantially set the context for the Brown Government's emphasis on expanding housing supply. The creation of an Infrastructure Planning Commission — as recommended by Barker and Eddington — is at the heart of the Planning Bill introduced to Parliament in the same month. The UK Government has toyed with a menu of options for local finance generation, and it remains to be seen what exact longer-term arrangements will emerge. The Comprehensive Spending Review and Pre-Budget Report of October 2007 confirmed the abandonment of the proposed Planning Gain Supplement; the intention to introduce a Supplementary Business Rate — the levy for local economic development proposed by Lyons; and the resumption of the 'local authority business growth incentive' (Labgi) scheme from 2009.[25]

JUDGING THE OUTCOMES?
GROWTH, SPENDING AND SPATIAL INVESTMENT

At this stage it is essential to ask if the strategy enshrined in institutional initiatives, the PSA target and the range of measures leading through to the Sub-National Review is actually showing signs of working. That requires a preliminary question: if the policy really is working, what consequences would we expect to find? We would certainly expect to see strong evidence of narrowing disparities between regions with the prospect of these being sustained into the longer term. We would also expect to see government incentives and resources applied to ensure fairer impact and distribution across regions. Given these considerations it is important to consider the extent to which progress has been made in reducing regional disparities, both in terms of regional growth and expenditure patterns.

---

[24] HM Treasury 2007, *Sub-National Review*.
[25] HM Treasury, *Meeting the Aspirations of the British People: 2007 Comprehensive Spending Review and Pre-Budget Report* (London: The Stationery Office, 2007).

Regional Disparities and Growth Patterns

To recap, the part of the Regional Economic Performance PSA target dealing with regional disparities aims to reduce the persistent gap in growth rates
— measured in Gross Value Added (GVA) per head — between the Greater
South East (defined as the East, South-East and London regions) and the six
remaining regions of the North, Midlands and West. The target will be met if
the gap is smaller in the period 2003–12 than it was in the baseline period of
1990–2002. In December 2006 the Treasury, the DTI and the DCLG
published their review of progress to date in meeting the target. Of course,
caution is needed because there are only two years of GVA data available.
Between 2003 and 2004, the first two years of the target period, the average
growth rate in the bottom six regions was 1 per cent higher than in the greater
south east, suggesting a reversal of the gap compared to the baseline period.
In 2004 itself, GVA per head grew by an average of 4.6 per cent for the
North, Midlands and South-West regions. In the Greater South-East, this
figure was only 3.5 per cent. This allowed the authors of the report to sound
an optimistic note, claiming that:

> There is emerging evidence of progress on narrowing the gap in growth rates
> between the regions. GVA per head data for 2003 and 2004 show that the North,
> Midlands and South West regions narrowed the gap in growth rates with London,
> the South East and Eastern Regions.[26]

Yet, as the review goes on to note, an assessment of whether the Regional
Economic Performance PSA target has been met can only be made over a
complete economic cycle — and frustratingly the definition of when this
will end is uncertain. The review concludes that it is simply 'too early to say
whether this recent narrowing reflects a narrowing in underlying trend
growth'.[27]

Indeed, a caution against an overly-optimistic view of progress emerged
in the same month with the publication of National Statistics data for 2005.
These indicate that between 2003 and 2005 GVA per head grew by an average of 4.2 per cent a year in the Greater South-East and by 4.3 per cent in the
North, Midlands and West. This allowed the Treasury to claim that 'these
figures show that all regions of the UK continue to grow strongly with signs
of convergence in regional growth rates in 2005.'[28] However, the figures
indicate that the positive gap enjoyed by the lagging regions began to close
by 2005 — from one per cent in the period 2003–4 — to only 0.1 per cent

[26] HM Treasury, DTI and DCLG, *Regional Economic Performance: Progress to Date* (London:
The Stationery Office, 2006), p. 6 and p. 9, available at www.treasury.gov.uk.

[27] HM Treasury et al 2006, p. 9.

[28] Anonymous Treasury spokesman quoted in S. Thorp, 'Government "on track" to close growth
gap', *Regeneration and Renewal*, 5 January 2007.

averaged across the period 2003–5.[29] The truth is that it is impossible to discern longer term trends from these data: the evidence on closing the gap is far too limited to support any sound conclusion one way or the other. Indeed, as the data in Figure 5.2 indicate, the southern regions still stand out starkly in terms of GVA per head, suggesting that the divide between the North and South remains substantial. On a more positive note, in light of the aspiration to raise all the regions' fortunes, GVA grew in all regions between 2004 and 2005. Growth in total GVA was highest in the North East, East Midlands and London (average 4.4 per cent), and lowest in the South East. Overall UK growth was 3.9 per cent.

Figure 5.2: Regional GVA, 2005[30]

Region	Total (£bn)	Growth on 2004 (%)	Per head (£)	Per head index (UK=100)
London	181.0	4.4	24 100	136
South East	166.3	3.5	20 400	115
East of England	104.9	3.7	18 900	107
South West	84.6	4.0	16 700	94
East Midlands	70.8	4.4	16 500	93
West Midlands	84.8	3.8	15 800	89
North West	106.1	3.7	15 500	88
Yorkshire and the Humber	78.1	3.7	15 400	87
North East	35.9	4.4	14 000	79
England	**912.7**	**3.9**	**18 100**	**102**

Public Spending and Spatial Investment

It is useful to complement the evidence quoted above on the fortunes of the English regions in GVA terms with the distribution of public expenditure. This might be expected to support the Government's policy aims in reducing regional disparities. Evidence prepared recently for the Communities and Local Government Select Committee's enquiry into the future of regional governance tells an interesting story. Overall, and excepting London, public expenditure is directed to the regions with most need (see Figures 5.2 and

[29] Thorp 2007.
[30] Source: National Statistics, *Regional, sub-regional and local gross value added*, 15 December 2006 available at www.statistics.gov.uk/pdfdir/gva1206.pdf.

5.3). But a regional breakdown of change in expenditure per head between 2000 and 2005 (see Figure 5.4) indicates that spending growth has been more favourable to the 'successful' regions. Indeed, it is most striking just how closely the ranking in Figure 5.4 mirrors that of Figure 5.2, with the exception of the South West. All of this suggests that UK Government's allocation of spending over this period is working directly counter to its stated aim of reducing regional disparities.

Figure 5.3: Total Expenditure on Public Services by Region, Per Head, 2004–5[31]

	Accruals £ total
London	7,530
North East	7,167
North West	6,930
Yorkshire and The Humber	6,363
West Midlands	6,291
South West	5,962
East Midlands	5,865
South East	5,624
Eastern	5,605
England	**6,361**

A similar picture emerges from a glance at the regional distribution of English Partnerships (EP) funding.[32] In the financial year 2001–2 just 31 per cent of EP's project budget was spent in the South. However, by financial year 2005–6 southern spending had risen seven-fold, taking 59 per cent of the agency's budget. The shift has largely been caused by extra funds given to EP to enable housing growth in the south, particularly that associated with the Thames Gateway. While this demonstrates a marked proportional shift in favour of the South, there was also a doubling in real investment in the North and Midlands — moving from £105 million in 2001–2 to £216 million by 2005–6. Only the budget for Yorkshire and Humberside has fallen, from £25 million in 2001–2 to £16 million in 2005–6. However, EP has denied it has

[31] *Source*: House of Commons Communities and Local Government Select Committee, *Is there a future for Regional Government? Vol. II: Oral and supplementary written evidence: Appendices* (Session 2006–7, 4th Report, HC 352–II) (London: The Stationery Office, 2007).

[32] J. Gardiner and S. Thorp, 'Going South (Special Report)', *Regeneration and Renewal*, 1 September 2006, p. 20–3.

shifted priorities to the South, and claims that provisional budgets for the next few years show funding swinging back to the North.[33]

Figure 5.4: Percentage Change in Total Expenditure on Public Services by Region, Per Head, 2000–1 to 2004–5[34]

	Total %
London	41
South East	39
Eastern	38
West Midlands	38
East Midlands	37
North East	37
North West	33
Yorkshire and The Humber	33
South West	31
England	**37**

This regionally selective picture of expenditure can be illustrated by looking at a number of significant locational spending decisions that have been taken over the last two years, all of which have long term implications for future public and private investment. By definition this kind of evidence is somewhat impressionistic, but nevertheless gives colour and substance to the picture painted by the GVA and public spending data noted above. Perhaps most prominently, the award of the 2012 Olympic Games to London involves substantial investment — in facilities, transport links and associated regeneration projects — to the east of London, and might be expected to exacerbate further the expenditure trends noted above. Not surprisingly, public debate has focused on the 'spiralling' costs of the Games. In November 2006 Culture Secretary Tessa Jowell informed the Department for Culture, Media and Sport Select Committee that the cost of building the Games facilities had risen by £900 million from the original Olympic bid estimate of £2.375 billion. The original understanding, agreed between the UK Government and London Mayor Ken Livingstone prior to the Olympic bid, envisaged cost overruns being met by the Lottery and London council tax payers, though those two key players have since made it clear that they do not wish to see an extra burden on London taxpayers for staging the

---

[33] Gardiner and Thorp 2006.
[34] *Source*: Communities and Local Government Committee 2007, as for Figure 5.3

Games. The worry is clearly that if the extra costs do fall on the Lottery this will significantly reduce the amount available for other 'good causes' both in London and the rest of the UK.[35] A further substantial rise in costs was announced in March 2007. Under the new calculations the Olympic Delivery Authority will be given a budget to cover construction costs of up to £5.3 billion until 2012. This will entail: £3.1 billion for building the Olympic park and venues, £1.7 billion for Olympic infrastructure and regeneration linking the park to the rest of the lower Lea valley — where the main facilities will be situated — and a £500 million allowance for programme contingency. This brought the bill to around £9 billion, or nearly treble the previous budget announced in 2006, the majority (£6 billion) coming from central government.[36]

The London Olympics' appetite for resources did not, as some had feared, hamper the provision of other existing major infrastructure projects in London, in particular Crossrail, the hugely complex east-west London rail link. The Crossrail Bill slowly progressed through Parliament between 2005 and 2007, and in October 2007 the UK Government committed to provide £5 billion towards the estimated £16 billion cost of the project. In early 2007, the Lyons review of local government finance offered a possible way forward for the further funding of Crossrail (and other infrastructure projects) in proposing that councils be allowed to levy up to 4p in supplementary business rates for special projects.[37] According to the *Financial Times*, if implemented by London's local authorities such a levy 'could help to raise more than £3 billion toward the estimated overall cost' of the project.[38] Crossrail offers a route through to Canary Wharf and will help to further open up the east end of the city, and is therefore a significant part of the Thames Gateway project, central to the UK Government's Sustainable Communities Plan.[39] In November 2006 the Thames Gateway interim regeneration plan was published setting out plans to expand the delivery team and push forward delivery. The plan involves the creation of 160,000 new homes by 2016, with over a third of these homes designated as affordable housing and with an extra 40,000 in the London part of the Gateway. The Thames Gateway is claimed to be Western Europe's largest regeneration project and the UK Government has invested £7 billion in the project since 2003.

---

[35] J. Gardiner, 'Overspend could up Games bill by 60% says Ken', *Regeneration and Renewal*, 17 November 2006, p. 1, and J. Gardiner, 'Lottery may have to pick up £900m Games bill', *Regeneration and Renewal*, 24 November 2006, p. 5.

[36] Statement by Tessa Jowell, Secretary of State for Culture, Media and Sport; HC Deb, 15 March 2007, col 451.

[37] Lyons 2007.

[38] C. Bryant, 'Crossrail boosted by rates top-up idea', *Financial Times*, Budget 2007 Supplement 22 March 2007, p.19. On overall costs see www.crossrail.co.uk.

[39] Office of the Deputy Prime Minister, *Sustainable Communities: Building for the Future* (London: The Stationery Office, 2003).

Outside of Greater London, there have also been spatial investment decisions which have benefited the less prosperous regions. Notably, the BBC finally announced in early 2007 its decision to relocate some of its staff from London to Salford at a cost of £250 million. Also in early 2007, the UK Government-appointed Casino Advisory Panel announced its decision on the siting of 17 new casinos. By far the most contentious aspect of that was the location of the single 'supercasino' from a shortlist of seven locations: Blackpool, Cardiff, Glasgow, Greenwich, Manchester, Newcastle and Sheffield. The award of the supercasino to Manchester took almost everyone by surprise — Blackpool and Greenwich were widely considered to be frontrunners — yet Manchester was judged to have stood out in the key criteria of the likelihood of securing maximum regeneration benefits from the casino, and providing the best test of social impact. The casino package, including the designation of East Manchester as the site for the first supercasino, was later voted down in the House of Lords and (as of Summer 2008) the plans for East Manchester were in limbo, awaiting decisions from the new Brown administration on how best to proceed.

In contrast, in December 2006 the Department of Health announced the creation of eleven new Biomedical Research Centres to be funded to the tune of £450 million over the period 2007–12. These are intended to drive the development and uptake of new and improved ways of preventing and treating illness. Both in terms of the delivery of their core research function and in spinning off commercial applications from that research, these initiatives are likely to have a substantial regeneration effect on the local economies of the areas in which they are to be located. However, in a decision which again appears to reinforce established research advantages of the greater south east, the bulk of the money will go into five comprehensive research centres: three of these will be in London, one in Cambridge and one in Oxford. The other six centres will be specialist research centres which will work in specific research areas — four will be in London, one in Liverpool and one in Newcastle-upon-Tyne.[40]

In sum, so far as outcomes are concerned, the GVA data are inconclusive — if disparities between the most and least successful regions have declined then it will be some time before this is evident. Added to this, expenditure figures suggest the trend is contrary to the Regional Economic Performance PSA target and that long term public investment seems more likely to exacerbate regional disparities rather than ameliorate them. Less reliable evidence on spatial decisions seems to support these conclusions. It is too early to be definitive about the success or failure of English regional policy. Certainly, the UK Government's explicit position, as expressed in the

---

[40] Department of Health, *New Health Research Centres of Excellence Announced*, 8 December 2006, press release 2006/0384.

Regional Economic Performance PSA target commitment to growth in all regions while also narrowing the gap between them, is contradictory and difficult to reconcile in practice. The UK Government's implicit position has been realised partly through policies and investments that respond to the market (Barker, Eddington, and housing growth areas, for example) and through active discrimination in favour of the London super-region (Olympics, Crossrail, Higher Education and pure and applied scientific research). It seems likely to drive further the growth of disparities rather than counteract them.

CONCLUSION

This chapter suggests that the UK Government's approach to territorial restructuring and spatial development within England remains largely dominated by the promotion and management of economic competitiveness, but has become less 'regional' over time. What has happened in the period since the North East referendum confirms that one element of the regionalisation 'package' originally adopted by post-1997 Labour administrations — the creation of substantial, new, directly elected bodies between the national and local levels — is now firmly off the political agenda, despite continued and somewhat disingenuous references to 'devolution'. Instead, the UK Government has embarked upon a further stage in the reform process in which a commitment to decentralisation — to unelected regional agencies but also to local authorities and, potentially, to sub- or city-regional bodies — is being paralleled by the introduction of greater democratic oversight of regional public sector activity, though mainly by Ministers and MPs rather than sub-national politicians.

There, however, the clarity ends. In other respects, the future shape and effects of English decentralisation — of which regionalisation remains an important but less dominant part — is characterised by three substantial paradoxes. First, it appears that a devolutionary 'solution' to sub-national development issues has been abandoned in eight of the nine English regions at precisely the time when it is gathering pace and momentum in the remaining one — London. Second, a contradiction remains at the heart of the approach to spatial development in England: the two elements of the PSA target on regional economic performance are difficult, if not impossible, to reconcile, and it continues to be unclear precisely what mechanisms are being used to bring about the longer-term aspiration to reduce the gap in economic growth rates between the regions. And third, even assuming that the latter paradox could be resolved, there continues to be dissonance between the explicit elements of the decentralisation/regionalisation agenda, which presuppose even-handed treatment of the regions at the very least, and a trend towards the concentration of productive spending in the best-performing regions.

It is theoretically possible that the latter two paradoxes could be overcome as the implications of the Sub-National Review, the plethora of policy reviews on which it drew, and the CSR 2007 unfold. It may be, for example, that explicit emphasis is placed upon the longer-term element of the Regional Economic Performance PSA target and that a larger number of Whitehall departments will be required to set out, with greater clarity than has been apparent thus far, precisely how they will adjust their priorities to support its realisation. Far more likely, however, given recent spatial economic and policy trends and some major investments to which the UK Government is already committed, is that 'implicit' regional policy, as we have conceived it, will continue to benefit the best-performing regions disproportionately and that disparities between regions will again start to widen. Should that prove to be the case, the robustness of the emerging decentralisation/regionalisation 'settlement' is likely to depend upon two things: the degree of cross-party consensus that it commands (or, put another way, the likelihood of major change under any future government), and the extent to which future growth in inter-regional disparities generates a significant political response.

With regard to the former, there are some differences between the major parties on the issue of sub-national institutional restructuring. It remains possible, for example, that a future Conservative administration will test the mood of regional business communities in deciding whether or not to retain RDAs. The Conservative Party is increasingly placing stress upon local autonomy and leadership, the importance of 'place-shaping' and stronger local economic development and regeneration policy, the need for cross-district collaboration on sub-/city-regional strategy and so on.[41] In this respect, the Tories appear, if anything, to be moving closer to Labour. Even on the issue of regional economic 'balance', a Conservative government will need to keep its core southern England constituency happy whilst retaining its appeal in the North. This means that any future Conservative administration is unlikely — albeit for very different political reasons — to shift more than marginally the balance between explicit and implicit regional policy that has pertained under Labour since 1997.

What might happen under rather different economic circumstances is a more open question. There is little doubt that one of the reasons that long-run growth in inter-regional disparities has not triggered more in the way of popular concern and mobilisation is that it has occurred within a long period of unbroken, national economic growth. With an economic downturn, this

---

[41] Cities Taskforce, *Cities Renaissance: Creating Local Leadership*, Submission to the Shadow Cabinet (London: Conservative Party, 2007), available at www.conservatives.com/pdf/City Leadership.pdf.

might change. It is interesting to speculate, for example, whether the outcome of the North East referendum would have been different had it taken place in a context of economic recession. The post-devolution settlement that is emerging, however, is not one that is likely to give the dog that is English regionalism another chance to bark, at least not in the foreseeable future. For all of its difficulties and shortcomings, one of the promises of the ill-fated move towards ERAs was that it potentially created a new, more visible and accountable form of territorial politics *within* England. To the extent that it presents opportunities for a different sort of territorial politics at all, the settlement that is now emerging is likely to be one that relies heavily upon voluntaristic, 'bottom up' leadership and coalition building, effective but largely invisible lobbying at the national level and the brokering of selective 'deals' between government departments and particular sub-national interests. The story of the next stage of decentralisation and regionalisation in England will doubtless be a fascinating one, but a Ph.D. in political science may be needed to follow it.

BIBLIOGRAPHY

Official Documents and Primary Sources

Association of Greater Manchester Authorities (AGMA), *City Regions Governance in Greater Manchester: The Way Forward* (Wigan: AGMA, 2007), available at www.agma.gov.uk/ccm/agma/AGMA_Initiatives/governance.en.

Barker, K., *Barker Review of Land Use Planning: Final Report — Recommendations* (London: The Stationery Office, 2006), available at www.hm-treasury.gov.uk/media/4EB/AF/barker_finalreport051206.pdf.

BERR, *PSA Target 7 — Regional Economic Performance* (London: The Stationery Office, 2007), available at www.berr.gov.uk/files/file14298.pdf.

Cities Taskforce, *Cities Renaissance: Creating Local Leadership*, Submission to the Shadow Cabinet (London: Conservative Party, 2007), available at available at www.conservatives.com/pdf/CityLeadership.pdf.

Department of Communities and Local Government, *Strong and Prosperous Communities: The Local Government White Paper* (London: The Stationery Office, 2006).

Department of Health, *New Health Research Centres of Excellence Announced*, 8 December 2006, press release 2006/0384, available at www.dh.gov.uk/PublicationsAndStatistics/PressReleases/fs/en.

Eddington, Sir R., *The Eddington Transport Study* (London: The Stationery Office, 2006), available at www.hm-treasury.gov.uk./independent_reviews/eddington_transport_study/eddington_main_report.cfm.

Gershon, Sir P., *Releasing resources to the frontline: Independent Review of Public Sector Efficiency* (London: The Stationery Office, 2004).

HM Treasury, 'Department of the Environment Transport and the Regions' in *Spending Review 2000: Public Service Agreements 2001–2004* (London: The Stationery Office, 2000), available at www.hm-treasury.gov.uk./spending_review/spending_review_2000/psa/pss_psa_detr.cfm.

HM Treasury, *Productivity in the UK: 3 — the Regional Dimension* (London: HM Treasury, 2001).

HM Treasury, 'Office of the Deputy Prime Minister' in *Spending Review 2002: Public Service Agreements* (London: The Stationery Office, 2002), available at www.hm-treasury.gov.uk./Spending_Review/spend_sr02/psa/spend_sr02_psadeppm.cfm.

HM Treasury, *Productivity in the UK: 4 — the Local Dimension* (London: HM Treasury 2003).

HM Treasury, *2004 Spending Review PSAs* (London: The Stationery Office, 2004).

HM Treasury, *2004 Spending Review: Meeting Regional Priorities — Response to the Regional Emphasis Documents* (London: The Stationery Office, 2004), available at www.hm-treasury.gov.uk./media/C/E/sr04_regpriorities_220704.pdf.

HM Treasury, *Terms of Reference for the Sub-National Economic Development and Regeneration Review,* available at www.hm-treasury.gov.uk./media/5/E/csr07_subnatecon_tor.pdf.

HM Treasury, *Sub-National Review of Economic Development and Regeneration* (London: The Stationery Office, 2007).

HM Treasury, Department of Trade and Industry and Office of the Deputy Prime Minister, *Devolving decision making: 3 — Meeting the economic challenge: The importance of cities to regional growth* (London: The Stationery Office, 2006).

HM Treasury, Department of Trade and Industry and Department of Communities and Local Government, *Regional Economic Performance: Progress to Date* (London: The Stationery Office, 2006), available at www.hmtreasury.gov.uk./media/7B7/0F/pbr06_regionaleconomicprogress_365.pdf.

HM Treasury, *Meeting the aspirations of the British people; 2007 Comprehensive Spending Review and Pre-Budget Report* (London: The Stationery Office, 2007)

House of Commons Communities and Local Government Select Committee, *Is there a future for Regional Government? Vol. II: Oral and supplementary written evidence* (Session 2006–7, 4th Report, HC 352–II) (London: The Stationery Office, 2007), available at www.publications.parliament.uk/pa/cm200607/cmselect/cmcomloc/352/352ii.pdf.

Lyons, Sir M., *Inquiry into Local Government: Place-shaping: a shared ambition for the future of local government. Final report* (London: The Stationery Office, 2007).

Ministry of Justice, *The Governance of Britain* Cm 7170 (London: The Stationery Office, 2007).

National Statistics, *Regional, sub-regional and local gross value added*, 15
    December 2006, available at www.statistics.gov.uk/pdfdir/gva1206.pdf.
Office of the Deputy Prime Minister, *Sustainable Communities: Building for the
    Future* (London: The Stationery Office, 2003).
Royal Commission on Local Government in England, *Report, Volume 2, Memo-
    randum of Dissent*, Cmnd 4040–I (London: HMSO, 1969).

Secondary Sources

Adams, J., P. Robinson and A. Vigor, *A New Regional Policy for the UK*,
    (London: IPPR, 2003).
Adams, J. and P. Robinson, 'Regional Economic Policies in a Devolved United
    Kingdom' in A. Trench (ed.), *The Dynamics of Devolution: The State of the
    Nations 2005*, (Exeter: Imprint Academic, 2005), pp. 225–51.
Bryant, C., 'Crossrail boosted by rates top-up idea', *Financial Times*, Budget
    2007 Supplement, 22 March 2007, p.19.
Gardiner, J. and S. Thorp, 'Going South (Special Report)', *Regeneration and
    Renewal*, 1 September 2006, pp. 20–3.
Gardiner, J., 'Overspend could up Games bill by 60% says Ken', *Regeneration
    and Renewal*, 17 November 2006, p. 1.
Gardiner, J., 'Lottery may have to pick up £900m Games bill', *Regeneration and
    Renewal*, 24 November 2006, p. 5.
Hazell, R. (ed.), *The English Question* (Manchester: Manchester University
    Press, 2006).
Institute for Public Policy Research, *City Leadership: Giving city-regions the
    power to grow* (London: IPPR, 2006).
Sandford, M. and P. Hetherington, 'The regions a the Crossroads: the Future for
    Sub-National Government in England' in A. Trench (ed.), *The Dynamics of
    Devolution: The State of the Nations 2005* (Exeter: Imprint Academic, 2005)
    pp. 91–113.
SURF-CUPS, *A Framework for City-Regions* (London: ODPM, 2006).
Thorp, S., 'Government "on track" to close growth gap', *Regeneration and
    Renewal*, 5 January 2007.

6

Financing Devolution
2008 and Beyond

John Aldridge[1]

The Barnett formula, or, to be more precise, the combination of block funding plus population related adjustments, for financing territorial spending in the UK seemed only a temporary expedient when it was introduced in 1978. It was to be reviewed or replaced following the 'Needs Assessment' exercise then being conducted to determine the spending of the new devolved Assemblies. That exercise came to nothing, along with institutions it was to support, and since then the temporary funding formula has proved remarkably durable. It has become more embedded over the years, more strictly applied, and for territorial Secretaries of State both a measure of success and a touchstone of fairness.

So embedded had Barnett become by 1999 that it was the automatic choice for funding all three new devolved institutions. What started as administrative convenience has become something of high political salience and near-constitutional status, though like many elements of the UK constitution it is written down only in descriptions of actual practice. And like some other elements of the constitution, it is all things to all men. To some it embeds overgenerous public spending levels in Scotland, Northern Ireland and perhaps Wales; to others it ensures unfairly low levels of growth in that spending; to others again it promotes fiscal profligacy and poor accountability, or even fails to promote economic growth. A lot of characteristics for a bit of simple algebra.

Now, however, the future of Barnett is once again under review. A SNP minority administration in Edinburgh aspires to greater fiscal autonomy, and has laid claim to oil revenues in particular; and the other parties in Scotland also call for changes to the funding arrangements. The Labour-Plaid Cymru coalition in Cardiff sets up a funding review, and the new administration in Northern Ireland hankers after flexibility in business tax levels. This chapter, therefore, reviews the arguments about Barnett, and considers the options for the UK in developing it.

---

[1] I am very grateful to Professor Jim Gallagher, who was co-author of an earlier version of this chapter before returning to the Civil Service.

NEEDS-BASED BUDGETING

Broadly speaking there are two alternative principles which might be employed in determining the budget of a sub-national government: either allocation related to the spending needs of the relevant area, or funding by some reference to its taxable capacity. In the UK, relation to need is key to almost every funding mechanism that distributes resources across areas, almost always with the aim of securing equity or equalisation in the provision of services or benefits. As Walker notes, there are powerful forces in British public life which demand equity in public resource allocation, and even though this might be seen as broadly a left-of-centre concept ('to each according to his needs'), it has in practice been put into effect by UK Governments of all complexions.[2] Indeed, in more recent years the idea of broad general equity across parts of the country as a guiding principle has begun to be supplanted by demands for universalism: that each citizen in the same circumstances in any part of the country should be treated in the same way.[3] This applies not merely in areas such as benefits, where uniformity has long been the pattern so that equals are treated equally by law, but in other areas of the welfare state such as health — an approach which, as Greer has noted, is antithetical to devolution. [4]

Equity in resource allocation inevitably implies 'horizontal' fiscal equalisation across regions, as need for spending and taxable capacity is unlikely to arise equally in each area. The UK has a long history of highly centralised and unhypothecated tax collection which makes this possible. Taxes are almost all collected centrally, with local government taxation at about 8 per cent of total revenue the only significant exception, and virtually none is hypothecated to a particular use.[5] The UK centre therefore has unusually wide scope to redistribute tax revenues according to need. But horizontal equalisation is not by any means a purely British notion. To take only two examples, the German federal Basic Law (constitution) requires the state to ensure 'uniformity of living standards' in different parts of the country (Article 106 (3) of the Basic Law). In Australia, the elaborate equalisation processes of the Commonwealth Grants Commission (probably the most

---

[2] D. Walker, *In Praise of Centralism: A critique of the new localism* (London: Catalyst Forum, 2002*)*.

[3] See for example G. Stoker, *Transforming Local Governance: From Thatcherism to New Labour* (London: Palgrave Macmillan, 2004).

[4] S.L. Greer, *Territorial Politics and Health Policy* (Manchester: Manchester University Press, 2004).

[5] The television licence is the one genuinely hypothecated tax as the road and national insurance funds are only notionally so allocated. However, as Chancellor, Gordon Brown in his Budget of March 2002 raised a special 1 per cent national insurance levy to invest in increased health spending.

sophisticated example of its kind) are aimed at ensuring that allocations are made to State governments so that 'if each made the same effort to raise revenue from its own sources and operated at the same level of efficiency, each would have the capacity to provide services at the same standard.'[6]

The fundamental problem of course is that needs are contestable: what constitutes need for public spending depends on contestable propositions about what services should be provided publicly, to what standard and in what way. And even where there is broad consensus on the services involved, how need should be assessed or measured is problematic also. Sometimes this is done by straightforward negotiation — as, for example, inside government when needs for different programmes compete with one another; often it is also done by formulae, usually themselves contested and negotiated, when resources are allocated to different areas, as in local government finance or in the NHS. There are quite profound technical problems about the measurement of spending need in practice, in addition to the value laden assumptions about what constitutes need. In particular, it is unusual to be able to identify measures of need which directly map on to spending requirements. Thus, allocating budgets according to need is easier said than done.

Nevertheless, a strong criticism of the Barnett arrangements is that they do not allocate public spending according to need. The most obviously problematic comparison is between Scotland and the North East of England, which is overall a poorer region but appears to enjoy lower levels of public spending than Scotland, and indeed lower spending than several regions of England as well. The data underlying these assessments, however, appears to be of mixed quality: Adams and Robinson, for example, have indicated that Public Expenditure Statistical Analysis (PESA) figures show that public spending in the North East of England is actually significantly higher than previous publications have suggested.[7] Indeed, they suggested that public spending was in fact growing in 2004, just when the 'Barnett squeeze' (see below) was beginning to reduce spending leads in devolved areas. McLean has nevertheless argued that higher spending in Scotland in particular is fundamentally unjustified, and constitutes a 'crisis' for the UK.[8] This may seem paradoxical when the higher levels of spending in Scotland, Wales and

[6] Set out in Commonwealth Grants Commission, *Report on State Revenue Sharing Relativities 2004 Review* (Canberra: Commonwealth Grants Commission, 2004), chapter 2, para. 3. See also I. McLean, *The Fiscal Crisis of the United Kingdom* (Houndmills: Palgrave Macmillan, 2005). For Germany, see C. Jeffery, 'Fiscal Equalisation in Germany', *Regional and Federal Studies*, 13 (4) (2003): 22-39.

[7] J. Adams and P. Robinson, 'Regional Economic Policies in a Devolved United Kingdom' in A. Trench (ed.), *The Dynamics of Devolution: The State of the Nations 2005* (Exeter: Imprint Academic, 2005), pp. 225-248. For the latest data, see HM Treasury *Public Expenditure Statistical Analyses 2008* HC 489 (London: The Stationery Office, 2008), especially table 9.2.

[8] McLean 2005.

Northern Ireland, embedded by Barnett, have been justified by successive UK Governments as fairly reflecting need. The original Block budgets, to which population-based additions have been made, were negotiated inside government to meet apparent needs for spending in the respective territories. There is a discussion later about why it is that, after 30 years of population increments, total spending is not uniform per capita, but for the moment it is worth noting that part of HM Treasury's motivation for Barnett was to avoid being rolled over by territorial interests.[9] Perhaps perversely, it is of course the fact that growth in budgets is proportionate to relative population, and not to existing budgets, that allows scope for criticism of the 'Barnett squeeze', resulting in lower growth.

REVENUE-BASED BUDGETING AND
THE DEBATE ABOUT FISCAL AUTONOMY

For many years, debate about devolved funding has been dominated by these arguments about relative fairness. Recently in Scotland, more attention has been devoted to arguments which stem from the alternative funding principle, that of 'vertical' fiscal equalisation, that a sub-national government's spending should be funded by the taxes it raises. This debate is helpfully summarised in a paper by Professors Charlie Jeffery and Drew Scott for the SCDI.[10] The shorthand for this debate is 'fiscal autonomy'. Total fiscal autonomy is tantamount to political independence, and it is therefore unsurprising that political nationalists tend to support greater tax and spending powers for the Scottish Parliament. A number of other arguments are however advanced for some lesser degree of fiscal autonomy for Scotland.

Of these the most persuasive is that funding the Scottish Parliament wholly by grant undermines its accountability to the electorate as it is not responsible for taxation decisions, only spending ones. At the margin it is unable to take the economically efficient decision between increased spending and increased taxation. At a level of principle this argument is unanswerable; the Steel Commission makes the point a little more pompously, saying that it is not right that one Parliament should be dependent on grants from another.[11] However, despite its force, this argument merits some critical scrutiny.

---

[9] See Jim Ross, formerly of the Scottish Office, quoted in J. Mitchell 'The Principles and Policies of Devolved Financial Arrangements'. Paper presented at conference on Comparative Fiscal Federalism, Birmingham, January 2002.

[10] D. Scott and C. Jeffery, *Scotland's Economy: The fiscal debate. A discussion paper* (Edinburgh: Scottish Council for Development and Industry, 2007). Available at www.scdi.org.uk/pi/2007/2584.pdf

[11] Scottish Liberal Democrats, *The Steel Commission: Moving to Federalism. A new settlement for Scotland* (Edinburgh: Scottish Liberal Democrats, 2006). Available at www.scotlibdems.org.uk/pages/publications

As a matter of fact the Scottish Parliament is not wholly dependent on grants from another. It determines — or virtually determines — the two local taxes, non-domestic rates and the council tax, which together in 2006–7 raised £4 billion, compared with a total Scottish Executive budget of less than £30 billion (so about 13 per cent of the whole). The same is broadly true for the National Assembly for Wales. These taxes do not, however, allow for ready accountability to voters. The impact of business rates on voters is indirect and so the tax is not perceptible, and accountability for the highly perceptible council tax is shared in a confusing way with local councils. They do, however, allow for decisions at the margin between tax and spending, and it is interesting that after a period of giving priority to maintaining revenue from business rates, the Scottish Executive has been pursuing a policy of reducing the tax. Similarly, the trajectory of council tax rises in Scotland has been significantly lower than in England largely because of the grant decisions of the Executive, so much so that average council tax is now lower in Scotland than in England or Wales. The new SNP administration promises to freeze council tax levels, has achieved the agreement of councils in Scotland for that in 2008–9, and may well continue to fulfil that promise if they can maintain their concordat with local authorities.

It has been argued, for example by Hallwood and Macdonald, that the lack of fiscal autonomy means that the Executive and Parliament have weak incentives to promote economic growth, as their budgets do not depend on locally-raised taxation and so on domestic growth.[12] This argument rests on ideas of 'public choice' economics, that politicians will be motivated to take policy decisions to promote growth more if that increases their own budgets. Such incentives may exist, though if so they will already operate for non-domestic rates and council tax (10 per cent plus of devolved budgets) which are directly linked to growth through property rental values and house building. It is also hard to assess whether they are in fact significant compared to the incentives created by the hope of re-election; certainly the Scottish Executive under Jack McConnell stated that economic growth was its top priority, a commitment repeated by John Swinney for the new administration, despite the limited powers of the Scottish Government and Parliament in this area.

It is also argued that as fiscal autonomy would mean decision-making power over more taxes, these would be available as policy levers to promote growth, notably by setting competitively low rates of corporation tax. Examples of small countries such as Ireland and the Baltic states promoting inward investment by setting competitively low rates of corporate taxation are often cited. Seeking such policy scope is an obvious argument for

---

[12] P. Hallwood and R. MacDonald, *The Economic Case for Fiscal Autonomy: With or Without Independence (Edinburgh:* Policy Institute, 2006), available at http://policyinstitute.info/research-publications/economy/the-economic-case-for-fiscal-autonomy/

nationalists, but there are constraints on the extent to which corporate tax rates may be varied inside a single member state of the EU. Recent jurisprudence of the European Court of Justice suggests that this may be possible without infringing the EU's 'state aids' rules, though this is not wholly certain and would appear to require the 'cost' of the tax reduction to be borne wholly within the region concerned. [13] A further challenge is the scope for transfer pricing and other tax management by companies operating inside the UK which could reduce tax take with no real effect on the Scottish economy. Gallagher and Hinze suggest that if corporation tax was to be made available to the Scottish Parliament as a policy tool, then it might in practice be better confined to the reduced rate of corporation tax payable by small companies which have less scope for legal tax avoidance. [14] They estimate the yield from this as potentially about £670 million a year in Scotland, £320 million a year in Wales and £190 million in Northern Ireland. What this does *not* do of course is improve accountability; corporation tax is paid only by profitable businesses, and is not readily perceptible to ordinary voters.

FISCAL AUTONOMY AND THE GERS DEBATE

Opponents of fiscal autonomy, and unionist commentators generally, often refer to the annual publication of Government Expenditure and Revenues in Scotland (GERS).[15] GERS attempts to account for all spending and revenues in Scotland; it uses HM Treasury data and of necessity makes assumptions and approximations, and shows a substantial fiscal deficit for Scotland. It starts with 'identifiable' public expenditure in Scotland, such as social security, health and education, including all Scottish Executive spending. This is spending which can be separately identified as being for the benefit of Scottish residents, and comprises about 86 per cent of total spending: in Scotland in 2004-5 the per capita figure is 15.8 per cent higher than in England. Wales is 10.4 per cent higher and Northern Ireland 25.4 per cent. ('Identifiable' spending includes both 'comparable' and 'non-comparable' spending, only the former being determined in total by Barnett.)

To estimate an overall fiscal balance to this is added a share (mostly pro rata to population) of 'non-identifiable' spending, such as the defence budget and debt interest payments. This total is then compared with estimates of locally raised revenue. Estimating revenue is more difficult than

---

[13] Case C-88/03 *Portugal v Commission of the European Communities*) [2006] 3 C.M.L.R. 45 (sub nom *Re Income Tax Reductions in the Azores*). For a summary of the Azores case see Scott and Jeffery 2007.

[14] J. Gallagher and D Hinze, *Financing Options for Devolved Government in the UK* (Glasgow; School of Law, University of Glasgow, 2005); available from www.gla.ac.uk/Acad/PolEcon/pdf05/2005_24.pdf.

[15] *Government Expenditure and Revenues in Scotland 2005* (Edinburgh: Scottish Executive, 2005).

expenditure and GERS explains the basis for its estimates. Overall (apart from North Sea revenues, which are treated separately) Scotland is estimated to produce slightly lower revenues per head than the UK as a whole: 8.1 per cent of total revenues for 8.5 per cent of population. GERS 2005 therefore estimates 'net borrowing' for Scotland — in substance, a transfer of funds— as amounting to about £11 billion in 2005–6. This number varies: in 2001–2, when the UK as a whole was in surplus, it was about £5 billion. These figures take no account of oil revenues (petroleum revenue duty and corporation tax on North Sea oil). These are volatile, peaking in 1984–5 at £12 billion, but running at about £5 billion in 2004–5.[16] There is no agreed method of allocating these to Scotland or other parts of the UK so GERS illustrates a range of assumptions. For example, allocating two-thirds of them reduces the deficit to £7.7 billion in 2004–5.

No comparable figures are published for Wales or Northern Ireland but, apart from oil revenues, their position is likely to be similar to Scotland's. Indeed, evidence suggests that economic performance in Wales and Northern Ireland is poorer than in Scotland. Consequently tax receipts are lower: income tax receipts are estimated at 62 per cent of the UK per capita level in Northern Ireland and 65 per cent in Wales; VAT yields in each case about 86 per cent per capita of the UK level compared to Scotland's 93 per cent. With identifiable spending per capita at 12 per cent and 29 per cent higher than UK levels, both countries' deficits might indeed be proportionately larger.[17]

GERS is of course highly controversial. The Scottish National Party asserts that Scotland is in fiscal surplus.[18] Cuthbert and Cuthbert have challenged the quality of the data and identified at least one error, which overstates Scottish relative spending by 1 per cent.[19] Certainly, GERS should be treated with caution. It was instigated under the Conservative UK Government in the 1990s by Ian Lang, then Secretary of State for Scotland, to demonstrate to the Scottish population the benefits of the Union, and the scale of fiscal transfers which Scotland enjoyed. It cannot be taken to illustrate what the position of an independent Scotland would be; that is dependent on too many other variables— the terms of any separation, the spending polices of an independent country on, say, defence or social security or taxation, and the amount of government borrowing regarded as prudent each year. And the data and methods used produce estimates subject to uncertainties, not actual fiscal balances. But nor does it seem rational to seek to wish away the broad picture which it shows - that Scotland (like Wales and Northern Ireland) enjoys levels of public spending supported by substantial fiscal

[16] Scottish Executive 2005.
[17] See Gallagher and Hinze 2005.
[18] Scottish National Party, *Scotland in Surplus — Past, Present and Future, December 2006.*
[19] J. Cuthbert and M. Cuthbert, *A Constructive Critique of the Treasury's Country and Regional Analysis of Public Expenditure* (Glasgow: Fraser of Allander Institute, 2005).

transfers from elsewhere in the UK. Advocates of greater fiscal autonomy have to take this into account if their propositions are to be taken seriously.

At the time of writing, the latest edition of GERS covering 2005–6 and 2006–7 is awaited, which will no doubt seek to take account of the comments made on earlier versions (for example by Cuthbert and Cuthbert) and will reflect the recent substantial increase in oil prices. The figures may therefore differ noticeably from earlier editions, but the overall picture is unlikely to be different.

EQUITY AND ACCOUNTABILITY: HAVING OUR CAKE AND EATING IT?

It is reasonable to ask whether it is possible to devise a system which secures both equity in public spending and the increased accountability which greater fiscal autonomy might bring. In the UK this has of course been the aim of the local government finance system for many years, and it might offer some guidance. Its history is tortuous, but overall it would not be unfair to say that in both England and Scotland there has been greater success in achieving equity than accountability. Local government has long been dependent on grants from the centre for a majority of its revenue. The proportion supported by local taxation has varied over the years, but nowadays when non-domestic rates are a national tax in all but name, it is as low as 20 per cent. The grant distribution system takes account of different needs for spending and of different taxable capacity.

Need, or more exactly relative need, is assessed by complex formulae which are substantially based on population, so taking into account the 'clients' for different services. The 'client group' approach is intended to be objective by assessing those factors which indicate need through regression analysis, to identify which factors outwith management control determine spending. It is possible to do this as there are many authorities involved in the system, though the results are often controversial. The total spending which the government carrying out the exercise considers is affordable is then shared out amongst authorities in proportion to this assessed need, and grant is distributed so that if councils spent at this level their local taxes would all be equal. Thus, if a council chooses to spend more or less than this level the effect will be seen on its local tax, and the change is heavily geared— that is to say that a 2 per cent increase in spending above assessed need results in a 10 per cent rise in council tax. (In practice of course, councils as a whole all spend more than this so all taxes are higher.) The attempt to equalise for both different needs and tax capacity works at present only if councils spend at assessed need.

Some lessons for devolution finance can be learnt from the local government system. First of all, this simple account disguises that the system is not intrinsically stable from year to year. The assessment of relative need will change as data, indicators or methodology change so, in the local government context, government finds it necessary to underpin a council's grant by a guaranteed minimum increase. Otherwise, for example, a council with a rapidly shrinking population may be forced to have unsustainably large tax rises if spending reductions fail to keep pace with grant decreases. The simple clarity of the connection between spending and tax is swiftly lost: the single largest influence on local tax levels is government grant decisions— at both aggregate and individual levels. And of course, until now, much grant has been distributed separately from the formulaic system, by specific grants or challenge funds tied to particular projects or programmes determined by government. In Scotland this has now changed. The SNP administration's concordat with Scottish local authorities trades off the removal of most such specific grants against a commitment by local authorities to freeze council tax levels. It will be interesting to see how, and to what extent, this increases or is seen as increasing local authorities' accountability.

The history of the local tax system is one of repeated efforts to improve accountability while still having equity. This issue was critical to the magisterial analysis of the Layfield report of 1976; improved accountability was the expressed aim of the unhappy interlude of the poll tax in the 1990's; and squaring this circle has been the objective of the recently published Lyons review in England, and to some degree the Burt review in Scotland — neither successfully.[20] And the history of central-local relationships which matches it is one of conflict and an unacknowledged drift towards greater central control by government.[21] Some general lessons for devolution finance might however be drawn. First, when grant predominates in any mixed system, any volatility in it will seriously undermine accountability, while conversely stability will tend to increase it. Second, both needs and tax capacity have to be taken into account, but complete equalisation for both is a will of the wisp and cannot wholly be achieved. Third, he who pays the piper is repeatedly tempted to call the tune. A persistent theme in the history of central-local relations is of resistance to hypothecated grant from government and assertion by councils of the need for freedom in spending decisions. A remarkable feature of the Barnett arrangements is that they do not

[20] Layfield Committee, *Report of the Committee of Inquiry into Local Government Finance* Cmnd 6543 (London: HM Stationery Office, 1976); Local Government Finance Review Committee, *A Fairer Way: Report on Local Taxation of the Local Government Finance Review Committee* (Edinburgh: Local Government Finance Review Committee, 2006), available at www.scotland.gov.uk/Publications/2006/11/06105402/0; Sir M. Lyons, *Lyons Inquiry into Local Government: Place-shaping: a shared ambition for the future of local government. Final report,* (London: The Stationery Office, 2007)..

[21] For an account of 30 years of central-local relations in Britain see J. Gallagher, K. Gibb and C. Mills, *Rethinking Central Local Relations in Scotland: Back to the future?* (Edinburgh: David Hume Institute, 2006).

have this characteristic. That, and the stability produced by Barnett, can in part be attributed to the fact that it deals with marginal increments of spend.

THE BARNETT FORMULA AS A THIRD WAY

Bizarrely enough, the Barnett system of resource allocation is based on neither equalising for measured need nor allowing fiscal autonomy. It contains some elements of both principles, and is criticised for its failures in meeting each. In fact, it is a classic piece of incremental policy-making, just as it is an example of incremental budgeting. Incremental budgeting has long been the way in which UK public spending has been allocated. The Public Expenditure Survey process initiated after the 1961 Plowden Report intro- duced the language of baselines with annual review.[22] The use of population to determine the increments to Scottish programmes also predates Barnett, and has it roots as far back as Chancellor Goschen in the nineteenth century, though he used population to determine total shares rather than incremental changes.[23] The block-and-formula system became thoroughly embedded under the Conservative governments of the 1980s and 1990s, as a practical device both to determine the Scottish and Welsh budgets, and as a way of allowing some spending discretion to the territorial Secretaries of State and to reduce the opportunities in Scotland and Wales for special pleading. So it is hardly surprising that it moved smoothly into being the funding mecha- nism of choice for the new devolved bodies: indeed it was the only one seri- ously considered. As Heald and McLeod note, devolution finance remains deeply embedded within the UK public finance system, which is primarily driven by the allocation between and control of spending programmes.[24]

Against this background it is worth reviewing some of the characteristics of Barnett that do not emerge from the debates about equity and accountabil- ity. The first, and often least-noticed, is the remarkable degree of spending autonomy that Barnett allows for. This is a result of its evolution. The Block budget for territorial Secretaries of State needed no strings attached: they were bound by UK Cabinet collective responsibility, and it was intended to allow them scope to adjust priorities within that. This lack of earmarking has been carried across into the devolved system, where of course it is even more appropriate. However, by international standards such unconstrained spend- ing freedom is unusual and deeply envied, not only in itself, but also because it avoids the need for the bureaucracy and boundary problems associated with specific or conditional grants. The second characteristic, in contrast

[22] Plowden Committee, *Control of Public Expenditure* Cmnd 1432 (London: HM Stationery Office, 1961) and see D. Heald, *Public Expenditure* (Oxford: Martin Robertson, 1983).

[23] See McLean 2005 for a good account of this.

[24] D. Heald and A. McLeod, 'Embeddedness of UK Devolution Finance within the Public Expenditure System', *Regional Studies* 39(4) (2005): 495-518.

with a system based on revenue or indeed with the local government finance system, is that Barnett offers remarkable stability. The baseline is much larger than the population adjustments. This is like a UK spending department, which of course is what the devolved administrations grew out of.

BARNETT AND CONVERGENCE

It is instructive also to review the actual effects of the Barnett system over its existence, and in particular since devolution. One of the criticisms made of Barnett is that it has sustained the high levels of relative spend which were reached by the 1970s to the present day. On the face of it, that ought not to happen, as a population-related increment will tend to equalise spend per head of population. This famous convergence or 'Barnett squeeze' is said to have been an intention of the arrangements. Given that the formula was introduced as an interim measure pending a needs assessment, it seems erroneous to talk of intentions, but it is clear that convergence ought arithmetically to be the effect of determining budgets in this way. In fact, as the data below will show, convergence was not seen for some years, but has in recent years been seen to a marked degree.

Chart 6.1: Per capita identifiable expenditure on services (excluding social protection and agriculture; England = 100)[25]

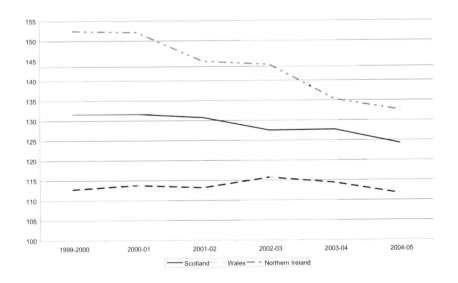

---

[25] Gallagher and Hinze 2005, chart 2.

This chart shows, as a proxy for devolved expenditure, identifiable services less social protection and agriculture (those budgets are not determined by the Barnett formula). From 2001 onwards, marked convergence is seen in Northern Ireland's spend, some in that in Scotland and less in Wales's, as would be predicted from their relative levels of inherited spend. Longer-run data is harder to obtain but the figures below for heath spending in Scotland show a striking trajectory.

Chart 6.2: Per Capita expenditure on the NHS in Scotland (England =100)[26]

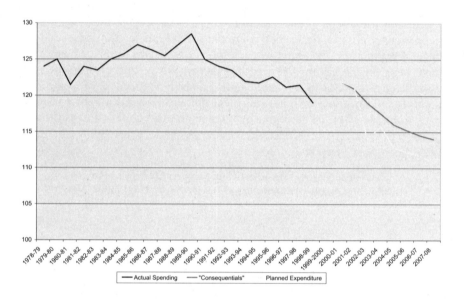

What is seen here is that Scottish health spending (approximately one-third of devolved spending) began to converge toward English levels in the 1990s, but that convergence accelerated after devolution. (Data are not accessible for Northern Ireland or Wales but for the reasons given below similar trends might be expected.) The calculation of 'consequentials' accruing to the Scottish Block parallels the actual budgetary decisions which suggests strongly that this is a consequence of the resources made available via Barnett, rather than decisions to give lower priority to health than England. Indeed Scottish Secretaries of State and since devolution First Ministers have made a virtue of allocating at least all the 'health consequentials' to health spending in Scotland (although the definition of 'health spending' has been broadened in recent years to include some

[26] *Ibid.*, chart 3.

spending which may be expected to improve public health but is not managed by the Health Department). This reflects the similar public pressure to allocate resources to health (particularly when the NHS in England was being allocated substantial extra resources for which the UK Government sought publicity) and the constraint that consequentials from other programmes were not readily available to add to those attributable to increases for the English NHS. This assessment is confirmed by the data in GERS, which shows relative health spending in Scotland at 110 per cent of the English level. The forecast convergence effect is working.

It is worth a brief detour to understand why this is a recent phenomenon. There are two reasons connected with the fact that Scotland's population has been declining relative to England. The first is that the population proportions used had only been reviewed infrequently and were therefore out of date until the early 1990s and so slightly over-generous to Scotland. (The population proportions are now revised for each UK Spending Review). Additionally, even when exact population proportions are used, because Scotland's population has been relatively declining the baseline element of the budget will increase in relative per capita terms. Since Barnett was first introduced, Scotland's population has declined by about 10 per cent relative to England, while the relative populations of Northern Ireland and Wales have not shown the same decline.

More significant, however, has been the mechanics of public expenditure calculation, well understood inside government but not outside it. To understand these it is necessary to delve into the history of administering public finance in the UK.[27] Until the early 1980s Public Expenditure Surveys were conducted in 'real terms', with inflation factors used to determine Parliamentary Estimates and Cash Limits. This system was known as 'volume planning'. When real growth was low, or even negative, no convergence should therefore have been expected. In effect, the increases to which Barnett applied were any marginal increases (or decreases) above or below the inflation allowance applied. In other words, Barnett applied only to a very small proportion of the cash changes to spending plans. Even when the system shifted to cash planning in the 1980s, the practice was to create the baseline for 'year three' by rolling forward the year two baseline uprated by an inflation factor, usually an assumed GDP deflator. Barnett was not applied to that. In addition, for some years some elements of the former 'volume planning' arrangements continued into the 'cash planning' regime. For example, in some years NHS pay increases were fully funded by non-Barnett increases to the Scottish Block (in parallel with similar arrangements for the Department of Health, then the DHSS, and the Welsh and Northern Irish health programmes). Given Scotland's already substantially higher per

[27] See Heald, 1983.

capita spending on health, reflected strongly in the numbers of doctors and nurses, this damped any convergence effect. Thus, the practice for most of the history of Barnett was to allow some growth in nominal expenditure approximating to inflation as well as the Barnett consequentials. Only since 1997, when public spending has been determined on a biennial basis in cash terms with Barnett rigorously applied, has marked convergence taken place. This is because each year the devolved administrations get less allowance for inflation as well as for real growth than comparable English programmes. Rigorous application of Barnett and significant convergence of spending is, then, essentially a post-devolution phenomenon.

The fact of convergence is however highly significant, particularly in the context of relative need. Identifiable public spending per capita in Scotland and Wales is now at 116 and 110 relative to England. In the 1979 Needs Assessment (for a different bundle of services and using methodology that might not stand up today) relative need was assessed at 116 and 109, while spending was at 122 and 106. These numbers need to be treated with a lot of care, but a lazy assumption that Barnett has fossilised relative spending levels at those of the 1970s is now wholly wrong. This is especially true for Northern Ireland, where relative need was assessed in 1979 as 135, but identifiable expenditure in 2004–5 was at 125.

MOVING BEYOND BARNETT:
WHAT MIGHT A WISE TREASURY WANT?

Two further significant factors will influence the future of devolution finance. First, it is clear that the unprecedented growth in public spending which has occurred at the same time as the new devolved bodies is now ceasing. Secondly, there is the fact of political divergence. Each of the actors in this system may have different views, but it is worth looking at the question from the perspective of HM Treasury, who remain the dominant force in UK public spending. Against this background, what might a wise Treasury want?

First of all, the Treasury will continue to want control of total spending. Barnett has delivered that with remarkable ease for HM Treasury, and the local tax discretion has been no more problematic in the devolved territories than in English local government. It seems undeniable that the Treasury will want to keep substantially the same amount of influence on total spend as it currently has. There is an obvious tension here with greater fiscal autonomy, though it is worth noting that the Government has been willing to allow some cautious increased flexibility to local government for some aspects of spending.

At the same time, the Treasury has a strong interest in promoting efficiency in devolved services. The wholly unhypothecated nature of Barnett allows, in principle, for the allocation of resources that most closely matches voter preferences, and so should be efficient in that sense. Similarly, the marked reduction in spending growth, now evident following the outcome of the 2007 Comprehensive Spending Review (CSR), will force hard choices on devolved administrations and increase the pressure for operational efficiencies. These pressures were moderated in Scotland by the Scottish Government's ability to draw down some £900 million of resource unused in earlier years and consequently 'banked' with the Treasury. There will, however, be pressure for the increased incentives of tax responsibility to improve accountability. The most practicable option here is increased income tax discretion, probably in the form of an increased number of tax points, that is to say, allowing the devolved body to alter the basic rate of UK income tax by more than three pence in the pound. Income tax is perceptible, and raises noticeable sums of money, and powers already exist for it to be different in Scotland. There might also be arguments for assignment of a proportion of income tax revenue, so that the devolved body can benefit from the (purportedly) beneficial effect of its policies on tax revenue. That would require careful consideration of how to deal with revenue volatility, which is currently absorbed by the UK Treasury. The more dependent an administration is on own source revenue, the stronger the argument for increased borrowing powers, possibly conflicting with Treasury expenditure control. There might also be some scope to provide devolved administrations with more flexibility on capital spending, analogous to the prudential capital regime for local government, whereby an administration could access resources for capital projects as long as they were satisfied that they could meet the costs from future revenue streams. That might also open the way to a wider range of unconventional financing arrangements for capital projects beyond the private finance initiative which may become less attractive in the light of new accounting requirements.

It is interesting to consider how far the 2007 CSR outcome supported this approach. At first sight, it would appear not to do so. If anything, the outcome of the CSR seems to point to a tightening of attempts by the Treasury to control the Scottish Government's spending. For example, while the Treasury allowed the Scottish Government access to end-year flexibility resources which had built up since devolution (at least partly due to deliberate decisions taking account of the different timing of spending requirements north and south of the border) the indications are that any similar sums that might build up in future would not be readily available.

Second, there had been a long standing tussle between the Treasury and the devolved administrations about the balance between capital and revenue resource allocation. The Treasury broadly wished to insist that changes to the capital baseline should be determined by the formula consequentials of changes to capital resources for comparable Whitehall departments. In other words, the Barnett consequentials of increases in capital spending for the UK as a whole should go to capital spending — which in turn meant allocating a proportion of the whole of the Block grant to capital spending, rather than allowing the whole block to be allocated as the devolved administration saw fit. The devolved administrations took the view that the devolution settlement allowed them to switch resources between capital and revenue as they chose. While the devolved administrations have not resiled from their principled position, their allocation decisions appear in practice to satisfy the Treasury's criteria.

Third, following the pattern since devolution, the formula has been applied even more rigorously in CSR 2007. For example, the Treasury has taken the view that spending on the 2012 Olympics (which will predominantly benefit London and southeastern England) should be regarded as non-comparable because there will be some, albeit small, benefit throughout the UK. Furthermore, the Treasury has agreed some major increases in resource for Whitehall departments on devolved services, notably to cope with the consequences of prison overcrowding in England, which they assert have been agreed outwith the CSR process and therefore do not generate formula consequences. This despite the fact that the Scottish Prison Service faces a similar growth in prisoner numbers.

All of this suggests a hardening of the Treasury line. However, a sensible Treasury will not act or pursue innovations in the fiscal framework for Scotland capriciously, but rather seek to shift the system in a strategic way. So far as fiscal autonomy is concerned, it is reasonable to ask: why cede additional tax powers to a body that has been unwilling to exercise the ones it already has? And improving the accountability of the system through greater taxation would fail to address the concerns which remain about equity. A new needs assessment would be a major undertaking over several years, but might be worth undertaking to increase the acceptability of the distribution of spend, even if in practice — given where convergence has now reached - it did not hugely change it. Addressing both issues simultaneously would be a highly complex task, though not necessarily impossible. Any change to the system would require a process agreed between all the relevant parties — the Treasury, Scottish Parliament, Northern Ireland Assembly and National Assembly for Wales, and, potentially, the English regions, which might demand a say in any new system.[28] The body reviewing the arrangements would need to be seen to be independent, and would therefore take some time to reach conclusions; and it would face the kind of problems discussed above in deciding on measures of need which would command universal

---

[28] Although the lack of elected regional governments and the dismantling of the appointed regional chambers might inhibit this, the regional ministers appointed in the June 2007 reshuffle could act as regional advocates for this purpose.

agreement, exacerbated by the inadequacy of the data available to measure many aspects of need. Furthermore, any changes would need to be phased in, so even proposals to reduce spending levels would be unlikely to release funds except over a long period, and there is a real risk from the Treasury's point of view that any new system could have costly unforeseen effects.

Most important, the financial mechanisms put into place by the UK Government have supported the UK's constitutional and political aims, and will no doubt continue to seek to do this. Barnett supported administrative devolution, and has allowed for genuinely autonomous devolved bodies. But devolution — rather than some more far-reaching approach — is what it allows for. The challenge for the UK, in finance as elsewhere, lies in supporting the policy of devolution and the autonomy of devolved administrations even when the UK Government has weak political links with the devolved bodies, or where devolved Ministers believe in separation from the UK. Barnett, deeply embedded in the UK finance system, is by any standards a unionist solution.

Finally, however, the Treasury will need a pragmatic, stable and workable system: government must go on. Because Barnett changes are incremental, it offers stability, and it gives relative clarity and ease of explanation. These factors may go some way towards explaining its remarkable endurance. Certainly, stability in public spending is an unremarked virtue: the UK Government has in the last decade moved to a system of two or three yearly spending reviews, with budgets stable between them, which has managerial advantages for the efficient planning of spending. A wise Treasury will not want to lose these benefits.

Nevertheless, demands from both the SNP administration in Scotland and the Labour/Plaid Cymru administration in Wales for some change to the financial settlements for their respective countries will put pressure on the Treasury to propose at least some amendment to the current arrangements. As the new Northern Ireland administration settles in, concern is likely to be expressed there too that some change is required. But the pressures will be for different things. The SNP administration has launched its 'National Conversation' in Scotland on the case for increasing the powers devolved from Westminster, an important element of which would be more fiscal powers. The three major opposition parties in Scotland have co-operated in establishing the Commission on Scottish Devolution chaired by Sir Kenneth Calman to review devolution for Scotland 10 years on. As well as considering changes in the powers which are devolved or reserved, the Commission will be considering in particular the financial arrangements. There is an expectation on the part of each of the Labour, Conservative and Liberal Democrat parties that increased revenue-raising powers will be proposed; and demands for a new needs assessment are growing. Although Wales may also seek more fiscal autonomy, its main concern is the way in which it perceives itself as disadvantaged by the Barnett formula, leading to proposals for a commission to review the Barnett arrangements. Northern Ireland seeks relief from a swift convergence effect of the Barnett squeeze to allow the recently-reinvigorated devolution process there to be consolidated. So the Treasury face a difficult balancing act. Doing nothing risks pressure building up to an extent where change is forced on it, with a loss of the control and certainty of the existing system. On the other hand, to propose changes too soon runs the risk of giving more away than it needs to in order to satisfy the devolved administrations. With its serious tightening of the purse strings, the 2007 CSR has provided further impetus to those arguing for change, but so far, the Treasury under Chancellor Darling has not revealed its hand. Nevertheless, funding of devolved administrations is bound to generate complex political debate, and there is a strong, if unfocussed feeling that something should be done. But, in the short and medium term, expect more continuity than change.

BIBLIOGRAPHY

Official Documents and Primary Sources

Commonwealth Grants Commission *Report on State Revenue Sharing Relativities 2004 Review* (Canberra: Commonwealth Grants Commission, 2004).

Layfield Committee, *Report of the Committee of Enquiry into Local Government Finance* Cmnd 6543 (London: HM Stationery Office, 1976).

Local Government Finance Review Committee, *A Fairer Way: Report on Local Taxation of the Local Government Finance Review Committee* (Edinburgh: Local Government Finance Review Committee, 2006), available at www.scotland.gov.uk/Publications/2006/11/06105402/0.

Lyons, Sir M., *Inquiry into Local Government: Place-shaping: a shared ambition for the future of local government. Final report* (London: The Stationery Office, 2007).

Plowden Committee, *Control of Public Expenditure* Cmnd 1432 (London: HM Stationery Office, 1961).

Scottish Executive, *Government Expenditure and Revenues in Scotland 2005* (Edinburgh: Scottish Executive, 2005).

Scottish Liberal Democrats, *The Steel Commission: Moving to Federalism. A new settlement for Scotland* (Edinburgh: Scottish Liberal Democrats, 2006). Available at www.scotlibdems.org.uk/pages/publications

Scottish National Party, *Scotland in Surplus— Past, Present and Future*, December 2006.

Secondary Sources

Adams, J. and P. Robinson, 'Regional Economic Policies in a Devolved United Kingdom' in A. Trench (ed.), *The Dynamics of Devolution: The State of the Nations 2005* (Exeter: Imprint Academic, 2005).

Cuthbert, J. and M. Cuthbert, *A Constructive Critique of the Treasury's Country and Regional Analysis of Public Expenditure* (Glasgow: Fraser of Allander Institute, 2005).

Gallagher, J., K. Gibb and C. Mills, *Rethinking Central Local Relations in Scotland: Back to the future?* (Edinburgh: David Hume Institute, 2006).

Gallagher , J., and D Hinze, *Financing Options for Devolved Government in the UK* (Glasgow: School of Law, University of Glasgow, 2005), available from www.gla.ac.uk/Acad/PolEcon/pdf05/2005_24.pdf.

Greer, S. L., *Territorial Politics and Health Policy* (Manchester: Manchester University Press, 2004).

Hallwood, P. and R. MacDonald, *The Economic Case for Fiscal Autonomy: With or Without Independence* (Edinburgh: Policy Institute, 2006), available at www.policyinstitute.info/AllPDFs/MacDonaldApr06.pdf.

Heald, D., *Public Expenditure* (Oxford: Martin Robertson, 1983).

Heald, D. and A. McLeod, 'Embeddedness of UK Devolution Finance within the Public Expenditure System', *Regional Studies* 39(4) (2005): 495–518.

Jeffery, C., 'Fiscal Equalisation in Germany', *Regional and Federal Studies* 13 (4) (2003): 22–39.

McLean, I., *The Fiscal Crisis of the United Kingdom* (Basingstoke: Palgrave Macmillan, 2005).

Mitchell, J., 'The Principles and Policies of Devolved Financial Arrangements'. Paper presented at conference on Comparative Fiscal Federalism, Birmingham, January 2002.

Scott, D., and C. Jeffery, *Scotland's Economy: The fiscal debate. A discussion paper* (Edinburgh: Scottish Council for Development and Industry, 2007). Available at www.scdi.org.uk/pi/2007/2584.pdf

Stoker, G., *Transforming Local Governance: From Thatcherism to New Labour* (Basingstoke: Palgrave Macmillan, 2004).

Walker, D., *In Praise of Centralism: A critique of the new localism* (London: Catalyst Forum, 2002).

7

Policy Styles and Devolution

Scott L. Greer and Holly Jarman[1]

The story of post-devolution politics in the UK is one of policy divergence. Policy-makers in Scotland and Wales have responded to pent-up desires to do things differently while facing, like their counterparts in England, new challenges and policy debates.[2] And, we argue, they solve their problems and pursue their ends by relying on already distinct, and powerful, images of what policy should be and how it should work. In other words, they have distinct policy styles.

A policy style is the repeated choice of policy tools, and the adoption of the same tools in different policy fields.[3] There are many ways to approach a given set of policy problems, be they funding universities, getting an equitable and efficient health service, or manipulating local government to produce central government's chosen outcome. When a government chooses one tool or another, over and over again, in different sectors, that makes a policy style.

The concept of a policy style is a tool of forestry, not of botany; it is about patterns. Policy experts face the danger of missing the fact that most politicians and many advocates deal with multiple issues. Students of politics and political institutions — and not a few politicians — are often deaf to what their institutions actually do in policy terms. That is where the concept of a policy style comes in; a given government will customarily apply the same basic tools, be they competition, partnership, or networks, to a wide range of

[1] We would like to thank Paul Cairney, John Curtice, Grant Jordan, Allan McConnell, Neil McGarvey, David Raffe, Alan Trench, and Robin Wilson for their comments, and Connie Rockman for help with the bibliography. Part of the research was funded by the Nuffield Trust, which we would like to thank for its support. All errors remain ours. Although this chapter was completed in the summer of 2007 and takes no account of developments since then, we consider that this does not materially affect the argument advanced here.

[2] K. Schmuecker and J. Adams, (eds.), *Devolution in Practice 2006: Public policy differences within the UK* (London: Institute for Public Policy Research, 2006). A. Trench and H. Jarman, 'The Practical Outcomes of Devolution: Policy-making across the UK', in A. Trench (ed.), *Devolution and Power in the United Kingdom* (Manchester: Manchester University Press, 2007).

[3] This is a narrower definition than the classic one presented by Jeremy Richardson, which incorporates both political processes and policy choices; J.J. Richardson, 'Convergent Policy Styles in Europe?' in J.J. Richardson (ed.), *Policy Styles in Western Europe* (London: George Allen & Unwin) pp. 197–210. We focus on policy styles as outputs – as the policy tools that are chosen over and again. This avoids tautology.

different policy areas. A style is the kind of policy that political logics impose *regardless of the policy issue.*[4]

POLICY STYLES IN DEVOLUTION

Literature using the concept of policy styles has not thrived recently. After some high-profile publications in the early 1980s it largely dropped out of policy analysis and comparative politics.[5] More recently, though, a good number of scholars have used it to identify not just the regularities of policy-making process that many fields study, but also regularities of policy choice and baselines from which to study changes such as those caused by Europeanisation or leadership changes, and, most recently, devolution in the United Kingdom.[6]

Why should we care? Analytically, a policy style is an outcome. If a political system chooses the same options over and over again in different fields, that is a product of its internal functioning, which enables us to do two things. One is to establish a baseline; if England routinely opts for markets over networks, we can expect that it will continue to do so. The other is that styles have lives of their own. They are the standard operating procedures of policy makers and shape policy unless updated. These two characteristics are of particular interest now, when we are clearly leaving behind the initial period of all-UK Labour dominance. We submit that, while some part of the explanation of each country's trajectory will be explicable by its particular leadership, another part will reflect the politics, administration, and policy climate of that country.

The next sections review policy in the areas of education, local government and health. On this basis, we argue that there are distinct Scottish,

---

[4] P. Katzenstein, *Policy and Politics in West Germany: The growth of a semisovereign state* (Philadelphia: Temple University Press, 1987) pp. 6–7.

[5] Richardson 1982.

[6] For the concept generally, see J. Blondel, *Comparative Government* (New York: Harvester Wheatsheaf, 1995); A. Jordan, 'Environmental Policy', in I. Bache and A. Jordan (eds.), *The Europeanisation of British Politics* (Basingstoke: Palgrave Macmillan, 2006), pp. 231–47; C. Knill, *The Europeanisation of National Administrations: Patterns of institutional change and persistence* (Cambridge: Cambridge University Press, 2001); R. Sturm, 'Policy-Making in a New Political Landscape', in S. Padgett, W.E. Paterson and G. Smith (eds.), *Developments in German Politics 3*, (Basingstoke: Palgrave Macmillan, 2003), pp. 101–20; C. Woll, 'Lobbying in the European Union: From *sui generis* to a comparative perspective', *Journal of European Public Policy* 13(3) (2006): 456–69; D. Vogel, *National Styles of Regulation: Environmental policy in Great Britain and the United States* (Ithaca, NY: Cornell University Press, 1986). For its use in relation to the UK, see S.L. Greer. and H. Jarman, 'Devolution and Policy Styles in the United Kingdom'. Paper presented at conference of the Political Studies Association Specialist Group on Territorial Politics, Queen's University Belfast, 11–13 January, 2006, and P. Cairney, 'What Is This Thing Called 'Policy Style? A comparative analysis of Britain since devolution'. Paper presented at University of Aberdeen, Department of Politics and International Relations research-in-progress seminar, February 2007.

Welsh and English policy styles with deep roots.[7] The key is the combination of powers, policies, and politics that explain policy divergence within any country; in reality, much of what affects policy remains constant from government to government.[8]

> *Powers*: What can a given government do, in terms of formal powers, financial capabilities, and access to key resources? This is mostly institutional and formal. In the UK, there are considerable powers for Scotland and, increasingly, Wales. Block funding through Barnett and weak central instruments make it difficult for Westminster to intervene in their core spending areas. Over time the institutional conditions of this autonomy are evolving, as policy-makers privately work out solutions to their various problems while publicly competing for credit and strategically picking fights. But compared to most central governments, Westminster starts out ill-equipped to intervene in Northern Irish, Scottish, or Welsh policy.[9]
>
> *Policies*: What is the political agenda? What policy options are on the table? No policy idea survives unless somebody advocates for it and unless it is promoted and defended in the running discussions of policy that take place among experts in every system. Understanding who the advocates are, whether lobbyists, academics, or journalists, is key to understanding what can get and stay on the agenda and what policy tools look sensible and workable to them.
>
> *Politics*: Party politicians do something because it enhances, or at least looks unlikely to damage, their party's standing and electability vis-à-vis its competitors. This means that understanding party strategies and positions is crucial to understanding what politicians will do — while they have bases and resource dependencies to satisfy, they must also seek voters who might change their minds. Often what politicians seek is simple — the votes of blocs of voters whose loyalty they contest with other parties.

Note that all three factors change slowly, and often scarcely change at all. Devolution clearly changed the powers, and created new political arenas. However, its effects on party systems were less striking (it increased the importance of the SNP in the Scottish arena, but did not create it), and its effects on policy communities were diluted by other influences as diverse as university hiring and the organisation of local government associations.

Two of the three key factors do not automatically change with changes of government, such as happened between May and July 2007. We will know

---

7 We regretfully exclude Northern Ireland for two reasons. One, it has a fairly distinct policy style, which one of us calls 'permissive managerialism', but given Northern Irish history, should anybody be surprised? Two, the mechanisms creating Northern Ireland's highly distinctive approach to public policy have more to do with direct rule and sectarian politics than with the democratic mechanisms at work in the other jurisdictions. Among other things, that might mean that it will change significantly with established devolution.

8 S.L. Greer, 'The politics of policy divergence', in S.L. Greer (ed.), *Territory, Democracy, and Justice* (Basingstoke: Palgrave Macmillan, 2006).

9 S.L. Greer, 'The Fragile Divergence Machine: Citizenship, policy divergence, and inter-governmental relations', in Trench 2007.

when powers change — when the Scotland Act is rewritten in a major way, or the Barnett formula publicly changed, or a new legal precedent established, or major physical resources transferred, then powers will have changed. Policy communities change at the margin, as obstinate purveyors of policies the government does not like lose influence and more labile ones start to speak the government's language. But the basic infrastructure of a policy community is generally sturdy. While party politics obviously change — the SNP is now in office in Scotland, not Labour — party competition and the issues that win and lose elections in given places changes much more slowly. Other forms of politics change, less, differently, and sometimes not at all.

DEVOLUTION'S ANCESTORS: THE HISTORICAL ROOTS OF POLICY STYLES

The fact that policy communities, party systems, and many other social institutions survive constitutional changes and elections means that the policy styles of today were often the policy styles of yesterday. Policy styles are responses to the political and administrative structures in a place. They are ways to deal with political and policy problems that worked before and will probably work again because they fit with the political logic of the system. These logics are deeply-rooted, and the nature of those roots (and slowness to change when they change), mean that the political logics of England, Scotland and Wales have long differed in ways that had real policy consequences. That point depends on remembering the distinction between administrative and political devolution — a distinction that is vanishing into history with remarkable speed and very little justification as the doings of 'territorial offices' during their heyday recede into the realm of academic historians and nostalgics. Under administrative devolution, 'territorial offices,' the Scottish Office and the Welsh Office, combined in their respective territories a range of functions that were carried out in England by line departments such as those responsible for education, agriculture or health.[10]

The exact extent of divergence under administrative devolution can be both over and under-stated; on the one hand, the UK did have one government whose writ ran across Great Britain, but on the other hand the interaction of distinctive administrations and societies in Scotland and Wales left distinctive policy communities, and often a more consensual, insider approach to politics and public policy. Furthermore, there was also some

---

[10] R.M. Deacon, *The Governance of Wales: The Welsh Office and the policy process, 1964–1999* (Cardiff: Welsh Academic Press, 2002); J. Mitchell, *Governing Scotland* (Basingstoke: Palgrave Macmillan, 2003); R. Rose, *Ministers and Ministries: A functional analysis* (Oxford: Clarendon, 1987).

substantive policy divergence in fields as diverse as the national curriculum in schools, Scottish water, Welsh mental health policy and Scottish schools testing. Even if the power of the territorial offices and their associated communities lay mostly in implementation, much can happen in implementation.[11]

One of us, giving talks in Scotland about devolution and health, is often asked whether devolution influenced health policy at all — whether the change from a Conservative UK Government to a Labour-led Scottish government really influenced policy. This question, dumbfounding to a student of politics, reflects the extent to which Scottish institutions had always preserved an aura of autonomy and sense of themselves, and to which they had understood their ability to implement and advise as a question of Scottishness rather than implementation.[12]

Political devolution did not just create elected governments where there had only been the Secretaries of State for Scotland and Wales; it also gave Scotland and Wales much more autonomy. Political devolution (just plain devolution now) increases the autonomy of devolved governments, placing them under new political influences, and giving them new electoral reasons to diverge, but it by no means wipes out the influence of inherited institutions.[13] It therefore gives us an opportunity to test for the existence and impact of policy styles. Logically, policy styles should be driven by policy communities. Scottish and Welsh policy communities existed before devolution and influenced the details and implementation of policy. So did party systems, and part of the job of a territorial Secretary of State was to be sensitive to the distinctive political problems UK parties faced in the Scottish and Welsh electoral arenas. If the policy after political devolution — when powers radically changed — uses the same tools as policy in the limited space for divergence before devolution, then that evidence indicates the existence of a policy style. Every political system affords us the opportunity of being able to see whether policies span different sectors; the UK also gives us a longitudinal study of the importance of ideas, independent of electoral politics. The following sections apply both these tests. In each case the policy tools used are similar across different fields, and were foreshadowed before political devolution in 1999.

---

[11] P. Cairney, 'New Public Management and the Thatcher Healthcare Legacy: Enough of the theory, what about the implementation?', *British Journal of Politics and International Relations* 4 (3) (2002):375–98.

[12] S.L. Greer, *Nationalism and Self-Government: The politics of autonomy in Scotland and Catalonia* (Albany, NY: State University of New York Press, 2007).

[13] J. Mitchell, 'Scotland: Devolution is not just for Christmas', in A. Trench (ed.), *The Dynamics of Devolution: The State of the Nations 2005* (Exeter: Imprint Academic, 2005), pp. 23–42.

ENGLAND: MARKETS AND MANAGERIALISM

The English policy style can be characterised as the routine preference for 'managerialism' (the use of managerial techniques rather than reliance on professionals) and 'welfare pluralism' (the use of public and private providers and efforts to increase consumer influences on public services).[14] It has for over two decades emphasised public choice logics that stress the virtues of contracting and competition. Its characteristic policy tools are diversity of providers, contracts and 'contestability'. While this style, often associated with New Public Management, is new since the 1980s, it fits in with long traditions of English institutional differentiation and fragmentation (especially in local government and education). This is combined with a strong tendency toward top-down policy-making, with consultation limited in many important decisions.[15] The approach is made coherent by suspicion of 'vested interests,' above all public-sector employees who enjoy much less elite political support in England than elsewhere.

This results in an English policy style characterised by institutional differentiation, top-down policy, low trust in providers and a faith in market mechanisms such as contracting and competitive tendering (if not necessarily markets). A further technique of control is use the use of central audit mechanisms. It is often characterised now as a sequence, with Tory privatisation giving way to top-down control in the first years of the Blair governments and a later shift to markets.[16] But what stands out in devolved comparison is the constant combination of top-down and market-based mechanisms in pursuit of a technical, self-sustaining system that will do what the centre wants without making the central government actually do it. Many tools have changed — from state-run firms and civil service circulars to quangos, autonomous regulators, and elaborate and highly regulated 'mimic markets'.[17] A few remain the same — inspection regimes and technocratic commissions. But what they have in common is the English difficulties balancing central power and central autonomy — finding ways to produce central government's desired outcomes without forcing central government to do everything. And that is hardly new.[18]

---

[14] C. Pollitt, *Managerialism and the Public Services* (Oxford: Blackwell, 1993); N. Rao, *Towards Welfare Pluralism: Public services in a time of change* (Aldershot: Dartmouth, 1996).

[15] The best statement is still S. Jenkins, *Accountable to None: The Tory nationalisation of Britain* (Harmondsworth: Penguin, 1995).

[16] M. Barber, *Instruction to Deliver: Tony Blair, the public services, and the challenge of delivery* (London: Politico's, 2007).

[17] R. Klein, *The New Politics of the NHS* (London: Longman, 2000).

[18] J. Bulpitt, *Territory and Power in the United Kingdom: An interpretation* (Manchester: Manchester University Press, 1983); J. Bradbury, 'Territory and Power revisited: Theorising territorial politics in the United Kingdom after devolution', *Political Studies* 54 (3) (2006); 559–82.

Education

English education policy has for many years relied on diversity, competition and standards. England has often established new types of school while at the same time maintaining older styles, incorporating educational diversity and stratification as a key part of the system.[19] Private ('public') schools have survived the spread of publicly funded secondary education and subsequently comprehensive schools, and the selective element of the tripartite system (via testing at age 11) still persists in some regions. The Callaghan government sought greater central control of the education system (from both local authorities and individual schools) and the Thatcher and Major governments won it. They combined this search for control with a strong belief in introducing market forces into the education system. In particular, they created a new category of 'grant maintained' schools which could 'opt-out' of local authority control to be maintained by central government and managed by their own boards of governors.

Since 1997 Labour has built upon this with a multitude of initiatives: Specialist Schools, able to attract additional public and private funding, Beacon Schools to spread best practice, Foundation Schools with greater financial autonomy, privately-sponsored 'City Academies' in deprived areas (now spreading to other sites as just 'Academies'), and increasing numbers of faith schools. Voluntary and private sector providers can step in to run failing schools on short-term contracts, while local authorities have a duty to advertise requirements for new schools.[20] The result is an extraordinary degree of differentiation among schools — that is, a wide range of categories created by the centre.

Differentiation comes with competition. England retains statutory testing at ages 7, 11 and 14, and the only school 'league tables' (performance rankings) in the UK, combined with a slimmed down national curriculum that focuses on key skills such as literacy and numeracy. After extended arguments over the continuing validity of A Levels, in the Curriculum 2000 reforms, A Levels and GCSEs will be supplemented by vocational diplomas by 2008. All these policies have soured relations with teachers unions. The highly controversial 2005 White Paper on education gives a taste of the thinking; it sets out plans to 'improve the system by putting parents and the needs of their children at the heart of our school system, freeing up schools to innovate and succeed, bringing in new dynamism and new providers, ensuring that coasting, let alone failure, is not an option for any school'.[21] The Blair governments ensured close Prime Ministerial control of this policy

---

[19] B.S. Silberman, *Cages of Reason: The rise of the rational state in France, Japan, the United States, and Great Britain* (Chicago: University of Chicago Press, 1993), pp 376–93.

[20] C. Chitty, *Education Policy in Great Britain* (Basingstoke: Palgrave, 2004), p. 75.

[21] Department for Education and Skills, *Higher Standards, Better Schools for All: More choice for parents and pupils* (London: The Stationery Office, 2005), p. 7.

area, which is predictable. Number Ten viewed 'education, education, education' as the key to electoral success, and kept a tight grip on policy initiation within the party. It was sometimes difficult for Department for Education and Skills officials to learn about policies such as school autonomy. The result of these efforts to make schools operate like diverse firms in a mimic of the market was the effective nationalisation of English school funding in 2006 — with consequences expected to include an increase in the differentiation of schools and their closeness to central government, and yet another reduction in the importance of local government.

In higher education and research policy, English policy-makers have also opted for policies that differentiate their universities and set them to compete. In terms of student finance, this means allowing each university to set fees subject to a cap of £3,000 per annum (although most institutions set their fees at the maximum permitted level initially). The Higher Education Act 2004 allowed universities to charge such variable fees for the first time, in return for negotiating 'access agreements' aimed at widening participation through bursaries for low-income students; students will repay the money after graduation. This is expected to drive universities to offer differentiated services and quality, in keeping with their fees (especially if, or when, the fees cap is raised) — and transfer more responsibility for student finance onto students and their families, in direct opposition to the universalistic goals Scotland would pursue. In research funding, the UK Government has similarly sought to differentiate English universities, with money increasingly targeted at a few major institutions that are thought to be internationally competitive and decreasing research support for the institutions deemed to be focused on teaching. In contrast to Scotland and Wales it has shown little interest in promoting networks of universities that would allow them to pool resources.

Local Government

Territorial equity — and the potential loss of Westminster seats in areas with bad local authorities — forecloses competition between local governments. No recent government has truly sought to discipline local governments via the exit option; rather than encouraging people to leave badly run local authorities as they do with schools or hospitals, they combine top-down policy and control with an affection for differentiating between good and bad councils. Historically, English local government policy is deeply marked not just by a history of institutional differentiation, but also by the traumatic experiences of the 1980s and 1990s. During those years, headlines were often dominated by rebellious, questionably competent, and possibly corrupt local governments and their conflicts with Conservative governments. The Conservatives tried to control them through legislation and judicial enforcement; local governments tried to wiggle through gaps in the new laws, and the main result was local government constraint, ill will, widely distributed contempt, and a remarkably complicated legal situation.[22] Efforts by the government to control local government, which led so far as the 'poll tax' that helped bring down Thatcher, gave Thatcher's Conservatives an even deeper distrust of local government.[23] Labour, entering office, also distrusted local government, partly because of the same experiences with embarrassing governments in places such as Lambeth and Liverpool, and partly because of a sense that good (local) public services would be decisive in establishing voters' faith in Labour.

Both parties consequently were interested in reducing local government's ability to check central government policy, and obliging it to provide the services and conform to the priorities sought by central government. These battles, and a shared central government frustration with local government, created a demand for novel policy that would make local government *want* to behave as central government wished. That demand eventually was met by a policy community versed in central-local control techniques and which has been encouraged to think of radical local government reform ideas such as elected regions and elected mayors. This produces a constant flow of ingenuity, such as plans for elected mayors of various sorts, or the late Blairite bagatelle of 'double devolution', which includes devolution of powers to sub-local-government units.

Drawing on those ideas, Labour has been keen to promote diverse local solutions and forms of representation to local councils. But it has done this from the centre. Vertical central-local links remain very hierarchical, with the centre expressing conflicting desires for both strong local leadership and enhanced democracy and local conformity with central policy. Unlike in Scotland and Wales, concepts of 'partnership' in English local government are usually horizontal, a means of local working rather than a device to enhance relations with higher tiers of government. Local Strategic Partnerships, established in deprived areas to coordinate service provision between authorities and the private and voluntary sectors are a generalised form of the many types of partnership that involve local government such as Action Zones, the New Deal for Communities, Learning, Sure Start, Youth Offending Teams, and Crime and Disorder partnerships.[24]

A policy of creating differentiation by offering a menu of institutional forms comes with a policy of tough, centrally driven standards and a level of

[22] M. Loughlin, 'The Restructuring of Central-Local Government Relations', in J. Jowell and D. Oliver (eds.), *The Changing Constitution* (Oxford: Oxford University Press, 2000), pp. 137–66.

[23] D. Butler, A. Adonis and T. Travers, *Failure in British Government: The politics of the poll tax* (Oxford: Oxford University Press, 1994).

[24] Office of the Deputy Prime Minister, *Evaluation of Local Strategic Partnerships: Report of a survey of all English LSPs*, February 2003 (London: ODPM, 2003); D. Wilson and C. Game, *Local Government in the United Kingdom* (Basingstoke: Palgrave Macmillan, 2002), p. 124.

scrutiny that easily exceeds what Whitehall applies to itself. The National Framework for Audit and Inspection allows central government to compare performance across the board. Better performing councils are given more freedoms, but failing councils, however, could see key responsibilities handed over to the private or voluntary sectors. Councils are in general extensively audited and tracked by Whitehall officials as well as accountants. Central enforcement of councils' Best Value (outsourcing and competitive tendering) obligations is also tough compared to Scotland and Wales. Under the Local Government Act 2000, councils were given the opportunity to raise standards, transparency and scrutiny through new political structures, but only by choosing from a set of fixed options including a cabinet system or a directly elected mayor.

The 2005 White Paper on local government reinforced many of these ideas with a call for further organisational reform of local government. Its approach to organisation and inter-organisational relations had the same themes: more organisational reform with stronger leadership and elected mayors (para. 3.19), a focus on working with and spinning off functions to private or non-profit organisations (chapter 2), a call for greater partnership between local governments, an extensive range of targets agreed with central government for local governments to hit (chapter 6) as well as efforts to create new mechanisms such as a 'Community Call for Action' that will make local governments more responsive (paras. 2.29–30).[25] These are all top-down reforms that expect, and are likely to build, little trust between central and local government. They also, of course, increase differentiation. Chris Game has summarised the New Labour record to date thus:

> central controls have become even more tiresome and excessive, the supervision of detail even more fussy; rate — and budget — capping are still in place and effectively determine the parameters of every council's budget-making; there was no quango cull and new quangos were created; democratically elected councillors have less direct control today over a more restricted range of services than they did a century ago.[26]

Gordon Brown's first statement to Westminster as Prime Minister, on 3 July 2007, called for a 'concordat' between central and local government. Blair was also emollient when he came to power. And, during the centralising 1980s and 1990s most Conservatives kept their vaguely Burkean, largely rhetorical affection for localism even as their government contemplated the abolition of the local authorities it was so fiercely opposing.[27] The political

[25] Department for Communities and Local Government, *Strong and Prosperous Communities: The local government white paper* (London: The Stationery Office, 2005).

[26] C. Game, 'Mayors, Monitors and Measurers: Blair's legacy to local democracy'. Paper presented at British Politics Group conference on 'Britain After Blair', Chicago, 28 August 2007, p. 6.

[27] Jenkins 1995, p. 60 and p. 254.

logic of England will probably continue to be stronger than any policy logic that would point to cooperation.

Health

The tidal-wave of money that hit the NHS in England from 2001 onward made possible a great deal of policy experimentation — and also created a rising frustration among policy-makers who found that improvements in their statistical performance or press coverage came nowhere near to matching the extra money spent. Again, the answer was a combination of diversity, efforts to harness competition, and a mixture of standards and targets set at the top.

Alan Milburn's accession as Secretary of State began the large-scale project of NHS reform that would preoccupy the Blair government for the rest of its time in office. These involved both strengthening command and control and putting in place the mechanisms that would produce a market, which would in turn produce responsiveness, efficiency, and quality. That began with the 2001 speech on 'Shifting the Balance of Power' which led to stripping out intermediate territorial levels, and the pushing of responsibilities to the centre and 'front-line' organisations such as hospital trusts.[28] Then came patient choice of hospital and the 'treatment centres' program in which the government signed (fixed-volume!) contracts with private firms to supply simple operations on an industrial basis. The justification for treatment centres or patient choice of hospital was never voter or patient demand. The object was to break the monopoly of NHS provision, allowing commissioners of services to play hospitals off against each other. This, in turn, would erode the power of hospitals and their doctors. The special advisor to Blair who is credited with formulating this narrative, Simon Stevens, called it 'constructive discomfort' — and left government to work with a large American company that was interested in entering the lucrative English market.[29]

The focus on competition and fragmentation also gives us a distinctive English approach to the problems of reconfiguration. Reconfiguration means closing existing facilities, often centralising services in larger facilities, and replacing local hospitals with clinics and various outpatient facilities. While it is possible to argue about the clinical desirability of this approach, the strength of elite clinical lobbies and the appeal of budget cuts to managers and ministers mean that it is common to all the systems. It is also politically explosive, since it means asking communities to exchange much-loved hospitals and A&E services for the promise of something better, different, and generally in the future. Activists opposed to reconfigurations

[28] A. Milburn, *Shifting the Balance of Power in the NHS*. Speech given at the launch of the NHS Modernisation Agency, London, 25 April 2001.

[29] S. Stevens, 'Reform Strategies for the English NHS', *Health Affairs* 23 (2004): 37–44.

typically have no trouble pointing out that this means jam tomorrow, and real sacrifices today.

How does England reconfigure? English policy often tries to make a machine that will go of its own — that will carry out the tasks of resource allocation, closures, and changes in services without burdening the centre.[30] In principle, the competitive disciplines of 'choice', the tariff for services and increased local pricing, the purchaser-provider split between primary care trusts and other trusts, the strict fiscal monitoring of foundation hospitals, the presence of competition from treatment centres, and the rise of practice-based commissioning will do the trick, and when a hospital closes it will be because it lacked demand. In reality, it is still difficult and politically contentious to close hospitals, and major reconfigurations have been held off on more or less explicit orders from ministers.

SCOTLAND: PROFESSIONALISM AND CONSISTENCY

The key word of post-1999 Scottish policy, according to policy-makers, is usually 'partnership'. Before political devolution there was no such code term, but it was well-documented that the Scottish elites had a more consensual, if distinctly insiderish, way of implementing policy.[31] The established policy communities in education, health and local government remained in existence, such that post-devolution Scottish policy largely resembles pre-devolution Scottish implementation. This has meant that the Scottish Executive has formed partnerships with incumbent public-sector providers, seeking to use their existing resources and advice, using rather than trying to reform inherited professional hierarchies and roles. It has emphasised good relations with provider groups, made efforts to democratise local decision-making and tried to simplify administration (but in doing so has not been averse to public-private partnerships). Rather than try to create competition, it prefers to build networks and encourage the shared use of resources. In short, the Scottish public policy style since devolution is deeply rooted in the history of Scottish politics and social policy, and is based on universalistic, directly provided, undifferentiated public services that use networks rather than competition and are governed based on a high degree of trust in the professionalism of providers.[32]

Education

[30] S.L. Greer, 'A very English institution: central and local in the English NHS', in R. Hazell (ed.), *The English Question* (Manchester: Manchester University Press, 2006), pp. 194–219.

[31] D. McCrone, *Understanding Scotland: The sociology of a stateless nation* (London: Routledge, 1992), pp. 137–8; C. Moore and S. Booth, *Managing Competition: Meso-corporatism, pluralism, and the negotiated order in Scotland* (Oxford: Clarendon, 1989).

[32] M. Keating, *The Government of Scotland* (Edinburgh: Edinburgh University Press, 2005), pp. 216–7.

Scotland's educational system has been distinctive for a very long time, reflecting first its different religious history and the politics of Union with England, and later because of its own institutional momentum and distinctiveness.[33] Since devolution, policy has presumed the existence of a partnership between schools, local government, and the Executive and then tried to build on it. Local government is a key partner in the 3–18 curriculum review, even if the Scottish Executive has given it a supporting rather than policy-making role. The Scottish Executive has largely dismantled the formal testing and oversight regime inherited from before devolution. It has also abolished school league tables and promoted greater local accountability for schools. The first education legislation to pass the Scottish Parliament placed new duties on councils to raise standards (rather than doing it directly, as in England).[34] The powerful Schools Inspectorate, long the mainstay of Scottish educational standards, remains in place, but the top-down performance management regime is otherwise gone.

Respect for professions has also had financial manifestations. Scotland has decided to pay teachers better than in England and offer them shorter hours, additional staff support and better pay in the wake of the 2001 McCrone review.[35] This professionalist approach has its limits, principally in its refusal to abandon Scotland's use of public-private partnership for schools infrastructure despite the objections of unions.[36]

The most polemical issue has been higher education funding, where Scotland's Labour-led governments (and Scottish Liberal Democrats) differentiated themselves from England by eliminating up-front fees and replacing them with an 'endowment' of (initially) some £2,000 repayable after graduation. The SNP, on 13 June 2007, then differentiated Scotland further by abolishing the repayable endowment. England would later adopt a similar repayment scheme but would not follow Scotland in subsidising students' maintenance costs with loans and generous means-tested grants.[37] The UK-wide introduction of tuition fees, driven by the UK (English) Department for Education and Skills and the Prime Minister himself, did not recognise that Scottish degrees (unlike English or Welsh ones) last four years. This 'Scottish anomaly' was eventually resolved in March 2000 when the

---

[33] A. McPherson and C.D. Raab, *Governing Education: A sociology of policy since 1945* (Edinburgh: Edinburgh University Press, 1988); L. Paterson, *Scottish Education in the Twentieth Century* (Edinburgh: Edinburgh University Press, 2004).

[34] *Scotland Devolution Monitoring Report*, November 1999 (London: The Constitution Unit, 1999). Available at www.ucl.ac.uk/constitution-unit/research/devolution/devo-monitoring-programme.html

[35] *Scotland Devolution Monitoring Report*, November 2001 (London: The Constitution Unit, 2001), p. 62.

[36] *Scotland Devolution Monitoring Report*, January 2006 (London: The Constitution Unit, 2006), p. 119.

[37] *Scotland Devolution Monitoring Report*, November 2000 (London: The Constitution Unit, 2000), p. 25.

Scottish Executive agreed to pay the fourth-year tuition fees of English, Welsh and Northern Irish students attending Scottish universities.

This Scottish refusal to embrace tuition fees left the problem of how to maintain and improve the quality of university research without the additional autonomy of variable tuition fees. The Scottish policy response was to change inter-organisational relationships: to integrate funding streams more closely (especially between higher and further education) and to try to organise research into wide networks. This meant pooling resources and staff that belong to different institutions.[38] It ultimately led to the Further and Higher Education (Scotland) Act 2005, which unified further and higher education funders into a single Scottish Funding Council, and allowed Scottish ministers to introduce variable tuition fees — justified by a concern that English students would study medicine in Scotland and then leave.[39]

Local Government

Scottish local government traditionally has been both a pillar of the Scottish Labour Party and a recognised force in Scottish politics and public administration. Even when it did not win battles with the Conservative governments, it was consulted more than its English counterparts.[40] Against much Scottish opposition, the Major government restructured local government into a single-tier of 32 unitary authorities in 1996, revising the two-tiered structure created by the Local Government (Scotland) Act in 1973 and transferring some of the functions of the second tier of regional councils to the (then) Scottish Office.[41] This change created distinctively Scottish, and distinctively close, central-local connections.[42] They were formalised with devolution in the first ever written protocol between two levels of government in Scotland, the Scottish Partnership Framework of May 2001. Although councillors still perceive the Executive as a centralising force, they generally see it as less so than its predecessor, the Scottish Office.[43]

Compared to England or the pre-devolution system, value for money standards and audits of councils give greater weight to local government autonomy, are more appreciative of different starting points particularly concerning levels of deprivation, and are less inclined to hold councils to

---

[38] M. Keating, 'Higher Education in Scotland and England after Devolution', *Regional and Federal Studies* 15 (4) (2005); 423–36.

[39] *Scotland Devolution Monitoring Report* January 2006, p 118.

[40] P. Carmichael, *Central-Local Government Relations in the 1980s: Glasgow and Liverpool compared* (Aldershot: Avebury, 1995); P. Hennessy, *Whitehall* (London: Fontana, 1989).

[41] A. McConnell, *Scottish Local Government* (Edinburgh: Edinburgh University Press, 2004).

[42] M. Bennett, J. Fairley and M. McAteer, *Devolution in Scotland: The impact on local government* (York: Joseph Rowntree Foundation, 2002); *Scotland Devolution Monitoring Report*, November 2005.

[43] M. McAteer and M. Bennett, 'Devolution and Local Government: Evidence from Scotland', *Local Government Studies* 31 (3): (2005), 285–306.

particular standards of behaviour than in England.[44] In a nice touch of symmetry, Best Value is less tough, and is applied to the Scottish Executive as well as local government. In other words, while partnership in English local government is horizontal, in Scotland it is also supposed to be vertical.

In finance, the Executive has substantially increased its direct funding of local government. But the Executive has as much power over local government as Westminster. So when the council tax began to be a political problem, the Executive was also able and willing to state that there should be no council tax increases above 2.5% in 2006–7. This statement caused tensions in the partnership between the Executive and local government.[45] It also presaged major future conflict over the council tax, which came to a head when the SNP called for its abolition and replacement with a local income tax.

While the Scottish Executive can be expected to shift the funding base in accord with SNP promises, which may cause strife, the real rifts seem likely to be a result of policies on local government structure. This is an area in which Scotland's one really activist local government policy should have significant effects. The Scottish Executive has been fairly consistent in its treatment of local government organisation; it respects local government autonomy much more than England. First of all, it has done less. It rejected the prescriptive reform options offered to councils in England, opting instead to allow each authority to conduct its own review (Scottish local government after 1996 was much less diverse anyway). Only a few authorities came out in favour of English-style strong executives or elected provosts (mayors).[46] The major change, and the one that will reshape central-local relations was the Local Government (Scotland) Act 2003, driven by the Liberal Democrats and a few Labour reformers. This cleared a path for the introduction of STV in the 2007 local elections, despite opposition from COSLA.[47] This new electoral system produced coalition governments and is sure to alter local-devolved relations and parties (and has prompted a wave of retirements by councillors). The new councils will have to work out their new relationship with the central government, both sides learning anew. They will do this, however, in conditions that are likely to produce more comity and talk of partnership — coalition governments increase the likelihood of SNP representation in council leadership.

[44] McConnell 2004, pp. 161–78.

[45] C. Jeffery, 'Devolution and Local Government', *Publius: The journal of federalism* 36 (1) (2006): 57–74; Jenkins 1995; N. McGarvey, 'Intergovernmental Relations in Scotland Post Devolution', *Local Government Studies* 28 (3) (2002): 29–48; *Scotland Devolution Monitoring Report*, January 2006, p 95.

[46] McGarvey 2002.

[47] McConnell 2004.

Health

If foundation hospitals, as well as many other English health policy innovations, are about fragmenting the system in order to introduce competition, Scottish health policy has been about unification.[48] Rather than develop markets, NHS Scotland has consistently unified organisations in a way that precludes competition, and instead focused on partnership working as the most efficient way to run a health service. This meant unifying all the various health trusts into large territorial boards, and running some services (especially in cancer) on the basis of three large 'clinical networks'. It also meant some very tangible demonstrations of faith in professionals such as quicker introduction of pay increases for nurses in 2007 (to the irritation of UK ministers preoccupied with balancing the books of the English NHS).

In other words, Scotland's organisational strategy focused on integration within the NHS. Rather than differentiation and competition, it opted for integration and centralised priority-setting. Along with the elimination of the trusts came the reduction in managerial power — the larger health boards gained strategic capacity but lost managerial control over the front lines — management came to mean distant health boards rather than the Chief Executive in the next building over. The new SNP government, insofar as its health promises focused on policy rather than reconfiguration, promised more of what Labour had claimed to do: reduce the role of the private sector; create and extend partnership rather than competition; and focus on public health and the determinants of a healthy society.[49] A perfectly typical 21 June 2007 statement by new health minister Nicola Sturgeon combined the themes that Scottish parties share (despite Labour's quiet but intense affection for PFI): 'We believe it is sensible to deliver healthcare on the basis of collaboration and cooperation, rather than division and competition. We oppose the use of public money to help the private sector compete with the NHS'. And the distinctive addition of the SNP was to internationalise an interest shared by the Scottish parties; she concluded the statement by inviting other health ministers (regional, or even member-state) to a conference on the reduction of health inequalities in Europe.

How does this system deal with reconfiguration? In 2001, a Scottish interviewee, high-level then and higher-level now, commented in an interview that a reconfiguration will always be political, so (in contrast to England), it makes no sense to design a health system around periodic reconfigurations. Rather, systems should be designed to run efficiently on a day-to-day basis and ministers should brace themselves to sign off on reconfigurations. This

[48] D. Kerr and D. Feeley, 'Collectivism and Collaboration in NHS Scotland' in S.L. Greer and D. Rowland (eds.), *Devolving Policy, Diverging Values? The values of the United Kingdom's National Health Services* (London: The Nuffield Trust, 2007), pp. 29–36.

[49] S.L. Greer, 'The Fragile Divergence Machine: Citizenship, policy divergence, and intergovernmental relations', in Trench 2007.

interviewee captured the logic of Scottish health policy — the actions of a Health Board stick to a minister just as much in Scotland as elsewhere, and very little about policy-making shields the minister. After being tested once in the reconfiguration of Greater Glasgow services the centralised politics of reconfiguration got a larger outing in 2006–7.[50] The 'Kerr report' which mapped out a future for Scottish health services after extensive consultation, promised an attractive destination but included a number of closures.[51] Simultaneously, unrelated reconfigurations (including one in Lanarkshire, John Reid's territory) became politically contentious. Local communities organised, and in mid–2006 Scottish interviewees were worried that hospital closures would cost Labour the election. They arguably did. In 2003 this produced a number of strong independent candidacies; in 2007 the SNP seems to have successfully brought anti-reconfiguration campaigns under its wing. It also promised 'to keep health local', which means no further closures.

WALES: CARROTS AND COMMUNITARIANISM

If Scottish medical audiences can ask whether devolution affected Scottish public policy, nobody studying Wales could fail to notice the difference with devolution. The basic repeated style of Welsh policy-making is the use of inherited mechanisms such as contracting in health services or the basic local government style while bending them to reflect a strikingly Welsh focus on partnership with local government, communities and employees. It is manifest in efforts to work closely with local government (such as through the Partnership Council that links ministers and local authorities, or by tightening its relationships with NHS Wales) and in broader partnerships to achieve policy ends as well as in a well-articulated unwillingness to pursue confrontational English policies towards the public sector. Welsh policies share with Scotland a trust in partnership with providers and professionals, but differs in its relative lack of willingness to construct or reinforce quality control and discipline through professional leaders.[52] These differences are, in technical terms, often about things like the structuring of public services commissioning. However in political terms, the communitarian background rhetoric of Welsh politics makes them soon very different, as potentially they are.

What happens in practice is that Welsh policy style is focused on inducing partnership behaviour, with carrots and efforts to design communitarianism and cooperation into policy. The NAW and WAG are hampered by a lack of

[50] S.L. Greer, *Territorial Politics and Health Policy: UK health policy in comparative perspective* (Manchester: Manchester University Press, 2004).

[51] Scottish Executive, *A National Framework for Service Change in the NHS in Scotland: Building a health service fit for the future* (Edinburgh: The Stationery Office, 2005).

[52] Welsh Assembly Government, *Making the Connections* (Cardiff: Welsh Assembly Government, 2004).

both money and legislative authority, but when they have an option, they typically opt for the carrots that they have available over the sticks that they could use. The result is a system designed to promote joint working across sectors and local responsiveness, but without much use of the tougher coercive tools that are the focus of, for example, English policy.

This is likely to continue even despite the fact that the scale of political change in Wales is impressive and impressively quick. The single corporate body structure of the National Assembly for Wales, when it was created, was half utopia and half local government. Institutions were designed to promote unity and consensus rather than the politics of government and opposition. The next eight years of Welsh history were then spent untangling this arrangement and creating distinction to provide greater accountability for policy. But as the National Assembly and the Welsh Assembly Government have become disentangled, electoral politics has built pressure for increased consensus. That is because minority and coalition governments demand compromise. The voters and the electoral system are imposing the kind of bargained policy-making that the single corporate body was supposed to generate. It helps that the Welsh parties, which all need to get elected in Wales, share many policy ideas. The tortured negotiations in the early summer of 2007 over a possible 'Rainbow coalition,' as well as the Plaid Cymru-Labour talks, highlighted a very considerable amount of consensus on policy issues. It proved surprisingly easy to identify a coherent common platform between the different Welsh parties — far easier than their differing ideological families, activists, or social bases might suggest.

Education

Welsh medium schools have long been the most distinct feature of education in Wales, with other policy tracking England for a long time. This is partly because the modern Welsh education was split from a homogeneous England and Wales system rather than developing in parallel as happened in Scotland; the first major difference that anglophone students would have noticed was the different Welsh National Curriculum, introduced with the National Curriculum in 1986. Since devolution, though, Wales has diverged prominently in the organisation of education and use of testing as an instrument the centre uses to control schools. Compared to the English emphasis on raising standards through testing, Wales has used less 'stick' and more 'carrot': replacing tests at 7, 11 and 14 with teacher assessments, abolishing government-organised league tables, and focusing on the reduction of junior class sizes. Diversity and markets are also absent, with the Assembly Government pledging no new private sector schools and no specialist schools.[53] Wales is increasingly breaking away from its historic tendency to follow England with policies such as a new 14–19 program with a wider range of vocational options, an early years agenda including integrated childcare centres, or developing the Welsh Baccalaureate; a consultation on 'The Learning Country 2: Delivering the Promise', conducted in 2006, should lead to more such policies, including the creation of a 3–7 Foundation Phase.[54]

This distinct agenda took time to emerge, because Welsh political debate had further to travel from its pre-devolved state. The first Assembly spent much of its time in protracted legal arguments over its ability to make decisions on performance related pay, attempted to function with different ministers responsible for pre- and post-16 education, and chose a non-Welsh speaker with little background in education as one of those ministers.[55] The turning point came in 2001, with the publication of *Wales: The Learning Country*, which set out partnerships between local education authorities, schools, and the Assembly, made possible by Wales's small size. It emphasised raising standards by 'valuing and supporting the teaching system' within a 'fully comprehensive system of learning that serves all our local communities well'.[56]

A broad review of higher education followed in 2002. Finding itself in the unenviable position of controlling Welsh higher education spending but not student support, the Assembly Government successfully lobbied Westminster to extend its powers, then announced that there would be no top-up fees in Wales until at least 2007. It then introduced 'Assembly Learning Grants' to provide up to £1,500 per person per year for 'home' students, as well as finding means (the Assembly fees grant) to cushion the impact of variable fees on students resident in Wales attending Welsh institutions of higher education. This still left a funding gap between Welsh and major English universities, one that opposition parties claimed would damage Welsh higher education and led to the Welsh Assembly Government having great difficulty passing its budget in December 2006.

---

[53] *Wales Devolution Monitoring Report*, November 2001 (London: The Constitution Unit, 2001),, p. 17.

[54] D. Wincott, 'Devolution, Social Democracy and Policy Diversity in Britain; The case of early-childhood education and care', in K. Schmuecker and J. Adams (eds.), *Devolution in Practice 2006: Public policy differences within the UK* (London: Institute for Public Policy Research, 2006), pp. 76–97; *Wales Devolution Monitoring Report*, September 2006 (London: The Constitution Unit, 2006),p 13.

[55] *Wales Devolution Monitoring Report* August 2000 (London: The Constitution Unit, 2000).

[56] National Assembly for Wales, *The Learning Country: A Paving Document: A comprehensive education and lifelong learning programme to 2010 in Wales* (Cardiff: National Assembly for Wales, 2001).

Local Government

In local government, Wales is particularly distinctive for the good relations between the central and local; there is nothing like the Scottish Executive's arguments about rates, let alone the kinds of policy disputes found in England. Although legislation has tended to parcel Wales with England, a distinct Welsh local government policy community existed before devolution, as did separate Welsh branches of London-based local government organisations. The 1996 reorganisation that merged all Welsh local government into 22 unitary authorities enhanced Welsh distinctiveness. The relationship between the Welsh Office and local government was informal and consultative.[57] This partly reflected the small size of the policy community; the Welsh Office officials, far fewer than their equivalents in the UK departments responsible for local government, tended to develop better relationships (and possibly weaker oversight) as part of their adaptation to Welsh administrative conditions.

After devolution, the relative strength and professionalism of local government, and its connections with the Welsh Labour Party, made it a power. Relationships between local government and ministers in the Welsh office and the embeddedness of Welsh Labour within local councils all created fertile ground for future networks. Local government could supply policies that were distinctively Welsh — by virtue of being localist — and could fit with a political narrative of distinctive Welsh communitarianism. This gave it influence even beyond its unquestionable importance in the Welsh Labour Party.

Devolution increased the access and influence of local interests.[58] In inter-organisational relationships, the Welsh Assembly Government relies heavily on local authorities to deliver services and provide information.[59] Local government in Wales has therefore developed extensive collaborative partnerships with the Assembly which are less codified than their counterparts in Scotland. This closeness has been most clearly expressed in the 'Welsh way' as espoused by the former Minister for Finance, Local Government and Communities, Edwina Hart.[60]

'Freedom and Responsibility in Local Government,' published on St David's Day, 2002 emphasised clear national priorities, but expressed a

---

[57] G.A. Boyne, P. Griffiths, A. Lawton and J. Law, *Local Government in Wales: its role and functions* (York: Joseph Rowntree Foundation, 1991).

[58] Jeffery 2006; Jenkins 1995.

[59] *Wales Devolution Monitoring Report*, May 2002 (London: The Constitution Unit, 2002),, pp. 36–42; S. Thomas, 'Local Government and the National Assembly: a "Welsh Way" to public sector reform?', *Wales Law Journal* 2 (2002): 41–50.

[60] R. Rawlings, *Delineating Wales: Constitutional, legal and administrative aspects of national devolution* (Cardiff: University of Wales Press, 2003).

wish to determine these through local-regional partnerships.[61] The Local Government Partnership Council established in 1998 and the Welsh Local Government Association (WLGA) have been the main facilitators of this ideal. The result is a preference for softer regulation combined with reluctance to use more formal hypothecation.[62] 'Policy agreements' link local priorities with the national level since 2001, allowing for small variations across local authorities, while 'community strategies' provide a Welsh slant to the horizontal provider networks found in England. The process of evaluating and inspecting councils, compared to the English version, is also conciliatory and Wales has the lowest total capital stock of local government PFI schemes in Great Britain.[63] Northern Ireland, with a smaller population, has slightly fewer, and Scotland, by contrast, has the largest PFI local government stock in the UK.[64] In 2006 the Welsh Assembly Government bid for Westminster to pass a Local Government (Town and Community Councils) (Wales) Bill that would, among other changes, increase the partnership working abilities of Welsh local authorities.[65]

Health

Welsh health policy after devolution showed that politics abhors a vacuum.[66] Without the medical elites found in Scotland, or the management and economics infrastructure of English health policy, groups excluded from health policy in the rest of the UK came to the fore in Wales. This meant, above all, public health activists, local government, and the more communitarian, egalitarian parts of the Labour Party. Their health policy has had two major pillars. One was a shift of priorities towards public health and the reduction of health inequalities; the currency of such a commitment is the difficult-to-count one of budgets and policy initiatives such as Health Challenge Wales.[67] The other was a reorganisation intended to make NHS Wales operate in partnership with local government, addressing community needs and working in a joined-up way. That reorganisation put the core of commissioning in local health boards, which were made coterminous with local governments. The councils and local health boards (LHBs) were then given

[61] *Wales Devolution Monitoring Report*, May 2002 (London: The Constitution Unit, 2002), pp. 36–42.

[62] Rawlings 2003, p. 339.

[63] On inspections, see M. Laffin, G. Taylor and A. Thomas, *A New Partnership? The National Assembly for Wales and local government* (York; Joseph Rowntree Foundation, 2002).

[64] M. Hockridge, *Powering Ahead? A critique of the impact that the new freedoms and responsibilities available to local authorities are having on improved local service provision in Wales* (London: SOLACE Foundation Imprint, 2006), p. 20.

[65] *Wales Devolution Monitoring Report*, May 2006 (London: The Constitution Unit, 2006), p 51.

[66] P. Michael and D. Tanner, 'Values vs. Policy in the NHS Wales', in Greer and Rowland 2007, pp. 37–54; Greer 2004.

[67] S.L. Greer, 'Devolution and Public Health Politics in the UK' in S. Dawson (ed.), *Health Policy Futures* (Basingstoke: Palgrave, forthcoming 2008).

a variety of joint statutory responsibilities. This remains the form, although the inadequacies of LHBs mean there is constant talk of something different. Welsh policy-makers interviewed in 2002 agreed that 22 local health boards is too many, but argued that the goals of localism, partnership — and co-terminosity — were worth pursuing despite the problems of overly small commissioning organisations.

Assembly and Assembly Government faith in local partnership has been fairly consistent, even if it means loyalty to policies which are plagued by problems. The Welsh health plan was striking in its rhetoric — unlike the Scottish and English plans, it spoke not of the NHS but of health, and ways that the NHS and others could contribute.[68] This is still the push of policy; while the alternative Welsh parties all called for better management of the NHS itself, none of their manifestos disagreed with the argument that better health comes from a broad range of strategies.

Localism was supposed to provide the means for identifying and carrying out service reconfiguration. In theory, local needs identification through the LHBs would do the trick. It did not; LHBs for many reasons proved incapable of creating consensual reconfiguration. The system came under fire for inefficiency and poor quality. Eventually, finances, bad media, and poor quality scores meant that Labour put forth a strategy with conclusions that meant closures.[69] Shortly afterwards came the announcements of closure or downgrading for several hospitals; and local resistance. Other parties immediately pounced on Labour, opposing the local hospital closure plans in the run-up to the May 2007 elections. This probably contributed to the erosion of Labour seats — especially in the west. It also highlighted the extent to which localism can frustrate locals as much as the centre.

CONCLUSION: THE FUTURE

[Policy areas] are like the different windows of a house. Each window provides us with a different glimpse of the inside. Those who argue that the political logic of the problem is more important than the political logic of the country would expect the furnishings of each room to differ drastically in shape and color; after all, the living room serves a different purpose than the dining room or bedroom. Those who argue that the political logic of the country is more important than the political logic of the problem, on the other hand, would expect a uniform style throughout the house because the same people live, eat and sleep in different rooms. Some, finally, might agree [that] even though the political logic of the country is more compelling than the political logic of the problem, that political logic does not explain all policy cases equally well; deviations and exceptions do

---

[68] National Assembly for Wales, *Improving Health in Wales: A plan for the NHS with its partners* (Cardiff: National Assembly of Wales, 2001).

[69] Welsh Assembly Government, *Designed for Life: Creating World-class health and social care for Wales in the 21st century* (Cardiff: National Assembly for Wales, 2005).

exist ... Although each house has a distinctive style, it also has a couple of rooms filled with odd pieces and comfortable junk. Needless to say, these are not the first rooms shown to guests when they arrive.[70]

Devolution in the UK is about difference as much as anything else. In its origins and in the mindsets of many policy-makers, it is about doing things differently in different places.[71] It is, at a minimum, about putting barriers in that will preserve Scotland and Wales from future English policies. Institutional structures, meanwhile, promote difference, with distinctive party systems and policy communities pushing policies apart, and a nebulous system of intergovernmental relations permitting their divergence.[72]

The UK's four systems were always different on some level; administrative devolution created, if not much real autonomy, at least autochthonous elites who gave policy formulation and implementation a very different feel. The interaction of those elites with Westminster and nationalist parties created many of the distinctive policies of administrative devolution. And those elites, along with the distinctive parties of the different jurisdictions, matter because they remained when political devolution came.

Foreshadowed by administrative devolution, entrenched in the generally unspoken assumptions of policy elites, and often remarkably immune to party competition, these styles are distinctive and strong models of public administration. The governors of England, a large country with a small elite, have long focused on what Bulpitt called 'the autonomy of the centre'. This means a powerful central government trying to sculpt the system that will make subordinate units such as the NHS or local governments do what it wants. Since Thatcher, the chosen techniques have been delegation to quangos, top-down orders, and the development of markets within and across the public sector. Seemingly immune to paradox and irony, English policy-makers gather public sector organisations closer to them and exert ever greater control over their organisation in an effort to make them innovative and autonomous.

Scotland, by contrast, a small country with an impressively dense growth of elites, has opted for partnership between the major institutions. Above all, this means a more egalitarian relationship between the Executive and local government than law (or the attitudes found in England) would demand, and a respect for the teaching and health professions. It also works out, given the constraints of size and a lack of faith in competition between hospitals or universities, to a distinctive and promising Scottish reliance on networks of shared resources in fields as disparate as cancer care and university science research. Wales, meanwhile, has with surprising speed, filled in a policy

[70] Katzenstein 1987, pp 362–3.
[71] A. Kay 'Evaluating Devolution in Wales', *Political Studies* 51(1) (2003): 51–66, makes the argument that this is the appropriate way to judge devolution.
[72] Greer 2007, 'Fragile Divergence Machine'.

style of its own as policy-makers work out the policy approaches that will 'work' in the particular politics and administrative structure of Wales — with a focus on partnership and communities, in rhetoric and efforts to appeal to producers and communities alike through joint working, consultation, and efforts to increase democracy into the public services.

Policy styles can change, of course, because they are reflections of and adaptations to politics. Whether quickly or glacially, party cleavages freeze and melt and policy communities change. Those changes will change the policies that can work politically and administratively, as well as the makeup and power of policy communities; the greater balance between legislature and executive in Scotland and Wales should make it slightly harder.[73] The consensus about Britain in the 1970s, including among the inventors of the concept of a 'policy style,' was that Britain was bound to constant negotiations and consensus among interest groups.[74] Twenty years later, the policy style in England, the nearest inheritor of 'British' politics, is one of imposition, markets, and management — and we seek the ancestry of Thatcher and Blair in the once-repressed figures of Bentham and Gradgrind. Party politics and changes in the structure of policy-making explain the transition; the changing policy style captures the depth and nature of the change. Devolution brought about such changes, with, for example, Wales becoming much more friendly to local government and localism once freed of the influence Whitehall once exerted over the Welsh Office.

What could change them now? The structures of party competition and policy advice are difficult to change; the transformation of London's policy communities under Thatcher, and the shift by the Labour Party that consolidated the new English policy style, took around twenty years. The early years of devolution are likely to prove to be a 'critical juncture,' a moment in which politics and policy styles took the form that they will retain for a long time.[75] The policy styles that evolved in England, Scotland, and Wales are policy-makers' adaptations to their realities — their established ways of making policy that fit with the politics and administrative constraints that they face. Over and over again, networks and professionalism work for policy-makers as a way to produce Scottish policy, as do the various forms of technocratic disengagement that English policy-makers choose. The policy styles, as tools to deal with the characteristic issues in policy-making, reflect their politics today as well as their administrative and political histories. They are good and well-adapted tools for the real political problems of

---

[73] J.J. Richardson, 'Government, Interest Groups and Policy Change', *Political Studies* 48 (5) (2000): 1006–25.

[74] S.H. Beer, *Modern British Politics: Parties and pressure groups in the collectivist age* (London: Faber and Faber, 1982); G. Jordan and J.J. Richardson, 'The British Policy Style or Logic of Negotiation?' in Richardson 1982, *Policy Styles,* pp. 80–110.

[75] P. Pierson, *Politics in Time: History, institutions and social analysis* (Princeton, NJ: Princeton University Press, 2004).

policy-makers, however obnoxious the tools may be to policy analysts, and however self-inflicted the problems.

The question of whether they will change, then, requires identifying what might change the politics and policies of the three systems. What could force change or convergence? The striking thing about party political competition is the extent to which it does *not* change policy styles. Nobody could mistake the SNP's policy choices for those of the Conservatives, or even UK Labour, but it would be easy to confuse many of them with Scottish Labour's policies. The same holds for England and Wales. The major UK parties are more like each other than they are like the major Welsh or Scottish parties. In addition, it is difficult to change policy communities; while the rise of managerialist, pro-market, policy communities in England is a striking case of change, it was also a highly contested twenty-year evolution from 1979 to the first years of the Blair government.

What, then, are the prospects for change in policy styles from outside? There are forces for convergence. The principal one at present is the European Union, which is increasingly regulating policy choices by governments.[76] EU law demands that member state and regional governments, in their policy choices, comply with the requirements of EU law (most easily summarised as the freedom of movement of goods, services, capital and people). It might rule out some options by imposing EU competition and state aid law (which, crudely, ban discrimination in favour of public providers when they are in competition with private providers). It might rule out others by, for example, regulating health services under the law of the single European internal market. And it is striving mightily to produce coordination through 'soft law' mechanisms such as the 'open method of coordination'. This is a thinly-veiled effort to produce EU-wide harmonisation, and the differences between Scotland and Wales (mere regions) are even harder to protect than the differences between member states like France and Finland.

A second source of potential change would be changes in intergovernmental relations — in the permissive structure that allows the devolved administrations such latitude to adopt their own welfare state policies within the limits of a block grant. Their autonomy is vulnerable because the Barnett formula does not necessarily safeguard it (and could be changed), and because a UK Government, with more or less ingenuity and determination, could circumscribe the autonomy of the devolved governments. Such efforts by central governments to impose policy priorities on other governments are the stuff of intergovernmental relations elsewhere, and as the other chapters of this book make clear they could easily happen in the UK. So people who

[76] Greer 2005, pp. 201–24.

care about the distinctive policy trajectories of the UK should care about the
technical and oddly cloudy area of intergovernmental relations.

But, for now, any intelligent observer can note the different 'feel' of politics in Cardiff, Edinburgh, and London. Not just the size, manners, and
personalities change, but the issues taken seriously, the people taken seriously, and the arguments taken seriously change. Contempt for local government is loud in SW1 and quiet, or loud but private, in Cardiff Bay. McKinsey
staff have passes to Whitehall buildings, not to Cathays Park or St Andrew's
House, and that is not only because of the relatively greater contracts available in Whitehall. Respect for private providers of health care is *de rigueur*
at London health policy events, and hard to gauge at events elsewhere
because Humana or UnitedHealth are not invited. Almost everybody but the
ministerial special advisors and private consultancies can be seen in London
as 'vested interests'; policy-makers in Scotland and Wales are much less free
with that term, and far more prone to talk of 'stakeholders'. These differences do not just add up to different ways of working; they are also the mark-
ers of different political processes that give us what we see today - different
policy styles.

BIBLIOGRAPHY

Official Documents and Primary Sources

Department for Communities and Local Government, *Strong and prosperous
  communities: The local government white paper* (London: The Stationery
  Office, 2005).
Department for Education and Skills, *Higher Standards, Better Schools for All:
  More choice for parents and pupils* (London: The Stationery Office, 2005).
National Assembly for Wales, *Improving Health in Wales: A plan for the NHS
  with its partners* (Cardiff: National Assembly of Wales, 2001).
National Assembly for Wales, *The Learning Country: A Paving Document: A
  comprehensive education and lifelong learning programme to 2010 in Wales*
  (Cardiff: National Assembly for Wales, 2001).
Office of the Deputy Prime Minister, *Evaluation of Local Strategic Partner-
  ships: Report of a survey of all English LSPs*, February 2003 (London:
  ODPM, 2003).
Scottish Executive, *A National Framework for Service Change in the NHS in
  Scotland: Building a health service fit for the future* (Edinburgh: The Statio-
  nery Office, 2005).
Welsh Assembly Government, *Making the Connections* (Cardiff: Welsh Assem-
  bly Government, 2004).
Welsh Assembly Government, *Designed for Life: Creating world-class health
  and social care for Wales in the 21st century* (Cardiff: National Assembly for
  Wales, 2005).

Secondary References

Barber, M., *Instruction to Deliver: Tony Blair, the public services, and the challenge of delivery* (London: Politico's, 2007).

Beer, S.H., *Modern British Politics: Parties and pressure groups in the collectivist age* (London: Faber and Faber, 1982).

Bennett M, J. Fairley and M. McAteer, *Devolution in Scotland: The impact on local government* (York, Joseph Rowntree Foundation, 2002).

Blondel J., *Comparative Government* (New York: Harvester Wheatsheaf, 1995).

Boyne, G.A., P. Griffiths, A. Lawton and J. Law, *Local Government in Wales: Its role and functions* (York: Joseph Rowntree Foundation, 1991).

Bradbury, J., 'Territory and Power Revisited: Theorising territorial politics in the united Kingdom after devolution', *Political Studies* 54: 559–82, (2006).

Bulpitt, J., *Territory and Power in the United Kingdom: An interpretation* (Manchester: Manchester University Press, 1983).

Butler, D., A. Adonis and T. Travers, *Failure in British Government: The politics of the poll tax* (Oxford: Oxford University Press, 1994).

Cairney, P., 'New Public Management and the Thatcher Healthcare Legacy: Enough of the theory, what about the implementation?', *British Journal of Politics and International Relations*, 4 (3): (2002):375–98.

Cairney, P., 'What Is This Thing Called 'Policy Style? A comparative analysis of Britain since devolution'. Paper presented at University of Aberdeen, Department of Politics and International Relations Research-in-Progress Seminar, February 2007).

Carmichael, P., *Central-Local Government Relations in the 1980s: Glasgow and Liverpool compared* (Aldershot: Avebury, 1995).

Chitty, C., *Education Policy in Great Britain* (Basingstoke: Palgrave Macmillan, 2004).

Deacon, R.M., *The Governance of Wales: The Welsh Office and the policy process, 1964–1999.* (Cardiff: Welsh Academic Press, 2002).

Game, C., 'Mayors, Monitors and Measurers: Blair's Legacy to Local Democracy'. Paper presented at British Politics Group conference on 'Britain After Blair', Chicago, 28 August 2007.

Greer, S.L., *Territorial Politics and Health Policy: UK health policy in comparative perspective* (Manchester: Manchester University Press, 2004).

Greer, S.L., 'Becoming European: Devolution, Europe and Health Policy-Making', in A. Trench (ed.), *The Dynamics of Devolution: The State of the Nations 2005* (Exeter: Imprint Academic, 2005), pp. 201–24.

Greer, S.L., 'The politics of policy divergence', in S.L. Greer (ed.), *Territory, Democracy, and Justice* (Basingstoke: Palgrave Macmillan, 2006).

Greer, S.L., *Nationalism and Self-Government: The politics of autonomy in Scotland and Catalonia* (Albany: State University of New York Press, (2007).

Greer, S.L., 'The Fragile Divergence Machine: Citizenship, policy divergence, and intergovernmental relations', in A. Trench (ed.), *Devolution and Power in the United Kingdom* (Manchester: Manchester University Press, 2007).

Greer, S.L., 'Devolution and Public Health Politics in the UK', in S. Dawson (ed.), *Health Policy Futures* (Basingstoke: Palgrave, forthcoming 2008).

Greer, S.L. and H. Jarman, 'Devolution and Policy Styles in the United Kingdom.' Paper presented at the Political Studies Association Specialist Group on Territorial Politics conference, Queen's University Belfast, 11–13 January, 2006.

Hennessy, P., *Whitehall* (London: Fontana, 1989).

Hockridge, M., *Powering Ahead? A critique of the impact that the new freedoms and responsibilities available to local authorities are having on improved local service provision in Wales* (London: SOLACE Foundation Imprint, 2006).

Jeffery, C., 'Devolution and Local Government', *Publius: The journal of federalism* 36 (1): (2006), 57–74,

Jenkins, S., *Accountable to None: The Tory nationalisation of Britain* (Harmondsworth: Penguin, 1995).

Jordan, A., 'Environmental Policy', in I. Bache and A. Jordan (eds.), *The Europeanisation of British Politics* (Basingstoke: Palgrave Macmillan, 2006), 231–47.

Jordan, G. and Richardson, J.J., 'The British Policy Style or Logic of Negotiation?', in J.J. Richardson (ed.), *Policy Styles in Western Europe* (London: George Allen & Unwin, 1982), 80–110.

Katzenstein, P., *Policy and Politics in West Germany: The growth of a semisovereign state* (Philadelphia: Temple University Press, 1987).

Kay, A., 'Evaluating Devolution in Wales', *Political Studies* 51 (1) (2003): 51–66 .

Keating, M., *The Government of Scotland* (Edinburgh: Edinburgh University Press, 2005).

Keating, M., 'Higher Education in Scotland and England after Devolution', *Regional and Federal Studies* 15 (4) (2005): 423–36.

D. Kerr and D. Feeley, 'Collectivism and Collaboration Values in NHS Scotland' in S.L Greer and D Rowland (eds.), *Devolving Policy, Diverging Values? The values of the United Kingdom's National Health Services* (London: The Nuffield Trust, 2007), pp. 29–36.

Klein, R., *The New Politics of the NHS* (London: Longman, 2000).

Knill, C., *The Europeanisation of National Administrations: Patterns of institutional change and persistence* (Cambridge: Cambridge University Press, 2001).

Laffin, M., G. Taylor and A. Thomas, *A New Partnership? The National Assembly for Wales and Local Government* (York: Joseph Rowntree Foundation, 2002).

Loughlin, M., 'The Restructuring of Central-Local Government Relations', in J. Jowell and D. Oliver (eds.), *The Changing Constitution* (Oxford: Oxford University Press, 2000), pp. 137–66.

McAteer, M. and M. Bennett, 'Devolution and Local Government: Evidence from Scotland', *Local Government Studies* 31 (3) (2005): 285–306.

McConnell, A., *Scottish Local Government* (Edinburgh: Edinburgh University Press, 2004).

McCrone, D., *Understanding Scotland: The sociology of a stateless nation* (London: Routledge, 1992).

McGarvey, N., 'Intergovernmental Relations in Scotland Post Devolution', *Local Government Studies* 28 (3) (2002): 29–48.

McPherson, A. and C.D. Raab, *Governing Education: A sociology of policy since 1945* (Edinburgh: Edinburgh University Press, 1988).

Michael, P. and D. Tanner, 'Values vs. Policy in the NHS Wales', in S.L Greer and D Rowland (eds.), *Devolving Policy, Diverging Values? The values of the United Kingdom's National Health Services* (London: The Nuffield Trust, 2007), pp. 37–54.

Milburn, A., *Shifting the Balance of Power in the NHS*. Speech given at the launch of the NHS Modernisation Agency, 25 April 2001 (London: Department of Health, 2001).

Mitchell, J. *Governing Scotland* (Basingstoke: Palgrave Macmillan, 2003).

Mitchell, J., 'Scotland: Devolution is not just for Christmas', in A. Trench (ed.), *The Dynamics of Devolution: The State of the Nations 2005* (Exeter: Imprint Academic, 2005), 23–42.

Moore, C. and S. Booth, *Managing Competition: Meso-Corporatism, Pluralism, and the Negotiated Order in Scotland* (Oxford: Clarendon, 1989).

Paterson, L., *Scottish Education in the Twentieth Century* (Edinburgh: Edinburgh University Press, 2004).

Pierson, P., *Politics in Time: History, institutions and social analysis* (Princeton: Princeton University Press, 2004).

Pollitt, C., *Managerialism and the Public Services* (Oxford: Blackwell, 1993).

Rao, N., *Towards Welfare Pluralism: Public services in a time of change* (Aldershot: Dartmouth, 1996).

Rawlings, R., *Delineating Wales: Constitutional, legal and administrative aspects of national devolution* (Cardiff: University of Wales Press, 2003).

Richardson, J.J., 'Convergent Policy Styles in Europe?', in J.J. Richardson (ed.), *Policy Styles in Western Europe* (London: George Allen & Unwin, 1982), pp. 197–210.

Richardson, J.J., 'Government, Interest Groups and Policy Change', *Political Studies*, 48: 1006–25, (2000).

Rose, R., *Ministers and Ministries: A Functional Analysis* (Oxford: Clarendon, 1987).

Schmuecker, K. and J. Adams (eds), *Devolution in Practice 2006: Public policy differences within the UK* (London: Institute for Public Policy Research, 2006).

Scotland Devolution Monitoring Reports, 1999-date, available at www.ucl.ac.uk/constitution-unit/publications/devolution-monitoring-reports/index.html

Silberman, B.S., *Cages of Reason: The rise of the rational state in France, Japan, the United States, and Great Britain* (Chicago: University of Chicago Press, 1993).

Stevens, S., 'Reform Strategies for the English NHS', *Health Affairs* 23 (2004): 37–44.

Sturm, R., 'Policy-Making in a New Political Landscape', in S. Padgett, W.E. Paterson and G. Smith (eds.), *Developments in German Politics* 3 (Basingstoke: Palgrave Macmillan, 2003), 101–20.

Thomas, S., 'Local Government and the National Assembly: a 'Welsh Way' to Public Sector Reform?', *Wales Law Journal* 2 (2002); 41–50 .

Trench, A. and H. Jarman, 'The Practical Outcomes of Devolution: Policy-Making Across the UK', in A. Trench (ed.), *Devolution and Power in the United Kingdom* (Manchester: Manchester University Press, 2007).

Wilson, D. and C. Game, *Local Government in the United Kingdom* (Basingstoke: Palgrave Macmillan, 2002).

Wincott, D., 'Devolution, Social Democracy and Policy Diversity in Britain; the case of early-childhood education and care', in K. Schmuecker and J. Adams (eds.), *Devolution in Practice 2006: Public policy differences within the UK* (London; Institute for Public Policy Research, 2006), 76–97.

Woll, C., 'Lobbying in the European Union: From *sui generis* to a comparative perspective', *Journal of European Public Policy* 13(3) (2006): 456–69.

Vogel, D., *National Styles of Regulation: Environmental policy in Great Britain and the United States* (Ithaca, NY: Cornell University Press, 1986).

Wales Devolution Monitoring Reports, December 1999-date, available at www.ucl.ac.uk/constitution-unit/publications/devolution-monitoring-reports/index.html

8

Lost Souls in the Lobbies?
Backbenchers from Scotland and Wales in Post-Devolution Westminster

Akash Paun[1]

Long before devolution, students of territorial politics were familiar with the notion that the UK should be considered a 'union' rather than a 'unitary' state.[2] This reflected the fact that 'the nation-building process in the UK was not a simple story of centrally-imposed homogeneity' but rather that each part was integrated into the UK state in a different and asymmetrical way.[3] In institutional terms the essence of a union state is the absence of administrative standardisation across the entire territory of the nation, and the 'survival in some areas of variations based upon pre-union rights and infrastructures'.[4] This includes, in the UK case, the separate legal systems for Scotland and Northern Ireland and the existence of the three territorial offices of state in Whitehall.

At Westminster, the asymmetrical union state was embodied in a raft of specialised structures and procedures established to fulfil the representative, legislative and scrutiny functions of Parliament along territorial lines. All three 'Celtic' territories had separate grand committees, select committees and question times, enabling members of the different territories to scrutinise legislation and executive activity applying to their part of the UK. In addition, two Scottish Standing Committees undertook the committee stage of many bills emanating from the Scottish Office and the Scottish backbenches.

From the perspective of MPs from constituencies in Scotland, Wales or Northern Ireland, one could speak of two separate 'levels' or 'spheres' of politics within which to operate.[5] One is of matters relating solely to their

[1] I would like to thank Robert Hazell and Alan Trench for their comments and suggestions, and René Holbach and Maria Stemmler for research assistance.
[2] See S. Rokkan and D.W. Urwin, *Economy, Territory, Identity: Politics of West European peripheries* (London: Sage, 1983); and J. Mitchell, 'Scotland in the Union, 1945–95: The Changing Nature of the Union State', in T.M. Devine and R.J. Finlay (eds.), *Scotland in the Twentieth Century* (Edinburgh: Edinburgh University Press, 1996).
[3] M. Laffin and A. Thomas, 'The United Kingdom: Federalism in Denial?', *Publius: The Journal of Federalism*, 29 (3) (1999): 89–107, p. 91.
[4] Rokkan and Urwin 1983, p. 181.
[5] In the main, this chapter does not consider the roles or behaviour of MPs from Northern Ireland. The specific political circumstances (including the long suspension of devolution between 2002 and

own territory, and the other is that covering UK-wide policy domains, which could have a more or less direct impact on the separate territorial spheres.[6] Scots in particular were sometimes said to inhabit a 'parliament within a parliament', with the Grand Committee described, and sometimes even addressed, as 'Scotland's Parliament'.[7] The significance of the Scottish committees as a parallel sphere of legislative activity is underlined by the high proportion of bills that followed the territorial path through the House of Commons.[8]

Pre-devolution analyses confirmed that the behaviour of Scots in the House of Commons was different in significant ways from that of their colleagues from elsewhere in the UK:

> Scottish MPs are a distinct group in the House of Commons. They have their own Bills to discuss; their own committees to sit on; and their own ministers to question. These activities set them apart from other members, who do not share their duties and interests.[9]

Scottish members typically focussed more on domestic and local issues, and less on international affairs or macroeconomic policy than their English counterparts. The majority of Scottish members were described as operating principally at the Scottish level where they 'concentrate on securing benefits for Scotland and are not fully integrated into the UK political system'.[10] An analysis of Scottish members' participation in question time similarly concluded that 'Scottish MPs devote the overwhelming proportion of their activity to Questions specifically concerned with Scotland.'[11]

There is also evidence that Welsh MPs could be considered a distinct group, though this is less well documented. As early as 1978 it was noted that the demands of committee work forced most Welsh MPs 'either to specialise in...Welsh Affairs or to increase their work-rate in order to participate in other areas of government activity'.[12] However, the smaller sphere of responsibility of the Welsh Office compared with its Scottish sister, coupled

2007) and the separate party system of Northern Ireland raise an entirely different set of issues which are beyond the scope of this chapter.

   [6] M.J. Keating, 'Parliamentary Behaviour as a Test of Scottish Integration into the United Kingdom', *Legislative Studies Quarterly*, 3 (3) (1978): 409–30 at p. 409.

   [7] G.E. Edwards, 'The Scottish Grand Committee, 1958 to 1970', *Parliamentary Affairs*, 25 (4) (1971): 303–25, p. 322.

   [8] One study found that of 23 bills certified by the Speaker as relating exclusively to Scotland in the 1966–67 and 1967–68 sessions, 12 received their second reading in the Scottish Grand Committee and 17 were considered in Scottish Standing Committee at the committee stage. See J.G. Kellas, *The Scottish Political System* (Cambridge: Cambridge University Press, 1984), pp. 88–9.

   [9] Kellas 1984, p. 81.

   [10] Keating 1978, p. 409.

   [11] D. Judge and D.A. Finlayson, 'Scottish Members of Parliament: Problems of Devolution', *Parliamentary Affairs*, 28 (1) (1975): 278–92 at p. 283.

   [12] W. Mishler and A. Mughan, 'Representing the Celtic Fringe: Devolution and Legislative Behaviour in Scotland and Wales', *Legislative Studies Quarterly*, (3) 3 , (1978): 377–408 at p. 380.

with the greater scepticism among Labour MPs about specific Welsh solutions, meant that Welsh members were more integrated into the UK mainstream. The Welsh Grand Committee provided less focus for Welsh politics than that of Scotland due to the absence of Wales-only bills. Consequently, it was not widely considered an important institution either in its first incarnation in the 1960s and 1970s or as part of John Major's anti-devolutionist 'Grand Committee strategy' in the 1990s.[13] The Committee on Welsh Affairs established in 1979 had a greater impact, although accounts of its early years reveal an ambivalence among members about its *raison d'etre*.[14] It was also criticised as 'largely ineffective' at holding accountable the institutions of Welsh government.[15] At the same time, the ongoing process of 'administrative devolution' saw those institutions — the Welsh Office and its associated 'quangocracy' — steadily growing in importance, thereby creating the space for a more extensive Welsh sphere of political action at Westminster.[16] In addition, the new, if fragile, ascendancy of Labour's pro-devolutionist wing, combined with the decline of the Conservatives in the principality, supports the idea of a growing focus on Welsh issues among Welsh members over the twenty years preceding devolution (albeit it that this was insufficient to keep pace with the widening 'democratic deficit').

However we understand the pre-devolution Scottish and Welsh political spheres at Westminster, what is clear is that with devolution, many of the key policy areas where MPs from Scotland or Wales might have different interests and preferences from England have been transferred to Holyrood and Cardiff Bay. This could have been expected to herald the demise of the separate territorial political spheres at Westminster. However, as discussed in previous volumes in the *State of the Nations* series, the institutional architecture of territorial representation at Westminster has remained largely untouched, with standing orders still providing for separate territorial committees, legislative procedures and question times.[17] This may reflect the 'counterintuitive and messy' nature of British institutional reform, and the survival of the territorial offices of state in Whitehall, whose contours are reflected in the committee system.[18] Alternatively, it may indicate that the

---

[13] J.B. Jones and R.A. Wilford, *Parliament and Territoriality: The Committee on Welsh Affairs, 1979–1983*. (Cardiff: University of Wales Press, 1986), p. 9; J.B. Jones, 'Changes to the Government of Wales' in J.B. Jones and D. Balsom (eds.), *The Road to National Assembly for Wales* (Cardiff: University of Wales Press, 2000), p. 24.

[14] Jones and Wilford 1986, p. 17.

[15] R. Rawlings, *Delineating Wales: Constitutional, legal and administrative aspects of national devolution* (Cardiff: University of Wales Press, 2003), p. 30.

[16] See K. Morgan and K. Mungham, *Redesigning Democracy: The making of the Welsh Assembly* (Bridgend: Seren, 2000), p. 45.

[17] G. Lodge, M. Russell and O. Gay, 'The Impact of Devolution on Westminster' in A. Trench, (ed.) *Has Devolution Made a Difference? The State of the Nations 2004* (Exeter: Imprint Academic, 2004), p. 194.

[18] Lodge, Russell and Gay 2004, pp. 212–3.

territorial structures and processes of the House of Commons have adapted
to the new circumstances in which they find themselves.

This chapter seeks to shed further light on this issue. But rather than
posing the question of what functions are played by the territorial machinery
at Westminster, it focuses instead on the *behaviour* of MPs from different
parts of the UK. As noted, pre-devolution research found that representatives from Scotland and Wales acted differently from the English in significant ways. Following in the footsteps of these studies, it addresses three
questions:

1. whether there are significant quantitative differences in the work-
    load of the three national groups of MPs;

2. whether the three national groups differ in terms of the activities and
    policy areas on which they focus;

3. after examining empirical evidence about the current situation,
    which factors are likely to have an impact on Scottish and Welsh
    members' behaviour in future.

One possible finding would be that Scottish, Welsh and English MPs now
behave in an indistinguishable manner from one another. Given the extensive evidence that this was not the case prior to devolution, this would imply
that since the establishment of the devolved bodies, there has been an *integration* of the previously differentiated activities of the various groups of
MPs. Arguably, this might represent a 'reintegration' process, with territory
and nationality resuming its former status as 'embellishment and detail',
marginal to the principal cleavages within the British political system.[19]

However, it is in fact highly unlikely that we would uncover integration in
the pure sense of essentially identical behaviour by MPs from across the
country. At the least, we would expect to find variation in the workload of
Scottish, Welsh and English MPs. In particular, this is likely to be reflected
in terms of constituency casework and legislative scrutiny given that much
of this relates to matters that are now devolved in Scotland or Wales. These
categories of work are largely reactive tasks from an MP's perspective, and
for Scots at least, both are likely to have fallen as a result of the transfer of
major policy areas to the new devolved bodies. What we might call the
underemployment hypothesis was posited prior to the failed 1970s devolution project, when it was predicted that devolution might lead to a 'Scottish
[and Welsh] group of 'lost souls' at Westminster'.[20] Evidence that Scottish
and Welsh members have less work to do would support this prediction.
Arguably, it would also represent a reversal of the pre-devolution situation

---

[19] Pulzer cited in W. Mishler, 'Scotching Nationalism in the British Parliament: Crosscutting
Cleavages among MPs', *Legislative Studies Quarterly,* 9 (1) (1983): 5–28, p. 5.
[20] Judge and Finlayson 1975, p. 292.

when non-English members were said to suffer from 'relative overwork', at least if they wanted to play any role in UK-wide matters as well as meeting the demands of territorial scrutiny.[21]

A more positive interpretation of the likely effects of devolution was made by the Kilbrandon Commission on the Constitution in 1973. It suggested that Scottish and Welsh members would 'be freed of a great deal of constituency business', and would therefore 'have more time to devote to the reserved matters like constitutional and external affairs, defence, finance and trade and industry, and to European Affairs'.[22] The idea that devolution would create a new cohort of *'national [UK] Members of Parliament'* was deemed naïve by some, given the pre-devolution focus on constituency and domestic policy matters among many MPs.[23] Evidence of a disproportionate emphasis on UK matters among Scottish and Welsh members, however, could support this thesis. It is worth noting that the 1990s blueprints for devolution — the report of the Scottish Constitutional Convention and the White Paper on *Scotland's Parliament* — did not address this issue.[24]

Alternatively, it may be that Scottish and Welsh MPs have diverted their efforts to UK (or England-Wales) policy issues but with a view to advancing the interests of their territory rather than as members of a UK-wide polity. This would suggest the emergence of *'territorial advocates'* rather than UK-focussed 'national MPs'. This was in fact, one of the roles that pre-devo-lution Scottish members often played. Keating found that although Scottish MPs in the 1970s acted predominantly at the 'Scottish level', when they did participate in UK-wide policy and legislative debates, it was usually in policy areas 'in which there was scope for promoting Scottish material inter-ests' such as agriculture and industrial policy.[25]

A final possibility is that MPs have responded to devolution by seeking out new roles in keeping with the 'multi-level' character of contemporary Scottish and Welsh governance. Specifically, MPs may play a role in facili-tating *linkage* between the central and peripheral tiers of governance. This might entail developing relations with members of the Scottish Parliament or National Assembly, scrutinising the intergovernmental aspects of post-devolution governance, or engaging in policy debates that are no longer the responsibility of Westminster. This last option is the most difficult to find

---

[21] Mishler and Mughan 1978, pp. 379–80. Mishler and Mughan also point out that the greater per capita representation of Scotland and Wales did not compensate for this as 'Notwithstanding their substantial overrepresentation...the absolute number of Scottish and Welsh MPs is quite small'...

[22] Royal Commission on the Constitution [The Kilbrandon Commission] *Report on the Constitution* Cmnd 5460 (London: The Stationery Office, 1973), p. 246.

[23] Judge and Finlayson 1975, p. 292.

[24] Scottish Constitutional Convention, *Scotland's Parliament, Scotland's Right* (Edinburgh: Scottish Constitutional Convention, 1995); Scottish Office, *Scotland's Parliament* Cm 3658 (London: The Stationery Office, 1997).

[25] Keating 1978, p. 419.

evidence for, as this chapter is concerned with observable behaviour and many 'linkage' type activities would be likely to take place behind the scenes, for instance through intra-party channels. Nonetheless this possibility needs to be kept in mind and we will return to it in the final section of the chapter.

Prior to that, the chapter discusses three types of empirical evidence. First, it examines data about the quantity of work that MPs from the different nations undertake. This is relevant not only as a test of the 'underemployment' and 'integration' hypotheses, but also for placing in context discussion about the search for new post-devolution roles. Secondly, it explores the territorial elements of the House of Commons' legislative process; in this area, as with constituency relations, devolution was expected to strip Scottish and (to a lesser extent) Welsh MPs of much of their workload. However, it is also possible that devolution has thrown up new legislative scrutiny tasks for MPs. The third section looks at the use of parliamentary questions for insight into the policy and executive scrutiny activities of MPs. Here we discuss whether a new-found UK focus is apparent among Scots and Welsh members and whether this points toward the emergence of either 'national (UK) members' or 'territorial advocates'.

Three caveats should be made at this point. First, the various scenarios mapped above are not mutually exclusive; rather, elements of each are likely to be discernible. Secondly, although short-hand descriptions used may sometimes lump Scotland and Wales together, it is likely that the behaviour of Scottish and Welsh MPs differs in significant respects, as indeed it did prior to devolution. Thirdly, given the wide range of activities undertaken by MPs that are beyond the scope of this discussion, much of the texture and detail of parliamentary life's rich tapestry is omitted. For instance, there is no consideration in any detail of the role of select committees as our interest lies in the behaviour of MPs as individuals. Nonetheless it is possible to reach some preliminary conclusions about behavioural differences between the various national groups in the Commons. This in turn will enable us to sketch the contours of the Scottish and Welsh political spheres as they operate at Westminster today.

THE WORKLOAD OF MPS:
TESTING THE UNDEREMPLOYMENT HYPOTHESIS

Measuring the overall amount of work done by MPs is a difficult task. However, two different sources of data are available to give us some indication of whether there is variation in the average workload of English, Scottish and Welsh members.

First, an objective record of certain aspects of MPs' work comes from the publication (by the House of Commons) of expenses claimed by MPs. Of the different categories of expenses listed, the one that might be considered the most useful proxy for MPs' workloads is the postage expenses claimed. Here the data clearly show that English MPs claim significantly more than either the Scots or Welsh. This difference is even more striking when a straight comparison is made between Labour backbenchers from the three countries, which corrects for any bias that might result from behavioural differences between MPs of different parties or between ministers and backbench MPs (as both are to be found on Labour, but not opposition, benches). The most likely explanation for this is that the volume of constituency casework has fallen as a result of devolution, with much of this workload now being handled by members of the devolved legislatures.

The second source of relevant data is from surveys of MPs conducted by Russell and Bradbury.[26] According to these figures (which are self-reported and partial), Scottish MPs do work fewer hours than their English counterparts. Breaking these data into different categories of activity reveals that the discrepancy is predominantly located in the field of work related to the constituency. As for Welsh members, although they claim to work more than their English counterparts overall, they too spend significantly less time on constituency business.

Comparing survey data from before and after devolution, Russell and Bradbury suggest that there is a significant, and probably widening, disparity between English and Scottish/Welsh MPs in the time devoted to casework though 'the gap is not as large as might have been expected if casework were distributed between the [devolved and UK] institutions on the basis of policy relevance alone.' They conclude that 'MPs in Scotland and Wales are reluctant to give up their constituency activities' and may undertake proactive measures to boost their constituency profile in the face of competition from MSPs and AMs, or may simply spend longer on the cases they receive.[27] And indeed, the final row in Figure 8.1 shows that Scottish and Welsh members claim to hold constituency surgeries more frequently than the English, which could be interpreted as part of an attempt to generate additional constituency work. Alternatively, it could reflect a differential propensity to focus on constituency work either between the different national groups of MPs or between the political parties (with Labour over-represented in Wales and Scotland).[28]

[26] M. Russell and J. Bradbury, 'Devolution, Elected Representatives and Constituency Representation in Scotland and Wales, 2000–2005', database SN 5443 at Economic and Social Data Service, (2006).

[27] M. Russell. and J. Bradbury, 'The Constituency Work of Scottish and Welsh MPs: Adjusting to devolution', *Regional and Federal Studies*, 17 (1) (2007): 97–116,, pp. 104–5.

[28] This would tally with pre-devolution findings that Scottish MPs — and those from the Labour Party in particular — concentrated on local and constituency matters more than other members (Kellas 1984, p.84; Judge and Finlayson 1975, pp. 282–3).

Table 8.1: MPs Workload by Nation[29]

		England	Scotland	Wales
	Postage Expenses claimed (all MPs) (2005–6)	£3,633.47	£2,885.41	£2,554.90
	Postage Expenses claimed (Labour backbenchers only) (2005–6)	£4,137.26	£2,866.48	£2,773.57
S	**Hours Spent on Different Activities (weekly)**			
u	*Constituency casework*	15.3	11.8	12.2
r v	*Other local constituency work*	16.5	12.6	15.4
e y	Total local/constituency workload	31.8	24.4	27.6
D	Parliamentary workload	25.4	26.2	28.3
a t	Dealing with UK wide organisations	3.8	3.6	5.8
a	Dealing with regional/ Scottish/Welsh organisations	1.4	2.1	3.8
2 0	**Total hours worked***	**68.2**	**61.1**	**71.3**
0	Communications received	216.1	94.6	115.3
4	Number of constituency surgeries per month	3.8	5.1	4.3
	For survey data, N =	103–49	22–28	12–16

* Total hours worked does not equate to a sum of the previous categories of activity because respondents were asked separately how many hours they worked overall as well as how many they spent on specific activities.

More striking is the difference in the average number of communications received per MP: English MPs receive more than double the number reported by Scottish MPs and nearly 90 per cent more than members from Wales. One minor caveat to be added is that in 2004 Scottish and Welsh constituencies were on average around 20 per cent smaller in per capita terms than those in England so a lower volume of constituency work is to be expected (redistribution means this is no longer the case in Scotland, but it is

[29] Source: House of Commons 2006, *Members' Allowance Expenditure April 2005 – March 2006*, column 7a 'Stationery: Associated Postage Costs', at: www.parliament.uk/documents/upload/ HoCallowances0506current.pdf; Russell and Bradbury, 2006.

still the case in Wales).[30] The discrepancy in constituency casework is far wider than the different sizes of electoral quota however, which strongly suggests that the existence of the devolved legislatures has reduced the volume of work in this area for Scottish and Welsh members.

Of course, dealing with constituents' casework is not in itself a 'political' activity and, as such, tells us little about the existence or absence of separate territorial political spheres at Westminster. What it does provide however, is suggestive evidence that in the post-devolution environment, Scottish and Welsh MPs must look elsewhere for functions to fulfil if they are to escape the fate of post-devolution 'underemployment'.

W(H)ITHER THE TERRITORIAL LEGISLATIVE SPHERES AT WESTMINSTER?

As noted above, a major responsibility of Scottish MPs prior to devolution was scrutinising legislation relating to Scotland, whether exclusively or not and whether or not that legislation passed through the special Scottish legislative machinery. In the decade before devolution, an average of over five Scottish bills was passed in each session. Since 1999 there have been only two in total. To put this in context: the UK Parliament passed an average of over 50 Acts per year in the decade prior to devolution and approximately 40 per year since devolution.[31]

With virtually no primary legislation to consider, the Scottish committee system — which lay at the heart of 'the Scottish political system in its parliamentary aspect' — has largely fallen into abeyance.[32] (The exception is the Scottish Affairs Committee which plays no role in the legislative process.) Neither of the two Scottish Acts passed since 1999 — the Sunday Working (Scotland) Act 2003 and Scottish Parliamentary Constituencies Act 2004 — were referred to the Scottish Grand Committee for second reading stage or to a Scottish Standing Committee for committee stage proceedings.

As shown in Table 8.2, in the aftermath of devolution the Scottish Grand Committee did continue to meet for debates on non-legislative matters, although less frequently than before devolution. Since 13 November 2003, however, there has been not a single meeting of this body. To a limited extent — and as anticipated by the Commons Procedure Committee — the parallel parliamentary chamber in Westminster Hall has provided an alternative outlet for specific Scottish and other sub-national debates, such as the debate on the Arbuthnott Report on electoral systems and boundaries in Scotland

---

[30] National Statistics, *Parliamentary electors on the 2000 and 2001 electoral registers — Revised Figures,* at: www.statistics.gov.uk/StatBase/xsdataset.asp?More=Y&vlnk=3258&All=Y&B2.x=61&B2. y=11

[31] Data from Office of Public Sector Information at: www.opsi.gov.uk/acts.htm.

[32] Kellas 1984, p. 85.

held on 20 July 2006.[33] Westminster Hall, however, is not generally seen as a high-profile arena, hence occasional calls for such debates to be referred to the Scottish Grand Committee instead.[34]

Table 8.2: Territorial Grand Committee Meetings per Session

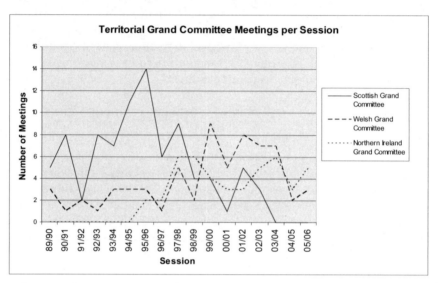

The situation faced by Welsh MPs is somewhat different in that Wales-only Acts at Westminster were a rarity before devolution — with just 10 such pieces of legislation passed between 1988 and 1998. Since 1999 a further seven Wales bills have been enacted meaning that devolution has not had a significant effect on the legislative scrutiny workload of Welsh MPs. No provision has ever been made for second reading debates on Wales bills to be taken in Grand Committee but non-Welsh members will generally leave the floor to Welsh members during Commons debates on such legislation, even on the constitutionally-significant Government of Wales Act 2006.[35] Likewise, specific Welsh standing committees have never been constituted but Welsh members can expect to comprise a large proportion of the membership of standing committees on Wales-only bills. In the 2005 Parliament, for instance, two Wales bills have been sent to a standing

---

[33] House of Commons Procedure Committee, *The Procedural Consequences of Devolution* (Session 1998–9, 4th Report, HC 185) (London: The Stationery Office, 1999), para. 17.

[34] House of Commons Scottish Affairs Committee, *Putting Citizens First: The Report from the Commission on Boundary Differences and Voting Systems* (Session 2005–6, 3rd Report, HC 924) (London: The Stationery Office, 2006), para. 13.

[35] 41 speakers in all participated in the Commons second reading debate on this bill, of which 28 (68 per cent) represented Welsh constituencies.

committee: the Transport (Wales) Bill and the Commissioner for Older People (Wales) Bill, with Welsh MPs making up 87.5 per cent and 58.8 per cent of the respective committees.[36] Welsh members represent just 6 per cent of the House as a whole. In addition to standing committee scrutiny, Wales bills are sometimes scrutinised (for instance in draft form) by the Welsh Affairs Select Committee which provides an additional element of an active, if limited, Welsh legislative sphere at Westminster. The Welsh Grand Committee has also continued to meet quite frequently, often to discuss broad issues such as the implications for Wales of the Budget or the UK Government's legislative programme rather than to consider specific legislative measures. Like its Scottish counterpart it has seen the frequency of meetings decline since the first term of devolution. During the long suspension of devolution up till 2007, the Northern Ireland Grand Committee became, for the first time, the most active of the three territorial Grand Committees.

By another measure, however, the amount of Welsh legislation has fallen significantly: with the National Assembly for Wales able to enact delegated legislation, the number of Statutory Instruments passed at Westminster that 'apply exclusively or primarily to Wales' has fallen from over 150 in two years before devolution to just 22 in the two years up to May 2007.[37] Even more dramatically, the number of statutory instruments (SIs) applying to Scotland has fallen from over 400 in two years before devolution to just 27 between 2005 and 2007. The total number of SIs passed annually at Westminster is over 3000, meaning that Scottish and Welsh SIs collectively represent under 1 per cent of the total. Thus secondary legislation offers very limited sustenance for separate Scottish and Welsh political spheres at Westminster, although when instruments applying solely to a single territory are committed to delegated legislation committees, it is the norm for there to be greater than proportional representation of that territory on the committee.[38]

Although exclusively Scottish legislation has become very rare and exclusively Welsh legislation has remained so, there are also various categories of legislation that apply to Scotland and/or Wales in specific ways as well as to other parts of the UK. Scrutiny of such legislation could potentially provide scope for political activity within discrete territorial spheres at Westminster.

---

[36] The bills for the Government of Wales Act 2006 and the Public Services Ombudsman (Wales) Act 2006 (both introduced in 2005) had their committee stages in Committee of the Whole House.

[37] Data from Office of Public Sector Information at: www.opsi.gov.uk/stat.htm.

[38] For instance, in the first six months of the 2006–7 session three committees were appointed to consider Wales-only SIs with an average of 47 per cent Welsh membership, compared with 6 per cent of the House as a whole. The level of Scottish representation on committees considering Scottish SIs varies quite widely, but orders modifying the legislative competence of the Scottish Parliament appear to have a particularly high percentage of Scots among their members: orders amending the list of non-devolved matters in 2005 and 2006 comprised respectively 55 per cent and 44 per cent Scottish members, compared with 9 per cent in the House as a whole.

For instance, from the 2005 UK general election till the end of the 2006–7 session (May 2005 to November 2007) a total of 16 bills passed at Westminster came under the ambit of the legislative consent (or 'Sewel') convention, meaning that they legislated for Scotland in devolved areas or amended the powers of the devolved institutions.[39] Many predominantly English bills also have provisions applying to Wales in non-trivial ways. Since the 2005 commitment to drafting legislation 'permissively' there have been four Acts of Parliament — in addition to Wales-only Acts — that have contained 'framework powers' granting significant policy discretion to the National Assembly.[40]

While Scottish and Welsh members may take an interest in such legislation, potentially acting as territorial advocates, they face a major structural problem in that the 'Sewel elements' or 'framework powers' in bills such as the Further Education and Training bill introduced in 2006 (which was subject to the Sewel convention as well as containing framework powers for Wales) are of minimal concern to the majority of members of the House. As a result, legislative proceedings are inevitably dominated by English concerns and English voices. In his analysis of parliamentary treatment of Sewel bills, Winetrobe found that they are 'treated just like any other bill' with little awareness of the Scottish implications of the legislation and limited Scottish representation on standing committees set up to scrutinise them.[41]

Indeed, of 16 standing committees set up to scrutinise bills subject to the legislative consent convention between May 2005 and November 2007, seven had no Scottish representation at all, and most of the others had just one Scot. Overall, Scots made up just 4.5 per cent of these committees — half the level of Scottish representation in the House. Page and Batey argue that 'the danger must be that against the background of devolution the Scottish element of such legislation will attract even less attention' than did Scottish elements of pre-devolution UK bills.[42]

Similar problems apply to scrutiny of the Welsh elements of predominantly English bills. Of the four bills containing 'framework powers' in the 2005–6 and 2006–7 sessions, there was, on average, just one Welsh member on each standing committee. In all cases this was a Labour backbencher. Nearly 80 per cent of Scots on Sewel bill committees were also from the

[39] Scottish Parliament Information Office, *Sewel Motions / Legislative Consent Motions: Session 2*, Scottish Parliament Fact Sheet, (Edinburgh: Scottish Parliament, April 2007).

[40] The commitment to permissive drafting was made in: Wales Office, *Better Governance for Wales* Cm 6582 (London: The Stationery Office, 2005). The four Acts in question are: the Education and Inspections Act 2006, the Further Education and Training Act 2007, the Local Government and Public Involvement in Health Act 2007, and the the NHS Redress Act 2006.

[41] B. Winetrobe, 'A Partnership of the Parliaments? Scottish law making under the Sewel Convention at Westminster and Holyrood' in R. Hazell and R. Rawlings, (eds.), *Devolution, Law Making and the Constitution* (Exeter: Imprint Academic, 2005), pp. 55–6.

[42] A. Page and A. Batey, 'Scotland's other parliament: Westminster legislation about devolved matters in Scotland since devolution', [2002] *Public Law* (autumn): 501–23, at pp. 522–3.

Labour Party, suggesting that there is limited critical scrutiny of UK Government legislation in terms of its implications for the devolved tier of government.

Table 8.3: Overall Voting Records of MPs by Nation[43]

	English MPs	Scottish MPs	Welsh MPs	Northern Irish MPs	Total
Participation in divisions (all MPs) (%)	71.2	68.3	71.4	28.2	69.7
Participation in divisions (Labour backbencher) (%)	76.0	76.9	75.6	n/a	76.0
Rebelliousness (all Labour MPs) (%)	2.5	1.5	1.6	n/a	2.3
Rebelliousness (Labour backbenchers) (%)	3.4	1.8	1.9	n/a	3.1

N (all Labour MPs): England = 284, Scotland = 39, Wales = 29.
N (Labour backbenchers): England = 176, Scotland = 24, Wales = 22.

A final method of assessing whether Scots or Welsh MPs play a distinctive role in the legislative process is by reference to voting records in divisions in the Commons. Table 8.3 shows that MPs from the three part of Great Britain have similar voting records in terms of the proportion of divisions they participate in. This is the case even when we correct for potential party bias by looking only at Labour backbenchers from the three nations. The implication of this is that whether an item of business affects an MP's constituency has little effect on whether the MP turns out to vote on it. An interesting contrast can be found in the third and fourth rows of the table, which demonstrate that English Labour MPs are much more likely to vote against the leadership line than their comrades from north and west of the border. While this may partly result from genuine differences of opinion, it probably also reflects the fact that many controversial votes have been on essentially English-only matters. On such divisions Scots and Welsh members have limited electoral incentives to cast their votes against their whips on grounds of principle. This is, in fact, further circumstantial evidence of the existence of Scottish and Welsh 'lost souls' on the backbenches of the House of Commons, with limited territorially-specific business on which to focus, restricted opportunities to act as advocates for Scotland and Wales during consideration of bills that apply in part to their

---

[43] Figures derived from www.theyworkforyou.com.

territories, and many divisions to vote on that have no relevance to their constituents.

PARLIAMENTARY QUESTIONS AND MPS' POLICY INTERESTS

Save for the limited opportunities available for Private Member's Bills, backbenchers themselves have little influence over what legislation comes before the House of Commons. Neither do individual MPs have a great deal of say over whether they are placed on committees considering specific pieces of legislation. As such, the amount of territorially-focussed activity for members to engage in during the legislative process is largely determined by factors out of their control. The evidence presented in the preceding session therefore gives a good indication of the differential opportunity structures faced by members from England, Scotland and Wales but says little about their interests or motivations.

The parliamentary question, on the other hand, represents a tool that MPs can wield at will. PQs (in their oral variety) were once described as 'almost the only vestige of the rights backbenchers enjoyed in the nineteenth century'.[44] As members of the UK Parliament, Scottish and Welsh members have the right to table questions to any government department, including on policy areas that have been largely or entirely transferred to Edinburgh or Cardiff. There is also no limit to the number of questions that MPs may table so data about written questions can provide direct insight into members' personal political interests and role perceptions, thereby helping us answer the question of what Scottish and Welsh MPs do post-devolution. The pre-devolution finding that Scottish MPs' parliamentary questions were largely focussed on Scottish Affairs is powerful evidence of Scottish members' non-integration into the UK-wide political sphere.[45] Post-devolution evidence of significant differences between national groups of MPs in terms of PQ usage would undermine the 'integration' hypothesis, that post-devolution Scottish, Welsh and English MPs behave in an indistinguishable manner.

Comparing the raw figures reveals that Scottish and Welsh MPs table significantly fewer written questions than their English counterparts. This pattern is confirmed - especially for Scottish members - when we restrict the data to Labour backbenchers only.[46] Specifically, between May 2006 and

---

[44] D.N. Chester in *Report of the Select Committee on Parliamentary Questions* (Session 1971–72, HC 393) (London: Her Majesty's Stationery Office, 1972), p. 87.

[45] See Judge and Finlayson 1975, p. 282; and D. Judge, 'Backbench Specialization — A study in parliamentary questions', *Parliamentary Affairs*, 27 (4) (1973): 171–86,. As noted earlier, Welsh MPs were less detached from UK politics, though comparable figures on PQ usage are not readily available.

[46] Restricting the sample to Labour backbenchers discounts any potential party bias, for instance deriving from a greater propensity of Opposition members (disproportionately from England) to table

May 2007 English Labour backbenchers tabled an average of 66 questions, while Welsh members tabled 51 and Scots just 22. This corresponds to Russell and Lodge's finding for the 2002–3 parliamentary session that Scottish MPs tabled significantly fewer questions on average than both English and Welsh members.[47] One interpretation of this discrepancy, and in particular the low usage of parliamentary questions among Scottish members, is that this further supports the 'underemployment' hypothesis. On the other hand, however, parliamentary questions are a rather blunt proxy for members' workload. They take minimal time to write and table and are often seen as a cost-free way for members to demonstrate (for instance to local media) their interest in or commitment to a particular issue. It is possible that Scottish members table fewer questions overall but spend more time on other related parliamentary activities. Indeed the evidence is that MPs from the three territories of Great Britain spent a similar number of hours on 'parliamentary work' (see Table 8.1). They also appear to participate equally frequently in oral question time in the House.[48]

Thus the main value of written parliamentary questions from a research point of view is as an indicator of MPs' priorities and interests. Past studies of the use of parliamentary questions have emphasised this point: Chester and Bowring's classic text pointed out that PQs are 'the most personal of all the activities of the House, reflecting much more closely than any other form of procedure the everyday activities of members, the problems that concern them, their predilections and idiosyncrasies'.[49]

Table 8.4 shows the 'most popular' departments among the current crop of Labour MPs in terms of those to which members addressed the most questions between 2001 and October 2007.[50] This reveals significant qualitative differences in the scrutiny activities of the different territorial groups of MPs. English members focus to a large extent on 'domestic' policy areas

questions. It also reflects the fact that government ministers do not table questions. Figures are derived from www.theyworkforyou.com.

[47] M. Russell and G. Lodge, 'The Government of England by Westminster', in R. Hazell, (ed.), *The English Question* (Manchester: Manchester University Press, 2006), pp. 66–9.

[48] We looked at oral questions on the order paper from January to December 2006 relating to a selection of 13 departments including the three territorial offices. For these departmental question times we found that 83 per cent of questions were tabled by English MPs (representing 82 per cent of the House) 9 per cent by Scots (9 per cent of the House) and 8 per cent by Welsh (6 per cent of the House). Hence English and Scottish MPs participated proportionately to their numbers in the House while the Welsh were overrepresented at the expense of MPs from Northern Ireland. These figures do not take into account differential representation in government.

[49] D.N. Chester and N. Bowring, *Questions in Parliament* (Oxford: Clarendon Press, 1962).

[50] These data come from www.theyworkforyou.com, specifically the 'topics of interest' section on the individual page for each MP which lists the five departments to which the MP in question has asked the most written questions. Figures cited in the text and in table 4 refer to the proportion of MPs for whom the department in question ranked in the top five. These figures therefore relate to the balance of interests between the different national groups of MPs, rather than to the overall volume of questions received by departments.

with health, home affairs and education taking the top three spots, and UK-wide policy areas of less interest.

For Scottish Labour MPs, in contrast, major UK-wide departments such as the Treasury, the Foreign Office and the Department of Work and Pensions score highly, as does the Scotland Office. Also of interest to Scottish members are home affairs, trade and industry, and defence — all areas where there are distinctive Scottish, and in some cases constituency-specific, interests that MPs might seek to promote. Many questions on the (largely Scottish-based) oil and gas industry, for instance, have been addressed to UK-wide departments such as the Department for Trade and Industry (now the Department for Business, Enterprise and Regulatory Reform) and the Treasury by Scottish MPs. Similarly, the Ministry of Defence has had to respond to questions on the status of Scottish regiments in the British army, and the Department of Work and Pensions has been questioned on the effects on benefits entitlement of the introduction of free long term care for the elderly by the Scottish Parliament. On the other hand, many other questions to these same departments from the same members contain no specific Scottish focus. It is also notable that trade and industry and environmental matters seem to be of less interest to Scottish than to English members, despite the fact that these were the areas where pre-devolution studies found strong evidence of Scottish interest.[51] It is hard to say what the balance is between UK-focussed 'national members' in the Kilbrandon sense on the one hand, and advocates for specific territorial interests on the other. Only further detailed research into the content of parliamentary questions could help to resolve this question.

Welsh MPs too appear to focus on reserved policy areas to a greater extent than English members. Interestingly, in the Welsh case there is a greater emphasis on those policy departments where there is greater scope for territorial advocacy. By far the most popular target of Welsh Labour MPs' questions is the Home Office, which is responsible for policing in Wales and receives a high number of specifically Welsh questions, for instance on its controversial attempt to merge the four Welsh police forces in 2006.[52] Trade and industry — another area where clear opportunities exist to defend particular territorial interests — is also a focus for far more Welsh Labour MPs than either English or Scots. Another interesting figure is the far higher number of Welsh than Scottish members asking questions to predominantly English departments such as those responsible for health and education. This

[51] Keating 1978, p. 419.

[52] Evidence of the strength of feeling among Welsh members can be found in: Welsh Affairs Select Committee, *Proposed Restructuring of the Police Forces in Wales*, (Session 2005–6, 2nd Report, HC 751) (London: The Stationery Office, 2006); and Welsh Affairs Select Committee, *Current Restructuring of the Police Forces in Wales*, (Session 2005–6, 5th Report, HC 1418) (London: The Stationery Office, 2006).

reflects the fact that these policy areas are more extensively devolved in the case of Scotland. For instance the National Institute of Clinical Excellence provides guidance on health technologies and clinical practice for the English and Welsh NHS only. As such these data indicate that Welsh members remain more closely integrated with English members. However once again, only detailed content analysis could ascertain what proportion of questions on any of these subjects pertain exclusively to Wales, and what level of territorial advocacy can be found among Welsh members.

Table 8.4: Proportion of Labour MPs with Scrutiny Focus on Various Departments (2001–7, as per centage)[53]

	England	Scotland	Wales	All
Health	76	24	56	69
Home Office	69	39	80	67
Education and Skills	54	6	24	46
Trade and Industry	43	39	72	45
Work and Pensions	37	52	28	38
Communities and Local Government[54]	36	9	8	31
HM Treasury	33	58	36	36
Environment, Food & Rural Affairs	32	24	36	31
Foreign and Commonwealth Office	31	58	28	34
Transport	21	21	20	21
Defence	15	36	28	18
Culture, Media and Sport	12	9	4	11
International Development	10	24	20	12
Constitutional Affairs / Justice	7	0	0	6
Other	5	6	0	5
Northern Ireland Office	5	9	0	5

[53] Figures refer to the percentage of members for whom the department in question was one of their top five in terms of the number of written questions posed. Departments are ordered by popularity among English members. Source: www.theyworkforyou.com.

[54] Includes previous incarnations of this department such as DETR and ODPM.

Wales Office	0	0	44	4
Scotland Office	0	48	0	5

CONCLUSIONS AND FUTURE PROSPECTS

The picture painted so far is a messy one, as is to be expected when presenting averages representing the behaviour of dozens or hundreds of individuals. Nonetheless, a few conclusions can be drawn about the extent to which each possible scenario for Scottish and Welsh MPs' roles in the post-devolution House of Commons is supported. This final section also considers factors that may bear upon the situation in the future.

First, in terms of the 'reactive' workload faced by MPs we found unambiguous evidence that in some senses Scottish and Welsh members suffer from *underemployment*. Constituency casework is lower for Scottish or Welsh members than for English ones, a disparity which may widen, given the probability that further responsibilities will be devolved from Westminster. This latter factor will also impact upon the Welsh legislative sphere, which we found to be livelier than the moribund Scottish equivalent. Particularly if the National Assembly for Wales acquires 'primary legislative powers' by 2011 (as the new Welsh Assembly Government intends) the quantity of Wales-only primary legislation at Westminster is likely to slow to a trickle.[55] Prior to that point, legislative competence is to be transferred to the National Assembly on a case-by-case basis, which will generate some scrutiny work for Welsh members, but only on the principle of whether the powers in question should be transferred, rather than the use to which they will be put by the Assembly in Cardiff.[56]

The workload faced by each Scottish and Welsh MP depends not only on the overall quantity of territorial tasks but also on the number of MPs from each territory. This is liable to change. Pre-devolution overrepresentation of Scotland was partly justified by reference to the demands of Scottish legislative and committee work. Now that this has all but evaporated, it may even make sense for the Scottish quota to be reduced to less than that of England. In addition, Wales might lose its present overrepresentation (at least in per capita terms) at some future date if Cardiff Bay acquires primary legislative powers. Reducing the number of Scottish and Welsh MPs to less than pure proportionality has also been advocated as a plausible *faute de mieux* solu-

---

[55] Labour and Plaid Cymru Groups in the National Assembly, *One Wales: A progressive agenda for the government of* Wales (Cardiff, 2007), p. 6.

[56] As some MPs were reminded to their frustration in the first scrutiny of a draft LCO. House of Commons Welsh Affairs Committee, 'Proposed Legislative Competence Orders in Council: Additional Learning Needs', Uncorrected Transcript of Oral Evidence, 7 November 2007, to be published as HC 44–I.

tion to the West Lothian question.[57] Should it be implemented, a side-effect would be that it would partially compensate for the declining workload of Scots and Welsh MPs.

Another relevant factor, as noted in the introduction, derives from the institutional symmetry of Westminster and Whitehall. Specifically, so long as Whitehall retains a territorial dimension in the shape of the Scotland, Wales and Northern Ireland Offices, Westminster will presumably reflect this in its organisation of question time and select committees. However, as differences between the three devolution settlements decline, the government may one day merge the three territorial departments into a single department for devolution, as some commentators have advocated.[58] Even if separate territorial select committees were to outlive the departments they shadow, they would probably struggle to find a coherent role, as some would say the Scottish Affairs committee already does. Like the Scottish Grand Committee, these bodies may slide gradually into irrelevance.

An alternative path these committees may seek to follow is that of forging closer relations with the respective devolved institutions. For instance, the Scottish Affairs Committee recently suggested the establishment of a '"super" Scottish Grand Committee' involving MPs, MSPs and MEPs, to consider 'Sewel bills' and other matters of joint interest.[59] The Welsh Affairs Committee, for its part, has already experimented with joint meetings with National Assembly committees when scrutinising draft legislation. However for a number of reasons the potential of this *linkage* role for Scottish and Welsh MPs' seems limited. First, the government is sceptical about formal inter-parliamentary structures like the proposed 'super Scottish Grand Committee'.[60] Second, there is some evidence of a lack of enthusiasm among MSPs and AMs themselves about the development of such links.[61] Third, the need for cooperative action is likely to decrease in future as legislative and policy 'delineation' between the two tiers of governance accelerates.

---

[57] I. McLean, 'Barnett and the West Lothian Question: no nearer to solutions than when the Devolution Programme started'. Paper presented at ESRC Devolution and Constitutional Change Programme Conference, London, December 2005, p. 11.

[58] R. Hazell, *Three into One Won't Go: The future of the territorial Secretaries of State* (London: The Constitution Unit, 2001); House of Lords Select Committee on the Constitution, *Devolution: Inter-Institutional Relations in the United Kingdom* (Session 2002–3, 2nd Report, HL 28) (London: The Stationery Office, 2003), para. 68.

[59] House of Commons Scottish Affairs Committee, *The Sewel Convention: The Westminster Perspective* (Session 2005–6, 4th Report, HC 983)) (London: The Stationery Office, 2006) para. 43.

[60] House of Commons Scottish Affairs Committee, *The Sewel Convention: The Westminster Perspective: Government Response* (Session 2005–6, 2nd Special Report, HC 1634) (London: The Stationery Office, 2006) paras. 10–12.

[61] In 2005 the Scottish Parliament Conveners' [committee chairs'] Group turned down an invitation to hold a meeting with the Scottish Affairs Committee, advising the Westminster body instead to arrange separate meetings with Scottish Parliament subject committees as appropriate. See: House of Commons Scottish Affairs Committee, *Work of the Committee in 2005* (Session 2005–6, 1st Report, HC 836) (London: The Stationery Office, 2006), paras. 35–8.

It is possible that despite these hurdles, the territorial committees may develop new and innovative inter-parliamentary modes of working. For instance, there may be scope for joint scrutiny of intergovernmental relations, which to date has operated predominantly beneath the radar of parliamentary scrutiny.[62] But these committees comprise only a fraction of the Scottish and Welsh parliamentary groups. What new roles they develop will therefore be of limited import as far as describing the behaviour and roles of Scottish and Welsh backbenchers as a whole is concerned. Of course, in a more informal sense MPs do fulfil the linkage function to some extent as individual members, through intra-party and constituency-level relations with members of the devolved legislatures. But this is unlikely to extend to playing an active role in debates around devolved policy matters, partly because of simple geographical and institutional isolation from those debates, and partly because the Scotland and Wales branches of the Labour and Conservative parties, for instance, may defend their autonomy against serious encroachment by MPs.[63]

The implication of this is that as political actors Scottish and Welsh MPs will predominantly be confined to the Westminster stage. As territorial legislative and scrutiny tasks decline, is there any possibility that they might be able to *(re)integrate* themselves into the 'mainstream' of political activity in the Commons? In one important sense, most Scottish and Welsh MPs do remain integrated by virtue of their membership of UK-wide political parties. It is undoubtedly the case that Scottish and Welsh Labour, Liberal Democrat and Conservative MPs perceive themselves as largely, if not primarily, participants in the partisan conflict that characterises Westminster life. Yet as confirmed by the behavioural analysis above, this does not mean that full integration — in the sense of identical patterns of activity among the different national groups of MPs — is plausible. For instance, the lower levels of rebelliousness found among non-English (and particularly Scottish) Labour MPs implies a semi-detached relationship with many of key political conflicts at Westminster. Analysis of parliamentary questions indicates that some Scots and Welsh members do continue, to a limited extent, to participate in debates in devolved policy areas (note for instance, the 6–24 per cent of Scottish members with an interest in health, education and local government). But although Scottish and Welsh MPs can table PQs in any area they wish, their influence on the 'English' policy-making process will be limited. Both select and bill committees on 'English' policy areas tend to

---

[62] R. Hazell and A. Paun, 'Parliamentary Scrutiny of Multi-Level Governance'. Paper presented at conference of the International Association of Centers for Federal Studies, University of Tübingen (Germany), 30 June 2006.

[63] Although it remains a point of debate how extensive autonomy has in fact been gained by the sub-national branches of the main parties (see M. Laffin, E. Shaw and G. Taylor, 'The Parties and Intergovernmental Relations', in A. Trench (ed.), *Devolution and Power in the United Kingdom* (Manchester: Manchester University Press, 2007).

be English-only zones.[64] And the prospects of integration in this sense could be set back further by attempts to tackle the West Lothian question, in particular by progress towards the Conservative goal of leaving English matters to English MPs.[65] Even if 'English votes on English laws' is not implemented, political constraints on the participation of Scots and Welsh members in English policy-making will persist.

This suggests that the most plausible options for Scottish and Welsh MPs may be to play the roles of UK-focussed *national members* or *territorial advocates*. Evidence presented here suggests that both these proclivities are present to some extent, though the balance between them is hard to discern. However, this chapter has focussed principally on Labour MPs, as no other party is represented in significant numbers in all three Great British territories. This may change. For instance, the SNP contingent in the Commons certainly consider themselves to be defenders of the Scottish rather than the UK national interest, so any growth in their number at future elections (likely on current polling evidence) would boost the *territorial advocacy* inclination of Scottish members. The same goes for Plaid Cymru, and perhaps the Scottish and Welsh Liberal Democrats too. But the most significant potential development would be the election of a Tory government, whose majority would almost inevitably rest principally on English seats. The upshot might well be to transform Scottish and Welsh Labour MPs into territorial advocates just as a decade and a half of Thatcherism convinced many of the need for devolution in the first place.

If Labour remains in power and dominant in Scotland and Wales, territorial advocacy is likely to be more muted as party considerations prevail, but some scope for this role will remain. This is particularly likely to be the case on the issue of finance. It is apparent that public spending growth over the coming decade will be lower than in the Blair years, and, partly as a result, pressure on the Treasury to revisit the financial structure of devolution is growing. Should a genuine rethink of the Barnett formula commence, it will be at Westminster where competing territorial interests will make their cases. In such circumstances, even otherwise loyal Labour MPs might find it hard to maintain support for the UK Government if their part of the country looked like losing out, particularly in the face of a strong electoral challenge from nationalists, Lib Dems or (in England) Conservatives.

As for the UK-focussed *national member* role, the pre-devolution prediction was that Scottish and Welsh MPs would find it hard to reinvent themselves en masse into specialists in foreign policy and the economy, and this has no doubt been a genuine difficulty for some members. To some extent, however, it could be a transitional problem, in that aspiring

[64] Russell and Lodge 2006, Figure 4.3, p. 69.
[65] Conservative Party, *Are you thinking what we're thinking? It's time for action.* Conservative Election Manifesto 2005 (London: The Conservative Party, 2005), p. 22.

politicians of the post-devolution era might be more likely to come to Westminster if they were interested or had expertise in UK-wide matters, while those with an interest in healthcare in Wales or policing in Scotland would be more likely to head for Edinburgh or Cardiff. Thus the number of 'national members' among the non-English contingent at Westminster may increase over time. But such a development would not compensate for the fact that Westminster will remain dominated by English political concerns, and increasingly so, should further powers be transferred to the three devolved capitals. Only a radical shift towards federalism — with either an English parliament or strong regional assemblies dealing with domestic policy matters — could change this, by transforming all MPs into UK specialists. But so long as the UK remains an asymmetrically-devolved union state, Scottish and Welsh MPs will continue to struggle to define their role, and as a result will continue to face calls to reduce both their numbers and their powers.

BIBLIOGRAPHY:

Official Documents and Primary Sources

Conservative Party, *Are you thinking what we're thinking? It's time for action.* Conservative Election Manifesto 2005 (London: The Conservative Party, 2005).

House of Commons Procedure Committee, *The Procedural Consequences of Devolution* (Session 1998–99, 4th Report, HC 185) (London: House of Commons, 1999).

House of Commons Scottish Affairs Committee, *Putting Citizens First: The Report from the Commission on Boundary Differences and Voting Systems* (Session 2005–6, 3rd Report, HC 924) (London: House of Commons, 2006).

House of Commons Scottish Affairs Committee, *The Sewel Convention: The Westminster Perspective* (Session 2005–6, 4th Report, HC 983) (London: House of Commons, 2006).

House of Commons Scottish Affairs Committee, *The Sewel Convention: The Westminster Perspective: Government Response* (Session 2005–6, 2nd Special Report, HC 1634) (London: House of Commons, 2006).

House of Commons Scottish Affairs Committee, *Work of the Committee in 2005* (Session 2005–6, 1st Report, HC 836) (London: House of Commons, 2006).

House of Commons Welsh Affairs Committee, 'Proposed Legislative Competence Orders in Council: Additional Learning Needs', Uncorrected Transcript of Oral Evidence, 7 November 2007, to be published as HC 44–I (London: House of Commons).

House of Lords Select Committee on the Constitution, *Devolution: Inter-Institutional Relations in the United Kingdom* (Session 2002–3, 2nd Report, HL 28) (London: House of Lords, 2003).

Labour and Plaid Cymru Groups in the National Assembly, *One Wales: A progressive agenda for the government of Wales* (Cardiff, 2007).

Royal Commission on the Constitution [The Kilbrandon Commission] *Report on the Constitution* Cmnd 5460 (London: The Stationery Office, 1973).

Scottish Constitutional Convention, *Scotland's Parliament, Scotland's Right* (Edinburgh: Scottish Constitutional Convention, 1995).

Scottish Parliament Information Office, *Sewel Motions / Legislative Consent Motions: Session 2*, Scottish Parliament Fact Sheet, (Edinburgh: Scottish Parliament, April 2007).

Wales Office, *Better Governance for Wales* Cm 6582 (London: The Stationery Office, 2005).

Welsh Affairs Select Committee, *Proposed Restructuring of the Police Forces in Wales* (Session 2005–6, 2nd Report, HC 751) (London: House of Commons 2006).

Welsh Affairs Select Committee, *Current Restructuring of the Police Forces in Wales* (Session 2005–6, 5th Report, HC 1418) (London: House of Commons, 2006).

Secondary Sources

Chester, D.N. in *Report of the Select Committee on Parliamentary Questions* (Session 1971–72, HC 393) (London: House of Commons, 1972).

Chester, D.N., and N. Bowring, *Questions in Parliament* (Oxford: Clarendon Press, 1962).

Edwards, G.E., 'The Scottish Grand Committee, 1958 to 1970', *Parliamentary Affairs*, 25 (4) (1971): 303–25.

Hazell, R. and A. Paun, 'Parliamentary Scrutiny of Multi-Level Governance'. Paper presented at conference of the International Association of Centers for Federal Studies, University of Tübingen (Germany), 30 June 2006.

Hazell, R., *Three into One Won't Go: The future of the territorial Secretaries of State* (London: The Constitution Unit, 2001).

Jones, J.B. and R.A Wilford, *Parliament and Territoriality: The Committee on Welsh Affairs, 1979–1983* (Cardiff: University of Wales Press, 1986).

Judge, D. and D A Finlayson, 'Scottish Members of Parliament. Problems of Devolution', *Parliamentary Affairs*, 28 (1) (1975): 278–92.

Judge, D., 'Backbench Specialization — A Study in Parliamentary Questions', *Parliamentary Affairs*, 27 (4) (1973): 171–86.

Keating, M.J., 'Parliamentary Behaviour as a Test of Scottish Integration into the United Kingdom', *Legislative Studies Quarterly*, 3 (3) (1978): 409–30.

Kellas, J. G., *The Scottish Political System* (Cambridge: Cambridge University Press, 1984).

Laffin, M. and A. Thomas, 'The United Kingdom: Federalism in Denial?' *Publius: The journal of federalism* 29 (3) (1999): 89–107.

Laffin, M., E. Shaw and G. Taylor, 'The Parties and Intergovernmental Relations', in A. Trench, (ed.), *Devolution and Power in the United Kingdom*
(Manchester: Manchester University Press, 2007).

Lodge, G., M. Russell and O. Gay, 'The Impact of Devolution on Westminster'
in A. Trench, (ed.) *Has Devolution Made a Difference? The State of the
Nations 2004*. (Exeter: Imprint Academic, 2004).

McLean, I., 'Barnett and the West Lothian Question: no nearer to solutions than
when the Devolution Programme started'. Paper presented at ESRC Devolution and Constitutional Change programme conference, London, December
2005.

Mishler, W., 'Scotching Nationalism in the British Parliament: Crosscutting
Cleavages among MPs', *Legislative Studies Quarterly*, 9 (1) (1983): 5–28.

Mishler, W. and A. Mughan, 'Representing the Celtic Fringe: Devolution and
Legislative Behaviour in Scotland and Wales', *Legislative Studies Quarterly*,
(3) 3 (1978): 377–408.

Mitchell, J., 'Scotland in the Union, 1945–95: The Changing Nature of the
Union State', in T.M. Devine and R.J. Finlay, (eds.), *Scotland in the Twentieth Century* (Edinburgh: Edinburgh University Press, 1996).

Morgan, K. and K. Mungham, *Redesigning Democracy: The Making of the
Welsh Assembly* (Bridgend: Seren, 2000).

Page, A. and A. Batey, 'Scotland's other parliament: Westminster legislation
about devolved matters in Scotland since devolution', [2002] *Public Law*
(autumn), 501–23.

Rawlings, R., *Delineating Wales: Constitutional, legal and administrative
aspects of national devolution* (Cardiff: University of Wales Press, 2003).

Rokkan, S. and D.W. Urwin, *Economy, Territory, Identity: Politics of West
European peripheries* (London: Sage, 1983).

Russell, M. and J. Bradbury, 'The Constituency Work of Scottish and Welsh
MPs: Adjusting to Devolution', *Regional and Federal Studies*, 17 (1) (2007):
97–116.

Russell, M. and J. Bradbury, 'Devolution, Elected Representatives and Constituency Representation in Scotland and Wales, 2000–2005', database SN 5443
at Economic and Social Data Service, (2006).

Russell, M. and G. Lodge, 'The Government of England by Westminster', in
R. Hazell, (ed.), *The English Question* (Manchester: Manchester University
Press, 2006).

Winetrobe, B., 'A Partnership of the Parliaments? Scottish law making under the
Sewel Convention at Westminster and Holyrood' in R. Hazell and
R. Rawlings, *Devolution, Law Making and the Constitution* (Exeter: Imprint
Academic, 2005).

9

The Practice of Multi-Level Government
How Intergovernmental Relations Work in Federal Systems

Alan Trench

INTRODUCTION: THE CHALLENGES OF WORKABLE SYSTEMS OF INTERGOVERNMENTAL RELATIONS

The 2007 elections brought home the reality of devolved politics to the United Kingdom. The SNP's narrow lead in the Scottish Parliament, and subsequent formation of a minority government, meant that Labour in London at last had to deal with a non-Labour government — and its worst fear, of a politically adroit nationalist government which was broadly left of centre but otherwise shared few of the presumptions about politics common to Labour or the Liberal Democrats. In Wales, Labour's 11-seat lead was not enough to create a stable government, and after protracted horse-trading led to a coalition between Labour and Plaid Cymru. And with the restoration of devolution in Northern Ireland, and an executive dominated by the Democratic Unionists and Sinn Fein, Labour faces a coalition which may be curiously composed, but which is also quite willing to rock the boat. Ten years after its UK election victory, Labour has to deal with governments which do not share either the party label or its ideological approach, and whose electoral mandate it cannot belittle. To put it slightly differently, it has been apparent for several years that the real challenges of devolution would emerge in the UK when Labour sometime, somewhere lost an election. The time was 2007 and the places were Scotland and Wales.

The challenge this presents for all the various governments in the United Kingdom is to find ways of dealing with each other, despite their political and ideological differences, so that the business of government gets done. For some time the attitude of many elected politicians (and many officials) has been that there would be such an overwhelming interest in serving the electorate that nothing much would need to change, and that the UK's existing machinery and ways of managing intergovernmental relations would function perfectly well with some small tweaks and adjustments. This view has been widely resisted by many outside observers.[1] Even the immediate

---

[1] For example, C. Jeffery 'The Unfinished Business of Devolution: Seven open questions', *Public Policy and Administration*, 22(1) (2007): 92–108; House of Lords Select Committee on the

aftermath of the 2007 elections suggested the outsiders were right, as within a few weeks of taking office the SNP minority government in Scotland found itself publicly falling out with the UK Government over a range of matters. The excessive reliance of the existing system on 'goodwill', underpinned by shared Labour dominance of all the three governments in Great Britain (and lack of real opposition in Northern Ireland), was particularly culpable in this respect: such a quality can at best be a lubricant in the practice of such relations, but instead it was made to serve practically as the totality of them, substituting for institutional machinery of co-ordination.

The spats that emerged in the first few months of the SNP government are touched on in chapter 1. Almost without exception, the UK has handled these matters badly; even if it has been in the right on them on formal or constitutional grounds, it has failed to acknowledge that the Scottish Government is entitled to make itself heard about such matters, or that its arguments may have merit even, perhaps especially when, it rejects them. Instead, on one hand the UK Government has sought to treat the Scottish Government as a subordinate level of government of limited authority, refusing to accept its autonomy except within the limits defined by the 1998 settlement, while on the other trying to maintain the sort of informal, ad hoc approach to the process of intergovernmental relations that it has taken since 1999. Intergovernmental issues relating to Wales are entirely different, underpinned by complex party politics and a convoluted set of institutional relationships put in place by the Government of Wales Act 2006.[2] Thanks to the peace process, the interest of the Irish Government as well as the UK's, and the north-south dimension, so are those for Northern Ireland. The upshot is that there are three sets of bilateral relations with only limited overlap or common ground between them. The UK Government has sought to maintain this state of affairs, so it appears it prefers this situation to any alternative. The UK's response has instead been a combination of fragmentation of institutional relationships and constitutional debates, coupled with a largely rhetorical insistence on 'Britishness'. This reflects the piecemeal and incremental approach that has characterised devolution at UK level to date, but it has not involved any assessment of whether these approaches are in fact still appropriate or a different one might now be better.

The UK's pattern of intergovernmental relations is very different to how things work in other federal or decentralised systems, where intergovernmental relations are an everyday part of government. Various authors have pointed out the differences between the UK's approach, accurately characterised as still 'interdepartmental' in nature, from the 'quasi-diplomatic'

Constitution, *Devolution: Inter-Institutional Relations in the United Kingdom* Session 2002–3 2nd Report, HL 28 (London: The Stationery Office, 2003).

  [2] See A. Trench, 'Old Wine In New Bottles? Relations between London and Cardiff after the Government of Wales Act 2006', *Contemporary Wales,* 20 (2007): 31–51.

approach common in federal systems.[3] Comparisons of such systems with the UK are hard to maintain, despite some institutional similarities — something which is revealing in itself. However, these may offer experiences on which elected politicians, civil servants, the public at large and the media in the UK can draw as they start to think about how these relations work.[4]

This chapter will discuss how such relations commonly work in a range of parliamentary federations, which display a striking degree of similarities in the 'grammar' of intergovernmental relations even if the issues and political contexts vary dramatically from system to system.[5] In particular, this chapter will look at practice in Australia, Canada, Spain and Germany, with occasional references to Belgium.[6] These systems all exhibit a form of 'executive federalism' in their intergovernmental relations that resembles each other, and makes their use as common reference points worthwhile. Indeed, perhaps the first research finding is that this group of systems exhibits a extensive range of similarities to each in the way they approach and deal with intergovernmental relations.[7] The actors in such relations, the mechanisms and processes of them, the issues that arise in them (and very often the solutions adopted) are all very similar — intriguing in itself, given the many differences between them, for example, in political parties and party systems, or whether they are multi-national federations.[8] In this respect, the

---

[3] E.g. R. Parry, 'The Civil Service and Intergovernmental Relations', *Public Policy and Administration* 19 (2004): 50–63. The classic account of the 'quasi-diplomatic' approach is R. Simeon, *Federal-Provincial Diplomacy: The making of recent policy in Canada* (Toronto: University of Toronto Press, 1972), reprinted 2006 with a new introduction.

[4] See e.g. L. Hunter, *Managing Conflicts after Devolution: A Toolkit for Civil Servants* (London: the Constitution Unit, 2000). Available at www.ucl.ac.uk/constitution-unit/publications/unit-publications /65.html

[5] 'Parliamentary federations' are federal systems based on principles of parliamentary democracy, rather than presidential systems with a separation of powers between the executive, legislative and judicial branches of government. Such systems — notably the United States — exhibit a very different form of intergovernmental relations. See R. Watts, *Executive Federalism: A comparative analysis* Research Paper 26 (Kingston, Ont: Institute of Intergovernmental Relations, Queen's University, 1989).

[6] This chapter is based on research undertaken as part of a project on intergovernmental relation in the UK and comparatively as part of the programme on 'Nations and Regions: the dynamics of devolution' funded by the Leverhulme Trust and based at the Constitution Unit at University College London. It draws principally on interviews and field research carried out during three visits to Canada, two visits to Australia and shorter but more frequent visits to Spain and Germany between 2002 and 2005. My thanks to the Leverhulme Trust for their support.

[7] See A. Trench, 'Intergovernmental Relations: In search of a theory' in S. Greer (ed.), *Territory, Democracy and Justice: Regionalism and federalism in western democracies* (Basingstoke: Palgrave Macmillan, 2006).

[8] In this context, and much of the comparative literature, 'multinational federation' means a federal system founded upon more than one group claiming national identity within the boundaries of the federation, and which the federal system is intended to enable to live together within one state for the purposes of international law. See Burgess 2006, particularly chapter 4. Such states may also be multi-ethnic in the sense that there are people, usually recent immigrants or their descendants, of other nationalities within them – but they are not territorially concentrated and do not constitute a distinctive group with claims to constitutional recognition as a result. In this sense, Canada, Spain and Belgium are

general institutional characteristics of a federal system play a significant role in structuring the behaviour of actors within the system, while the specific constitutional and institutional arrangements of particular systems are much less important. Otherwise, it is impossible to explain why such other-wise-divergent systems continue to use the same repertory of techniques and methods. The practice of a broadly similar system of intergovernmental rela-tions is not just common to most federal systems, but does not depend on the formal characteristics of the systems to which much attention has histori-cally been given.[9] In order to do this, however, it is necessary to skim over many of the details of each specific system; this chapter focuses on the wood, not the trees.

One way of putting the UK into this broader context is to use a distinction between three models of intergovernmental relations: 'functional', 'finan-cial', and 'summit-oriented'.[10] 'Functional' intergovernmental relations are dominated by specific policy matters and interactions, and are concerned with largely technical issues of how one government's policies affect another's. It therefore concerns ministers and officials for that policy area but seldom spills over to affect other ministers or departments. Consequently there is little or no interest in intergovernmental relations from the centre of government. Financial intergovernmental relations are concerned with financial matters (either the allocation of finance from the federal/central government to constituent units, or the management of fiscal relations between them), and means that the key actors become finance ministers and ministries, with other considerations (notably legal and constitutional ones) taking a back seat, and the finance minister making the running on intergov-ernmental matters more generally. Summit-oriented intergovernmental rela-tions develop when high-stakes political issues come onto the agenda. It leads to the direct management of intergovernmental relations by heads of government, and their close and ongoing interest in it. This may well happen

multinational federations; Australia and Germany (and, for that matter, the United States) are not. For practical purposes such states are what Michael Keating and others call 'plurinational' states. Cf M. Keating, *Plurinational Democracy: Stateless nations in a post-sovereignty era* (Oxford: Oxford University Press, 2001). Constitutional asymmetry is commonly associated with such multinational systems, as a way of accommodating demands for recognition of the distinctive sub-state national minorities. There is obviously a parallel here with the UK's extreme asymmetry, the distinctive nationhood of Scotland and Wales, and the contested place of Northern Ireland within the United Kingdom.

[9] The classic example of this approach is K.C. Wheare, *Federal Government* 4th edition (Oxford: Oxford University Press, 1963). For a more up-to-date comparative discussion, taking into account issues of society and political theory as well as institutions, see M. Burgess, *Comparative Federalism: Theory and practice* (London: Routledge, 2006).

[10] This model is essentially that of Stefan Dupré: see J.S. Dupré, 'The Workability of Executive Federalism in Canada' in H. Bakvis and W. Chandler (eds.), *Federalism and the Role of the State* (Toronto: University of Toronto Press, 1987). Dupré distinguishes between financial, functional and constitutional intergovernmental relations: the modification to refer to summit-oriented intergovernmental relations is my own. See Trench 2006, pp. 236–8.

when constitutional issues — increases in constituent unit powers, or the possibility of secession/independence — come onto the agenda, but can arise in other circumstances such as a general desire by heads of government to remain engaged in such important matters, which may affect their own standing in their domestic arenas.[11] (Australia is a good example here, with the establishment of the Council of Australian Governments or COAG as a forum for the federal Prime Minister and state and territory Premiers to meet, at least annually, for discussions on important, usually policy matters — health, water resources, climate change, and so forth.) On this scale, until May 2007 the UK barely made it to having 'functional' intergovernmental relations, given the level of disengagement of even most departmental ministers and their senior officials from intergovernmental issues. The summit-oriented nature of intergovernmental relations in Canada, marked during the 1980s and early 1990s, has declined considerably since the late 1990s and Canada would probably now fall around the 'financial' stage of the continuum (though even that is debatable, as financial issues have receded in importance in the last year or so), as would Australia.

First of all, this chapter will discuss the role of some of the key actors in intergovernmental relations. Second, it will survey some of the key issues in such relations, and the ways these are dealt with. Then it will look at some of the common mechanisms and process of such relations. Finally, it will consider the application of these comparative experiences to the UK.

It is worth clarifying the terminology that will be used here. 'Federal/central government' should be self-explanatory, but 'constituent unit' may not be — this refers to states, provinces, Länder and similar governments. To try to avoid using 'level' or 'tier' to distinguish between these sets of governments (and so avoid the implication of a hierarchy in which one is higher than the other), I have used 'sphere' or 'order' (the former is often used in South Africa, the latter in Canada).

ACTORS

First Ministers

The political heads of governments usually take a close and keen interest in intergovernmental matters, indicating the political (as well as constitutional

---

[11] Dupré's category of 'constitutional' intergovernmental relations conflates the importance of summitry (which can have other causes) with the emergence of legal and constitutional issues as the dominant ones. This conflation is understandable in a Canadian context, but is less valid for other systems. I have argued elsewhere that the role of law and legal issues in intergovernmental relations is related much more to societal characteristics, and (although the relationship is complex) where political systems are highly legalised that this will cause the emergence of constitutional issues as a major factor. See A. Trench, 'Legalisation and the Practice of Intergovernmental Relations in Federal Systems'. Paper presented at ECPR Joint Workshops, Helsinki, May 2007.

importance) of them. In many governments, especially smaller ones, first ministers will take on the role of acting as minister for intergovernmental affairs (for example, most Canadian Provinces or Australian States). Larger governments, with more complex relations, may have a special minister for the function, but that minister is usually directly answerable to the head of government and works closely with him or her (e.g. in Canada in both the federal and Quebec governments). But in most federal systems, the head of government takes a personal interest in intergovernmental matters and is closely engaged with them. This is obviously important when high-stakes matters are on the table — constitutional negotiations, for example, or discussions about changing systems of financial redistribution. On the day to day level, their role is understandably more marginal, but it is interesting that they remain engaged and give direction from the heart of government. It is also interesting that this is generally as true for federal/central governments as for state or provincial ones, with federal prime ministers needing to ensure that they are in control of the process and manage relations with states or provinces which are usually much weaker constitutionally and in other ways.

Ministers

Ministers with specific portfolio responsibilities — for health, energy, or whatever — will similarly be closely engaged in intergovernmental matters. Many items in their portfolio will have intergovernmental aspects, and they will need to keep close contact with their counterparts in other governments as a result. For federal governments, this often provides a way to steer the overall direction of policy in a particular area, especially as they are likely to able to support favoured initiatives with federal money. Such contact will take various forms, but commonly involves regular meetings of ministerial councils or conferences. Ministers commonly seek to manage the politics of their particular portfolios, both in relation to the other sphere of government and (for ministers from constituent units) their counterparts in other constituent-unit governments.

Officials and Issues of Internal Governmental Organisation

Officials are the lynch-pins of intergovernmental relation in federal systems and have to do much of the work to enable those systems to function effectively. There is much liaison between governments to be done, and much co-ordination within a government as well. For that reason, internal organisation to deal with intergovernmental matters is an important aspect of understanding how intergovernmental relations are handled.

Part of this work is handled by central co-ordinating offices, located close to the head of government. Sometimes they are teams in the *Staatskanzlei*, the department of the prime minister or premier, or whatever the department directly serving the head of government is called. In other cases, they constitute separate departments or ministries. They can vary hugely in size, but are commonly much larger in federal/central governments than constituent units (although Australia is an exception to this). In Canada, the most advanced case, the federal government's Intergovernmental Affairs Office in the Privy Council Office has around 80 officials at present. Its largest provincial counterpart, the Quebec government's *Secrétariat aux affaires intergouvernementales canadiennes*, has about 70; Ontario, the next largest, about 35, and some of the smaller provinces have a mere handful of officials at the centre. But the presence of a central coordination capacity to advise the head of government and other intergovernmental affairs ministers, develop and co-ordinate intergovernmental and often constitutional policy within government, liaise with other governments and gather intelligence is general.

As well as central agencies, there are also intergovernmental specialists, concerned with the broader constitutional implications of policy issues, in each functional or line ministry. Again, such teams are usually quite small (single figures of staff, often fewer than 5), but they act as both a source of internal advice to their colleagues concerned with finance or social welfare, and act as a broader network with their colleagues from other governments.

In addition to all this, intergovernmental relations commonly forms a major part of the work of many officials whose main concern is with a policy issue, down to quite low levels (the equivalent of HEO in the UK). Such officials are likely at least to keep an eye on what other governments are doing, partly as a source of ideas for making better policy, partly because their ministers and the mass media are likely to be interested, partly out of general awareness. The upshot is that a very large number of officials in all governments are concerned with managing relations with other governments, and that this takes up an appreciable amount of their time and work. It may only be a designated full-time specialisation for a few, but it is a concern for many.

There are two other salient points about the working of officials in federal systems. First, a consequence of the high level of interaction between officials and the extent to which they keep an eye on developments in other jurisdictions is that what one might call a 'concertation reflex' develops, particularly among constituent-unit officials. The result is that officials, presented with a policy challenge or some initiative of the federal/central government, will tend to ask each other what the other governments are doing and how they do it almost immediately. It is a straightforward response to operating in an environment where governments can be easily outmanoeuvred. The phenomenon is not unique to federal systems (it can also be observed in the European Union, for example), but it becomes an important feature of how federal systems work.

Second, officials from one level of government usually work in distinct civil services from one another — the Australian Commonwealth (federal) government and New South Wales each have their own civil services. (Germany is peculiar in this respect, as the regulation and grading of the civil service have been treated as federal matters until the recent Federalism-I reforms, although each government employs its own officials). They have no difficulty in understanding each other as professional colleagues and bound by similar codes of conduct and accountability.

Federal and central governments enjoy a considerable number of advantages when it comes to the bureaucratic aspects of managing intergovernmental relations. They often have more officials. They often (though by no means always) have fewer responsibilities for delivering public services, so can take a broader, more synoptic view of what policies 'the country' should have and how to deliver it. They also have the time to do so. They may be helped in this by having greater awareness of developments elsewhere, and perhaps a better network of international contacts than their constituent-unit counterparts. They may well enjoy the benefits of constitutional powers that enable them to play some role (even if it is a very minor one) in many areas of policy, so they can involve themselves in a wider range of issues than constituent-unit governments or departments. And, thanks to a combination of personnel, constitutional and financial resources (the last itself the consequence of a vertical fiscal imbalance), they can promote indirectly and by suasion initiatives favoured by the centre even when they have to act through or in conjunction with constituent unit governments. In other cases, they may simply be able to bypass constituent unit governments altogether. The result is that federal/central governments are in a powerful position, structurally if not constitutionally, and can often achieve what they wish even if they need to approach their goal tactfully and indirectly.[12]

Parliaments and Back-bench Politicians

All federal systems worthy of the name are democracies, and many (including those discussed here) are parliamentary-type systems rather than presidential ones. But this does not mean that parliaments and legislatures play a major role in intergovernmental relations. Commonly, the executive takes control of this area (not surprising, as so many issues concern matters of

---

[12] Roland Sturm has pointed out the extent to which policies and institutional arrangements in federal systems come to resemble each other: see R. Sturm, 'The Adventure of Divergence: An inquiry into the preconditions for institutional diversity and political innovation after political decentralization' in S. Greer (ed.), *Territory, Democracy and Justice: Regionalism and federalism in western democracies* (Basingstoke: Palgrave Macmillan, 2006).

policy and administration), and parliaments are at best a poor second.[13] Inter-governmental relations are largely a game the executive arms of government, not territorial units as a whole, play. It is otherwise in presidential-type systems such as the United States, where each territorial unit has at least three actors for intergovernmental matters (the legislature, the governor or president, and the courts), and perhaps a fourth if state delegations to the US Congress are included.

Legislatures play a limited role for a number of reasons. One appears to be the lack of interest many elected members show in what are often complicated and arcane areas of policy. If the members are not full-time, or not of high calibre, this is exacerbated. A second factor is information, and accessibility of information; federal systems often give rise to complaints about how executive-dominated intergovernmental relations operate beyond the range of normal accountability to parliament.[14] The result is that legislatures seldom play a serious or active role in intergovernmental matters, whether by building direct links with other legislatures or by scrutinising their own government carefully and holding it to account for its actions in the intergovernmental arena.

Political Parties

Political parties are important forces in intergovernmental relations, and many students of them following 'rational choice' approaches emphasise the importance of an integrated party system in maintaining unity across the country as a whole.[15] In many federal systems — particularly multinational ones (Spain, Canada, Belgium, for example) — there is no state-wide party system. While some political parties may operate across the whole of the state, the existence of parties for some particular parts of it (minority nationalist parties are the obvious example, but not the only one) mean that the conditions of party-political competition vary considerably depending on which jurisdiction (federal/central or constituent unit) is involved, and from constituent unit to constituent unit. Spanish elections are very different in Catalonia and Andalusia; Canadian federal elections are quite different from provincial ones.

There are two interesting points about how the practice of party politics in such complex environments affects the practice of intergovernmental relations. The first relates to party organisation. To operate effectively in such

---

[13] See Watts 1989.

[14] See R. Simeon and D. R. Cameron, 'Intergovernmental Relations: An oxymoron if ever there was one' in H. Bakvis and G. Skogstad (eds.), *Canadian Federalism: Performance, effectiveness, and legitimacy* (Toronto a Oxford: Oxford University Press, 2002).

[15] See for a recent example M. Filippov, P.C. Ordeshook and O. Shvetsova, *Designing Federalism: A theory of self-sustainable federal institutions* (New York and London: Cambridge University Press, 2004).

varying political environments, it is necessary for particular parts of state-wide political parties to have considerable financial, policy-making and campaigning autonomy to be able to adapt to the environment in which they function. What helps the CDU win votes in North Rhine-Westphalia is not the same as what wins them votes in Baden-Württemberg. In some cases (Canada is the most extreme) this results in a fragmentation of the party system, with different parties not only in federal and provincial elections but, at provincial level, varying widely from province to province (there is little similarity between the provincial Liberals in Ontario and British Columbia, for example). That sort of way of working is simply a fact of life in such systems. Parties concerned with a single constituent unit (particularly minority nationalist parties) have it much easier in this respect, as their focus is only on one specific part of the system — and they can often work better as an integrated party, using their strength in several spheres of government to advance the interests of their part of the country.

Second, even where there organisational or ideological links between the various parts of a state-wide party, it is hard for politicians to do favours to their party colleagues in another jurisdiction, whether that be from one constituent unit to another or from the federal/central level to a constituent unit (or vice versa). As one senior Australian Labor (state) politician put it privately, 'I don't win an election in [my state] by helping out the party nationally. I have to stand up for the interests of [my state].' The focus on winning the elections that one contests takes precedence over the desire (which exists) to help out party colleagues operating in other domains. One will help them if one can, without it causing any harm in the domestic arena — but a politician's concern is with that arena first and foremost. Standing up for the voters in one's own jurisdiction is the best way that politicians can demonstrate that.

Courts and Judges

Courts, particularly supreme and constitutional courts, play a surprisingly limited role in intergovernmental relations in parliamentary systems, especially common-law ones.[16] (They are much more important in presidential systems, where the separation of powers gives them both greater autonomy and greater scope to affect other actors.) The reason is that courts are not autonomous actors with control of a wide agenda in the way that governments are (and even parliaments, to some extent). While they have room for manoeuvre in deciding the issues that do come before them, they have very little control over what those issues are. Even courts which have jurisdiction

---

[16] For a comparative discussion of different approaches to federalism issues by the courts in three common-law federations, see G. Baier, *Courts and Federalism: Judicial doctrine in the United States, Australia and Canada* (Vancouver: UBC Press, 2006).

to give advisory opinions on important but abstract issues (and which are not simply limited to resolving cases actually in dispute between the parties) can only consider a case if a) there is a point which is legally unclear and b) the parties wish them to resolve it. Governments have the initiative when it comes to bringing such cases. They cannot wholly control the issues that a court might determine, as other public bodies, commercial interests and private individuals may all have concerns about the lawfulness or constitutionality of government actions or legislation, but they are the most active litigants when it comes to questions of how powers are divided between the different spheres of government in a federal system. If they can find other ways of resolving an issue in a way that is both legally secure and practicable, they may well do so. Litigation is a protracted and inherently unpredictable way of securing an outcome, so tends not to be preferred if there is a choice.

The result is that governments are unlikely to have recourse to the courts if they have a better alternative which they can control more effectively — if they can reach an agreement and ensure it will be legally binding, that is often preferable to going to court. The comparative unpredictability of the courts means that even litigants who generally do well before them are reluctant to undertake the risks of litigation.[17] Civil-law systems, like Germany or Belgium, work somewhat differently as the conception of what is 'legal' is broader, and the constitution is seen first and foremost as legal rather than political in nature. (A good example is the recurrent litigation before the Federal Constitutional Court in Germany about financial equalisation between the *Länder*.) There is therefore a greater need to ensure that any changes are lawful, and the courts (and lawyers) are more prone to assert their role in such systems.

This is not to say that courts cannot play a major role in intergovernmental relations. Many matters of legal but not political importance will be regularly before the courts, either because third parties bring them or because governments want an outcome that is legally certain even if they do not know what that outcome might be. More important is that courts define constitutional boundaries, and periodically those boundaries shift. As a result, court decisions play a significant role in reshaping the constitutional environment within which intergovernmental relations take place. (The opinion of the Supreme Court of Canada in the *Reference regarding Quebec Secession*, discussed below, is a good example.) This is, however, a role that is played on relatively rare occasions; having the power to reshape the boundaries of intergovernmental relations does not make the courts into actors in the more routine practice.

---

17 The argument advanced here is developed at greater length in Trench 2006, pp. 244–6.

ISSUES

Finance: the Power of the Purse

Finance is a key issue in every multi-level system. There are a number of problems. One is to find ways of dealing with different levels of prosperity and economic performance, and to reconcile that inequality with at least some commonality in the provision of public goods and services. The second is to deal with the different taxing powers of different layers or orders of government, as commonly the federal or central government has both wider taxing powers and greater fiscal capacity than state or regional governments. The first of these usually leads to some form of horizontal fiscal equalisation, which is usually undertaken by the central or federal government, and involves allocating funds to poorer regions at the expense of richer ones. The second results in some measure of vertical fiscal imbalance, which enables the federal or central government to engage in horizontal fiscal equalisation, and perhaps leads to a 'fiscal imbalance' between the two spheres of government.[18]

Federal systems usually manage these conflicting objectives in a way that has similar elements in substance, if not in form. What usually emerges is a system in which:

- States or regions raise a substantial amount of their own *tax*, principally through personal income tax, but also other taxes and charges (for example, property taxes or stamp duties). In decentralised systems like Canada or Switzerland, this can account for as much of 70–80 per cent of overall constituent unit spending (which itself is typically 45–60 per cent of total public spending). In some cases, the taxing authority is the state or region under its own name; in others, a significant proportion of tax revenue (at least 30 per cent) is formerly allocated to the states or regions by the central or federal government, which on the formal level monopolises tax-raising powers.
- The federal or central government allocates *grants* to the states or regions for specific purposes. These grants are conditional, although how conditional they are varies a good deal; conditions are sometimes onerous and used to promote federal government policy, and on other occasions fairly limited and ensure country-wide application of a general sort of policy. They are usually related to welfare policies, notably health, perhaps also other social services or education. Such grants are usually calculated on a fairly crude basis — often simply on a per capita basis.

---

[18] For a recent comparative discussion of financial arrangements in federal systems see A. Shah (ed.), *The Practice of Fiscal Federalism: Comparative perspectives* (Montreal and Kingston: McGill-Queen's University Press, 2007).

- The federal or central government also allocates funding specifically to equalise the financial resources available to all governments. Such grants are unconditional, but the calculation of that is complex as it relates principally to need, and this manifests itself in various ways. Equalisation is of course a form of territorial redistribution: areas that are already prosperous can demonstrate little need, so receive relatively little from such funds, while poorer ones have both higher need and fewer resources of their own, so receive a larger amount.

How this broad framework is achieved varies a good deal from system to system. What is general is the use of a combination of instruments (by contrast, the UK's reliance on what is effectively a very large unconditional grant is highly unusual).[19] What is also general is that this then leads to complex and protracted debates about finance, which tend to be a running feature of financing federal systems. As any system means some constituent units are winners and others losers (and economic changes mean that the winner and losing constituent units change over time), there are recurrent attempts to re-open financial issues and revise the structure of finance (particularly the weight of the various instruments), and the formulae used. The questions this presents for a political system are significant: about money, and about the redistribution of money. One of the hazards they present is that what are essentially political questions become veiled in economic or financial terms, so the underlying issues become obscured — a hazard that is to some degree limited by the extent to which the questions are so clearly political that politicians become very closely interested in them.

Policy Making and Policy Overlaps

Overlaps between the policy functions of each sphere of government is another inevitable feature of federal and similar systems. However perfect the constitutional design may be (or have been), in the modern world it is inevitable that there are overlaps between policy, which need to be handled in some way. Executive intergovernmental relations — the processes described above — are one way this often happens. Litigation is sometimes another, with the courts called on to determine which sphere of government has authority over a particular matter. But however such overlaps are resolved, they are a routine occurrence, needing to be managed at the level of day-to-day policy and to be understood as reflecting larger political struggles at a more profound level.

---

[19] For further discussion of the importance of finance and the instruments available, see A. Trench, 'Tying the UK Together? Intergovernmental relations and the financial constitution of the UK' in R. Hazell (ed.), *Constitutional Futures Revisited: Britain's Constitution to 2020* (Basingstoke: Palgrave Macmillan, 2008 forthcoming).

The question is how such overlaps are managed, in both substantive and process terms. Substantive outcomes depend on a range of factors, including the constitutional powers of each sphere of government, differences in the policies they wish to pursue and their ideological approaches generally, party-political linkages, and the general balance of power between the two spheres of government. Unsurprisingly, outcomes vary a good deal. But the processes are remarkably similar across systems: a process of negotiation and brokerage, along the lines sketched out in this chapter, organised around ministerial meetings and involving a wide range of actors within governments. (Recent academic writing, particularly in the US, has often focussed on such issues of 'intergovernmental management', as though this has not always formed a significant part of the work of officials concerned with the practice of intergovernmental relations.)

On the constitutional level, it is worth noting that the UK is distinctive in one important respect. Most federal systems have built their welfare states (in particular) around federal institutions: the constitutional framework of federalism preceded the welfare state, and the welfare state was therefore fitted into a pre-existing constitutional framework that would be tweaked if needed, but seldom fundamentally adjusted as a result. The UK's welfare state was built in the context of a much more centralised state, with common policies even if aspects of administration were handled by the Scottish (and later Welsh) Offices. Devolution has meant a spinning-out of centralised policies into the hands of the devolved institutions. Only one other system has done this: Belgium. Belgium's approach to intergovernmental relations is predicated on the exclusive grant of powers to each order of government, so in principle no government or legislature needs the consent of another in order to act, a marked contrast to the UK. However, the narrowness with which functions are defined for this purpose means that in reality extensive collaboration between governments is needed for the making of policy or the delivery of public services.[20] Thus, despite a completely different approach to the constitutional structure of federalism there, the overall outcome resembles the close entanglement of governments that one finds in the UK — and the mechanisms to manage these that are used in Belgium are generally similar to those used in other federal systems.

Constitutions and the Allocation of Competencies

The issue of which government is responsible for which matters is a contentious one in pretty much every system. Debates about this are best regarded as part and parcel of operating in a multi-level system rather than as a regrettable intrusion. However, in most of federal systems, the issue of the

---

[20] See J. Poirier, 'Formal Mechanisms of Intergovernmental Relations in Belgium', *Regional and Federal Studies,* 12 (2002): 24–54.

'internal' constitution of a state or region is not part of this pattern. The constitutions of German *Länder*, Australian States, or Canadian Provinces (or for that matter US States) are internal matters; issues like the proper relationship between executive and legislature, the regulation of the legislature or the proper conduct of state or regional elections are internal matters, not federal ones, and change in these matters is similarly an internal matter. (Spain is an exception here, as the individual statutes of autonomy of the autonomous communities are matters of legislation by the central state, even if they are negotiated between individual autonomous communities and the central state.) The constitutional issues that are raised in intergovernmental relations mainly concern the division of powers between the two spheres of government, which requires a broader consensus. A secondary issue may be formal recognition of constitutional distinctiveness, and the granting of 'special treatment' or 'special regimes' for particular constituent units.

Constitutional politics are the most difficult area for the practice of intergovernmental relations. One issue is the difficulty of reaching agreement between parties with very different interests and views, when formal amending formulae often mean that unanimity or near-unanimity is needed to effect change. A second issue is that the relatively private and closed nature of intergovernmental processes makes it hard to build support for proposed changes among the general public. As the process tends to present a compromise outline agreement at a relatively advanced stage of intergovernmental negotiations, it is hard to re-open complex issues if that is needed to build public support, let alone have a process that involves the public and invites wider participation from the outset.[21]

National Minorities and Demands for Autonomy and Independence

The place of minority nations in larger multinational or plurinational systems creates a perennial form of intractable constitutional politics in all such systems.[22] Such constitutional politics affect broader aspects of intergovernmental relations — quite apart from ongoing constitutional debates, they are an undercurrent in more routine intergovernmental relations too, and problems in making the system work as a whole can be used to support demands for further constitutional change, while demands for such change may be undermined if the present system can be shown to work effectively.

A major issue for central/federal states is the extent to which they accept, or encourage, asymmetry — differential treatment of some constituent units

---

[21] For a hugely valuable account of these processes in Canada, see P. Russell, *Constitutional Odyssey: Can Canadians become a sovereign people?* 3rd edition (Toronto: University of Toronto Press, 2004). These problems particularly bedevilled the Meech Lake and Charlottetown accord processes there in the late 1980s and early 1990s; see chapters 9–11.

[22] For a comparative discussion of some of the issues see S. Tierney, *Constitutional Law and National Pluralism* (Oxford: Oxford University Press, 2004).

compared with others, and the reaction of less favoured constituent units to this. Asymmetry causes (but may also be caused by) bilateral rather than multilateral relationships. Asymmetric constitutions add complexity, and may introduce a logic of 'catch-up' to the state as a whole — less-favoured units seek greater autonomy, prompting the previously-advantaged ones to seek yet further advantages (usually in the form of enhanced powers, either legal or financial) which have the effect of re-establishing a differential between that unit and other ones. Asymmetry runs the risk of opening up broader debates about territorial justice and injustice — whether one part of the state is doing 'better', and this is regarded as being at the expense of other parts. By and large, it would seem that central states seek to promote constitutional symmetry rather than asymmetry, though they may not be able to sustain that; apart from anything else, having all constituent units with similar powers makes life somewhat easier for them.

Debates about independence can similarly continue indefinitely. From the point of view of the central/federal state, the fact that the debate continues is an indication of success not failure — it means that constituent units in question have not, in fact, become 'independent' (whatever that may in fact mean). Yet the ground rules for such debates are often hard to identify — the yardsticks set by the Supreme Court of Canada in its landmark opinion on Quebec secession remain, however, of great importance.[23] These are, in essence, that there was no right to secede unilaterally in international or Canadian law, but that the demonstration of a clear desire to secede in response to a clear referendum question created a duty on the federal government to negotiate in good faith the terms of independence. Such a ruling, while the subject of much contention, has led to greater clarity about the processes of secession than in any other part of the world.

PROCESSES AND INSTRUMENTS

Intergovernmental Meetings

It is probably evident from the discussion of actors above that meetings are a key part of the framework of managing intergovernmental relations. They occur regularly, routinely, at almost all levels of government from middle-ranking officials responsible for particular files or specialist areas of policy through more senior officials to ministers. The level at which meetings are rarest and least used is the summit level, of heads of government, discussed below.

---

[23] *Reference re Secession of Quebec*, [1998] 2 S.C.R. 217. For a discussion, see D. Schneiderman (ed.), *The Quebec Decision: Perspectives on the Supreme Court Ruling on Secession* (Toronto: Lorimer, 1999).

Ministerial meetings occur with varying frequencies, according to need; in some policy areas they may only be annual events, but in others might happen every two or three months. Ministerial meetings are, of course, the highest and most visible part of a network of broader collaboration between governments, involving preparation by senior and, below them, more junior officials. Meetings tend to be somewhat more frequent at working levels, especially when a policy issue becomes active (as with the pensions file in Canada in the late 1960s and early 1970s).[24] This can itself become an issue: the amount of time, energy and money that regular meetings take up is considerable, and may become a source of concern to governments that are keen to exercise autonomy (Quebec is a notable example here). Moreover, if such regular meetings lead to the development of system-wide 'policy communities' that embrace officials from federal/central and constituent-unit governments, developing a common idea of what would make 'good policy' that they then seek to effect in their respective spheres of government, they can act as a powerful force for convergence.

The heavy reliance on meetings is a useful tool for the central or federal government. It often convenes meetings, takes the chair at them (or co-chairs them with a representative of the constituent unit governments), and in practice can shape both agenda and outcome (for example, by offering financial support for some options but not others). Yet they do not get matters entirely their own way. Much depends on the extent to which constituent units are able to agree and stick to a common position. It is routine for constituent-unit governments to meet ahead of time to work out a common position. (Particularly at summit level, it is also common for the federal/central government to try to find ways to break up the unity of the constituent units.)

Intergovernmental meetings structure intergovernmental relations (junior officials develop detailed policy among themselves and may also meet to prepare for senior officials' meetings, which in turn prepare ministerial meetings), and become part of a web of government activity managing policy across the country. They are central to the practice of intergovernmental relations, not just because of their immediate role but because they structure much wider forms of interaction. Perhaps this explains why (other than in Germany) few constituent-unit governments have representative offices in the federal/central capital; they are not needed to represent views or act as a focus for co-ordination, as the relevant officials are in regular contact by phone, email as well as routine meetings in any event. (In Germany, the very intensity of official contact, particularly around the

---

[24] Discussed in Simeon 1972.

Bundesrat, appears to be the reason for the large offices that each *Land* maintains in Berlin.[25])

Perhaps the most important aspect of intergovernmental meetings is their role in relation to disputes and disagreements between governments. Disagreements are a natural part of the practice of intergovernmental relations. The practice of working through a large number of meetings, at a variety of levels, provides a set of mechanisms for dealing with such disagreements. It enables issues to be clarified, and in many cases for them to be resolved by negotiation or compromise.

Summitteering

Summit meetings of the first ministers or heads of government in federal/central and constituent unit levels are always significant events. In some systems, such meetings never happen at all (e.g. Spain — although there are bilateral meetings, there are no multilateral ones). In others (such as Canada), they happen sporadically; others, like Australia and Germany, hold them annually as a matter of routine.[26] All such meetings are inevitably politically charged — it is an opportunity for politicians from all governments to hold the public stage and seek to advantage the interests of their government, and the tensions are such that Canadian prime ministers have sought to hold such meetings as rarely as possible, knowing that they may well be embarrassed even if they secure the sorts of agreements or outcomes they sought, and will probably have to make significant concessions to get such outcomes. Summit meetings between federal/central and constituent unit governments are not just the rarest form of intergovernmental co-ordination but also the least useful aspect of it. Their value is partly symbolic (showing the efforts to which the federal/central government will go to seek endorsement of its proposals, the role all governments play in the overall governance of the country, and so its unity as well as diversity). It is also partly practical. Such meetings can be the only way to secure progress on important country-wide issues — whether it be major policy issues such reform of health care systems and financing arrangements or financial arrangements for equalisation systems, or constitutional change — as well as to secure agreement on particularly thorny disputes. But they are the tip of an iceberg of much wider co-ordination.

---

[25] See U. Leonardy, 'The Institutional Structures of German Federalism' in C. Jeffery (ed.), *Recasting German Federalism: The legacies of unification* (London: Pinter, 1999).

[26] The frequency of first ministers' meetings in Canada has declined since the end of the rounds of 'mega-constitutional' negotiations, and first ministers' conferences have ceased altogether since then. See Russell 2004.

Horizontal and Vertical Relations

Intergovernmental relations are not simply about vertical relations — between the federal/central government and those of constituent units. An important aspect are horizontal relationships, between the various constituent units among themselves. This can take a number of forms: meetings where the constituent units have (normally exclusive) formal competence, as with culture in Germany, meetings to develop and co-ordinate common positions ahead of meetings with the federal/central state as well, or meetings of constituent-unit heads of government covering a wide agenda and not simply oriented toward meetings of all first ministers in the country. This last approach has been adopted in Canada, with the Council of the Federation, and extended to Australia, with the Council for the Australian Federation.[27] In Germany, there are pre-meetings for the pre-meetings, with *Land* governments of different political complexions caucusing together before the *Länder* as a whole meet.

Although horizontal relations can be concerned with matters in which the federal/central government has no (formal) interest, they are generally principally focussed on relations with the federal/central government. Their intensity consequently depends chiefly on the extent to which constituent units collectively find that they are strongest when they act together, rather than manage their relations with the federal/central government bilaterally. The Council of the Federation in Canada arose from a determination of the incoming Quebec Liberal government in 2003 to prove collective provincial strength, both in acting together where co-ordination of policy was desirable but the matters involved were exclusively provincial, and in developing common positions of the provinces toward the federal government. Its impact has been limited not just by differences in interests and views among the provincial governments, but also by a changed approach to intergovernmental relations by the federal governments under Paul Martin and Stephen Harper.

Intergovernmental Agreements

Intergovernmental agreements are a routine instrument for handling intergovernmental relations. They have a number of common features in most systems: they tend to numerous, used in a variety of contexts (making generalisations difficult to make), and described as not legally enforceable.[28] Legal enforceability would raise constitutional problems — it would entail one government purporting to bind its successor, and also binding its

---

27 For details of the two Councils' activities, see their websites – at www.councilofthefederation.ca and www.caf.gov.au respectively.

28 The most comprehensive discussion is J. Poirier, 'The Functions of Intergovernmental Agreements: Post-devolution Concordats in a Comparative Perspective', [2001] *Public Law*, 134–57.

legislature. Although classifying such agreements is hard and generalising about them is difficult, there are clearly two distinct sorts of agreement. One sort are those that are general in content and political in intent, embodying a high-level agreement (usually at the level of heads of government) about a constitutional or policy matter. A good example might be the Canadian 'Social Union Framework Agreement'. Such agreements are public, and meant to be — their purpose is at least as much to declare general political intentions as it is to shape the details of policy, and they may be enforceable before public opinion but not in the courts. What is often more important is what such agreements omit as what they say. Their level of ambiguity and generality is such that, even if they were legally enforceable in principle, it would be very hard for a court to identify their legal meaning. The second sort are much technical and intended to make practical arrangements work. They tend to be professionally drafted, in legal form and with legal precision, so that they could be construed and enforced by a court if need arose (and if they were intended to be legally enforceable). These deal with areas where collaboration between governments needs to be clear and precise, for example when one government provides services to another (e.g. collecting taxes). These are a common tool of the practice of government, negotiated in detail if not in general outline by officials and drafted by government lawyers.

Legislation

By definition, federal systems do not have the overlap and duplication of legislative competence that, legally speaking, underpins devolution in the UK. Even where legislative powers are expressed as concurrent rather than exclusive, legal doctrines arise to govern the exercise of legislative power — such as the precedence of federal/central legislation in areas where two pieces of legislation conflict, or that of 'occupation of the field', meaning that constituent units may not legislate in fields where the federal/central government has legislated (which itself raises the question of what exactly such a field is). Where legislation does need co-ordination (as arises in Australia, with the power of the state parliaments to refer matters to the federal parliament under section 51 (xxxvii) of the Australian constitution), the result is a highly formal process to control the use of that power, involving legislation passed by state parliaments and legally-drafted, detailed intergovernmental agreements with the proposed legislation annexed between the federal and state governments.

It is common for federal/central governments to have powers relating to constituent-unit legislation, to ensure that such legislation only relates to functions constitutionally allocated to the constituent units. These powers usually include the ability to refer legislation that the federal/central government considers exceeds those limits to the courts, for a decision about whether it is *intra vires* (within powers) or not. But the existence of such powers does not mean that one sphere of government will spend much time pre-emptively scrutinising legislation proposed in another sphere; they have too much 'real' work to do for that. While a government is likely to take considerable care over the constitutionality of legislation before its own legislature, checking other legislation is simply too much work. Such legal sanctions are therefore only likely to be invoked reactively, when there is reason to suspect that there is a problem.

CONCLUSION:
LESSONS FOR THE UNITED KINGDOM FROM FEDERAL SYSTEMS?

It will be clear from the discussion above that the way intergovernmental relations work in the UK does not resemble that of federal systems to any very great extent.[29] In the key areas — of the processes used, of the actors involved, or the main issues — the UK continues to manage its intergovernmental relations in a very different way to such systems, one which owes much to pre-devolution forms of interdepartmental relations and to forms of ad hoc management devised when Labour dominated all three British governments. Such an approach is no longer appropriate, as different political parties come to hold office in the various governments and to use power in increasingly different ways. The fact that such a wide range of federal systems have converged on similar ways of working is itself intriguing, and suggests that those systems may afford valuable lessons for the UK in the coming years. The UK has hitherto placed heavy reliance on trust and goodwill — important factors in the practice of intergovernmental relations, but not the sole factor by any means. These have been required to take the place of established institutional ways of working, rather than augment them.

Perhaps the most important issue is whether the system adopted in the UK is workable. 'Workability' is the concept used by Dupré to assess how effective intergovernmental relations were in Canada.[30] It asks, in essence, whether intergovernmental institutions and processes provide a forum conducive to negotiation, consultation or simply an exchange of information, or handicaps these aspects of intergovernmental relations. It may be enhanced by trust and regular contact between the various parties, but the key issue is whether overall the system in fact can operate given the demands placed on it. Whether the UK's system as it operated before May 2007 was workable was open to some debate, but by and large it met the demands

---

[29] For further discussions of the differences between the UK and federal systems, see chapters 11 and 12 (by Watts and Trench) in A. Trench (ed.), *Devolution and Power in the United Kingdom* (Manchester: Manchester University Press, 2007).

[30] See Dupré 1987.

placed on it — the problem was that those demands were likely to change, and indeed have. In some ways, the UK's systems met the standards Dupré sets for workability; the reliance on bilateral contacts, and the ability of specialists in particular areas to deal directly with their counterparts rather than have such people of differing professional backgrounds try to find common ground, are aspects of the UK's system that work well. But when it comes to more political matters, and especially ones where the complexities are technical as well as political, the UK's present arrangements fail to manage these complex relationships well, to recognise the nature of the devolved UK as a state, or to deal with the disputes and differences that naturally arise between governments.

Making the UK's arrangements more workable would not be easy but would be manageable. It would involve greater thought about constitutional powers, and what is a matter for each sphere of government. In this, it is particularly the UK Government and Parliament that need to change. They would also need to show greater acceptance of limits on what each can do as a result. That would imply administrative reorganisation in Whitehall, to differentiate more effectively and clearly between those functions of the UK institutions which related only to England (and were the counterpart of devolved function in Scotland, Wales or Northern Ireland), and those which were UK- or Britain-wide. It would also imply greater use of formal mechanisms, not because such mechanisms are inherently good but because they are an appropriate way to manage relations between governments with different functions and different approaches to policy whose interests and roles overlap or affect each other. That would enable common ground between administrations of different political hues to be identified, and differences managed. In that sense, the approach of the Scottish Government since May 2007 has been much in keeping with securing a workable form of intergovernmental relations than the UK Government's has been.

It is perfectly reasonable to ask what the interest of constituent unit governments might be in seeking to use techniques and processes that (from the account given above) often put them at a disadvantage compared with the federal/central government (although clearly that is not a view that the present Scottish Government shares). It will be apparent from this discussion that central or federal governments hold many of the cards in the practice of intergovernmental relations, and that it is not hard for them to secure favourable outcomes by a variety of means and by cumulating the effect of their various sources of influence. Part of the reason why this overall model is commonly followed is to do with habit and inertia, but that so many constitutionally-varied systems adopt similar approaches suggests that these are not the only factors. And while the question may be reasonable, it also misses the point, as it fails to ask what the alternative is. For most constituent units, the alternative to this approach is one that places them at an even greater disadvantage, prone to being picked off by the central/federal government when it chooses. What this sort of approach to the processes of intergovernmental relations offers to constituent units is a degree of consistency and stability in how things work, and the opportunity to form alliances that offer at least a prospect of greater influence overall. Central states get influence rather power; constituent units get influence too, in a different sort of way. In an age in which sovereignty is becoming increasingly diffuse and hard to locate in a single place, it is an appropriate way of managing differences. That the UK has taken a different approach so far tells us that the early years of devolution have been a transitional period. What happens in the next decade will tell us whether the UK is indeed part of this broader family, or continues to be an exception.

BIBLIOGRAPHY

Primary Sources and Official Documents

House of Lords Select Committee on the Constitution, *Devolution: Inter-Institutional Relations in the United Kingdom* Session 2002–03 2nd Report, HL 28 (London: The Stationery Office, 2003).

Secondary References

Baier, G., *Courts and Federalism: Judicial doctrine in the United States, Australia and Canada* (Vancouver: UBC Press, 2006).
Burgess, M., *Comparative Federalism: Theory and practice* (London: Routledge, 2006).
Dupré, J.S., 'The Workability of Executive Federalism in Canada' in H. Bakvis and W. Chandler (eds.), *Federalism and the Role of the State* (Toronto: University of Toronto Press, 1987).
Filippov, M., P.C. Ordeshook and O. Shvetsova, *Designing Federalism: A theory of self-sustainable federal institutions* (New York and London: Cambridge University Press, 2004).
Hunter, L., *Managing Conflicts after Devolution: A Toolkit for Civil* (London: the Constitution Unit, 2000).
Jeffery, C., 'The Unfinished Business of Devolution: Seven open questions', *Public Policy and Administration*, 22(1) (2007): 92–108;
Keating, M., *Plurinational Democracy: Stateless nations in a post-sovereignty era* (Oxford: Oxford University Press, 2001).
Leonardy, U., 'The Institutional Structures of German Federalism' in C. Jeffery (ed.), *Recasting German Federalism: The legacies of unification* (London: Pinter, 1999).
Parry, R., 'The Civil Service and Intergovernmental Relations', *Public Policy and Administration*, 19 (2004): 50–63.

Poirier, J, 'The Functions of Intergovernmental Agreements: Post-devolution Concordats in a Comparative Perspective', [2001] *Public Law*, 134–57.

Poirier, J., 'Formal Mechanisms of Intergovernmental Relations in Belgium', *Regional and Federal Studies*, 12 (2002): 24–54.

Russell, P., *Constitutional Odyssey: Can Canadians become a sovereign people* 3rd edition (Toronto: University of Toronto Press, 2004).

Schneiderman, D. (ed.), *The Quebec Decision: Perspectives on the Supreme Court Ruling on Secession* (Toronto: Lorimer, 1999).

Shah, A., (ed.), *The Practice of Fiscal Federalism: Comparative perspectives* (Montreal and Kingston: McGill-Queen's University Press, 2007).

Simeon, R., *Federal-Provincial Diplomacy: The making of recent policy in Canada* (Toronto: University of Toronto Press, 1972/2006).

Simeon, R. and D. R. Cameron, 'Intergovernmental Relations: An Oxymoron if Ever There Was One' in H. Bakvis and G. Skogstad (eds.), *Canadian Federalism: Performance, effectiveness, and legitimacy* (Toronto a Oxford: Oxford University Press, 2002).

Sturm, R., 'The Adventure of Divergence: An inquiry into the preconditions for institutional diversity and political innovation after political decentralization' in S. Greer (ed.), *Territory, Democracy and Justice: Regionalism and federalism in western democracies* (Basingstoke: Palgrave Macmillan, 2006).

Tierney, S., *Constitutional Law and National Pluralism* (Oxford: Oxford University Press, 2004).

Trench, A., 'Intergovernmental Relations: In search of a theory' in S. Greer (ed.), *Territory, Democracy and Justice: Regionalism and federalism in western democracies* (Basingstoke: Palgrave Macmillan, 2006).

Trench, A., 'Legalisation and the Practice of Intergovernmental Relations in Federal Systems'. Paper presented at ECPR Joint Workshops, Helsinki, May 2007.

Trench, A., 'Old Wine In New Bottles? Relations between London and Cardiff after the Government of Wales Act 2006', *Contemporary Wales*, 20 (2007): 31–51.

Trench, A., (ed.), *Devolution and Power in the United Kingdom* (Manchester: Manchester University Press, 2007).

Trench, A., 'Tying the UK Together? Intergovernmental relations and the financial constitution of the UK' in R. Hazell (ed.), *Constitutional Futures Revisited: Britain's Constitution to 2020* (Basingstoke: Palgrave Macmillan, 2008 forthcoming).

Watts, R., *Executive Federalism: A comparative analysis* Research Paper 26 (Kingston, Ont: Institute of Intergovernmental Relations, Queen's University, 1989).

Wheare, K.C., *Federal Government* 4th edition (Oxford: Oxford University Press, 1963).

10

Ever Looser Union

James Mitchell

INTRODUCTION

During the Scottish elections in 2007, as in all previous elections when the Scottish National Party (SNP) was an electoral threat, the Nationalists were portrayed by opponents in apocalyptic language. Perhaps because the SNP had never before held office, its opponents were able to invoke negative imagery unchallenged in large sections of the media — indeed, sections of the media displayed even more enthusiasm for absurd exaggeration than party political opponents of the SNP.[1] The reality of an SNP government has been remarkably sober by comparison, much to the surprise of many commentators. Far from ripping up the constitution, constantly picking fights with London or exploiting every difference, the SNP in office has been the model of moderate, responsible government. So, who are the SNP and what are the broader implications of an SNP government?

WHO ARE THE SNP?

A quarter of a century ago, the dominant paradigm for understanding the SNP was that of traditional left-right British class politics. In challenging this way of understanding internal SNP politics, it was suggested that the real tension within the party focused on devolution. Fundamentalists were identified as SNP activists who were suspicious of devolution, viewed it as a trap which would prevent advance to independence while gradualists, later described as pragmatists, were those who saw devolution as either a step towards independence or simply believed that devolution was better than the status quo.[2] The experience of the 1970s, particularly the perception that the '40 per cent rule' (the threshold of support from 40 per cent of the electorate as a whole) had rigged that 1979 referendum, only added to the value of this understanding of internal SNP debates. In this context, one of Alex Salmond's most remarkable achievements in his first term as SNP leader

---

[1] N. McGarvey and P. Cairney, *Scottish Politics* (Basingstoke: Palgrave Macmillan, 2008), p. 43.

[2] See J. Mitchell, 'Ideological Consistency and Strategic Change: The SNP in the 1980s'. Paper presented at Political Studies Association conference, Aberdeen, 1987; J. Mitchell, 'Recent Developments in the Scottish National Party', *Political Quarterly* 59(4) (1988): 473-477; J. Mitchell, *Strategies for Self-Government* (Edinburgh: Polygon, 1996).

was to line his party up behind the campaign for a 'double Yes' vote in the 1997 referendum — only a tiny band of hardliners opposed devolution — and successfully mobilise his party's vote behind devolution. This achievement had significant implications for the SNP and Scottish politics.

The establishment of the Scottish Parliament in 1999 was bound to have a profound impact on the SNP and called into question the fundamentalist-gradualist paradigm which had come to dominate not only academic understanding of the SNP but also journalistic and internal SNP understandings. It also created new opportunities for the SNP. The SNP was helped by operating within a Scottish political environment and by the more proportional electoral system. Nonetheless, George Robertson (then still Labour's shadow Scottish Secretary) predicted, presumably more in hope than expectation, that devolution would kill off the SNP and there were occasional academic attempts to confirm this view.

A number of hardliners were elected to the Scottish Parliament in 1999 but behaved impeccably, becoming model parliamentarians. This was hardly surprising. The SNP had no serious history of support for abstentionism and only a limited tradition of civil disobedience. That did not mean, however, that the old tensions disappeared — not least because old political enmities do not disappear even after their original cause has passed, including within political parties. But instead, the SNP's hardliners became rebels without a cause, quick to criticise the leadership when it faltered but unable to propose an alternative strategy. In time, the absence of an alternative strategy combined with the SNP's electoral advance to erode the hardline position.

Many of those previously associated with a hardline position moved on, taking account of the changed nature of Scottish politics. Kenny MacAskill, now Justice Secretary but previously one of the party's leading hardliners, produced a book in 2004 in which he suggested that there was no need for separate Scottish institutions for all public policy:

> Is there a need for a separate DVLA or even Ordnance Survey?... Does a bureaucracy need to be created in Saltcoats as well as in Swansea? Can we not simply pay our share as well as our respects? Do we need to reinvent the Civil Aviation Authority or other such Institutions as opposed to exercising control from north of the border even if the Institution remains located in the south of it... There are numerous other organisations and Departments where separation is not necessary but the right to direct and instruct is. [3]

In the past, such a view would have provoked serious rows within the SNP. Mike Russell, now another SNP Minister, co-authored a book published in late 2006, in which he conceded that independence was a long way off and called for 'Devolution Stage Two, a necessary staging post on

---

[3] K. MacAskill, *Building a Nation: Post devolution nationalism in Scotland* (Edinburgh: Luath Press, 2004), pp. 29-30.

the way to the future. Some might call such a staging post a New Union'.[4] 'New union' has traditionally been the language used by opponents of devolution, not to mention independence. It is difficult to identify many hardline SNP MSPs today and it is impossible to identify any hardliner amongst the team of Scottish Government ministers.

But more significant than the personnel are the politics of the SNP. The old 1970s position that a majority of SNP MPs amongst Scottish MPs constituted a mandate for independence never appeared credible beyond the party but lost all credibility post-devolution. It is conceivable that a hardline position might be articulated by some voices in the event of a SNP electoral or other setback. But this could hardly help the party. If some post-devolution version of SNP fundamentalism ever came to prominence, the party would suffer electorally and this is well understood within its senior echelons. Electoral incentives have forced the SNP to abandon any hint of fundamentalism. The possibility of a return of the hardliners cannot be dismissed entirely but the lessons of electoral history are clear — hardliners do not do well in elections.

Paradoxically, when the SNP amended its constitution in April 2004 it removed reference to 'self-government' as an objective and replaced this with 'independence'. This was the first time that independence has appeared in the party's constitution. Superficially, this might be seen as evidence of a continued hardline attitude. However, this change was necessary, as senior figures privately confirmed, because the party was intent on pursuing a pragmatic strategy and it was thought wise at the time to throw a symbolic gift to those who might have objected. In retrospect, it is uncertain whether it was necessary. Moreover, independence for the SNP today means something very different from sovereigntist notions of political power of the past. Its opponents will continue to portray it as supporting a nineteenth-century idea of independence, but there is little evidence of this. It is notable that mainstream figures in the SNP frequently express support for independence with caveats, references to interdependence, insistence that independence has many forms and that developing a more independent political culture and social structures are almost as important as constitutional independence. Indeed, it is striking how much more conventionally nationalist is the language of British politicians. It is difficult to imagine Alex Salmond making the equivalent of the 'British jobs for British people' speech that Gordon Brown delivered to the TUC in September 2007.

Lord Acton famously suggested that power corrupts — but in democratic politics it is more likely to tame and mature. The early years of devolution were transitional but reasonably smooth for the SNP. Today's SNP evolved from a loosely-organised oppositional force largely dependent on

---

4 D. MacLeod and M. Russell, *Grasping the Thistle* (Glendaruel: Argyll Publishing, 2006), p. 125.

volunteers, with few full-time politicians or officials and with very little prospect of governmental power. Devolution gave it the chance to become a governing party. Before the 1997 election, only eighteen SNP members were ever MPs (including one Labour MP who defected but never won an election as an SNP member). In 1999 alone, almost twice that many were elected to the Scottish Parliament. The first elections to the Scottish Parliament placed the SNP second behind Labour both in terms of seats and votes for the first time in its history. In 2007, it was the most sophisticated political party operating in Scotland, with a growing membership, a professional organisation and a modest programme for government. It had the profile of a party more in search of respectability than revolution. The Scottish Parliament has given it a new lease of life and a new credibility, but only because the party has come to terms with devolution.

INTERGOVERNMENTAL RELATIONS

There is no doubt that the SNP will seek to exploit opportunities available to it to make political capital. What is in doubt are which opportunities it will exploit and how it will do so. Its opponents' predictions have been confounded; the SNP has not sought to exploit every difference with London and SNP policy was not designed to manufacture divergence.

Some commentators have listed the policy differences between the new Scottish Government and those in London as if such policy differences will inevitably bring damaging conflict. It is hardly surprising that opponents of devolution should adopt this view, but others who had supported devolution might have been expected to appreciate that diversity is an expected consequence of devolution. The policy stances of the McConnell years may have created an expectation that devolution is about institutional diversity combined with public policy parity, similar to the old Stormont model of devolution, but there was little in the long campaigns for a Scottish Parliament to suggest that this was what Scots expected or wanted. Indeed, Henry McLeish's policy of free long-term care for the elderly and the Liberal Democrats' policy on university tuition fees would have to be seen as attempts to break up the Union if policy differences were a measure of manufacturing trouble.

'Year zero' assumptions, with commentators ignorant of past debates, continue to afflict much commentary on devolution. Where differences exist between the SNP and Labour, as for example over financing local government, nuclear energy and higher education, these exist for reasons other than attempts by either Labour or SNP to exploit constitutional conflict. SNP policy on each of these matters simply reflects public policy choices often rooted in debates of thirty years ago. The SNP has, for good or ill, been remarkably consistent in its stance on each of these issues since the 1970s. In addition, the suggestion that there are considerable policy differences between the SNP and Labour would not be recognised by serious scholars of Scottish politics who have long noted the extent of policy convergence of the two main parties on a vast range of issues. Assertions that policy differences are the result of some planned constitutional conflict simply do not stand up to analysis.

There are good reasons why the SNP would not wish to pick a fight. First, London holds more levers of power and would be expected to win in any contest. Secondly, such a battle would run contrary to the strategy that allowed the SNP to become Scotland's largest party in the 2007 elections. Creating a constitutional crisis or manufacturing conflict is not consistent with respectability and moderation. Thirdly, the SNP does not command a majority in the Parliament and would be blocked, if not removed from office, in any such endeavours.

This is not to suggest that relations have been trouble-free — but the source of the problem has usually been London, not Edinburgh. Former Prime Minister Blair's attempts to interfere in the devolved polities highlighted the absence of a deeper commitment to devolution. From his efforts to prevent Ken Livingstone becoming Labour candidate for London Mayor or blocking Rhodri Morgan's effort to become Welsh Labour leader to the refusal to acknowledge the election results in Scotland in 2007, Tony Blair's acceptance of devolution was always less than fulsome. Gordon Brown himself only called Alex Salmond to acknowledge the new First Minister four weeks after the election and well after David Cameron had done so. More worryingly, Blair's failure to keep the devolved government informed of the protocol with Libya regarding prisoner exchanges (and clearly affecting Abdelbaset al-Megrahi, convicted in a Scottish court of the Pan Am 103 bombing over Lockerbie) shortly after the election ran contrary to the spirit of devolution and the principles for the conduct of intergovernmental relations set out in the *Memorandum of Understanding* between the UK and devolved governments.[5] Blair's behaviour had more in common with Margaret Thatcher's integrationist conception of the Union than that of a convinced devolutionist. This suggests that while the UK has devolved institutions it has yet to develop a devolved political culture. While formal institutions may have been created, there remains a mindset that devolution should be symbolic rather than substantive in policy terms.

But, of course, while London might be inclined to pick a fight — and Tony Blair seemed intent on disrupting devolution in his dying days as Premier — there are reasons why Gordon Brown should be as keen to avoid conflict as Alex Salmond. Conflict with Edinburgh would only highlight Brown's

5 *Memorandum of Understanding and Supplementary Agreements between the United Kingdom Government, Scottish Ministers, the Cabinet of the National Assembly for Wales and the Northern Ireland Executive Committee* Cm 5240 (London: The Stationery Office, 2001).

Scottish background and support base. Gordon Brown's authority in Scotland is unlikely to be questioned but conflict with the devolved government may remind voters in England that Brown is a Scottish MP, unable to determine much Scottish domestic policy while more able to determine English domestic policy than any other MP at Westminster.

The perception that a Conservative government in London would result in damaging conflict with Edinburgh has diminished since devolution's establishment. The Conservative leadership today seems more at ease with devolution in Scotland though continues to have serious concerns regarding its UK dimension. Indeed, Conservatives may be keen to avoid any hint that they would damage the Union and could prove to be more relaxed in power than Labour has been. In his speech to the Scottish Tory conference in May 2008, David Cameron maintained, 'Whatever the outcome in Scotland of the next General Election, a Conservative Government will govern the whole of the United Kingdom, including Scotland, with respect. Whoever is Scotland's First Minister, I would be a Prime Minister who acts on the voice of the Scottish people, and will work tirelessly for consent and consensus so we strengthen the Union.'[6]

This may reflect the passing of the old pre-devolution generation of Conservative politicians. As Bagehot remarked, 'A new Constitution does not produce its full effect as long as all its subjects were reared under an old Constitution, as long as its statesmen were trained by that old Constitution. It is not really tested till it comes to be worked by statesmen and among a people neither of whom are guided by a different experience.'[7] Gordon Brown was not only schooled under the old constitution but cut his political teeth on devolution in the 1970s. It may take the political passing of the Brown generation before we see devolution operating unfettered by old attitudes and prejudices. Devolving institutional power without a concomitant devolutionary political culture at the centre has created difficulties, though these should not be exaggerated, and as the old guard make way for a new generation in each of the main parties at Westminster, we may begin to see a devolutionary culture develop.

There is a case for review after two terms of devolution. There is evidence that all is not well. Formal intergovernmental institutions such as the Joint Ministerial Committees were last-minute arrangements established to facilitate good relations, but have not been used as anticipated. Michael Aron's leaked paper outlining difficulties in European Union affairs suggests that matters are not operating according to expectations, at least in this sensitive

---

[6] D. Cameron, Speech to Scottish Conservative Party conference, Ayr, 23 May 2008. Available at www.conservatives.com/tile.do?def=news.story.page&obj_id=144993&speeches=1

[7] W. Bagehot, *The English Constitution* (London: Fontana / Collins, 1981), p.268.

area.[8] Tony Blair's style of government was often characterised as 'sofa government'. That implies informality and a willingness to sit down and talk. As far as intergovernmental relations are concerned, sofa government would be better than the refusal to pick up the telephone but whether such informal arrangements which have characterised devolution are better than a more rules-based system needs to be explored.

It was the SNP First Minister who called for the renewal of institutions designed to provide for good relations between components of the UK, while the British Prime Minister abandoned or at least downgraded them. But, of course, the withering of the various intergovernmental institutions should not be seen as the withering of intergovernmental relations, merely that other more traditional mechanisms (in the broadest sense) are being used. At times of crisis — the terrorist attack on Glasgow airport, the Foot and Mouth disease outbreak, and the Grangemouth oil refinery dispute — London has been willing to engage constructively with Edinburgh. Whitehall has adjusted to devolution reasonably well, and though there have been tensions and difficulties, these have been far fewer than the civil service anticipated in the 1970s, when devolution was first seriously contemplated. The problem appears to exist at the level of relations between politicians, not civil servants. The fact that Labour was in office in both London and Edinburgh between 1999 and 2007 minimised difficulties. But the real test has inevitably and predictably come when different parties are in power in London and Edinburgh and, crucially, financial pressures have increased.

There are also other matters that deserve to be reviewed to improve the operation of devolved institutions. The Howat Report, commissioned by the previous Scottish Executive to review Scottish Executive budgets in light of a tighter fiscal environment, observed that the partnership agreement between Labour and Liberal Democrats had created problems in managing budgets and setting priorities.[9] Howat and his team recommended that the Parliamentary timescale of 28 days to elect a First Minister 'effectively limits the negotiating time for the political parties' and creates pressures leading to Partnership Agreements that lack clear priorities and creates inconsistencies.[10] Howat's observation is made more pertinent given the difficulties that are involved in agreeing a programme for government when a minority is being established. The Gould Report's recommendations on

---

[8] See e.g. D. Fraser, 'Scotland "finding itself frozen out of Brussels"' *The Herald* (Glasgow) 22 January 2007.

[9] Budget Review Group, *Choices for a Purpose: Review of Scottish Executive Budgets* (Scottish Executive, 2006) available at www.scotland.gov.uk/Resource/Doc/178289/0050741.pdf

[10] Budget Review Group 2006, p.13.

electoral administration, reviewing the 2007 elections, also suggest a need for tidying-up measures.[11]

THE EVOLUTION OF DEVOLUTION

Separate from any discussion of improving intergovernmental relations and tidying up measures is the issue of whether Holyrood should gain more powers and responsibilities. On this, there is no 'settled will' of the Scottish people. The public appears to want more powers — although, understandably, it has no firm view on what these should be. Opinion within the main parties is in flux. The Liberal Democrats set up an enquiry under David Steel which produced a lengthy document advocating some significant changes pointing towards a fully federal system.[12] Even opponents of a fully federal system might find value in the Steel Commission report though it would be mistaken to assume that support for any of its provisions means endorsement of the Liberal Democrat's endpoint (something the Liberal Democrats may wish to ponder when they read the SNP Government's White Paper on independence). The Steel Report was not given the attention it deserved, partly because of its timing and partly because the report contained a number of gaffes that were pounced on by opponents, but all the signs are that the SNP Government has read it carefully. Liberal Democrats appear to have been caught off guard by the style of the SNP during and since the elections and have failed to notice how much of the Steel Report has found its way into the SNP's independence White Paper.[13]

The Conservatives in Scotland have found a new lease of life and, having seen off the Lib Dem challenge in three Scottish elections and with the prospect of a return to power at Westminster, now feel reasonably confident as Scotland's third party. They have gained confidence. There is some support within the Conservative Party in favour of increasing the powers of the Parliament. Even before David Cameron became leader, the Conservatives in London signalled a relaxed attitude on fiscal autonomy and more powers, leaving it to the party north of the border to decide for itself. However, grass-roots opinion in the party may not share this relaxed attitude toward

---

[11] Electoral Commission, *Scottish Elections Review 2007: The independent review of the Scottish parliamentary and local government elections* (London: Electoral Commission, 2007), available at www.electoralcommission.org.uk/files/dms/Scottish-Election-Report-A-Final-For-Web_27622-201 6_E_N_S_W_.pdf

[12] Scottish Liberal Democrats, *The Steel Commission: Moving to Federalism — A new settlement for Scotland* (Edinburgh: Scottish Liberal Democrats, 2006), available at www.scotlibdems.org.uk/files/steelcommission.pdf

[13] Scottish Executive, *Choosing Scotland's Future. A National Conversation. Independence and Responsibility in the Modern World* (Edinburgh: Scottish Executive, 2007). Available at www. scotland.gov.uk/Publications/2007/08/13103747/0

further devolution and the party is far from having a clear line on what it will support.

Labour today looks like the outsider — the position that the SNP and Conservatives seemed to vie for in pre-devolutionary times. Wendy Alexander has attempted to present the SNP as the outsiders with her 'constitutional commission', but this will not succeed if all that unites the parties in the Commission is opposition to the SNP. The idea of a commission was presented in what appears to have been a hurriedly-prepared speech on St Andrews Day in 2007.[14] The idea has evolved and lost much of its initial meaning as timetables have slipped and the original intention has been diluted. The commission has moved from being expert-led to largely party-based and from being the creature of Holyrood to being serviced and run by Whitehall. Each party will have to decide what it supports but there is currently no clear consensus in either Labour or Conservative parties around which agreement can be reached. Both parties are divided on whether there should be further devolution. The commission is the poor grandchild of Harold Wilson's Royal Commission on the Constitution — established to get a deeply-divided party out of a hole, thus giving the appearance of action while evading an internal debate.

Henry McLeish has come to understand what needs to be done better than most Labour politicians. McLeish is the Jimmy Carter of Scottish politics; the best part of his career began the day he stood down from office. Demitting office appears to have liberated the former First Minister, allowed him to think independently and engage constructively in political debate. In a recent co-authored book, McLeish has referred to the 'doggedly centralist attitude in Westminster' and even suggested that there is a 'natural bridging point to link the [SNP] gradualists with those in the Unionist parties who wish to move on from the status quo and the first phase of devolution'.[15]

Given the reaction to McLeish's views from some of his former Labour colleagues, it is hardly surprising that others within his party have not followed him. The results of the 2007 Scottish elections have not helped. Many Labour supporters (and MSPs) convinced themselves that the result was a fluke, that Labour did not do too badly and did not need to address the constitutional question. Initially, Wendy Alexander, Scottish Labour's new leader, argued simultaneously that there was no appetite for more constitutional debate and that she was open-minded on further reform. She formally engaged with the Tories to defend the Union, then days later attacked the Tories for being in alliance with the SNP to break the Union.[16] Subsequently,

---

[14] W. Alexander, 'A New Agenda for Scotland'. Speech at Edinburgh University, 30 November 2007. Available at: http://wendy.intraspin.com/2007/11/30/a-new-agenda-for-scotland/?cat=20

[15] T. Brown and H. McLeish, *Scotland: The Road Divides. New Politics, New Union* (Edinburgh: Luath Press, 2007), p. 10 and p. 5 respectively.

[16] See *The Herald* 20 September 2007; *The Times* 24 September 2007.

she recommended that the SNP 'bring on' a referendum but with a week reversed this position. Leaving aside Alexander's failings as leader, this confusion signifies Labour's difficulties and shows that the party is still in the process of coming to terms with the loss of power and accepting that Scottish politics has changed. These inconsistencies and incoherence may well be a necessary, if painful, early part in the process in developing the new thinking which Labour urgently needs.

THE SNP'S INDEPENDENCE WHITE PAPER

The SNP Government issued its White Paper on independence in August 2007.[17] From the perspective of the SNP of old, the document was as unexpected as its reception was predictable. The evidence that 'fundamentalism' and 'gradualism' are unhelpful terms in understanding the SNP today is strong from this document, but what is less clear is how we should understand the party today. It is difficult to imagine a government issuing a white paper on a matter so central to its *raison d'être* that is as balanced as is the White Paper on independence. There is even a passage stating, 'The effect of increasing Scotland's responsibility for its own economic and fiscal policies remains a matter of debate' (p. 10). The tone of the White Paper is evident in Alex Salmond's preface. At no point is there any claim that Scotland has voted for independence but that the 'people voted clearly for further development of the way we govern ourselves in Scotland' and though the SNP believes independence would be 'best for our country', there is a 'range of views in our country, and represented in the Parliament' (p. v). Some commentators have either been lazy in their reading of the White Paper or simply not understood it and have tilted at windmills, guilty of a fundamentalist unionist fallacy in refusing to treat debate on Scotland's constitutional future in anything other than absolutist terms.[18]

The most striking aspect of the White Paper is its pragmatism. More space is devoted to discussing the extension of devolution than independence. It is acknowledged that certain matters are 'fundamental to the United Kingdom as a state' and lists these as foreign affairs and defence, borders and citizenship, the UK Parliament and currency and central bank and notes that many of these are now 'affected by international treaties and membership of international organisations, particularly the European Union' (p. 8). Much emphasis is placed on interdependence. The evidence of this White Paper, along with the actions of the SNP Government since coming to power, indicates a willingness to engage in discussion on Scotland's constitutional

---

[17] Scottish Executive 2007.

[18] See J. Murkens, 'Response to the SNP's White Paper, Choosing Scotland's Future: A National Conversation', Constitution Unit press release, 16 August 2007. Available at www.ucl.ac.uk/constitution-unit/media/press-releases/2007.htm#1608

future, no doubt partly due to an appreciation that it does not command a majority in Holyrood nor would likely carry a majority in a referendum on independence at this stage. This contrasts with the other parties. The Liberal Democrats, the only other party seriously and wholeheartedly committed to reform, have refused to engage with the SNP despite obvious common ground.

THE PROBLEM OF SOVEREIGNTY

But we have a problem in how debates on Scotland's constitutional status can become meaningful. This is the sovereignty problem. Quite simply, how do we amend the constitution? At present, the only mechanism is through an Act of the Westminster Parliament. Even if a clear majority of Scots support more powers for the Scottish Parliament, this will not happen if a majority of MPs at Westminster disagrees. This was precisely the conundrum faced by campaigners for a Scottish Parliament before 1997. In the late 1980s and early 1990s, the Scottish Constitutional Convention asserted sovereignty of the Scottish people but this proved hollow.

Indeed, some of the Scottish Parliament's own internal procedures cannot be amended without the agreement of Westminster. Amongst its recommendations, the Steel Commission proposed that the Scottish Parliament should have exclusive competence over its own operation. As David Steel pointed out, the Parliament was unable to appoint a third Deputy Presiding Officer to fill the vacancy when he was ill during his period as Presiding Officer. The Steel Commission's solution was to recommend a new constitutional convention and this won the support of the *Sunday Herald* newspaper. The central problem remains exactly that which plagued the old Scottish Constitutional Convention. At the first meeting of the old Convention on 30 March 1989, Kenyon Wright, its co-convenor, asked, 'What if that other voice we all know so well responds by saying, "We say no, and we are the state"? Well we say yes — and we are the people.' John Major's response after the 1992 election was, in effect, 'We say No, and we are the state.' Wright's rhetoric proved empty. But there have been two significant changes since 1997: the Scottish Parliament can claim authoritatively to embody the will of the Scottish people, and London is likely to be wary of completely ignoring such a body given the difficulties that the Tories faced when they turned their back on Scottish opinion. A Scottish view endorsed by the Scottish Parliament would have greater authority than the old Constitutional Convention ever had but would require widespread support inside the Parliament. Of course, it would not have the legal capacity to determine Scotland's constitutional future — but no-one should confuse legality and legitimacy.

Three issues will need to be addressed. First, any changes short of independence will need to take account of the UK-wide dimension of devolution.

Parliament at Westminster will have to legislate for any significant changes and it is most unlikely that opposition will be as stilled as it was immediately after 1997. There are opponents of extending devolution in both Labour and Conservative parties. Secondly, it is not clear whether any further powers would require public consent in another referendum. It would seem odd that extensions to Welsh devolution should require a further referendum but potentially more significant changes in Scottish devolution could take place without one. This also raises the question as to when a referendum should take place — whether it should be before or after legislating for further changes (the 1979 or 1997 model) — and that would have a significant effect on the likely Parliamentary process. Thirdly, this debate raises the general issue of constitutional amendment and whether changes are to continue to be treated in an ad hoc manner or subject to new, more formalised mechanisms.

THE UNFINISHED BUSINESS OF DEVOLUTION

The main lesson of the current arrangements is that stability requires account be taken of state-wide implications — particularly the 'English dimension'. As well as pressure from Scotland for more powers, there is pressure from England to tackle the anomalies of the current arrangements, the unfinished business of devolution.[19] The real challenge will be to take account of both sets of pressures. Failure to do so may lead to frustration and instability. It should be possible to move forward by taking account of Scottish pressures and the need to accommodate the need for equity across the UK, though there may be losers who will resist any change for as long as possible.

Two sets of issues need to be addressed: the West Lothian question and territorial finances. The West Lothian question takes two forms: its older version focusing on Parliament, and its more politically difficult form focusing on UK Government ministers sitting for Scottish seats whose portfolios principally affect other parts of the UK. Some compromise might be arrived at, with the most likely response being a further reduction in the number of Scottish MPs. The only obstacle that currently stands in its way as far as Scottish representation is concerned is party political interest, though this cannot be dismissed lightly, as the Labour Party fears losing seats in Scotland, and other parties no doubt support this reduction for equally partisan reasons.

When the new Labour government decided in 1997 to reduce the number of Scottish MPs as part of the devolution package, there was a hope that the West Lothian question had been dealt with. It is possible that a further reduction will not deal with the problem now either. But the difference this time round must be that any reduction is done following serious deliberation and

[19] J. Mitchell, 'Devolution's Unfinished Business', *Political Quarterly* 77(4) (2006): 465–74.

consensually, with winners and losers alike agreeing on the numbers involved. Losers' consent is central to the long-term success of any constitutional arrangement. The problem in 1997–8 was that the Conservatives did not feel part of the decision-making process — the Scotland Act was steam-rolled through Parliament after the loss of all Tory seats in Scotland and after a decisive majority for devolution in the referendum. Henry McLeish, Scottish Office Minister responsible for devolution at the time, has acknowledged that it was 'felt that a referendum would improve the prospects of the legislation having a trouble-free passage through the House of Commons if the people of Wales and Scotland had given it their prior blessing.'[20]

The West Lothian question is not purely an English issue, but one that affects all parts of the UK. The establishment of devolved government appears to have removed issues of legitimacy of government in Wales and Scotland, but it may also simply have shifted the problem elsewhere.[21] Proposals for 'English Votes for English Laws' (EVEL) as supported at different times and in different forms by the Conservatives at Westminster might create new problems elsewhere. Part of the issue is financial, and the way the Barnett formula makes changes in funding for Scotland (and Wales and Northern Ireland) dependent on changes in spending in England. If Scottish MPs could not vote on policy that had a direct impact on the funding of services provided by the Scottish Parliament, through the Barnett formula, then EVEL would simply create a new problem elsewhere in the constitution. Unless a consensual solution can be found, we are in danger of a never-ending game of constitutional ping-pong.

It does not help Scotland if devolution ends up creating resentment in England. The alternative is that pressure for an English solution, involving EVEL, will build up and changes will be made that prove unstable or that Scotland suffers from an English backlash. No Scottish devolutionist could complain if the Conservatives played the English card in much the same way as SNP, Labour and Liberal Democrats played the Scottish card before devolution. But this is hardly conducive to resolving tensions.

The financial regime is also difficult to defend. There is something anomalous in Scotland having generous services unavailable in other parts of the UK while not having to pay for them. It is one thing to insist that public expenditure should be used to assist poorer areas, to compensate for economic and social deprivation, but Scotland is now a prosperous part of the UK. Devolution should involve Scotland having different priorities, but there is no case for allowing Scotland to have an advantage in better services without paying some cost — whether in reduced services elsewhere or through taxation. Devolved government can either be about encouraging

[20] Brown and McLeish 2007, p. 10.
[21] Mitchell 2006.

more independent responsibility or simply serve as a lever to wrest more resources out of the centre. English regions have long worried that devolution would be the latter. It is difficult to deny that this is what it looks like.

Scottish politics was dominated by a debilitating politics of grievance for much of the post-war era, during which success was measured by the resources that could be wrung out of London. Various parties, Labour and SNP especially, argued for devolution while simultaneously demanding more and more from London. There was a contradiction in these demands. The corollary of allowing Scotland to have more expensive policies must be that it should also have to pay for them unless such policies can be justified in terms of greater need.

The financial dimension of devolution is its least coherent and least stable element and requires attention. It might be tempting to let sleeping dogs lie, but in politics sleeping dogs have a habit of awakening at awkward moments. Of course, outlining a policy change such as this is easy. Providing the details and implementing it is another matter. It will not be possible to implement it over night and it may be necessary to set a timetable for its implementation. As Kenneth Wheare remarked many years ago,

> There is and can be no final solution to the allocation of financial resources in a federal system. There can only be adjustments and re-allocations in the light of changing conditions. What [is needed], therefore, is machinery adequate to make these adjustments.[22]

This applies equally to devolved financial relations. The absence of such machinery is a major deficiency in the current arrangements, and establishing such institutions should be a major objective of the next few years. There is a debate to be had on the precise details — the balance between tax and grant, for example. But the principle can be outlined and should find broad agreement.

CONCLUSION

Improved prospects for the SNP were among the most predictable consequences of devolution. Devolution created incentives encouraging the SNP to become more pragmatic; so long as public office was a distant prospect, the SNP had the characteristics of a typical pressure group and the SNP had few incentives to think seriously as an alternative party of government. It was relatively easy to frighten voters with apocalyptic predictions but the reality of an SNP government has been business-as-usual with the bonus of business-with-a-purpose. Many of the SNP's opponents have been left confused and befuddled. Their response has mirrored the fundamentalism of

---

[22] K.C. Wheare, *Federal Government*, 4th edition (Oxford: Oxford University Press, 1963), p. 117.

the SNP of old: suspicious, seeing traps and plots everywhere and unable to engage seriously. The electorate has accepted an SNP government and Scottish civil society has willingly engaged constructively with it. The danger for its opponents, especially Labour, is that unionist fundamentalism, most notably the failure to engage constructively with the governing party, will make them lasting political outsiders. Coming to terms with new political realities is challenging for all parties but particularly for those that were previously long dominant. Fundamentalist impulses incline parties to indulge in the political equivalent of the foetal position, refusing to face the world. Leadership can be measured by a willingness and ability to confront new realities. Labour across Britain learned that lesson in the 1980s but has still some way to go to learn this in Scotland today.

One theme of this chapter is that we have unfinished business, both in developing a culture to match the institutions of devolution amongst elements of the party political elites in London and in filling gaping institutional holes that remain in the framework of the devolved institutions. The London political elite's refusal to let go may prove a temporary problem associated with an elite whose formative experiences date from the pre-devolution period. This is not to say that all parts of the government machine has failed to develop a culture of devolution — Whitehall civil servants are more relaxed about it than anyone could have predicted based on past reactions. Likewise Scottish civil servants and civil society are remarkably at ease with devolution, indeed with an SNP administration.

Devolved government too needs to be encouraged and given incentives to develop a different culture. Devolved government must be about a degree of independent responsibility or self-government not creating a stronger voice in the machine. Speaking in Edinburgh in 2006, Peter Hennessy referred to the institutions which had wrung so much out of the Treasury over the years — the military, doctors and the Scottish Office. If devolution is to develop, it needs to develop beyond being a means of maintaining the success of the old Scottish Office. In this sense, Scotland needs more independence.

BIBLIOGRAPHY

Official Documents and Primary Sources

Alexander, W., 'A New Agenda for Scotland'. Speech at Edinburgh University, 30 November 2007.
Cameron, D., Speech to Scottish Conservative Party conference, Ayr, 23 May 2008.
Electoral Commission, *Scottish Elections Review 2007: The independent review of the Scottish parliamentary and local government elections* (London: Electoral Commission, 2007).

Memorandum of Understanding and Supplementary Agreements between the United Kingdom Government, Scottish Ministers, the Cabinet of the National Assembly for Wales and the Northern Ireland Executive Committee Cm 5240 (London: The Stationery Office, 2001).

Scottish Executive, '*Choices for a Purpose: Review of Scottish Executive Budgets*', *Report of the Budget Review Group*. (Edinburgh: Scottish Executive, 2006).

Scottish Executive, *Choosing Scotland's Future. A National Conversation. Independence and Responsibility in the Modern World* (Edinburgh: Scottish Executive, 2007).

Scottish Liberal Democrats (2006), *Report of the Steel Commission: Moving to Federalism — A new Settlement for Scotland*, (Edinburgh; Scottish Liberal Democrats).

Secondary Sources

Bagehot, W., *The English Constitution* (London: Fontana / Collins, 1981).

Brown, T. and H. McLeish, *Scotland: The Road Divides. New Politics, New Union* (Edinburgh: Luath Press, 2007).

MacAskill, K., *Building a Nation: Post devolution nationalism in Scotland* (Edinburgh: Luath Press, 2004).

MacLeod, D. and M. Russell, *Grasping the Thistle* (Glendaruel: Argyll Publishing, 2006).

McGarvey, N. and P. Cairney, *Scottish Politics* (Basingstoke: Palgrave Macmillan, 2008).

Mitchell, J., 'Ideological Consistency and Strategic Change: the SNP in the 1980s'. Paper presented at Political Studies Association conference, Aberdeen, 1987.

Mitchell, J. 'Recent Developments in the Scottish National Party', *Political Quarterly* 59(4) (1988): 473–7.

Mitchell, J., *Strategies for Self-Government* (Edinburgh: Polygon, 1996).

Mitchell, J., 'Devolution's Unfinished Business', *Political Quarterly* 77(4) (2006): 465–74.

Murkens, J., 'Response to the SNP's White Paper, Choosing Scotland's Future: A National Conversation', Constitution Unit press release, 16 August 2007.

Wheare, K.C., *Federal Government*, 4th edition (Oxford; Oxford University Press, 1963).

Index